By Donald N. Michael

*On Learning to Plan—and Planning to Learn:
The Social Psychology of Changing
Toward Future-Responsive Societal Learning*

*The Unprepared Society:
Planning for a Precarious Future*

*The Next Generation:
The Prospects Ahead for the Youth
of Today and Tomorrow*

*Cybernation:
The Silent Conquest*

*Proposed Studies on the Implications
of Peaceful Space Activities for Human Affairs*

On Learning to Plan—
and Planning to Learn

The Social Psychology of Changing Toward
Future-Responsive Societal Learning

Donald N. Michael

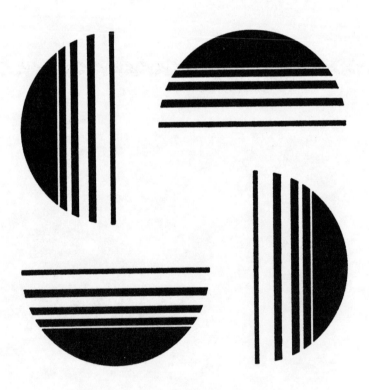

On Learning to Plan— and Planning to Learn

Jossey-Bass Publishers
San Francisco · Washington · London · 1976

ON LEARNING TO PLAN—
AND PLANNING TO LEARN
The Social Psychology of Changing
Toward Future-Responsive Societal Learning
        by Donald N. Michael

Library of Congress Catalogue Card Number LC 73-7153

International Standard Book Number ISBN 0-87589-187-X

Manufactured in the United States of America

JACKET DESIGN BY WILLI BAUM

FIRST EDITION
        First printing: October 1973
        Second printing: October 1976

Code 7329

The Jossey-Bass
Behavioral Science Series

*For
Geoffrey,
my son—
who
is
learning*

Acknowledgments

*T*he work underlying this report was supported by the Center for Studies of Metropolitan Problems, National Institute of Mental Health, first through a Special Research Fellowship for me and later through a special research grant, #MH 14629. I am indebted to the Center for its support, and especially to its former Associate Director, Dr. Matthew Dumont, and its Executive Secretary, Richard Wakefield, for their enthusiasm and help.

Among other things, the Center grant made it possible to create a Work Group for the study. Its purposes are described in the Introduction. Here I want to thank its members for their conscientious, imaginative, and critical contributions to the study; their influence pervades the report. Work Group members were Raymond Bauer, Henry David, Robert Kahn, Matthew Dumont, Philburn Ratoosh, Donald Schon, Allan Westin, and Melvin Webber.

At various times James Crowfoot, Joseph DiMento, Alan Guskin, Robert Olson, and Meridith Spencer were project staff members. Crowfoot and Guskin, as Assistant Project Directors, were deeply involved through about the first half of the project. Olson, as Research Associate, came in part way through that period. Crowfoot made fundamental contributions to our theoretical understanding, especially concerning the role of planning as an organizational guidance system (Crowfoot, 1972). Guskin clarified our understanding of the social psychological implications of advocate planning, and initiated our advance into the murky area of

ix

personal time perspectives and their relation to felt needs for planning (Ross and Guskin, 1972). Olson enlarged our understanding of the social psychology of political processes as a property of social systems. I write "our" because at that time the project was very much a team creation. While much of the study was carried out after the team members departed, their influence contributed greatly to my understanding of what I was struggling with. It has remained strong in my thinking. Of course their contributions went well beyond the subjects singled out here: they accomplished difficult field interviews, wrote working papers that enlightened me and the Work Group, and provided a day-to-day intellectual atmosphere and supportive mood that were crucial for coalescing the directions of this study. It was a deeply rewarding time for me, and the study and I are much the better for it. Early in the study, Meridith Spencer undertook some very helpful literature searches on various meanings of planning and analyses of them. Toward the project's end, Joseph DiMento was invaluable as a literature reader, abstractor, and evaluator.

Melvin Webber arranged for one of his graduate students in planning to listen to the tapes of the Work Group meetings and abstract them, emphasizing the topics and arguments that most impressed him as new, useful, or important. The resulting report and critique, prepared by James Sundberg, was most helpful to further Work Group deliberations and most informative, thanks to his own interpolated comments on how, as a planner-to-be, he saw these issues and judged our approach to them. (Mr. Sundberg later became involved in community development and planning activities in the San Francisco Bay Area. His insights into those activities were especially valuable, in part because he and I had the material from his report as a shared basis for my questions and his answers.) I strongly recommend that others seek the benefits of such assessments when undertaking analogous studies.

Throughout, my students in the various versions of my seminar on technology and social change provided a supportive and responsive context for trying out ideas—theirs and mine, and who is to say which is which. All I can do is thank them for sharing and making productive so much ambiguity and uncertainty. John Krogman, James Pelikan, and Neil Tudiver have devoted many hours of effort and imagination to interviews and working papers that extended far beyond the period of their seminar involvement. Their interview-based examples and insights into structural and perceptual determinants of long range planning in some large corporations in the greater Detroit area have been especially helpful.

At the end of this report is a list of respondents who were willing to be identified. The trouble with such lists is that the very format washes out a sense of the uniqueness of each respondent as a busy but helpful person. The time, thought, and courtesy each gave to me, face-to-face or in a few cases in correspondence, is nowhere evident in such a list. Yet their generosity was crucial to the development of the study.

Near the end of the study several people critically read a draft of this book. I have tried to be as responsive as I could to their many suggestions, and this version has greatly benefited from both their candor and support. In addition to members of the Work Group, draft readers were: Chris Argyris, Bayard Catron, C. West Churchman, Joseph DiMento, David Hertz, Alfred Kahn, Robert Olson, Richard Raymond, Geoffrey Vickers, and Dwight Waldo.

Of course I alone am responsible for what use I have made of the information, speculations, and advice offered by all those who have helped in this effort.

Throughout, Beverly Walter was the project administrative officer, comptroller, coordinator, caterer, note-taker, secretary, and overall integrator. She kept things together and going in the right direction at the right times in ways I only dimly understand but deeply appreciate. She comes closest to having been *the* indispensable person in the project.

In turn, our activities were effectively facilitated by the many human and material resources of the Center for Research on Utilization of Scientific Knowledge and its parent organization, the Institute for Social Research, at the University of Michigan.

I am especially grateful for the time, resources, and ambiance needed to revise the manuscript and to prepare it for copyediting and publication which were generously and efficiently provided in the form of a Visiting Fellowship at the Institute of International Studies, University of California at Berkeley.

Permission to reprint extended passages from the following books and articles is gratefully acknowledged. M. Rein, "Social Planning: The Search for Legitimacy," reprinted by permission of the *Journal of the American Institute of Planners, 35* (July 1969). Alfred J. Kahn, *Theory and Practice of Social Planning,* Chapter 2, Figure 1, and pp. 19–20, © 1969 by Russell Sage Foundation, New York. C. Argyris, "The Incompleteness of Social-Psychological Theory: Examples from Small Group,– Cognitive Consistency, and Attribution Research," *American Psychologist, 24* (1969) 10, copyright 1969 by the American Psychological Association and reproduced by permission. C. Argyris, "Resistance to Rational Management Systems," reprinted from *Innovation Magazine,* issue no. 10, 1970, by permission of *Business and Society Review/Innovation.* H. Wilensky, *Organizational Intelligence: Knowledge and Policy in Government and Industry* (New York: Basic Books, 1967), reprinted by permission of Basic Books, Inc. F. Emery, "The Next Thirty Years: Concepts, Methods, and Anticipations," reprinted from *Human Relations,* 1967, *20,* by permission of Plenum Publishing Corporation.

The seemingly endless editorial minutae involved in preparing the manuscript for publisher and printer were accomplished, and the accompanying exasperation kept bearable, through the gracious assistance of my wife Margot. Indeed, during the last many months of writing, the most thankless tasks have been born by her and by my son Geoffrey. All my bad moods and frustrations invariably came home to roost, but their moral support, good humor, and understanding prevented what could have been a miserable time for all of us and provided a setting in which I found refreshment and revitalization. Their caring was more important than I can say.

Berkeley, California   DONALD N. MICHAEL
February 1973

Contents

xiii

On Learning to Plan—
and Planning to Learn

The Social Psychology of Changing Toward
Future-Responsive Societal Learning

Mark it well, the communication of new ideas, new conceptions, new understandings, inventions, new ways of doing things, between individuals fixed in their ways and intent upon their separate objectives is difficult and rare. The intent to communicate is the exception rather than the rule; the more common motivation, indeed, is to hide and obscure. Nor need there be a common language. If there is a common language, it is likely to be inadequate for the task of conveying what is intended, for the very novelty of an idea sets it outside the common points of reference by which communication occurs. Even if the inventor wants to communicate and has the language that explains, others need not want to listen nor have the time and will to attend. These are the difficulties of communicating a new idea even between individuals, face to face, man to man. In fact the problem is far more difficult, for the communication of invention is rarely from man to man, from inventor to innovator, from source to destination directly. Rather it is a transmission of an idea "through channels," infiltrating, drifting, passed along through the layers upon layers of organization. Beyond the barriers that separate individual from individual, it must cross those which set apart groups and communities.

ROBERT A. SOLO
*Economic Organizations
and Social Systems*

Part One

The Problem

The Problem

Introduction

The study on which this book is based was undertaken with these assumptions in mind: (1) that long-range social planning (lrsp) is necessary (but not sufficient) for the humane development of our society; (2) that changing over to lrsp will require changes in the accepted norms and structures that characterize conventional organizational behavior; (3) that changes in norms and structures require changes in personal, interpersonal, functional, and technological aspects of organizational life and related changes in members of the organization's relevant environment; (4) that the typical ways in which people and organizations deal with innovations, especially social innovations such as lrsp, are to distort or reject them in order to make them compatible with the rewards for doing things in conventional ways for conventional reasons; and (5) that either rejection or distortion of lrsp would undermine precisely those humane and democratic values that make lrsp necessary in the first place.

This book is concerned with the circumstances of *changing toward* the application of lrsp. It is not concerned with conjecturing about the conduct of lrsp or the impact of lrsp when and if that mode of operation would be conventional. Whatever the eventual impact might be, if lrsp were to become standard operating procedure, and what forms lrsp might take would depend on how its evolution was influenced by formative circumstances. It is imperative, therefore, that we understand whether changing toward lrsp is occurring, and whether it can be influenced to occur, in ways that are compatible with human fulfillment. From such

3

an understanding we could learn what knowledge about people and institutions needs to be applied right now and what research needs to be done
in order to enlarge that base of applicable knowledge and to have it put
into use.

Organizations and their environments will of course resist and
subvert lrsp, or indeed any activity that can seriously be called planning;
this has been repeatedly demonstrated and variously explained. A body of
literature has explained why planning is a chimera, especially in government. It emphasizes the unpredictability of the future, the limited rationality of men, the logical and operational dilemmas of setting goals and
priorities, the pragmatic and expedient conduct of politics (both internal
to the organization and as it operates in the larger environment), and
the constraints of existing structures of governance and statutes.[1] Some
of this literature is devoted to arguing that planning is not only unfeasible
but also, if a democracy is governed by responsible and responsive people,
unnecessary and undesirable: negotiation and competing group interests,
the argument goes, will insure that what is missed by one disjointed and
incremental action will be attended to by another.[2]

While there is little question that "disjointed incrementalism" (to
use C. Lindblom's term) typifies the way organizations have behaved,
many observers are pointing out that this is a major reason why the plight
of the society is increasingly desperate. If there is to be an effective allocation
of intellectual, psychological, and material resources and humane results
from those allocations, then environmental revival and protection, Third-
World development, new city building, educational policy, arms control,
technological assessment, control of biotechnology and social technology,
all will require something radically different from policies based on reflexive mini-twitches, policies learned from past experiences.[3]

For many, then, the evidence seems overwhelming that disjointed
incrementalism is profoundly inadequate for dealing with the present and
the conjectured future. Indeed, much of the rapidly accumulating social
mess can be seen as the legacy of an indifference to the future that resided
in past applications of disjointed incrementalism to the production of
knowledge, as well as to the governance of society.[4] In an important sense,
that approach worked so well in a simpler society that it produced, either

---

[1] The arguments are succinctly summarized in Banfield (1962).

[2] The classics in this genre are Lindblom (1965) and Wildavsky (1964).

[3] See Caldwell (1972); Michael (1968); Peccei (1971); and Spilhaus
(1972).

[4] The adverse consequences of these *two* products of disjointed incrementalism are devastatingly summarized in Crowe (1969). On the adverse consequences for the authority and competence of democratic government of the
pluralist philosophy, operating as interest-group liberalism, in which disjointed
incrementalism plays a central role, see Lowi (1969).

through oversight or indifference, a state of affairs that may well be un-manageable now.

> *I do not wish to seem overdramatic, but I can only conclude from the information that is available to me as Secretary-General that the members of the United Nations have perhaps ten years left in which to subordinate their ancient quarrels and launch a global partnership to curb the arms race, to improve the human environment, to defuse the population explosion, and to supply the required momentum to world development efforts.*
>
> *If such a global partnership is not forged within the next decade, then I very much fear that the problems I have mentioned will have reached such staggering proportions that they will be beyond our capacity to control [U Thant, 1970, p. 9].*

  •   •   •

> *Given the scale of our operations, the changeability of our self-disturbed fortunes, and the limitations of our minds, [societal regulation] may well already have become impossible [Vickers, 1965, p. 144].*

It is not the purpose of this book to argue the virtues of planning as against those of some variant of disjointed incrementalism. Others have done this elsewhere.[5] My position is simply that evidence seems to be accumulating that the traditional approaches are not working well enough to keep society from being overwhelmed by the pile-up of old and new problems, and that it is necessary to take new kinds of risks in the direction of lrsp rather than assume that living with the old risks of in-crementalism will finally carry the day. (And I will assume that those who invest their time and thought by reading this book are at least sympathetic to this position.)

For several years now, a number of activities, which have been growing both in the formal attention they receive and in the popular imagery they generate, have given the strong *impression* that there is a growing concern with planning the development of society over periods ranging from five to twenty years or so. University courses, think-tank research projects, professional conferences, new professional journals, articles in magazines like *Fortune* and *Harvard Business Review,* proposed federal legislation, and an endless proliferation of books all argue that the

---

[5] The pros and cons of the incrementalist approach to societal guidance versus the "rationalist" approach are well summarized in Etzioni, 1968, Chapter Eleven; the bibliography for that chapter is an extensive as one could want on related arguments, exegesis, and apologia. Other contributions to the pro-lrsp position are found in Brzezinski, 1970; Caldwell, 1970; Dror, 1964, followed by the commentaries of Lindblom, Jones, McCleery, Heydebrand; Michael (1968); and Schick (1969).

comfortable mythology that the future will take care of us, and in a progressive manner at that, has less and less utility for more and more of those who define society's problems and opportunities and the means for dealing with them. Along with these activities have come an increasing number of sophisticated calls for an "experimenting society." Supporting this change in perspective and providing some of its substance are a cluster of prototechnologies such as societal simulation by computer or gaming, social indicator data and research, systems analysis, future studies, program budgeting and planning systems, decision theory, planned organizational change techniques, technological forecasting, and so on. Add to these developments the new appreciation of looming ecological crises, with all their human, technological, and ethical implications, as well as growing recognition that the future is our present responsibility, and it looks as if planning is rapidly becoming an "idea in good currency" (in D. Schon's phrase).

The meanings and purposes referred to as "planning" are usually vague and various. But such is the growing approbation attached to the idea that increasing numbers of organizations claim they have been planning all along and that they are either using or are about to use even more advanced techniques.[6] The federal government and some state and local governments have been among the enthusiasts, if they are judged by attempts or talk about intention to use components of the technology associated with lrsp. Program budgeting and planning has been introduced in domestic agencies, data banks have been established, cities have conducted "goals" studies (as did a National Goals Research Staff), a ten-year goal was established for a manned moon landing, and various proposed laws have been introduced which aim at effectuating long-range technological assessment. The operating status of these government activities—as distinct from the initiating actions—and their implications for government change-over to lrsp are crucial: it is public agencies that carry the responsibility for the public interest, and it would seem that it

---

[6] An "organization" may be an agency or a bureau within it, or an office or division within the bureau, and so on. While our chief interest will be in government organizations, we will also have occasion to comment on corporations and on "third-sector" organizations, especially, as important components of the environment. Third-sector organizations are those that are not government-owned or profit-making corporations or companies. Organizations differ in structure, subject matter preoccupation, relations with their environment, statutory mandate, and almost an endless number of other factors. Correlating organizational properties, purposes, and performance is a frequent exercise of researchers and theorists. To date, there is no model that differentiates organizations broadly in ways that also correlate well with a wide variety of performance measures. Like many differentiating concepts in the social area, "organization" is fuzzy at the edges but it will have to do for our purposes.

is government (at whatever level) that has the resources under law and the potential functional capability that must be marshalled for lrsp if it is to be done in the public interest.[7]

How serious, then, and how developed in fact are these impressions of intent and implementation? And, regardless of what the situation is today, what is likely over the next several years? Is there now or is there likely to be a change-over underway in public agencies toward lrsp values and operations? The findings of this study, both theoretical considerations and field experiences, indicate a somber and worrisome state of affairs, quite contrary in its characteristics and implications from what one would expect if the pro-planning imagery and initial activities were taken at face value. *Now or within the foreseeable future, lrsp does not seem possible unless there are radical changes in the structure of organizations and in the norms that guide and sustain the behavior of the people who work in them and who, in turn, sustain those structures.* The required radical changes seem most difficult to realize in government agencies; they may be slightly less difficult to realize in other organizations because of their limited or nonexistent responsibility for the public interest. This does not mean that people and organizations do not take actions intended to influence the future or anticipate it, or that they do not change in one way or another. Nor does it mean that none of these actions succeeds. It does mean that government organizations, concerned with human social development, are not deliberately and knowledgeably changing toward organizational arrangements that reward their members and their clientele for assuring that the organizations *continuously* operate so as to meet three requirements: that present actions be deeply influenced by sophisticated conjectures about relevant future *societal* (as contrasted to technological) contexts; that, at all stages of moving from present actions into the future, the social and natural environment be scanned and the feedback from it be controlling in the unfolding and alteration of the future-oriented plans; and that *explicit* social goals and the implementation of programs to realize them be intertwined conceptually and operationally, with the goals serving as highly salient regulators of social development rather than as rigid end-points.

[7] As will be clearer later, requirements for environmental participation in lrsp mean that the distinctions will become increasingly blurred between government responsibility for the public interest and that of other organizations, particularly those in the third sector. Indeed, I expect the very definition of the public interest to change, with or without lrsp efforts. Uncertainty over what constitutes the public interest and who should be responsible for pursuing and protecting it is a major component of the present social unrest, especially as expressed in the challenges from all sides to conventional claims of organizational legitimacy. Learning appropriate meanings for "the public interest" will be one of the things accomplished through lrsp efforts.

Typically, organizations, even those who favor or think they favor lrsp, do not meet these requirements. The social psychological reasons for this have been given very little attention in the conventional literature on organizational behavior. The conventional literature has not been concerned with organizations in the process of changing into forms that would meet these requirements, or with organizations that have felt the need to change in these directions, because these requirements have not been seen as necessary for the effective conduct of society.[8] These requirements carry within them disturbing questions, for those who would be involved, about their own natures, goals, perspectives, and their relationship to the people they work with or for. It is such personally and culturally disruptive matters—matters where the structural and legitimizing underpinnings are weak or absent—that we will examine here. Thus it is that the social psychological perspective is a necessary *addition* to those already available if we are to understand the circumstances and problems that would be associated with changing over to lrsp.

For this purpose we will explore three questions. What are the behaviors required of people and their organizations that can be deduced from the descriptions of what constitutes good lrsp? What does the organizational psychology and related literature suggest about how people would react when requested to behave as required in order to change toward lrsp? In this light, what can we conjecture about likely responses to efforts to move toward lrsp, starting from conventional situations, and what might be done to overcome resistances in ways compatible with lrsp as characterized here?

Purposes of the Book

Through this social psychological examination, I hope to serve three general purposes. The first is to introduce into the mix of ideas

[8] That neither organizations nor organization theory have had to deal very much with the requirements for lrsp is well evidenced by the continuing popularity of the classic work, Cyert and March (1963). It is used frequently to explain organizational behavior in government as well as in business, and is used as bedrock upon which to build more theory. But it is a theory that is *not* dealing with the situation we shall be looking at. With reference to business organizations on which their theory of the firm is based, Cyert and March say: "Whether we consider what we have said here about organizational goals or what we have said about organizational search, it is clear that the organizations described here devote rather little time to long run planning (that has operational significance for decision making), especially when that planning is dependent on long run estimates. They move from one crisis to another. At the same time they rely heavily on traditional methods, general industry practice, and standard operating procedures for making decisions" (p. 102).

about planning feasibility and desirability, a better understanding of the individual potential for change in the direction of lrsp. This includes understanding the nature of the difficulties to be overcome that derive from conventional definitions of what it means to be competent in complex situations under conditions of high uncertainty. Social psychological needs are created and met by operating in the present unplanned situation. These would be threatened by changing toward lrsp. By understanding better both these needs and the threats to their fulfillment I hope we shall be able to imagine what other ways there may be to meet or remove these needs in order to encourage changes toward lrsp.

The second purpose is to stimulate the application, *when appropriate,* of what we do know to overcoming resistances to innovation, to efforts to move toward lrsp. The evidence seems clear that, especially in government, what efforts there have been to try to move toward one or another aspect of lrsp have been undertaken with no sophistication about the sources and nature of resistance to innovation. As a result such efforts end in despair, cynicism, or ritual. Such experiences increase the possibility that some espousing planning will seek to force it, to hide or to gloss over failures, or to settle for ritualized planning that will undermine the very purposes of enhancing the human condition that should be the basis for planning efforts. This book, then, is intended to help would-be organizational innovators understand what they are getting into when they attempt to encourage changes toward lrsp. It is intended to help them see the burdens *they* will carry as well as those they will be asking others to carry.

The third purpose is to stimulate research on the social psychological aspects of changing toward lrsp. This book should be read as a compendium of hypotheses yet to be tested.

Methodology

With this statement of my beliefs and intentions I turn to describing the means by which the substance of this book was generated and organized. It is important to understand the status of the live and printed source materials, and the process by which they were selected for attention, since this book makes no claim to be definitive or value free. Quite the contrary.

I make no effort to fit the subject matter into some grand theoretical structure from behavioral science or pop sociology. There is no such structure in the realm of social psychology that is relevant to this study. In particular, most of the concepts to be used come from the eclectic and sprawling field of the social psychology of organizational behavior. Essentially all the research and theory in that area come from the study of organizations operating in comparatively tranquil environments, concerned with goals and means other than those that will preoccupy us. R. Bauer summarized the differences between the organizational issues emphasized in the literature compared to those in this book as follows:

> *I find it useful to think in terms of the history of organizational theory. One way was to look at the worker and the organization in which he is "confined" for a period of time and try to find what is making him unhappy or find ways to make them happier. Another way was to look at the worker as raw material for getting the organization to do what it should do. Then one looks at motivational incentive and selection and so forth. Then researchers began to look at the organization as an organization but as an organization which produces goods and services . . . certain organization forms, certain organizational processes, which make the organization more efficient in order to shove goods and services out the end. That is about where the literature stands now. We are talking about the organization as an information processing system which produces large decisions, and there is only a smattering of attention to this.*[9]

The very conditions that make lrsp necessary go beyond the conditions that have characterized the natural laboratory of organizational psychology. This does not mean that the findings are inapplicable, because the resistances to be discussed are not new: they arise when men in organizations face threatening changes, especially those changes needed to incorporate innovations. But trying to change over to lrsp will accentuate these resistances and elaborate them, because the requirements for lrsp and the very conditions that intrude on the organization, which make it necessary to try to change toward lrsp, will be different. In many cases these requirements and conditions will bring up questions about self, meaning, and values from which organizations typically protect their members.

The reader will have to forgo, therefore, the comforts that formal structure can afford, especially to professionals and especially in upsetting times. Instead I will use an eclectic and essay-like approach to the subject, and what is more I will argue with myself throughout: I want to believe that the resistances to learning how to undertake lrsp can be overcome, and since I find few reasons to think that they can, I work these reasons as hard as I can. (But the very limits of our understanding of complex societal dynamics means we cannot come to firm conclusions about the likely destiny of seemingly marginal favorable circumstances.) This style

[9] Remarks at a meeting of the Work Group that advised this study. Edited from the transcript.

of interpreting and reporting shows my preferred way of holding onto, if not of structuring, the world: the material we shall be examining must be viewed and reviewed from multiple perspectives, and I have tried to do this. I subscribe to K. Boulding's dictum: "all important distinctions are unclear."

The study, then, upon which this book is based was a "hunting expedition": there was important territory to explore. The intention was to bring back enough interesting reports and exotic specimens, and to generate enough stimulating questions and hunches about the contours of the terrain and the properties of the forces that produce it, to encourage others to make more focused and detailed studies. As a hunting expedition, the base of operations was always tentative and subject to change as activities fanning out from it suggested more interesting locations to explore. That is the way the study was conducted: a constant and deliberate interplay between speculation, reading, and interviewing. But this method had built-in dangers. The normative planning literature is quite detached from "the real world," and the literature of social psychology is seriously incomplete in its understanding of the dynamics of people and organizations undergoing change. Further, there were many opportunities for me to inject personal fantasy and follow a compulsion to invent meaning and order. Under such circumstances, especially in a study as heavily value-laden as this one, it was necessary to self-consciously try to reduce the risk of inventing an interesting reality that would, upon close examination, prove to be only a fantasy.

Two means were used. One was to check interpretations of the literature against what seems to be going on in the real world through interviews with people directly involved or whose credibility made them valuable secondary sources. The interviews were semi-structured, questions being directed to matters appropriate to the respondent and to our developing understanding of the topic. Some of the respondents were interviewed more than once over the three years of the study. Even though the interview material and the literature review seemed compatible, the likelihood of reality-inventing was only reduced in this way. There was still the possibility that we chose our respondents, or heard what they had to say, or asked questions, in ways that elicited answers compatible with our cognitive and emotional biases.[10]

The other means used to discourage self-fulfilling speculation was to enlist the help of colleagues concerned with the issue and knowledge-

[10] Again, the validity of what is reported here and its interpretation must be checked through systematic study and research. I cannot overemphasize that aside from the research cited here, the rest is offered in the spirit of hypotheses. In the interests of style, conjectures have not been cast in the form of questions, or as "if-then" statements in need of testing, but that is what they are.

able about it, who were prepared to put effort into refining and sophisti-
cating the study but who were not so involved that they would become
committed to a common intellectual position. These colleagues met as a
Work Group occasionally during the course of the project to review the
state of the project and steps to be taken next. Detailed background materials were prepared for them, and they read these before each of the
two-day meetings.[11] Between meetings Work Group members arranged
interviews, supplied relevant materials, and were separately involved in
further discussions. The Work Group was an invaluable reality-testing
instrument, though here too, selective perception doubtless influenced
what was said and what was heard.

It only remains to introduce the reader to some further caveats
about my intentions and their expression, as a guide to what follows.

A Guide for the Reader

These days no book on a topic as broad and exploratory as this one
can be read by itself. This book is one part in an elaborate mosaic being
pieced together in many places, and I do not intend it to stand by itself:
its usefulness will depend, in large measure, on the extent to which
readers know and use other concepts from related areas. To continue the
metaphor, I am contributing certain colors and shapes; how the reader
uses them will depend on how they are combined with other colors and
shapes in his own possession. Political scientists, sociologists, economists,
and even other social psychologists will have to combine their "pieces" with
mine to create satisfying additions to that mosaic. A sampling of related
ideas are cited or quoted. They in turn have their own quotations and
references and I depend on them to supplement my References. A number
of well known publications have not been cited. I assume that the reader
is familiar with them already or will come across them frequently. I count
on the reader to use information retrieval schemes that do not depend on
having everything in one place.

I have listed the people interviewed who were willing to be
identified, and their affiliations at the time of their interview; see the List
of Respondents. Like the bibliographical footnotes, they are references to
source materials, and like the notes they are potential sources of further
ideas and information.

I find distinct advantages in using many quotations. Sometimes
they emphasize a point I have made; sometimes they make the point. I

---

[11] A condition for membership, explicitly established when invitations
were proffered, was a moral obligation to be fully prepared when attending the
meetings.

see no reason to paraphrase someone else's observations if they have made them well. Quotations provide a change of stylistic pace; they show that others share the position I am developing (at least to the extent quoted); and they imply there is further understanding to be gleaned from the quoted reference. (All emphases within quotations are those of the authors.)

C. W. Churchman emphasized for me, and I fully agree with him, that the problem as defined and elaborated herein must be understood as an expression of my own psychology and its selective perception of what is happening. That others may agree proves little. But agreement—or disagreement—has the potential of creating ideas in good currency, and that is what attempting to share ideas is all about when one is, as I am, trying to be influential.

I have avoided trying to bolster my position by generalizing from single research studies, especially those done in the laboratory rather than in the field. Laboratory research, using student subjects or studies done under simulated and controlled conditions, does not carry the conviction of mirroring reality with sufficient richness.

At first I intended to pepper this book with formal hypotheses derived from the hunting expedition. I have decided against this, preferring to let the narrative stimulate the reader to his own formulations. While stating formal hypotheses would comply with one stylish standard for formal communication in the behavioral sciences, in this broad study it would be mainly a contribution to image-making. I know of no one who has ever tested a hypothesis as stated from someone else's collection of hypotheses. They are either too unqualified, or if precise enough, too trivial to be taken up in the form offered. Besides, creative hypothesis-testers want to invent their own hypotheses out of their unique sense of reality. I see my task as offering a reality that is sufficiently rich and compelling to stimulate others to draw their own questions from it, and their own schemes for answering them.

Given the linearity of language and pagination, the circularity of complex processes, and the absence of an over-arching theory or model, certain implications in one part of the book will not be sufficiently appreciated without the rest of it in mind. I know of no way around this, but a few observations may help some readers to approach the book more comprehensively. Matters that are taken up at one point are often taken up again later on. If I do not alert the reader that I will continue the topic or treat it more fully later, I run the risk of seeming to have ignored, at the point of introduction, obvious or important aspects. If I do alert the reader I run the risk of interrupting the reader's concentration on the matter at hand. I have chosen to run the former risk—most of the time. The detailed Table of Contents is intended to reduce that risk. Most of the book is about resistances to lrsp change-over efforts. Descriptions of

forces pushing for lrsp are concentrated in Chapter Three and the
Epilogue. Although from time to time I try to suggest how a certain
resistance might be overcome, the prevailing mood is depressing; readers
who find this hard to bear might turn to the Epilogue for a few encouraging words.

　　Throughout the book, individuals, groups, and organizations outside the ones we are focusing on at the moment will be subsumed under
the word "environment." When I mean the natural environment as
opposed to the social environment, I will so state. There is of course a
real risk in referring to human beings as "the environment": it deper-
sonalizes them. But I have already felt constrained, in the interests of
precision, to use conditional and future conditional tenses, and to use
"human" or "person" or "one" in order to avoid (at least some of the
time) "him" or "his" when I mean "him/her" or "hers/his"; to add
another sentence-lengthening requirement by referring each time to the
human incumbents that comprise the environment would be just too
much. I can only hope it will be clear from what I say about it that I
know there are people "out there."

　　It should be recognized from the outset by readers who are themselves proponents, and perhaps initiators, of change-over efforts, that the
changes in people and organizations required to move toward lrsp will
also be required of them personally. Sooner or later, then, the reader will
resist what is being said. Of course, the resistance may be appropriate
because an argument or conjecture is dubious. However, when reading
any book on this frustrating topic, it is worth keeping in mind that resistance may arise from a desire to avoid facing the personal threat to
beliefs, values, and sense of competence that each of us must inevitably
feel. P. Ratoosh (1966), an operations researcher, games theoretician, and
psychotherapist, after describing the resistances of executives to using new
information when it was introduced into a management game, has
speculated about why operation researchers avoid including psychological
factors in their models.

*The background of most workers in the field is largely engineering,
the physical sciences, and mathematics. Furthermore, the results and conclusions of the social sciences that can be fruitfully applied to this area
are meager. But this does not account for the lack of interest—an area of
ignorance will often present a challenge. It seems to me that there is
another reason that problems pertinent to the social sciences attract little
interest among most operational research workers. It is intimately related
to the reasons that our experimental groups reject the solution. It is that
the recognition that something that seems as complicated and uncontrol-
able as human psychology plays an essential role in operational research*

would lead to very grave doubts on the part of operational researchers about the potency of their techniques. And these doubts operational research workers are no more willing to entertain than were our chief executives willing to accept a solution when the acceptance would lead to doubts about their own competence [p. 254].

Much the same could be observed about anyone seeking to implement lrsp, myself included. Thus forewarned, perhaps readers may be better able to cope with their resistances to the implications of what follows.

Finally, this is *not* a book about the social psychological impact of lrsp on planners or planning staffs as such. The study on which this book is based began that way, but it gradually became evident that planning, as used here, is better understood as an organizational and societal condition. Planners and planning offices will be special resources in the planning process, but focusing on them does not seem to be the way to understand the problems or possibilities of changing toward lrsp. Occasionally, we shall pay specific attention to them because they will sometimes be seen, and will sometimes see themselves, as unique to the planning process, and this has some special social psychological implications. But the requirements involved in changing toward lrsp, as developed here, will put more common burdens on organizational members than unique burdens on planners, and it is these shared burdens that I will emphasize.

I

Overview and Context

In his extraordinary delineation of the nature of societal learning, and the need for it, E. Dunn (1971) observes:

The principal problem of social organization that confronts advanced societies . . . can best be seen by contrasting the organizational consequences of normal problem solving and paradigm shifts. In normal problem solving, system reorganization is purposive, anticipatory, and controlled. In contrast, paradigm shifts have historically been primarily reactive, unanticipated, and uncontrolled. They tend to arise out of a reaction to exogenously and endogenously generated boundary crises. They are frequently unanticipated by the management elite of the system. The reorganization is often defensive in character—that is, it is directed toward preserving and extending the life of the system in the face of change rather than taking the form of a directed self-transformation in pursuit of some higher order goal.

We appear to have arrived at a point in social history where this kind of uncontrolled social reorganization is taking on a rate and form that seem to threaten the viability of the social process itself. The reason for the special nature of the threat in advanced societies is the fact that we have formalized and mastered the process of normal problem solving in the physical sciences and in the design of physical systems to the point

16

that this very process is generating an accelerated and escalating series of boundary crises for established social systems [pp. 214–215].

If Dunn is right, and I believe he is, we must seek means for "directed self-transformation" or abandon ourselves to the consequences of drifting and muddling. Accepting this latter alternative as the dominant mode of response, it seems to me, would mean abdicating the essential human obligation to take responsibility for self and others, for today and tomorrow. The means for directed self-transformation which we will be concerned with is long-range social planning. But it will not be in the spirit and form usually associated with the term "normal problem-solving." Normal problem-solving won't work during "paradigm shifts," or whatever one prefers to call the turbulent and radical process of social change we seem caught up in. The very circumstances that lead to defensive behavior under such conditions strongly discourage the kinds of purposive and anticipatory performance appropriate to the situation. There can be an alternative meaning for lrsp: it can be seen as a procedure for accomplishing future-responsive societal learning (frsl). This is the meaning I intend lrsp to convey: purposes and procedures for learning how to cope constructively with the changing society; for learning what can be anticipated, chosen, and regulated; for learning how to overcome the defensive behavior that either tries to use lrsp for social engineering—or avoids it altogether, hoping to get through "as we always have."[1] In brief, I see *lrsp as a societal learning process for learning how to do lrsp.*

Lrsp could be a means, perhaps the only means, for accomplish-

---

[1] By "social engineering" I am referring to an attitude toward planning and society, held by those doing the planning, as much as to a method. It is elitist, top-down planning which assumes that the planers hold a monopoly on expertise. Those doing it are impatient with and resistant to any feedback from the environment that might upset their plans or the means used to implement them. Goals tend to be set rigidly and emphasis is placed on means for reaching them. It is more a "can-do" attitude in which the problem is assumed given and the task is to devise efficient means to "overcome," "breakthrough," or "war on" the problem. Careful assessment of what *is* the problem is usually bypassed on grounds of expediency, or because no one acceptable to the planners questions the problem definition that is in good currency. The definition of the problem tends to remain unexamined during the life of the engineering project. Too many expert reputations are at stake, and because the public was assured that the means used would work, too much is at stake politically. "Everybody knows what delinquency is. The trick is to get rid of it." Or "Everybody knows what causes delinquency. The task is to remove those causes." (Note that at various times over the years, "everybody" knew delinquency was caused by: inheritance, family, peer group, and lack of access to society's goodies, among other things.) For a knowledgeable and incisive summary of the weaknesses in the social engineering approach to social planning, see Rittel and Webber (1972).

ing Frsl. But the intention to do frsl will be necessary in order to permit the development of norms and organizational arrangements needed to learn how to do lrsp. Most of the activities that constitute lrsp would be located in organizations, but they would be dependent on an environment that believes and participates in learning to be a frsl society. This will be a dialectical process which evolves as we learn how to change toward lrsp and learn how to be a society that values frsl. To emphasize this interdependence, which in many ways amounts to an identity of activities and intentions, and especially to emphasize that lrsp is to be treated here as a learning procedure, I will sometimes use the terms lrsp and frsl interchangeably. The reader should know that whichever four letters are printed, the other four will probably fit just as well, at least in my mind.

What Will Be Required to Change Toward Lrsp?

In the chapters ahead I will try to demonstrate that *changing toward* frsl would require that people working in organizations, and in the social and natural environments linked to them, find it rewarding to learn how to do at least these six things:

1. Live with and acknowledge great uncertainty.
2. Embrace error.
3. Seek and accept the ethical responsibility and the conflict-laden interpersonal circumstances that attend goal-setting.
4. Evaluate the present in the light of anticipated futures, and commit themselves to actions in the present intended to respond to such long-range anticipations.
5. Live with role stress and forego the satisfactions of stable, on-the-job, social group relationships.
6. Be open to changes in commitments and direction, as suggested by changes in the conjectured pictures of the future and by evaluations of on-going activities.

To be able to learn these things will require basic changes in the ways people view themselves and others, and basic changes in the norms and structures of organizations that facilitate and reward some behaviors and punish others. To be able to learn them will also require changes in the way members of the environment view themselves and the organizations that serve them.

I will argue that changing people, organizations, and environments to meet these requirements can succeed, if it can succeed at all, only if it is done in a spirit which treats all aspects of changing over to lrsp as a learning process rather than as a social engineering technology. Everything that follows in this book rests on understanding why this is true. And whatever feasibility there may be for such changes will rest on the availability of circumstances that encourage such learning. It is thus appropriate to include in this overview a summary of my position on why lrsp must be a learning process.

First, the social technologies for facilitating this learning process are underdeveloped because social science theories and the data needed to refine and test them are inadequate for understanding and delineating complex and changing social systems. Indeed, it is not clear how much systematic and useful information about societal dynamics can be developed. We face a long period of learning how to create theories and technologies applicable to lrsp.

Second, we will have to learn how to introduce the requirements for lrsp into organizations in ways that will not result in their rejection, or their distortion into ritual or into rigid, dehumanizing, social engineering exercises. We will have to learn *how* to change toward lrsp. We will need to learn what organizations and their members need to do in order to function effectively as part of a frsl arrangement, and we will need to learn how organizations and their members can change over to functioning in those ways. Our theory and methods for organizational development, for felicitously relating the needs of humans to the techniques and structures of an organization, need much research and development. The development of personnel must be articulated with the development of organizational structures that are willing and able to redesign themselves continuously. And both personnel and organizational structure must be able to incorporate the evolving technology of lrsp. Therefore, a long period of learning how to apply organizational development techniques for introducing lrsp into organizations also lies ahead.

Third, a particularly difficult research and development activity will have to do with learning how to incorporate members of the environment into the lrsp process. Two reasons make incorporation mandatory. First, members of the environment share norms and expectancies that reinforce the very norms, structures, and self-images of members of organizations which will produce resistance to the introduction of lrsp. Shifting the norms and expectations of the environment so they permit or encourage organizations to experiment with learning how to meet the requirements for lrsp will itself require the environment to participate in the learning, and that in turn requires that it be part of the learning system. Second, at all stages of lrsp there will be need for ideas, arguments, perceptions, and information from those in the environment who presumably will gain and lose from the unfolding of particular activities guided by lrsp. But we do not know how to incorporate "inputs" from the environment in the lrsp process. What constitutes competence, relevance, and effective procedure have yet to be discovered, especially as we move into a time of partisans and confrontation politics. For more than one

hundred years we have been learning how to conduct an industrial democracy. We shall have to extend the societal learning process to learn
as a society how to learn in the situation that makes lrsp necessary. But
much more so than in the past, we shall have to be self-conscious and
committed to the learning process and learning experience as such.

Finally, we shall have to learn what in a turbulent world can be
guided and regulated and what it is necessary or desirable to regulate.
There are no ready-made, tested "solutions," nor, usually, even humane
coping procedures, for dealing with the major societal tasks. Even when
a wide-ranging "solution" can be proposed, candid examination reveals
that there are no available political, fiscal, and organizational means for
implementing the proposal. These need to be invented, developed through
the processes of frsl. We shall have to learn what it is that we can try to
manage through lrsp, as well as learning how to manage what we can
through lrsp.

In the light of these learning requirements, lrsp is needed to develop society's capabilities for meeting needs and opportunities that *cannot*
be quickly accomplished, that must work themselves out over a period of
ten to twenty years. Whatever approaches are developed will be developed
in the future and applied still later. Consequently the very goals for which
social research and development are undertaken, as well as the choice of
means to be used to move toward them, will have to be chosen with an
appreciation of what alternative longer-range futures seem worth achieving, and possible to achieve. But even if the organization's relevant future
is so close that it appears to harbor no new sources of uncertainty or requirements to rethink and refeel the value bases for the organization's
activities, responding to the requirements for lrsp seems prerequisite for
responsible organizational performance in the public interest.

Many sub-units in large government agencies will necessarily be
oriented in time and practice essentially to the next few years. But they
should be operating as part of a larger organizational perspective that
must have a longer orientation. If the overarching units are to be effective
in their lrsp, they will need knowledgeable interpretations and data about
what is happening in the present, from these sub-units, that is responsive
to a lrsp perspective. It would seem, then, that even if a government
organization's short-time perspective is appropriate, it will have to shift its
style of assessing purpose and procedure from looking at where it has been
to looking at where it is going. Hence decisions will have to be based on
appreciation of what needs to be done in a functional and temporal context that is more comprehensive than the disjointed incremental approach
permits. The incrementalist policy-maker, "typically a partisan, often
acknowledging no responsibility to his society as a whole, frankly pursuing

his own segmental interests" would have no place in such a setting (Hirshman & Lindblom, 1962, p. 220). Thus, while I will emphasize changing toward lrsp, because that is what we desperately need to do, the social psychological sources of resistance to changing would seem to apply as well to changing over to social planning with short-time perspectives.

The necessary learning tasks will be enormous and terrifying, as learning must be in threatening and confusing situations. We will look at only two facets of the task: first, the nature of the social psychological resistances to making the changes in organizations needed to meet the requirements that are necessary if lrsp is to be a societal learning procedure; and second, what might help overcome these resistances. One of the most difficult aspects of this learning task will be to discover when it will be appropriate to *resist* changes in the direction of lrsp. In Vickers' words, "the heritage we enjoy owes just as much to stout-hearted defenders as to fluid-minded innovators. . . . The slowing of change is one of our normal, as well as one of our pathological, responses and it is widely practiced for good, as well as bad reasons."[2] What are normal and pathological, or good and bad, resistances to changing over toward lrsp will depend on the context. Then too, the appropriateness of resistance to changing toward lrsp will be complicated by questions of ideological compatibility. C. W. Churchman has pointed out to me that some will argue that before planning can be humane each member of humankind must learn to obey the command "know thyself"; or that the proper way to deal with social issues is through politics, not planning; or that planning is just another way to deny or put off allocating resources *now* to the dispossessed and deprived. To some extent I share these positions, at least when I am apprehensive about the possible misuse of planning. On the whole, though, I believe frsl could further the ideological concerns of those who at first might consider lrsp antithetical to their interests. I will not, however, argue that here: I simply acknowledge that such concerns will be among the sources of resistance to lrsp. We will have to learn how to value them when they arise in particular situations.[3]

Of course there will be enormous obstructions to learning to change toward lrsp. Limited funds, technology, time constraints, manpower, contradictory and constricting laws, legislative prerogatives, conventional political aspirations, an obscene number of overlapping, com-

---

[2] G. Vickers, personal correspondence.
[3] While emphasis will be on resistances as they arise in organizations, by the very nature of lrsp as a societal learning procedure, it will be necessary to attend somewhat to complementary resistances that will arise in the organization's environment. Hopefully this book will stimulate others to give the environment the detailed attention it also deserves.

petitive, and obstructionist municipalities, jurisdictions, commissions, authorities, and so on, all will stand in the way. Some would say that if the legal, political, jurisdictional, and power issues could be resolved and if we were not to be plagued with the politics of confrontation, then the social psychological matters would take care of themselves. But these aspects and the social psychological matters comprise a self-reinforcing system. We are in J. Platt's term "locked in" (1969).[4] If interventions in one "part" of the system are likely to be successful it will be because attention was given to anticipating their impact on the other "parts." If there is to be system change there must be interventions, at least if we want to feel that changes in the system are deliberate rather than simply the product of "historical forces." Present arrangements were created by people, though not always with deliberation and not necessarily to produce the consequences they have; and they persist because changing them confronts people with the private and public costs of coping with innovation. Thus if changes are to be made in the direction of lrsp, they will have to be made by people choosing to do so, by people choosing not to resist innovations which may now seem natural or right to resist.

As a contribution, then, to overall understanding of what is required to change toward lrsp, I will examine herein the social psychological level of reactions to be anticipated for such change efforts. This level of description and analysis is not now part of the planning literature. Its usefulness lies in the fact that understanding and overcoming resistance to change has been amply demonstrated to be in significant part a social psychological matter in other settings involving other innovations, whatever other factors also operate.

I will try to show that the resistances to changing toward lrsp derive from images of man and his purposes, and from the organizational means for accomplishing them, that are incompatible with the requirements for lrsp. Historically, these images of man have brought us to where we are. They have resulted in ways of expressing and organizing human behavior characterized by hierarchical organizational structures, public organizations that try to avoid or at least minimize open contact with their relevant environment if it threatens them, and a host of negotiating procedures that reward closedness, resource preemption, power preemption, ambiguity, disjointed incrementalism, deceit, error-denying, distrust, interpersonal distance, pseudo-interpersonal collaboration, and pseudo-emotional support. They have resulted in setting organizational and sub-organizational survival above anticipatory responses to the future that are appropriate for environmental development; in seeking to attain and maintain power through aggressive and possessive actions;

---

[4] Also see Platt (1970) and Hoffer (1963).

in encouraging at least personal and organizational amorality; in avoiding feedback from the environment; and in waffling about serious future-responsive goal-setting. In other words, we reward forms of organizational life that at best discourage effective societal learning and at worst make it impossible. Instead, people are rewarded for behaving in the ways that are producing an ungovernable and unsatisfying world; which is made the more so because efforts to counteract this situation move in the very directions that exacerbate the situation—more novelty, distraction, image-making, security-seeking, more "nowness," more separatist "individuality" and splintering autonomy.[5]

I will also try to show that images of man and the good life that seem compatible with the social psychological requirements for frsl are now developing, most notably the definitions of man that derive from human potential explorations in psychology, philosophy, and theology, and that there are circumstances developing in our society that might make serious movement toward lrsp feasible. While the likelihood seems very small that this shift in definition of man and collateral changes in the structure of organizations will become dominant in the foreseeable future, we know far too little of what it takes to bring about massive social change to be sure the change cannot occur. We do not even know whether massive social change per se is necessary.

This perspective rests in turn on the position I accept regarding the nature of human nature and its expression in the way men organize themselves to compete or collaborate.

The Societal Expression of Human Nature: One Perspective

We are, after all, dealing with "human nature" when we examine the way people resist or respond favorably to change. Why and how people resist the changes associated with the requirements of lrsp will seem to be "natural," given the way people "are" and organizations "are." If so, it will seem that delineating why people resist is an idle exercise, since seeking to change people and their institutions so that they are able to meet the requirements of lrsp will seem to be trying to make people or organizations act "unnaturally." To appreciate why this is not an idle exercise it is necessary to understand that I am accepting throughout this book the well supported but poorly understood position that we make our own social reality.[6] That reality seems natural to us because we

[5] See, for example, Slater (1970).
[6] In what follows I am not arguing that man is infinitely plastic, unlimited by his biological nature. Doubtless there are limits on what he might be in himself and in his relations to others. But we do not know what these limits

are part of it, subject to the same reality-shaping processes as the people we shall be examining.

It is clearly true that both science and philosophy, by the concepts of human nature which they use and propagate, can powerfully affect men's views of themselves, their possibilities and their limitations, and may thus alter what human nature effectively is. A mistaken view of planetary motion, though held for centuries, had no effect on the motion of the planets. They continued on their elliptical way, undisturbed by human preference for circular motion; and even when men discovered their mistake, they had no means to bring the course of nature into line with their aesthetic predilections. A too restricted view of human nature, on the other hand, even though only briefly ascendant, can significantly alter the expectations and hence the behavior of men and societies and may thus provide its own bogus validation [Vickers, 1965, p. 17].[7]

In reviewing a study published by R. Titmuss that explains how it is that the British give their blood free and we sell ours, with the result that British blood is of better quality and more readily available than American blood, the reviewer observes: "Set up a social framework in which men are encouraged to be generous and most of them will rise to the occasion; set up one which encourages them to be selfish and most of them will sink to it. . . . Thus the assumption that man is motivated only by immediate self-interest . . . turns out to be merely another of the self-fulfilling hypotheses of social and political 'science'. . . . The utilitarian, having helped create a world in which human relationships have increasingly been brought—forced—into the marketplace, finds in it superb confirmation of his initial dogma; that man is governed by marketplace motives" (Claiborne, 1971, p. 4). C. Argyris (1969) makes a similar observation in arguing for research on interpersonal behavior that is more open, trusting, supportive, and feeling, for what he calls Pattern B behavior in contrast to Pattern A, the conventional mode of organizational behavior: "If one does not study the Pattern B world, one runs the risk of developing a conception of man in which the 'natural' behavior is hiding feelings, not taking risks, showing little concern, individuality, and trust. This will tend to occur naturally because individuals will turn to the descriptive research to develop their views about

are, or where they are, whereas we do know that through time and across cultures the demonstrated plasticity of man is far greater than any one culture has made use of.

[7] For a discussion of how psychological theory and psychiatry derive from and culturally reinforce given definitions of human nature, see Bart (1971, pp. 114–159). See also Kantor (1969).

man. What is becomes what ought to be. Existing theory is used to explain existing behavior. Thus black militants have defended their aggressive behavior by citing psychological research that 'proves' aggression is an expected response to frustration. The covert and silent analyzing of other people and unilaterally attributing motives to them can be shown to follow from present conceptions of attribution theory" (p. 901). Put in more abstract but more general terms:

> *It is important to keep in mind that the objectivity of the institutional world, however massive it may appear to the individual, is a humanly produced, constructed objectivity. . . . Despite the objectivity that marks the social world in human experience, it does not thereby acquire an ontological status apart from the human activity that produced it. . . . It is important to emphasize that the relationship between man, the producer, and the social world, his product, is and remains a dialectical one. That is, man (not, of course, in isolation but in his collectivities) and his social world interact with each other. The product acts back upon the producer [Berger and Luckmann, 1966, p. 60].*
>
> *The objectivity of the social world means that it confronts man as something outside of himself. The decisive question is whether he still retains the awareness that, however objectivated, the social world was made by men—and, therefore, can be remade by them. . . . Typically, the real relationship between man and his world is reversed in consciousness. Man, the producer of a world, is apprehended as its product, and human activity as an epiphenomenon of non-human processes. Human meanings are no longer understood as world-producing but as being, in their turn, products of the "nature of things." It must be emphasized that reification is a modality of consciousness, more precisely, a modality of man's objectification of the human world. Even while apprehending the world in reified terms, man continues to produce it. That is, man is capable paradoxically of producing a reality that denies him [p. 89].*

In reading and responding to this book it is critically important to appreciate that what we call the nature of man is only the nature he shows in a particular kind of man-made social structure that rewards and punishes him for behaving in certain ways, for seeing himself and his society in certain ways, and for expecting certain kinds of reciprocal behavior from others. "A culture is not only a reticulum of patterned means for satisfying needs but equally a network of stylized goals for individual and group achievement. Almost no human situations are viewed in ways which are altogether a consequence of the individual's experience. Culture is—among other things—a set of ready-made definitions of the situation which each participant only slightly retailors in his own idiomatic way;

Cultures create needs as well as provide a means of fulfilling them; cultures create problems as well as solving them." (Kluckhohn and Kelly, 1945, pp. 78–106).

If the reader even tentatively accepts this position it will be easier to see the behavior to be described as a product of culture and as such subject to change. If the reader persists in viewing typical organizational behavior as "natural," then what is called for in the following chapters will seem to counsel "saintliness" or perfection. It would be asking for that, by conventional standards. But alternative ways of being and doing, suggested along the way, need not be judged for acceptability according to some presumed standard of "naturalness." There *are* perceptual changes afoot not only with regard to planning but with regard to the nature of human nature and to the events that people attend to and consider important. Perhaps moves toward frsl can be facilitated if individuals try to accept and encourage as potentially "natural" certain arrangements of people and their activities that are different from those that seem so natural to us now.[8] Even if the establishment of new norms and structures seems highly problematic, if we see more clearly what needs to be done and what added knowledge is needed to try to do it we should at the very least enlarge the moral and intellectual setting in which to choose whether to take the clear risks of social disaster from drowning in our own disorder, or whether to take the new risks of social learning that might lead to a new social order.

To see *what* human nature may need to become and what organizational norms and structures would be needed to sustain and reward it, if lrsp is to become feasible, it is first necessary to be clearer about how and why the presently legitimated, hence rewarded, definition of human nature operates to resist changing over to lrsp. Since it is people who have to design and make the transition to living in the new structures that will sustain a different human nature, it is about people who are asked to change from their conventional structures that we need to know more:

---

[8] Such shifts in definition *have* happened before in what we call Western culture. For example, R. Heilbroner (1962) has described in a clear and fascinating manner the shift to the market-economy man from the definition of man that sustained and was sustained by the feudal culture of the Middle Ages. The required changes in values and organizational styles were enormous.

For a survey of the changes and continuities in Western definitions of societal reality from the "end" of the Middle Ages to the present, see Brinton (1953). For an even wider ranging perspective, see Mumford (1956). A summary of alternative definitions of "human nature" is in Drews and Lipson (1971, Chapter One). The enormous differences between ancient Greek and modern meanings with regard to ideas (and the "natural" behavior compatible with them) such as "freedom," "equality," "humanness," "work," and "privacy" are explicated in Arendt (1958).

people will have to change themselves and other people, sometimes through interpersonal skills, sometimes through less personal interventions in the forms of organizational arrangements and social programs. We need to understand why people act as they do in such situations of change; hence this social psychological exploration.

Environmental Turbulence as the Context for Lrsp

Ironically, appreciation of the need to cope with social turbulence has produced not only the beginnings of a technology intended to do so, but also a technology which on every hand brings to would-be planners information that emphasizes that things are much more complicated, interlocked, and seemingly intractable and unpredictable than they had appreciated when these evolving means were unavailable for probing societal processes; this information emphasizes the pathetic limits of our theory and methods for understanding what is going on "out there," for coping with societal turbulence.

Throughout, we will struggle with the question: Is there really any reason to believe that enough of our society *can* be contained, smoothed-out, anticipated, and studied so that we can learn enough through lrsp to find our way to preferred futures? An examination of the idea of the "turbulent environment" will help us cope with this question.

Two seminal papers (Emery and Trist, 1965; and Emery, 1967) have differentiated between four types of environments in terms of the kinds of transactions a system (in our case, an organization) must arrange in order to attain or avoid what the environment contains.[9] These transactions depend on whether the relevant contents of the environment are randomly or non-randomly distributed and whether they are active or passive in their response to the intervening system. Type 3 and Type 4 environments are important here. The Type 3 environment is the one within which organizations have operated for approximately the last two hundred years. For effective transactions within it, its members have developed the familiar hierarchically structured organizations and the corresponding supportive and legitimizing definitions of man. In the Type 3 environment "each system does not simply have to take account of the other when they meet at random, but it has to consider that what it knows about the environment can be known by another. That part of the environment to which it wishes to move is probably, for the same reason, the part to which the other wants to move. Knowing this, they will wish to improve their own chances by hindering the other, and they will know that the other will not only wish to do likewise, but will know

---

[9] Also see (Terreberry, 1968).

that they know this. In a word, the presence of others will imbricate some of the causal strands in the environment. The causal texture of the environment will, through the reactions of others, be partly determined by the intentions of the acting organization. However, the environment at large still provides a relatively stable ground for the arenas of organizational conflict" (Emery, 1967, p. 221).

The Type 4 environment is "the turbulent environment" which Emery and Trist argue now exists in our kind of society; it differs from Type 3 in having the profoundly important characteristic of "dynamic properties that arise not simply from the interaction of the systems [organizations], but also from the field itself." Emery continues:

There are undoubtedly important instances in which these dynamic field properties arise quite independently of the system in the field. . . . [However,] most significance attaches to the case where the dynamic field processes emerge as an unplanned consequence of the actions of the component systems. . . . We have recently become more aware of these processes through the intervention of the ecologists in problems of environmental pollution. . . . The emergence of active field forces (forces other than those stemming from the individual organizations or the similar organizations competing with it) means that the effects will not tend to fall off . . . but may at any point be amplified beyond all expectation. . . . Similarly, lines of action that are strongly pursued may find themselves unexpectedly attenuated by emergent field forces [p. 223].

This perception of what the world is like is what I shall mean when I refer to "turbulence" or the "turbulent environment." The Type 4 environment has evolved from Type 3 and is exemplified by societal conditions familiar to readers of this book; such is their momentum and pervasiveness and "these fields are so complex, so richly joined, that it is difficult to see how individual organizations can, by their own efforts, successfully adapt to them." (p. 223) Emery and Trist look at two modes of adaptation. The first mode "down-grade[s] complexity" by processes of "segmentation," "fractionation," or "dissociation." I will not use these terms, but later on we shall recognize these processes among the means for avoiding facing the requirements for changing over to lrsp. Emery's estimate of their utility for coping with a turbulent environment merits quoting: "(a) they are mutually facilitating defenses, not mutually exclusive; (b) they all tend to fragment the spatial and temporal connectedness of the larger social systems and focus further adaptive efforts on the localized here and now; (c) they all tend to sap the energies that are available to and can be mobilized by the larger systems and otherwise to reduce their adaptiveness" (p. 228).

Emery's second approach to a solution for coping with our Type 4 environment is to transform the environment by transforming the value system that defines it.[10] He proposes the redesign of social organizations as the most likely means of doing this comparatively quickly. He does so on the following grounds:

It is in the design of their social organization that men can make the biggest impact upon those environmental forces that mould their values (that make some ends more attractive, some assumptions about oneself and one's world more viable); further, it assumes that if these changes are made in the leading part, the socio-technical organizations, the effects will be more likely to spread more quickly than if made elsewhere. . . . We are suggesting that adults be the educators and that they educate themselves in the process of realizing their chosen organizational designs. This confronts us with the question of what values, and we are suggesting that the first decisions about values for the future control of our turbulent environments are the decisions that go into choosing our basic organizational designs. If we can spell out the possible choices in design we can see what alternative values are involved and perhaps hazard a guess at what values will be pursued by western societies [pp. 229–230].

Reasoning from cybernetic principles, Emery and Trist deduce that organizational redesign that emphasizes redundancy in an organization's response repertory has the most chance of succeeding in coping with turbulence, and that such redundancy is furthered by non-hierarchical, multiple-participation, organizational design. (As we shall see, there is evidence that supports their hypotheses.)

Emery and Trist do not claim that their analysis is complete or that their proposals for coping are sufficient: they simply think they are pointing in the right direction, and so do I. Their analysis is important because it tells us about a general and crucial characteristic of information from the environment with which organizations and members of the environment seeking to change toward lrsp will have to contend. And it is important because it raises a question about potential individual and organizational effectiveness that is bound to affect the social psychological context of those seeking to move toward or to avoid lrsp: Is it reasonable to expect that our Type 4 environment is *so* autonomous and unanticipatable that there really is very little reason to hope that actions taken in the present *can* be guided and revised by learning about the environment through lrsp?

[10] It is possible that error-embracing and the open acknowledgment of uncertainty, as explored in later chapters, may represent such value system changes.

In order to go through all the troubles involved in changing over to lrsp, the members of organizations would have to believe their relationship to the environment is such that undertaking actions in the present, aimed at attaining a chosen future, are likely enough to succeed to make the heavy burdens of trying worthwhile. Perhaps there is a tenable basis for hope if at any time we *believe* that the turbulent environment is comprised of three components.[11] These are:

(1) Those aspects that we believe are well enough understood in terms of present theory so that positions can be taken and acted on with some sense of the probability of outcomes, but which require for the development of such positions data that have not yet been collected and analyzed. (2) Those aspects that we believe are hypothetically understandable but for which theory has not yet been created: they must wait both for data and experiment to provide the basis for conceptualizing. (3) Those aspects of the environment which we believe are not understandable, controllable, or predictable by scientific means because they cannot be conceptualized within the ways of thinking available through science. These aspects would include emergent phenomena such as the "creation" of new social theory and images and phenomena which are important in their singularity but for which scientific methods supply only average or aggregated results.[12]

[11] Bell and Mau (1971) make beliefs about the past and present, causes and effects, and values central to their outline for a theory of social change. See especially pp. 18–23.

[12] An example may be helpful here. Scientific reasoning can predict with great precision what percent of a sample of radioactive material will disintegrate within a given time period. But the model that allows this can say nothing at all about *which* atoms will disintegrate in that time period, much less which one atom will be the next to do so. For humans, what we want to anticipate in many situations is precisely the outcome of a *specific* interaction between, say, eight committee members. Yet, except for certain classes of Newtonian relationships, scientific method can only supply theory with representations of aggregated or average outcomes of interacting events. What is more, the properties of a *system* of interactions cannot be predicted from the properties of the components. To describe these "emergent" properties seems to require a state of being or conceptualizing that is "outside" the system of components that comprise it (Polyani, 1966). Understanding men and their organizations would seem to be, to some important degree, not possible for men who are part of the social system they want to understand. These methodological and conceptual difficulties and their significance for the problems of anticipating futures are perhaps best symbolized by the perennial argument about the "great man" as maker or product of historical trends. It seems as if it is often *an* event or person that determines the nature of turbulence or tranquility. These seem to be the unexpected, the unanticipated devlopments that make obsolete previous predictions or expectations. But there is also a strong counter-argument. (A superb introduction to the question of the extent to which individuals make history or history makes

Changing toward lrsp could be a procedure for extending our ability to reduce turbulence to the extent that our beliefs about components (1) and (2) can be made to work. That is, frsl could be a means for inventing, and then coming to believe in, a social reality in which people and organizations would behave so that significant amounts of the turbulence they now generate could be understood (or could be learned to be understood) and could be regulated or eliminated: "Men in their dealings with men create and recognize another kind of regularity—rules of their own devising, imposed and accepted consciously and unconsciously. The only reason men are by and large more predictable than the weather is that they are concerned to be predictable; concerned to meet each other's expectations by accepting common self-expectations" (Vickers, 1970, p. 101).

As I have emphasized earlier, our social reality now operates as it does because we have "created" it that way, by our actions in response to the expectations we hold about what constitutes its "natural" modes of operation. We act out our own theory of reality. In time, we could hope that people and institutions could learn to define themselves in new ways and to expect responses from each other which would lead them to behave increasingly so as to make frsl possible: "The social processes involved in both the formation and the maintenance of identity are determined by the social structure. Conversely, the identities produced by the interplay of organism, individual consciousness, and social structure react upon the given social structure, maintaining it, modifying it, or even reshaping it. Societies have histories in the course of which specific identities emerge; these histories are, however, made by men with specific identities" (Berger and Luckmann, 1966, p. 173).

We are beginning to be self-conscious about this process of creating reality by believing it "really" is thus and such. For example, we apply fiscal and monetary theory in the light of a self-conscious effort to anticipate likely behavioral responses to its application. Many well educated people define themselves in psychoanalytic terms and respond to others in terms of psychoanalytic attributes they ascribe to them, such as paranoid, repressed, defensive, compulsive, neurotic, and so on. And recently anti-racists and anti-sexists have, with growing effect, explicated the usually unconscious beliefs, behaviors, and institutional arrangements that have resulted in a reality that guides blacks, women, homosexuals, and others into ways of being that maintain self-fulfilling prophesies about them.

The third component of a turbulent environment would remain

---

individuals is Berlin, 1957; a complementary classic is Hook, 1943.) Other observers have arrived at similar conclusions.

outside the direct purview of lrsp. But trying to cope with it would include two kinds of lrsp-facilitated behavior: First, a variation of "management by exception" but with the important difference that there could be more resources for coping with the exception because not so much would have been frittered away trying to manage by ad hoc or incremental means those societal circumstances that could be better managed through lrsp. And second, avoiding actions that an enlarged capability for and supportive sensitivity to lrsp would suggest are likely to have serious unanticipated or unregulatable consequences. The decisions to abandon nuclear testing in the atmosphere and to forgo the supersonic transport project are precursors of such avoidance actions. The societal rewards from learning through lrsp should encourage the development of values which themselves improve the setting for societal learning, and these values could enhance sensitivity to and discouragement of the production of turbulence we think we can't regulate.

Of course the unregulatable, unanticipatable component of turbulence could turn out to be overwhelming rather than residual. If so, we have produced for ourselves an environment in which our civilization or at least our present society cannot survive. There are, after all, more dead societies than live ones, and many apparently died as a result of conditions they themselves produced. But we are a very long way from knowing that our turbulence is so intractable: we have not instituted the lrsp or even the efforts to change over toward it that would allow us to learn the extent to which we can understand, transform, control, and cope with the turbulent environment which makes lrsp necessary in the first place.

Some Sources of Turbulence and Their Implications

Those involved in changing over to lrsp must be able to deal with several, often simultaneous, contributions from the overall turbulent environment. If organizations are going to try to discover to what extent and in what ways we can cope with turbulence, by learning with the aid of lrsp, they will have to begin by facing turbulence openly rather than avoiding its manifestations or refusing to recognize our finite capabilities for regulating it. But we have almost no tested organizational forms appropriate for engaging domestic turbulence.[13] To an important extent, organizational leadership typically has defined its competence by its ability to reduce or remove turbulence from the organizational setting, or, under conditions of its choice, to introduce it for special change-

---

[13] Combat military organizations, in contrast to peacetime military groups, have developed such forms under *some* combat conditions. It would be fruitful to compare both the conditions of turbulence and the means for responding to it (including the moral imperatives) with the domestic situation.

inducing purposes.[14] One of the powerful psychological rewards organizations provide their members is protection from turbulence: "One of the functions which formal organizations perform is to buffer the individual member from the impact of the chaotic interrelation of everything to everything. Ideally, organizations free the member effectively to deal with just so much of the environment as his intellect and psyche permit. The organization, through compartmentalization of tasks and responsibilities, circumscribes for each member the domain of environmental factors with which he must be concerned, and permits a match to be established between the complexity of the environment, the type of role and the modalities of decision-making which are appropriate in the functions performed by the members" (McWhinney, 1968, p. 269). At the least, the organization specifies what kinds and sources of turbulence a member is expected to cope with as well as how to cope with it through performance of an assigned role.

Much of our cultural emphasis on control probably grows from a desire for a stable, predictable, hence non-threatening life setting. Traditionally, the most approved models of behavior have been those who could control themselves, others, and nature. So deep is the satisfaction of feeling in control that, rather than risk loss of control by becoming involved with turbulence for which one has not learned the ritual or operative means for control, many people live on the edge of becoming or are in fact what I have elsewhere called a "petit Eichman." Most people avoid examining the ethical bases for their performance, partially, I think, because doing so exposes the ambiguous consequences of their actions. This in turn exposes the questionable extent to which they really do control their world. Thus they avoid, and are encouraged to avoid, reflection about the moral consequences of their role performance by believing that "that's not my job."[15] For them, somebody else in the organization or some other organization has the responsibility for the larger ethical issues behind what they do. But if turbulence invades the organization, the arrangements that protected individuals from facing up to the ethical implications of their actions will no longer be adequate. As a result, some will resist moves toward lrsp because by requiring openness to turbulence it will also pressure them to reexamine themselves, which they want to avoid.

Since information feedback from the environment will be mandatory for lrsp, it will also become a generator of turbulence within the

[14] Observed by Argyris, in personal conversation, on the basis of his wide experience with managers, administrators, and executives in all kinds of organizations. Other students of organizational behavior have made similar observations.

[15] On this endemic behavior, see (Arendt, 1963), especially p. 253. Two examples from today: (Vandivier, 1972), and (Terkel, 1972).

organization because it will provide continuing evidence of turbulence outside.[16] To some degree, this internal turbulence will mirror external turbulence, because many organization members, particularly those professionals in human welfare areas, will *also* be members of various contending and contentious groups in that environment. (Recall the civil servants who joined protests against the Vietnam war in defiance of the Hatch Act, and the many leaks of organizationally embarrassing reports.) In part, internal turbulence will result from members' reactions to efforts to change toward lrsp, the very change needed in order to respond creatively to information about the external environment. While evaluations of the usefulness of public agencies have been rare and are difficult to contrive, it is clear that the cause is at least as much because the organizations prefer it that way as because evaluation methodology is weak. Instead of seeking more feedback for better decision-making and evaluation, organizations use many defenses against feedback in order to avoid the disruption it inevitably must generate. (See Chapters Fifteen and Sixteen.)

In the future more voluntary organizations will provide consumer advocates, environmentalists, protesters, and advocate planners to serve special needs and interests (Chapman, 1968). There will also be more circumstances, value shifts, and voluntary organizations to incite and train members of the environment to marshall their data and force their feedback upon other organizations. Social indicator data and more sophisticated models of societal processes will make more information available to support differing interpretations of the meaning of the feedback. These interpretations will be part of the feedback forced on organizations. To the degree that internal and external interpretations differ, internal turbulence at least will increase, especially when interpretations are based on different and strongly held value priorities.

Attending seriously to feedback from the future—future studies—will also contribute to turbulence. Future studies inevitably raise questions about the longer-term utility of present activities. In doing so they also confront those involved in them with disturbing questions about their usefulness and commitments. Since future conjectures must change over time, and since they cannot be proven correct before the fact, their con-

---

[16] I am referring to internal upsets and disruptions as "turbulence" because some reactions will be unanticipated and will produce reverberating consequences within and among organizations and their environments not unlike those produced by turbulence in the environment outside the organization. The unanticipated nature of the responses and the difficulty in containing secondary and tertiary impacts from them will increase, because the very bureaucratic norms that expelled or at least limited turbulence will have to change in order to allow organizations to receive and respond to turbulent messages from the environment.

tribution to organizational turbulence will be repetitive as well as self-imposed.

In situations where turbulence is high and where its repression would be counterproductive, people in organizations will have to learn anew how to demonstrate competence, and those in the environment will have to learn how to assess it. They will have to learn how to respond to turbulence without overreacting or underreacting to it. Conventional reactions include avoiding feedback, tightening-up, firing the bearer of bad news, obfuscation, repression, and "fire-fighting."[17] Instead, leaders will have to see themselves as competent, and be seen as competent by their organizations and their environments, precisely because they seek out and engage environmental turbulence instead of seeking to avoid or repress it. Of course this poses formidable problems for the conventional politician, political appointee, or administrator; he expects to reduce turbulence, not seek it out, and believes that this is what his superiors and constituents expect of him. Others in the environment will have to forego seeking a leader who, by conventional definition, is able to protect them from turbulence. But we know that accepting the burden of freedom, of personal responsibility, is difficult (Fromm, 1941).

In all, making an individual and an organization accessible to turbulent input means living with larger overloads of information and more confusion about who one is and what one is supposed to do. In conventional organizations with conventional norms and rewards, when conditions of overload and ambiguity occur, tempers shorten, people and organizations play it safe and defensively close to the chest, values either surface irritatingly or are repressed dangerously, and management leans toward hierarchical command philosophies. "When the crunch comes you do what you know works—and no nonsense." Planning doesn't happen. Yet, it is societal turbulence that makes lrsp necessary and, if lrsp is to be tried, it is necessary to be open to it. The structures of organizations

---

[17] Fire-fighting is usually a consequence of actions previously taken to protect an organization, especially a government organization, from turbulence-generating feedback. Fire-fighting aims at getting things under control as fast as possible without much, if any, attention to the impact of the fire-fighting on any plans, much less long-range plans: it is disjointedly incremental in style and philosophy. Indeed, it has often been lamented that organizations use so many of their resources fire-fighting that they have none left with which to plan. It should also be noted, however, that one of the great rewards in fire-fighting is that it is an activity that removes one's sense of uncertainty and indecision—quite the opposite of the lrsp state of mind. Since fire-fighting is compatible with the rewards and structures of conventional organizations, it seems much easier to maintain the relationship with the environment which eventually results in fire-fights than to take on the social psychological burdens of deliberately changing over to internal and external arrangements that would reward long-range planning.

and the behavior of their members must be redesigned so that information overload and existential ambiguity do not produce resistances to efforts to change toward lrsp. Before undertaking a detailed examination of the social psychological nature of these resistances and what might be done to reduce or remove them, when appropriate, we need to be clear on the characteristics of lrsp. For it will be these specific characteristics, set against the fact of a turbulent social and natural environment, that will give us the clues as to what social psychological factors to focus on within organizations and among their members.

II

The Meaning and Purposes of Long-Range Social Planning—or Future-Responsive Societal Learning

*T*his chapter has three tasks: first, to establish an understanding of what I mean by lrsp; second, to demonstrate why, from the technological standpoint, lrsp can operate only as a means for societal learning rather than as a means for social engineering;[1] and third to explore in a general way certain terms and activities that will pervade later chapters.

What Is Meant by Long-Range Social Planning?

The conception of lrsp emphasized here grows from a variety of hopes, motivations, perceptions, and ambivalences. The evolving idea of lrsp is therefore very much a product of the times, but it is also a product of the history of planning per se. For many people the idea of lrsp carries with it a semantic freight of earlier, essentially elitist meanings: planning in which middle-class, "city-beautiful," or land-use criteria were established by experts working with those in power. People were "planned-for." If this old approach continues to be the image believed by profes-

[1] In later chapters I will try to show why, if the social psychological resistances to lrsp are to be overcome, lrsp must be valued as a learning procedure rather than as a social engineering method.

sionals and laymen, it will contribute an important and avoidable source of resistance to efforts to try the societal learning approach espoused here. However, while there is a broad consensus, among those in the camp to be quoted, about the normative and operational requirements for lrsp, the political consequences of what is being proposed are not clear. Given the real-world context in which trying to change over to frsl would take place, B. Gross's "friendly fascism" looms; and lrsp could indeed contribute to the arrival of fascism if it were to regress, as it easily might, into efforts to do social engineering (Gross, 1970).[2] One motive for trying to do lrsp will be to maintain the present distribution of power. Given the mixed motives behind the thrust to introduce lrsp, there is a real risk that alterations in organizational behavior made in the name of changing toward lrsp could be corrupted in the direction of social engineering. But learning how to avoid that eventuality is one of the risks involved in learning how to accomplish frsl. Not attempting this kind of learning, and continuing to try to muddle through, seems to carry a far higher risk of societal disaster—quite possibly of "friendly fascism," of increasing disruption and decay.

I begin, then, with an attempt to strip away misleading semantic freight by suggesting how I envision lrsp by quoting some who are struggling to invent purposes and activities that are appropriate for it, both now and in the kind of world we think we would like to seek.

H. Ozbekhan (1969, p. 118) has contrasted the "mechanistic" or "social engineering" planning concept with what he calls a "human action model":

Mechanistic Model	Human Action Model
Goals given from outside.	Selects values, invents objectives, defines goals.
Designed to solve specific class of problems.	Seeks norms, defines purpose.
Internal organization independent of purpose.	Higher order organization defined by purpose.
Controlled by external policy.	Self-regulating and self-adaptive.
Programmed actions toward given outcome.	Regulation of steady-state dynamic through change and governance of meta-system's self-adaptive and self-regulatory tendencies, through policy formation.

In an elegant summary of the inadequacies of the traditional concept of urban comprehensive planning, as prolegomenon to conceiving

[2] See also Gross (1971, especially pp. 283–287); and Morris (1948, pp. 166, 168).

planning (in the sense used here) as a mutual societal learning process,
J. Friedmann (1971) expresses the mood of this book's intentions regarding lrsp:

> *If knowledge about metropolis is revealed to us only in fragments and sequentially, a flow concept must come to replace the now outdated notion of learning as a fixed stock of knowledge. The policy analyst, accordingly, is not a man having a superior knowledge in some field, but a superior ability to learn. To be a rapid learner, he will need new tools for exploring complex problem situations, a facility at concept formulation, and a background of relevant theory that will help him integrate new observational data into ad hoc models useful for strategic intervention. But capability for rapid learning is not enough. Unless potential client groups can be taken along on this learning trip, the expert's models will . . . simply remain models. Expert and client must share in the learning experience so that a joint reconceptualization of problems can occur and the possibilities for concerted action be discovered. The policy analyst must thus be able also to structure the learning experience of others, to be a teacher and learner at the same time.*
>
> *Mutual learning involves a symbiosis of policy analysis and client group that should go beyond a single interaction and extend to a continuing relationship. It is not a limited deficiency that has to be made up. The metropolitan age imposes upon all organizations a requirement of continuous adjustment, of exploration, discovery, and learning.*
>
> *. . . In a situation of accelerated change and only limited autonomy, this will require a tightening of the feedback loops of information about change in both internal and environmental states, a general attitude of openness towards the future, and a quickening of the response times to new learning.*
>
> *. . . A willingness to explore alternative futures in the search for new possibilities of action is an important part of the learning orientation here proposed [Friedmann, 1971, p. 325].*[3]

E. Jantsch (1969) summarizes the contrasts between the old mechanistic, or social-engineering, concept of planning and those concepts we will attend to:

> *Three essential features of the "new" planning make it radically different from the "old" (non-creative) planning: (1) The general intro-*

---

[3] Friedmann (1973) elaborates a societal participation procedure. Its implementation, it seems to me, would depend on overcoming the resistances examined here. Also see the rest of the May-June 1971 issue of *Public Administration Review*, Mertins and Gross, Eds.

duction of normative thinking *and* valuation *into planning, make it non-deterministic and futures-creative, and places emphasis on invention through forecasting; (2) the recognition of* system design *as the central subject of planning, making it non-linear (i.e., acting upon structures rather than variables of systems) and simultaneous in its general approach; and, following from the two preceding points, (3) the conception of* three levels—*normative or policy planning (the "ought"), strategic planning (the "can"), and tactical or operational planning (the "will")* —*in whose interaction the "new," futures-creative planning unfolds.*

Planning *deals with system design at the levels of total system dynamics, system structures (goals), and changes of variables in given system structures. Planning provides the information basis, in dynamic terms, for decision-making.*[4]

J. Friend and W. Jessop of the Tavistock Institute argue:

In public planning, however, it is exceptionally difficult to formulate strategies in advance which are sufficient to cope with all conceivable contingencies; the complexity of the community system, and the imperfect understanding of it in the governmental system, combine to prevent any complete enumeration of the situations which the former might be expected to present. In these circumstances, planning must become in some degree an adaptive process. Although firm commitments may from time to time be required in particular sectors of a complex decision field, it may also become particularly important to retain an element of flexibility in other sectors in the expectation that, by the time commitment in these sectors becomes inevitable, the state of knowledge of the environment may be very different and the whole context of decision may have changed. This does not necessarily mean that the process has reverted from one of planning to one of unco-ordinated short-term response: by adopting a strategic approach, *involving formulation and comparison of possible solutions over a wide decision field embracing anticipated as well as current situations, the governmental system may find that it is led to select a very different set of immediate actions than would otherwise have been the case [Friend and Jessop, 1969, p. 112].*[5]

---

[4] A more readily available version of his position is in Jantsch (1972).

[5] Etzioni's (1968) concept of "mixed-scanning" seems entirely compatible with the approach proposed here. His point is: "What is needed for active decision-making is a strategy that is less exacting than the rationalistic one but not as constricting in its perspective as the incremental approach, not as utopian as rationalism but not as conservative as incrementalism, not so unrealistic a model that it cannot be followed but not one that legitimates myopic, self-oriented, non-innovative decision-making" (pp. 282–283).

A. Kahn (1969) has written the most searching examination of social planning.[6] As such, an extensive quotation from his work will help reinforce the concept of lrsp proposed here and also provide a sense of the scope of human welfare subsumed by the word "social":

> *The central goal of planning is not a blueprint but a series of generalized guides to future decisions and actions. It demands: (a)* selection of objectives *in the light of assessment of interests, trends or problems, social goals or values, and awareness of their broader implications; (b)* a willingness to act in foresight, *based on more or less faith and rigorous projections; (c)* constant translation of policies into implications for specific objectives and for programs and action; *(d)* constant evaluation and feedback.

His diagram, essentially a normative expression, of the "steps" or "phases" in lrsp (see Figure 1) summarizes the tasks to be accomplished and emphasizes the unavoidably cyclic and interactive nature of these activities (p. 62).

As to the matter of social planning:

> *Social planning at present addresses the following domains, appearing routinely in some and only occasionally in others. We move from smaller to larger societal units:*
>
> Planning within an agency or organization in social welfare. (*This is properly seen as administrative planning.*) *Planning has always been understood to be a function of administration. For example, a local welfare department needs (and some do have) a planning staff.*
>
> Planning for a concert of services on a community level. (*This is sectorial or categorical planning on the local level.*) *The focus is coordination and case integration. As an illustration, we might mention* Planning Community Services for Children in Trouble. *The point of departure for such planning might be a social problem (illegitimacy) or a service system (child welfare). The objective is the creation of a coordinated service system in the public or voluntary sectors or in both combined.*
>
> Planning to introduce (or correlate) social components into housing projects, or into local, city-wide, or regional housing and renewal

---

[6] In Dror's optimal model of policy formulation (1968, pp. 15–16), the policy-making stages and the post-policy-making stages seem entirely compatible with the position developed here. What he calls the "meta-policymaking stage" is compatible with the learning processes involved in learning how to carry out the policy-making and post-policy-making stages.

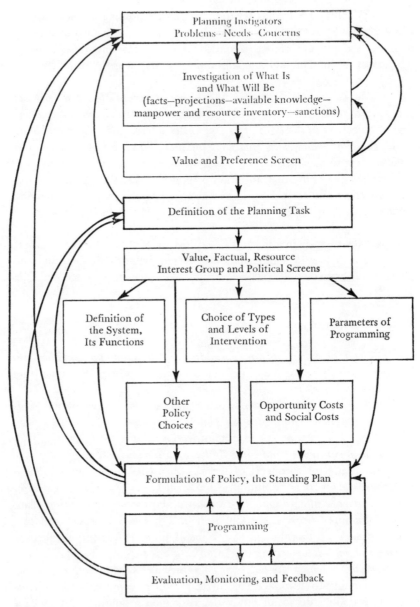

Interlocking Circles and Spirals: Planning in Action. From A. Kahn, *Theory and Practice of Social Planning*, Chapter Two.

activities. (*This is the* social *in relation to* physical *planning.*) *This category includes social planning in New Towns, social aspects of public housing planning, community social facilities in renewal areas, relocation, the Model Cities program.*

Planning nationally or regionally for an intervention system. (*This includes sectorial or categorical planning on a regional or national level; planning by functional fields.*) *Here, too, the concern might be with the public or the voluntary sectors, or with both combined. While the definition of boundaries of intervention systems is in itself subject to difficulty and controversy, one must periodically cope with such questions nationally, as in child welfare planning, next steps for the social security system, and the design of housing legislation.*

Problem-oriented or social-trend oriented planning. *This may also be seen as planning for the interrelationships among or restructuring of intervention systems, usually with reference to a broad national, state, or regional problem. This type of planning may encompass two or several intervention systems, and the outcome may involve their reconceptualization. For example, anti-poverty planning could result in new relationships among social security, public assistance, and tax programs. Coping with juvenile crime may involve and restructure several systems. Planning to cope with the consequences of automation or the causes of urban riots has broad ramifications. In these and other illustrations the outcome may be policy and institutional changes as well as the restructuring of direct services.*

Planning the social aspects of fiscal and monetary policy or other public programs not primarily defined as "social." *Included here are social and family policy concerns with reference to tax policy, tariff, road-building, etc.* [*Kahn, 1969, pp. 19–20*].

Dunn (1971) provides some observations that fuse the previous quotations and point toward individual and societal behavior, the social psychological sources of which will preoccupy us in later chapters:

Prediction takes the form of a developmental hypothesis, which may be expressed as follows: 'We hypothecate that if we undertake a certain course of action; the performance of the social system will be modified in such a way as to improve its efficiency in satisfying the goals or objectives of the system.' This is not known to be true on the basis of established deterministic laws. It is not an exercise in simple engineering design. It is an experimental design. Planning takes the form of conducting an experiment by embodying the new modes of behavior in the performance of the system. It can be viewed as testing the developmental hypothesis in action. If the developmental hypothesis is not falsified by the results of the experiment (i.e., if the performance of the system with reference to its goals is improved), the novel mode of behavior will be reinforced and persist. If the results call the hypothesis into question, a new or modified one will take its place and a new experiment in social action carried out.

It is not implied that social learning is always the product of a consciously designed and carried out social action experiment. During much of social history to date this has not been so. . . . Even where free from self-deception, those who are engaged in initiating a change in behavior often feel it necessary to represent the change proposal as a certified cure for social ills or a certified instrument of social gain. . . . As a consequence, the implementation of social action is rarely viewed as a test. Indeed, it is often carried out in such a way as to obscure the results of the test and render difficult, if not impossible, dispassionate evaluation" [*pp. 133, 134*].

Many of these intentions and descriptions converge in M. Webber's incisive description of activities that should constitute social planning.

1. The explication of goals, objectives, and targets for each subsystem under consideration including, in the public sphere, each of the publics that will be touched by the planned actions.

2. The continuous forecasting of both qualitative and quantitative changes that lie outside the planners' control.

3. The continuous forecasting of likely chains of consequences, within and especially among subsystems, resulting from each set of alternatively hypothesized planned actions.

4. The appraisal of investment costs and welfare payoffs attached to each alternatively projected history. If a reasonable fit is found between an hypothesized course of action and the value sets, a time-sequenced action strategy is synthesized, comprising shorter-run action tactics, each with its time targets. Each shorter-run tactic is carefully appraised for its likely net return, and is then expressed in the language of fiscal budgets.

5. The continuous monitoring of the systems being planned. A constant flow of information on actual outcomes is fed back into the planning system to signal forecasting errors and to actuate corrective steps. In addition, early warning of imminent danger or opportunity can alert deciders and, most important, the effectiveness of goal-directed actions can be empirically evaluated for each subsystem and each public [*Webber, 1968, p. 278*].

However, since the above phrasing tends to stress budgetary and fiscal criteria, it unnecessarily constricts our meaning here. Webber's reformulation provides a simplified summary of the requirements for lrsp which will serve our purposes as a quick reference check list:

1. Conjectures about future settings (differentiating exogenous and endogenous factors) for which the working out of the plan over time is relevant and desirable.

2. Analysis leading to goal setting.

3. Evaluation of the costs and benefits of alternative plans for goal seeking.

4. Tracing out the consequences for the chosen plan of pertinent circumstances outside the plan's direct operating environment.

5. Laying out and carrying out sequenced chains of actions that define the plan.

6. Evaluation of how the plan is working out on the basis of environmental feedback that permits recycling of the above steps.[7]

Carrying out bits and pieces of the list is not of itself lrsp—though succeeding with bits and pieces may create a supportive atmosphere for further attempts to change toward lrsp. Emphasizing the bits and pieces without appreciating what else is required encourages overlooking two crucial consequences inherent in the multiple requirements that characterize lrsp: First, in the context of the *set* of activities comprising lrsp, the social psychological implications for the people involved will always extend beyond those associated with a particular activity. Second, to be meaningful in an lrsp sense, implementing any one procedure requires that the other activities be implemented as well. All requirements need not be implemented by the same people or even by the same organization, but those involved in any given activity must know and understand why their activities are integrated into a deliberately contrived set of activities intended to lead toward frsl. During the period of changing toward lrsp it is particularly important that people understand that the intention is to fold their activities, over time and across and within organizations, into a lrsp "package." Thus, as described here:

It will not be lrsp if a systematic examination of relevant futures is not part of the basis of choosing goals and programs. Merely projecting or extrapolating from the past or present is not systematically looking at alternative futures. For example, it is now the fashion for colleges and universities to plan for their future. Almost invariably the issues examined have to do with new capital investments and faculty additions to service a projected future population of students. It is seldom considered that in the university of the future, faculties may be smaller with students dispersed geographically, possibly linked electronically (and through cheap

[7] As edited from the transcript of a Work Group meeting and approved by him.

and easy transportation) into several universities (or learning centers) rather than only one.

It will not be lrsp if future-responsive goals are not spelled out and priorities assigned as a basis for program design and resource allocation. This would include explication of both the social costs and benefits expected to be attached to a given goal, since all goals, if described so that progress toward their attainment can be evaluated, embody undesirable consequences as well. At present no such goal explications are made in areas such as power, pollution, education, employment, or transportation. For example, city planners typically set as a goal the capacity to accommodate a certain number of private automobiles ten to twenty years from now. They almost never expose the anticipated costs in public health that could result from automobile pollution increases, nor do they examine the possibility that in the future staggered work hours or much smaller commuting vehicles could relieve peak road capacity demands. In the federal government the activities closest to the explication of goals and their consequences are like those undertaken by Presidential Commissions. The trivial destiny of Presidential Commission studies, for all their careful analyses and qualified recommendations, is too well known to merit further comment.

It will not be lrsp if requirements (2) and (3)—analysis leading to goal setting, and evaluation of the costs and benefits of alternative plans for goal seeking—are not met. PPBS (planning, programming, budgeting systems) and related methods are a beginning. But, so far, not only are the techniques inadequate but there is a strong tendency to use PPBS to bolster the preferences of superiors rather than as a deliberate method for evaluating costs and benefits and then, in the light of these and other requirements for lrsp, acting in conjunction with other agencies. That agencies must prepare environmental impact statements, according to the Environmental Protection Act, bodes well; but the attempts, at this writing, to amend the Act into impotence and the Secretary of Commerce's rejection of the findings on the likely adverse impact of the Alaskan pipeline, make it clear that this move toward an lrsp philosophy will be strongly resisted.

It will not be lrsp unless the plan includes procedures intended to accomplish the plan. Typically, plans omit this requirement either because it has not been thought through or because of fear that explicating the procedures would also raise intransigent political, ideological, organizational, and goal-priority problems. But avoiding requirement (5)—carrying out a sequence of actions that define the plan—vitiates most of the usefulness of the other requirements. Implementation planning is of the essence for assessing goals and program feasibility, and in the case of frsl it is crucial for exposing the areas where learning will be necessary in order to discover implementation procedures. We do this phase of planning very well when scheduling the development of hardware, whether it be buildings, dams, or spacecraft. Indeed, much of the feasibility evaluation for the manned moon-landing program revolved around the question of sequencing the research and development and creating documentation procedures so that learning could and would occur. (Thus when three astronauts died in a space capsule fire, it was possible to pinpoint precisely what had gone wrong and what needed to be done to avoid another such tragedy.) In social planning, the strong tendency is to avoid exposing the implementation requirements for fear the plan will be rejected before it begins to be implemented. One reason that "plans" evaporate is because those involved have not tried to anticipate "what they are getting into" and shared this in advance, with others who would be in it with them, to get their understanding and commitment. (An exception worth careful attention has been the extensive explication in the preparatory studies of what would be required to implement the capital improvements proposed for the new Los Angeles master plan. To do so, Chief of City Planning, Calvin Hamilton, found it necessary to carry out a number of other requirements for lrsp. These will be referred to, as appropriate, later.)

It will not be lrsp if evaluation of both goals and means is absent. Evaluation, when it is conducted, is usually done in an adversary spirit, because organizations are reluctant to discover whether their preferred and publicized goals are meaningful and their programs effective. This is so because evaluation is perceived as a threat. If lrsp were the norm, however, negative findings would not need to be threatening. Nor would organizational efforts need to be represented in ways that would result in negative findings being a threat. Instead, untried programs and goals would be treated as experiments. If the findings were negative they would be treated as they are in the laboratory, as hypotheses that were not verified. Through the increased understanding thereby provided a new program or goal would be introduced. The resistance to evaluation under present norms emphasizes the second requirement if evaluation is to meet its requirements within the context of lrsp: organizations must be designed so that the evaluations do in fact systematically influence changes in program content and conduct and in the choice of goals. As of now, there is no certainty that evaluation results will be influential. Indeed, until very recently it was highly unlikely that evaluations would be undertaken.

Finally it will not be lrsp, in the spirit intended here, unless actions in fulfillment of the requirements are undertaken self-consciously for the specific purpose of facilitating frsl. In this, there is a precedent and perhaps a model in the self-conscious efforts of the writers of the Constitution to build in mechanisms to regulate the use and abuse of power.

That none of these requirements are in themselves lrsp, and that seldom is any one of them understood self-consciously to further the development of frsl, does not mean that they cannot further that development. The very fact that there are more efforts to attempt to implement some of the requirements, and increasing recognition that they are interdependent, suggests that there may come to be a cumulative positive thrust. The problem is, of course, that because the requirements are tied together the difficulties of implementing them (in part social psychological difficulties) will increase enormously. The strong incentive therefore, will usually be to meet these requirements in piecemeal fashion and hope that will be enough. Those difficulties and negative incentives are what this book is about.

What have been listed here are characteristics I would expect future forms of lrsp to include. But let me reemphasize that what forms lrsp would take if it were to become the norm are unknown: the whole societal setting would be different. Characterizing such a culture presents us with culture-bound conceptual limitations analogous to those which would have faced a feudal lord asked to describe the future characteristics of a society based on a market economy. Thus when I write here "changing toward lrsp," let the reader beware of reifying "lrsp" (or frsl). I do not mean it as a thing, a dogma, or a rigid program. Lrsp would be a societal condition characterized, I imagine, by these listed attributes the meaning of which would, during the period of changing toward that condition, partake of what are now their familiar meanings and whatever new meanings they came to have in the very process of trying and learning how to apply them.

The State of the Technology

Roughly, changing toward frsl will depend on willingness and ability to do so, on the capabilities of planning technology for aiding that human will and skill, and a data base that is appropriate for humane development aided by planning technique. Most people think planning technology and a data base are the necessary and sufficient conditions for lrsp. Very little attention has been directed to the human condition that must be created if the technology is to be developed and applied fruitfully. Since attention is first directed to technologies, and expectations are based on their potential, we will first look at the present and anticipated state of the art; and since technique and data are so interdependent I will treat them together.[8]

[8] One aspect of human willingness and ability to change toward frsl may be noted at this point. Over the next pages anger, anxiety, and perhaps re-

Describing the methods and means now being developed to assess the condition of society and to make estimates of the future as a basis for present action is not necessary for the purposes of our exploration. There is a large literature on these matters.[9] It is sufficient merely to name some of these methods and means: computer-based information systems (such as data banks and management information systems); social indicators; PPBS; economic and social modeling; simulation; gaming; future-conjecture methods (such as Delphi, cross-impact, and technology assessment); heuristic, linear, and dynamic programming; the systems approach; operations research; planned social change techniques; and program evaluation methods. What is important is to have a sense of how useful and valid can we expect these technologies to be over the next couple of decades and particularly in the near future.[10]

The trustworthiness and utility of the technologies will influence the degree to which most public organizations will be willing to accept the pains and the long periods involved in changing over to arrangements that can use them effectively for frsl. Less prudent organizations that succumb to fad or fancy and try to go beyond the capabilities of the technologies will face gratuitous frustrations and costs that will further discourage change-over efforts—not only in those organizations but in others that learn of their experience. While withdrawal from change-over efforts would be a rational response, technological limitations will also provide an excellent rationalization for avoiding changing toward lrsp, thereby inhibiting further refinement of the technologies because, as I shall argue later, for the most part these technologies can only be refined in the laboratory of the real world.

What then is the state of lrsp technology? It is rudimentary, in the light of what is needed, though certainly the components are, for the most part, improvements over what we could do and understand before they existed. In a report commissioned by the Conference Board (*Information Technology*, 1972) several authors examined the implications and state of information technology (a catch-all term for much of lrsp technology)

---

jection, will well up in some readers. Let this be "real life" evidence that changing over will be painful for those who think they *want* lrsp, not only for those who want to avoid the changes lrsp would require of them.

[9] For detailed reviews and extensive bibliographies, see Ackoff (1970) and Steiner (1969). Sophisticated technical articles are published in *Futures*, Guildford, Surrey, England, IPC House (32 High Street); and in *Technological Forecasting and Social Change*, New York, American Elsevier (52 Vanderbilt Avenue, 10017).

[10] Throughout I shall use "technology" as a catch-all word for this mixture of analytic modes, data systems, techniques, and technologies.

over the next two decades.[11] In my chapter of the report I summarized the mood of the other chapters as follows:

> *Information technology, as a monitoring and guidance system, will be unavoidably immature during much of the next two decades. A crucial inhibitor will be the inadequate social technology needed to develop organizations humanely so that they can make use of information technology proportionate to its potential. Also, much of the needed data base and theory for interpreting it will still be insufficient for many applications of information technology, especially in the public interest area. Necessarily, at least the 'seventies will be a time for fundamental information technology—pertinent research and development on manpower, legislation, organizational design, education, ethics, as well as on information technology hardware and software per se.*
>
> *For organizations and for society as a whole, the impact of information technology during these decades will be sporadic, uncertain, and uneven. Information technology's development and application will be aided and obstructed by the turbulent state of the society and by the felicitous and disrupting consequences of applying immature information technology when the laws and ethics pertaining thereto are only partially developed. That is, the turbulent society will both encourage the use of information technology to understand and guide it, and interfere with its rapid development because it will make difficult the simultaneous development of all the necessary parts of the organizational-data-hardware-legal-ethical-information-decision-making system. The resultant likelihood of undesirable consequences from using only a partially developed information technology system will also discourage its application and inhibit further development if it is misapplied [Michael, 1972, pp. 40–41].[12]*

A few examples will illustrate the interdependence and immaturity of these techniques, hence the need to plan for their simultaneous development.

The primitive state of social change theory is almost common knowledge. It is symbolized by our continuing inability to predict changes in birthrates.[13] In the words of the distinguished sociologist and pioneer

[11] See *Information Technology* (1972). The most formidable anthology of highly competent critiques and caveats about the state of information technology (particularly management sciences and data banks) and its applications and applicability is Westin, Ed. (1971).

[12] All chapters of this report merit the reader's attention.

[13] For critiques of, laments about, and proposals for a theory of social change see Bell and Mau (1971, especially Part I); and Blumer (1971), who says, "Current sociological theory and knowledge, in themselves, just do not enable the detection or identification of social problems. Instead, sociologists

in social indicator theory, Wilbert E. Moore, "We don't know what is the sequence of modernization: we do know history is no guide."[14] Our ignorance of the dynamics of change is more profound than commonly realized. We are quick to acknowledge that we cannot predict the future and we are prepared to argue about how the present is unfolding, but we usually overlook the fact that "the past is unpredictable" also.[15] Historians know that starting at any point in the past with all the information available on the situation up to that time it is not possible to predict what happened "next." The same branching tree of plausible but unpredictable alternatives faces the historian just as faces the futurist:

The history of human experience is not singular. It is plural, and the histories of human experience may be viewed as competitive and complementary. The burden and meaning of the past that establishes the present or initial state for the futures researcher is not given; it is a function of his choice. That choice will depend first upon how he perceives and defines his own task and, second, upon bodies of historical knowledge —within which are included angles of vision and assignments of meaning as well as 'hard' data created by others [David, 1970, p. 228].

. . .

Nearly every generation of literate peoples has some who desire to shape the world to suit themselves by rewriting their history. Even if intentional falsification does not take place, facts can be mustered to support different interpretations. No one would deny this who has read E. Wilson or A. Cobban on the historians' conflicting versions of the French Revo-

---

discern social problems only after they are recognized as social problems by and in a society" (p. 299). For illuminating and sobering critiques of the rudimentary state of model building and simulation in the behavioral sciences, by acknowledged leaders in the area, see R. Stogdill, *The Process of Model Building in the Behavioral Sciences* (Columbus, Ohio: Ohio State University Press, 1970). The summary chapter by C. W. Churchman is especially valuable. See also Buckley (1968); Buckley (1967); Deutsch (1966); and McNamara (1970, especially p. 10). Presumably social change is associated with changes in beliefs, attitudes, and values. As to the status of our understanding of these phenomena, "the present analysis suggests that, considered all together, [attitude researchers] are studying different parts of the same elephant, that they are concentrating on different kinds of inconsistent relations as represented within different cells of the matrix. The present analysis further suggests that a majority of all the possible experiences of consistency and inconsistency, especially those implicating the more central parts of the value-attitude system, still remain for the most part unexplored" (Rokeach, 1968, p. 166).

[14] In personal conversation, 1971. Quoted with his kind permission.
[15] Ascribed to Professor J. Minus, philosopher, by P. Ratoosh.

lution or who has compared the different scenarios that portray American history. . . . [Bell and Mau, 1971, p. 7].

Nevertheless, we act as if we knew how the past got from then to now, as if we really understood the dynamics of social change.

The inadequacies of economic theory are hidden behind a well-perpetuated mythology that acclaims its potency. Only occasionally do prominent economists assert its inadequacies in public places. One of these has written:

It comes down to this: The Establishment economics that is taught in the universities, proliferated in the journals, regurgitated in the councils of government, with all its mountains of published outputs, has not advanced our capacity to control our economy beyond what it was in the late 1930's.
. . . The real complexities of real economies elude us. Establishment economics provides no conceptual approach to measure and comprehend industrial performance, nor to reform, restructure, or control industry. The multifaceted dynamics of technological advance and industrial transformation—the underpinnings of increased productivity—are almost wholly excluded from the normal purview of Establishment economics. Nor does it offer any guide to a control of price that reflects a rational policy for allocation of resources, for the distribution of income, or for incentives for efficiency and technological progress [Solo, 1972, p. 47].[16]

In view of these limitations in economic and social theory, the well-publicized procedure of technology assessment is completely inadequate when the future social and economic context must be attended to as a necessary part of that assessment.

"Although much effort has been expended on technological forecasting," Dr. Albert T. Olenzak, manager of technical planning for Sun Oil, points out, "few people are satisfied with the results achieved relative to the effort expended. Many programs bog down in overcomplicated systems with excessive data handling and failure to communicate results to management in a meaningful way. The state of the art leaves a lot to be desired." Changes in public attitudes toward technology and the increasing interdependence of technological change with the rest of the social and physical environment, he adds, "have added new dimensions of difficulty and uncertainty to the fundamentals of technological forecasting" (Kiefer, 1972, pp. 11–12).

As of now, technological assessment is at most a method for choos-

---

[16] For other critiques of economics, see Boettinger (1967); Dale (1971); Heilbroner (1970); Kaysen (1968); and Thompson (1965).

ing a likely path to success in research and development on a technology per se, rather than a method for assessing the social consequences of the development of the technology.

Since, ostensibly, a chief reason for doing technological assessments is to detect second-order and third-order consequences, it should be emphasized here that the very concept of "second-order and third-order consequences" is snarled in epistemological dilemmas and semantic traps. The phrase has a kind of intuitive meaning probably based on an essentially linear rather than cybernetic imagery of causal processes. But when the matter is looked at systematically it turns out to be inordinately difficult to get either a conceptual or an operational fix on it.[17] Suffice it to say that this crucial reason for technological assessment is seldom dealt with at more than a metaphoric level, even though the methods for describing such impacts give an impression of rigor.

The conceptual and utilitarian limitations of cost and benefit analysis, which is also a major method used in planning, programming, budgeting system are well documented.[18] These limitations derive from lack of appropriate data for calculating costs and benefits of alternative approaches within a program; from the unavailability of other than economic criteria for measuring social value; and from incommensurables when costs and benefits are compared between different activities.

While the income and economic growth benefits of social action programs will probably become less important and less interesting to decision makers over the next few years, this does not mean that it will be impossible to compare the benefits of social action programs. Ingenious analysts will be able to place shadow prices on the nonincome benefits of social action programs. But these estimates are likely to be shaky and highly judgmental.

Once we leave the fairly firm ground of income we move into a kind of never-never land where we must set values on self-reliance, freedom from fear, the joys of outdoor recreation, the pleasures of clean air, and so forth. The result may not be worth the effort.

Even if we could compare the benefits of social action programs in commensurable terms, we would be left with the problem that different programs benefit different people. Social action programs typically produce both private and public benefits. The first accrue to individuals, who are, for example, cured of cancer or enjoy the better life a literate society provides.

The private benefits of different types of social action programs

---

[17] See Bauer with Rosenbloom and Sharp (1969), (Maimon, 1971); (Maimon, 1971).

[18] See Crecine (1970); Jones (1968); McKean and Anshen (1965); Rivlin (1969); Schick (1971); and Schultze (1968).

may go to entirely different groups of people. People who have cancer are not the people who cannot read. Even if we knew that the benefit-cost ratio was higher for reading programs than for cancer programs, we would not necessarily choose to devote more resources to reading. The decision would depend in part on the values attached to benefiting cancer victims and illiterates [Rivlin, 1971, pp. 57–58].

As for the utility of the mix of operations research and system design and analysis methods subsumed under the term "management science," the assessment of one of the founders and most distinguished contributors to that field merits repeating: "We have begun to see all around us the kinds of limitations on the techniques of management science. . . . The limitations show up most often as uncertainties and our inability to effectively sort out conflicting objectives. At the moment they appear to be quite unyielding. We need to discover better ways of dealing with uncertainty of all kinds and, in particular, with the complexities and interconnections of organized human behavior and the goals of institutions" (Hertz, 1971, p. 14).[19]

Inadequate data bases for choosing between programatic means, and for program evaluation, fuel the search for social indicators. Not only are the data lacking but the experts are quite clear on how enormously difficult it will be to design valid social indicators and to interpret them, especially for the purposes of coping with or conjecturing about social change. Two special difficulties presently burden this area. Understanding social change will depend on time series data which for the most part we presently do not have. And time series data inherently contain an assumed model of social change; otherwise there is no way to decide what it is important to collect data about.[20] This situation leads Wilbert E. Moore to conclude that in spite of sophisticated data collecting and data processing techniques, as of now, "our refinement in quantifiable data about society does not help us with understanding social change."[21] Dunn (1971) puts the task of generating relevant information for frsl this way:

[19] A most searching epistemological and ethical examination of the basis for and consequences of operations research and related activities is found in Churchman (1970). See also Dearden (1966), and Hoos (1969 and 1968).

[20] The data are also value-loaded. If time and money are spent collecting the data it must be because they are presumed to be socially important. "Important" is inevitably a value judgment except possibly where data are collected as part of the logic of testing a hypothesis—in which case the hypothesis will have to be deemed important if time and money are to be spent testing it. On these matters, see Bauer (1966, especially Chapter 2 by Biderman, and Chapter 3, by Gross); Etzioni and Lehman (1967); Gross and Spainger (1969); Milsum (1968).

[21] In personal conversation, quoted with his kind permission. A devastat-

Those forms and sources of information that have been traditionally exploited by social science do not adequately serve the study and practice of social learning.

What is needed is information about social system goals and controls that will reveal the degree to which the system's response to environmental signals is goal satisfying. The identification and definition of social problems require the ability to judge the consistency of social system goals and controls. Once the problem areas are identified and the need for boundary revisions established, information is needed about the behavioral options that are candidates for formulating a developmental hypothesis. This requires a means for becoming informed about the goals and controls and technologies employed by other systems that might be borrowed as well as inventive imagination. Once a developmental hypothesis is formed, one needs political information concerning the system's human constituents necessary to the formulation of a consensus. One needs a technology of organization for change. Once the social experiment is performed, one needs information that measures goal convergence and, hence, is necessary for reality testing.

Here we are talking about information about social system goals, the goals and attitudes of human components, machine technologies, organizational or control technologies, and similar matters. None of these are forms of information provided by the classical information systems of social system management or social science. The conventional internal accounting and reporting systems of management and the traditional general-purpose, general-parameter information systems conventionally employed by social science do not generate information of these kinds [pp. 254–255].[22]

Thus the development of valid social indicator data will take much research, development, and revision. It will take years to test theory against data. This testing itself will have to be planned even while the available data are used. Hopefully, the data will be used with a tentativeness appropriate to the limited understanding of their meaning. Whether they

---

ing critique of the theoretical and empirical footlessness underlying injunctions to use social indicators and expectations about their usability is found in Sheldon and Freeman (1970, pp. 97–111). In a similar vein, see Cazes (1972).

[22] A compact and sensitive description of the elements—description, explanation, valuation, and utilization—that would link social indicator data to policy and planning is found in Kahn (1972, especially pp. 156–161). An illuminating example of how complicated is the question of what should be measured by social indicators—that is, what is related to what—is found in Thomas and McKinney (1972).

are used in this way will depend in part on how successfully organizations come to cope with the requirements for frsl.

The absence of criteria for selecting or using data and the data themselves are reasons—we will examine others later—why data banks, which have played such a large role in the imagery of urban planning over the last few years, are presently inadequate for that task. "Scores of handsomely printed long-range plans and feasibility studies speak confidently of affecting higher decision-making levels by producing information geared to program evaluation, alternative policy formulation and testing, and information systems for top management. But no data bank has been found in civilian agencies of city, county, state, or federal government that is in fact delivering on such promises. . . . Most of the systems remaining in existence are geared to automation of existing program operations or of similar programs mandated to new legislation (Westin, 1972, p. 60).[23]

Finally, future studies—including this book, to the degree that it is a future study—suffer the conceptual and informational weaknesses of these methods and theory. Even though methodologically ingenious and operationally rigorous techniques are being developed, the simple fact is that logic and procedure cannot make up for ignorance about the present processes of society or for unanticipated developments whose interactions with the rest of society will follow dynamics whose properties we hardly understand at all. "The art of conjecture, however strict the scientific apparatus on which it rests, remains an art" (Salomen, 1971, p. 17).[24]

If the technologies are so rudimentary, why even bother trying to change toward lrsp? In the first place, crude as they are, the technologies

---

[23] Four years have passed since Dial's 1968 survey, but Westin's observations and my interviews indicate that the situation has hardly improved since Dial reported: "the author visited a number of the cities which had the longest experience in developing urban information systems. *In none of them did he find a computerized based urban information system in being.* Furthermore, after conferring by telephone with officials in selected other cities, and after attending a conference on the present 'state of the art,' it could only be concluded that *there are no such systems in existence today.*" [Italics in original.] Dial (1968, p. 6). See also Urban and Regional Information Systems (1968). The evaluation reports in Part IV of the document, prepared by users of the systems, make it quite clear that information useful for planning was not usually stored in the memory banks. See, for example, the reports of Alameda County, Calif. (p. 14), Alexandria, Virginia (pp. 24–25), Los Angeles (p. 60), and Santa Clara County, Calif. (p. 88).

[24] The classic examination of the epistemological issues is in de Jouvenel (1967). For critiques of future conjecture techniques, see Duncan (1968). For a survey of future conjecturing methodology, see de Hoghton, Page, and Streatfeild (1971); and Bell (1964).

are marginally and narrowly useful even now. Sometimes they help us know more about the present, and they surely provide more detailed images of the future than before. They have helped clarify social program options and some of the economic costs and benefits associated with the options. Future studies have influenced corporate actions. The technologies have produced new data and new concepts about what is happening in society, and these have influenced the recommendations of government commissions and committees. Complex simulations of social and ecological processes have stimulated international discussion and apparently broadened appreciation of the substance of the issues. Even these rudimentary technologies have aided the legitimation of a long-range perspective and furthered the expectancy that long-range planning can be done; here and there, they have even made possible more rational and informed decisions and allocations.[25]

In the second place, changing toward lrsp need not depend on fully developed and validated technologies. The human requirements for beginning to change are independent of the state of the technology, as we shall see later. Essentially lrsp is a philosophy, with operational consequences, for going about *learning* how to act in the present in light of continuously revised anticipations about the future. It is a philosophy of responsible, strategic, decision-making in a complex and changing society; it is inherently open and tentative but strongly committed to acting in terms of chosen futures.[26] However, the legitimation and application of these technologies can be expected to provide a pedagogy, a discipline, for thinking and acting in ways that are compatible with frsl. Thereby they will help undermine belief in the naturalness and sufficiency of disjointed, incremental, and ad hoc responses. These technologies can encourage belief in the need: to think systematically about the longer range future as a basis for present action; to look for many more options than arise when decisions are based on unexamined expectations about the future; to recognize that value issues inhere in facts and must be openly

[25] Again, using some of these technologies does not of itself constitute planning, much less lrsp. Much of the imagery which suggests that lrsp is underway results from using the technologies for scheduling, administration, public relations, and the like and then equating these uses with planning. For example, there is a strong tendency for organizations to encourage others to believe, and often to believe themselves, that by doing a future study they are planning, or that by installing a computerized management information system or data bank they are planning. Neither activity is planning, though such activities could deliberately or inadvertently facilitate changing over toward planning. So far, however, such activities usually become encapsulated or die.

[26] The preconditions for "perfect planning" are set out in Bauman (1967). It is precisely the *absence* of these conditions that makes frsl necessary.

faced; and to know that assumptions about the dynamics of society always need examination and that models and data can help that examination. By their very existence the technologies can be another source of moral and rational obligation to be much more deliberative, systematic, and strategic about getting from here to there, and about what constitutes "here" and "there."

There is a third argument for trying to change toward lrsp even though the technologies are weak. It is only through trying to change that there will be occasions to strengthen the technologies.

Let us accept the fact that man's deeply ingrained concept of cause is a product of biology, psychology, and evolution rather than a pure analytic concept. If so, it reflects the adaptive advantage of being able to intervene in the world, to deliberately change the relationship of objects. From among all the observable correlations in the environment, man and his predecessors focused upon those few which were, for him, manipulatable correlations. From this emerged man's predilection for discovering "causes," rather than mere correlations. In laboratory science, this search is represented in the experiment, with its willful, deliberate intrusion into ongoing processes. Similarly for the ameliorative social scientist: Of all of the correlations observable in the social environment, we are interested in those few which represent manipulable relationships, in which by intervening and changing one variable we can affect another. No amount of passive description of the correlations in the social environment can sort out which are "causal" in this sense. To learn about the manipulability of relationships one must try out manipulation. The scientific, problem-solving, self-healing society must be an experimenting society [Campbell, 1971, p. 14].[27]

Ultimately these technologies can only be tested in the real world and revised in the light of those tests: the only way they can be developed and refined is by going "back to the drawing board." But there has to be a place where the drawing board can be. Less metaphorically, research and development for lrsp technology itself will be a long-range planning task, a future-responsive learning activity. The research and development effort must be part of those relationships the organization has with its environment where it is intended that lrsp will become the modus operandi for effective responses to the environment's needs and wants. The financial, moral, social, and psychological support for developing the technology will come only from those who need the technology. But the technology will remain feeble if organizations avoid recognizing

[27] See also Kaplan (1970).

their need for lrsp technology, or if they recognize the need for it but nevertheless resist using it because it is weak. Not using it because it is weak will complete the vicious circle and will keep the technology feeble.

It is necessary to comment further on some characteristics of the lrsp philosophy to reduce whatever impressions remain about inherent elitism or rigidness.

The Relationship Between the Organization and Its Environment

In the Introduction I explained that "environment" refers to the environment of people and organizations that are associated with an organization. (When "environment" is the natural environment I will so refer to it.) It will be helpful to be a bit more explicit about the "content" of the "surround" of a given organization—for example, an agency, department, bureau, mayor's office, or planning commission. (Each could have an lrsp capability or requirement at a given time, and if the change toward lrsp were ultimately successful, most or all of them would.) The surround includes formally linked superior and subordinate organizations, organizations that supply resources, groups that are the beneficiaries of the organization, and groups that suffer adverse consequences from it, organizations it controls or regulates, and organizations and groups that are sometime allies, competitors, or enemies. Some components of the environment are essentially stable and permanent; others arise and disappear in response to the organization's actions or inactions or to other happenings in the environment that, rightly or not, implicate the organization. The "environment" then would be the interdependent cluster of persons, groups, organizations, political parties, and so forth, to which the organization must respond.[28]

[28] We will not be thinking exclusively about bureaus as such, but rather about *any* organizational entity involved in the consequences of changing toward lrsp. It is also worth emphasizing again that no purpose will be served by choosing one or another of the available schemes for differentiating organizations in terms of what they do, how they do it, who they do it to or for, how they are structured, legitimized, or funded, and so on, in order to compare their anticipated social psychological responses. There are elaborate arguments in the literature about how to classify organizations for the purposes of predicting their performance. And there are multiple interpretations of the "meaning" of correlations between various factors and measures of morale, "productivity," adaptiveness, bureaucraticness, and so on. But there is no validated comprehensive scheme for typifying organizations that would enlighten our task. I will draw attention from time to time to organizational differences—as, for example, between more or less hierarchically arranged organizations, or between those that have passive constituencies compared to those with active environments—and the implications

The set of requirements for lrsp represents a cybernetic system. These requirements relate to each other two sources of signals, namely: those from the planning activities and those from the plan-using activities —the planning organization and the planning-using environment—so that differences between what is intended and what is happening can be detected and serve as a basis for adjusting the relationship between the two sources so that the mismatch is reduced or at least kept from growing. Meeting these requirements becomes problematic when they are translated into human behavior, because this cybernetic scheme requires that people articulate the goals they seek in such ways that the nature and extent of error in pursuit of these goals can be detected. It requires persons and organizations to seek out their own errors and reward their detection rather than repressing errors in the hope of avoiding punishment for "failure." It requires that the activities involved in responding to the environment have the "requisite variety" built into them to make the needed responses. And this requires that organizations be designed with a large internal capability for modification. Thus lrsp has two areas of application: the first is reorganizing and controlling the internal structure and processes of an organization involved in trying to perform lrsp; the second is responding to and influencing the relevant environment in order to aid society in moving from "here" to "there" in time and content. Some substantial accomplishments must occur with regard to the first for the second to occur at all.[29]

Planning (whatever was meant by that word) was a much more comfortable activity for "planners" when it was assumed that the environment did the altering while the planning organization, which produced the conditions for alteration, stayed the same. When performed this way, planning inevitably was seen as elitist and often as manipulative and anti-

---

of these differences on certain processes, such as internal information flow. But a classification that would cluster organizations on the basis of multiple distinctions that uniquely differentiate them from other clusters simply does not exist, to my knowledge.

Using what is available would lose us more than we would gain if we moved very far from the position that, for our purposes, an organization is an organization, except when I suggest otherwise. (Hopefully others will try to cluster organizations in terms of variables that predict or explain their present or potential ability to respond to the requirements of lrsp; but that comes after this book.)

[29] Redesigning the environment so that its various groups and functions can effectively be part of a cybernetic societal learning process will involve large sociological considerations as well as social psychological aspects. A. Etzioni's *The Active Society* gives a corresponding emphasis to the complexities of environmental responses and participation at the sociological level of analysis.

democratic. The assumption of a passively responding environment was also comfortably compatible with a belief in the naturalness of a hierarchical model of human relations. This perspective has been abetted by our language structure, which implicitly assigns cause and effect, subject and predicate, and thereby implicitly treats social systems as if they were "naturally" linear rather than circular in process.[30] Throughout this book the reader should keep in mind that both syntax and brevity carry with them a linear, we–they hierarchical implication that is explicitly rejected here. Instead, a circular relationship between an organization and a potentially *active* environment is assumed here.[31]

Rather than conceive of lrsp as differentiating in an almost geographic sense between a planning activity and the environment that absorbs it, it is more useful to think of sequences of information and activity that tend to get processed and used by various persons or groups at different times. Some individuals and groups will functionally fill the same processing and utilization roles all or most of the time; others will fill these roles some of the time. At any given time the distraction between planning-doers and planning-users would to some degree refer to what are in principle temporary allocations of functions. Note, however, that endowing the environment with active, error-responding characteristics also imposes on that environment many of the same obligations that are required of the organizations doing their part of the process of changing toward lrsp. But social psychological sources of resistance to efforts to change-over to lrsp will operate in the environment too. Thus, relearning must characterize *all* parts of the system if the requirements for lrsp are to be met.

Lrsp will involve many more kinds of people than the "planner" as conventionally defined. "Planner, community organizer, and administrator are, then, in closely interrelated and interacting roles. The social policy analyst or policy scientist (an American variation) is sometimes a scholar of social policy, often a planner or administrator. All are interested in and draw upon the work of students of social change theory and organization theory. And, because the roles not only interrelate but also have unclear boundaries, each is readily found functioning in the domain of the other and defining it as his own" (Kahn, 1969, p. 23). Because of the kinds of requirements that must be met in changing toward lrsp, the activity would involve all levels and functions in an organization. Means and organiza-

[30] A superb anthology on this difficulty and related semantical problems is Lee (1949, especially Part VIII, "The Structural Patterns and Implications of a Language").

[31] With regard to the restructuring of the environment in the forms that might make it more responsive to societal learning, see Etzioni (1968, particularly Chapter 15).

tional structures for selecting goals, for conducting, revising, or eliminating programs, for generating and applying information from the present and the future will have to be created. Some could be done better by the "line," some by the "staff," some by the organization, and some by parts of its environment, depending on the competencies needed and the setting required to use them. Here the point is that lrsp would have to be a normative and operational characteristic of a *system* which includes the environment. Changing toward lrsp could not be the exclusive responsibility or perspective of planners, or a "planning staff," or management, or a consumer advocate group, and still be a means for frsl. At the same time the performance of change-over activities and the impact of these performances would be distributed differently according to function and competencies.

Since we are concerned here not with the final form of an organization-environment *doing* lrsp but rather with the *change-over* situation, it is important to add that the incentive to change-over could come from anywhere in the organization-environment where resources and rationale provide means to push for such changes. However, it does seem clear that top-level, sophisticated, enduring, and participative support will be required at least when change-over efforts are initiated within an organization.[32]

In addition, means will have to be invented for effectively utilizing environmental "participation" in lrsp processes. The appropriate forms for using different competencies, perspectives, representations, jurisdictions, and so forth and so on do not now exist. A major and continuing task during frsl change-over efforts will have to be research and development on such inventions.

On Incrementalism and "Satisficing" in a Lrsp Context

A major contributor to the disjointed incrementalist philosophy is H. Simon's argument that in the nature of things men are constrained to use what he calls "bounded rationality." Limitations of time, resources, access knowledge, and wits mean that men settle for less than what perfect rationality and perfect conditions for obtaining and using knowledge would lead them to. In his term they "satisfice," they settle for a "good enough" solution to the problem. He proposes that this is a reflection of limitations in human wits. Others argue that it is not wits but will that sets the level at which satisficing occurs (Banfield, 1962). The important point for this exploration is that, barring some absolute limit on concep-

---

[32] Steiner (1969, pp. 94–99) argues this persuasively, as does the literature on organizational development (which will be cited later).

tual abilities in the individual or in some augmented arrangement involving other people or machines, which it would be hard to argue we have reached, the degree to which a situation is examined and alternatives explored is culturally determined: what constitutes a satisficed solution or action is determined by what the society will settle for. If the demand goes up for more comprehensive searches and deliberations of a wider-ranging set of alternatives, then satisficing conditions won't be met at the old level which has served until now. This is what Y. Dror (1968) means when he writes, "The main weakness of the [satisficing] model is that it takes the satisfactory quality as given, and so ignores a main question it should be answering, namely, what the variables shaping the satisfactory quality are, and how much they can be consciously directed" (p. 48). Thus lrsp is quite compatible with the satisficing model of human behavior: it simply requires that the standards be set much higher.

From place to place in this book the requirements for frsl will be contrasted with those ascribed to incrementalism. When I refer to "incrementalism" I mean the disjointed incrementalism that is associated with what A. Schick (1969) calls "process politics" and "process budgeting" and which has been most articulately espoused in the writings of C. Lindblom (1965) and A. Wildavsky (1964). The learning approach described and promoted herein is of course incremental in the sense that experiments and program and goal alterations proceed step-wise. But the philosophy and the consequences of its application are the antithesis of what is called for and follows from disjointed incrementalism as conventionally described and justified. The "increments" involved in lrsp are defined by deliberate choices of goals; they are future-oriented, innovative, and implemented even though outcomes are uncertain; they are articulated rather than disjointed; and they are responsible and responsive to environmental needs at least as much as to considerations of organizational survival and aggrandizement. B. Gross (1970) put the difference this way:

While the great value of Lindblom's approach has been to emphasize the sequential nature of decision-making and the huge limits on thoroughly rational analysis, he went too far in stressing the disjointed nature of the process. He thereby ignored the necessity of focussing strategic decision-making, under certain circumstances, on major structural changes rather than a disjointed series of increments. The wisdom of Lindblom's analysis, however, lies in the fact that major structural change—even change of a revolutionary nature—cannot take place except through a series of small steps. These steps, however, must follow each other in accordance with some broad strategic considerations. They must be jointed, instead of dis-

jointed. *Hence, jointed incrementalism is one of the major principles of strategic decision-making*" [*p. 85*].

Distributive Equity and Lrsp

The simplified Webber list emphasizes that careful attention to distributive equity is a requirement for lrsp. It is more than a normative and logical requirement for lrsp; with growth in the social technology of social indicators and related information retrieval and feedback systems, there will be increasing capability to pay attention to "secondary" and "tertiary" consequences of actions, and there will be increasing efforts to try and anticipate them—which will encourage lrsp. Public pressure will insure that organizations pay attention to such consequences. Clearly, the requirement that lrsp be closely attentive to distributive equity issues would by itself make necessary substantial participation by members of the environment. Corporations have not traditionally taken innocent cost-bearers and gratuitous gainers into account in their planning and programming. Government has been more self-conscious about the problem and has depended on the processes of interagency negotiation and agency-executive-legislative negotiation to solve it. In recent years we have come to appreciate that this political and organizational process approach has very deep limitations. Thus, recognizing more explicitly and systematically who gains the benefits and who suffers the costs will be a rich source of personal and organizational pain in moving toward lrsp as well as a strong pressure for moving that way.

Evaluation of Social Experiments in the Context of Lrsp

To assess the continuing relevance of the chosen goals and the effectiveness of programs underway in the pursuit of them, evaluation must be a central and continuing part of frsl. Evaluation of evaluation methods themselves and of the purposes of evaluation would also be necessary to learn how, when, and what to evaluate. The process of designing social experiments so that they can be evaluated will be subtle and complex. Only in the last few years has this begun to receive the quality of attention it deserves.[33] Like the rest of lrsp technology, it is in a rudimentary state.

This reflects partly the state of behavioral science and partly the result of so few opportunities in the past to develop and try out adequate evaluation procedures. Those responsible for most public service programs

[33] See, for example, Borgatta (1966); Campbell (1971), Guttentag (1972); Lewin (1968); Rivlin (1971), Chapter Five); and Suchman (1967).

have resisted evaluating them. In those rare cases in which evaluation has been requested, it has usually been done after the program has been in operation. As a result, the evaluators were unable to get the information they needed to compare conditions before with conditions after, or to control properly the variables under consideration. Often the organization requesting the evaluation defined its object so narrowly that the evaluation was useless for the purposes of program redesign. Also, most evaluations have been made according to paradigms that simply were not sophisticated enough to handle the subject. "With the most minor exceptions, it can be said for the United States that none of our ameliorative programs have had adequate evaluations" (Campbell, 1971, p. 9).[34]

Overall, even when evaluation has been requested, the requestor's mood has been deeply ambivalent. There is always the fear that the evaluation may show that programs are not working. If so, the agency or persons who promoted the program would be "in trouble" and those committed to the program would have to shift their psychological investment. An open, supportive, experimental attitude toward program outcomes has not been the way members of organizations or their funding or administrative superiors have approached the challenge of public service performance. It is not surprising, then, that there are no built-in procedures to assure that evaluation findings will be used, or that the development of effective evaluation methods has been thwarted.

Two crucial but unsolved problems in designing evaluations appropriate to lrsp deserve mention here. First, what is to be the relationship of members of the environment who are the "object" of the experiment to the "experimenters"? Obviously, there are grave ethical and

[34] This situation is starting to change. Among other pressures of the sort described in Chapter Three are legislative directives allocating 1.5 percent of programatic funds for evaluation. But as of this writing, little has been done: much has been avoided since the funds need not be spent on evaluation; and what has been done is inadequate. (It has been estimated that human welfare programs require the equivalent of between 5 and 30 percent of the program budget to do a really worthwhile evaluation under the best of circumstances.) Also, evaluations are not integrated into organizational structures which assure that programs will be designed so they can be evaluated, or that evaluations will definitely affect subsequent program activities.

Another factor contributing to new pressures for evaluation is the small beginning of deliberate societal experiments such as those on the effects of a guaranteed minimum income, low-income rent subsidies, and educational vouchers. By the time this book is published, probably others will be underway. But these experiments are not yet imbedded in other lrsp processes which would give them the utility they need; they are more an attempt to deal with present problems than the product of future responsive goals studies. Nor are they linked to government agencies and Congress in ways that would *assure* their impact across government operations. Nevertheless, both are starts in the right direction.

ideological issues involved in the conventional arrangement in which the
objects of the experiment do not know what behavior of theirs is being
evaluated (because that knowledge would alter their behavior). There are
also deep methodological issues involved. The effect on subjects' behavior
of knowing they are experimental subjects without knowing what is being
studied compared to the effect on their behavior when they are co-experi-
menters or collaborators with the "experimenter" is just beginning to get
attention. There are reasons to believe that the classical "scientific" experiment has produced a body of laboratory findings that essentially distort or trivialize our understanding of human behavior simply because of
the stance the subject takes in the role of subject.[35] How useful will it be
to know how people behave under the experimental conditions when the
legitimating norms will be different when the behavior is accepted as normal and conventional? People who are part of an experiment in which,
for example, they receive a monthly supplemental income when such income is not acknowledged as the right of every citizen, may well act
differently than they would if such an income were legitimated as a right.

More fundamentally, there is the question of whether the purpose
of societal experiments—including the evaluation aspect—should be to
gather data and test hypotheses, or whether it should be to provide a
means by which "experimenters" and "subjects" alike learn new norms
and behavior? To my mind, lrsp, as a procedure for societal learning,
leans strongly toward the latter.

The fact that lrsp involves goals and public programs that would
have their fulfilment well in the future poses a second basic problem in
evaluation methodology and hence for the conduct of frsl. How is the
balance to be found between experiments that are comprehensive enough
in time and scope to be meaningfully evaluated and the social and economic costs that such comprehensive experiments might entail? Time
duration is a particularly knotty problem. *When* is the utility of the program to be evaluated? The end point—if indeed there is one—is too late
if it should turn out that the program is counter-productive. Trying to
make a definitive evaluation too early might subject the program to political and other pressures that could eliminate it for the wrong reasons.
In the process, attempts at changing over to lrsp would be undermined.
How then can we commit ourselves to long-term programs and goals and
at the same time evaluate and revise them continually without destroying
our very commitment? If there are answers, they will have to be discovered
in the process of trying to meet the requirements for frsl, and they will be

[35] See Rosenthal (1966) and a forthcoming volume sponsored by the
Social Science Research Council on evaluation of social experiments. Title and
editorship not yet decided on.

intimately related to ways of dealing with the social psychological resistances to changing toward lrsp.

Phases and Actors in Change-Over Processes

Impressionistic as it must be, it will be useful to have an image, a "map" or "program" of the kinds of phases and actors I have in mind when I refer to the process of "changing over" or "changing toward" lrsp. What follows derives from the circumstances and activities that seem to characterize organizations that are trying to move in the direction of lrsp and from the formal literature on organizational change and related matters. However, it should be noted that, while a good bit has been theorized about the patterns of organizational change and much has been written about what they should be, "there have been even fewer studies of the pattern of change than of its causes and consequences" (Hage and Aiken, 1970).[36]

The broad categories of influences bearing on the change-over processes are: (1) The characteristics of the environment as it impinges on the organization. (2) The state of lrsp technology, both as it is developing in an organization and as it is available outside it. (3) The ideas in good currency regarding the utility of lrsp and its technology. (4) The circumstances that determine (a) who is pushing for lrsp in the light of aspects of (1), (2), or (3), and why; and (b) the resources they can bring to bear in furtherance of their efforts (inside and outside the organization). (5) The circumstances that determine who opposes moving toward lrsp in the light of aspects of 1, 2, or 3, and why; and the resources they can bring to bear in furtherance of their efforts (inside and outside the organization.) (6) The personal, interpersonal, and organizational circumstances that determine what of (1), (2), and (3) are screened out or emphasized through the selective attention of members of (4) and (5).

That which is selectively attended to or ignored will change over time in part as a result of accumulated experiences, including those associated with the change-over effort, and in part as a result of exogenous influences from new personnel, changes in organizational structure, and feedback forced on the organization by the environment. This is the appropriate place to introduce the concept of "appreciation" as developed by G. Vickers (1965).

An appreciation involves making judgments of fact about the "state of the system," both internally and in its external relations. I will call these

---

[36] Their organizational change phases seem compatible with those used here.

reality judgments. These include judgments about what the state will be or might be on various hypotheses as well as judgments of what it is and has been. They may thus be actual or hypothetical, past, present, or future. It also involves making judgments about the significance of these facts to the appreciator or to the body for whom the appreciation is made. These judgments I will call value judgments. Reality judgments and value judgments are inseparable constituents of appreciation; they correspond with those observations of fact and comparison with norm which form the first segment of any regulative cycle, except that the definition of the relevant norm or complex of norms, like the identification of the relevant facts is itself a product of the appreciation. The relation between judgments of fact and of value is close and mutual; for facts are relevant only in relation to some judgment of value and judgments of value are operative only in relation to some configuration of fact (p. 40).

Throughout this book I will assume the ubiquitous operation of the appreciative process: indeed, lrsp can be thought of as a self-conscious working out of it at the organizational level. The process is operating when we call a human situation "natural" and draw attention to certain "facts" to validate that assessment. Thus under most circumstances it sustains the definition of reality society holds at a particular time. (See Chapter One). When enough compelling anomalies accumulate, the appreciative process is central to the creation of a new definition of human reality that in turn becomes self-sustaining.[37]

Among the most important appreciations in any group situation are those that have to do with what appreciations are permissible within the group: that is, there are limits about what one can question, or pay attention to, and still remain a team member. The constraints on what it is "permissible" to perceive as relevant or as fact may be different for groups within organizations and in the environment.[38] Different persons and groups have, to varying degrees, different appreciative systems, different selective attention characteristics, though within groups the social forces to perceive in a consensual manner are very high indeed.[39]

[37] Elsewhere Vickers emphasizes that although it is clear that we learn what to treat as information and what to value, we have very little understanding of how we learn these things. See Vickers (1967).

[38] For example, what is perceived by "establishment" law and order agencies as disruptive and threatening to societal stability may be seen by the dispossessed as new opportunities for access to membership in society.

[39] A somber and lucid history of a fateful contest between appreciative settings, and the limits of permissible appreciative settings, is found in Hoopes (1969). On how groups unconsciously collude to keep their members in line in terms of how they appreciate a situation, see Bion (1959) and Rice (1965).

With the appreciative process in mind, along with some of the circumstances that will affect its operation, let us look at the "phases" that might be abstracted from the on-going processes of changing toward lrsp. Five phases are delineated here in order to help emphasize that different needs and circumstances will be dominant as the effort to change toward lrsp progresses over time.

At some point circumstances and the felt needs of those involved would combine to produce a "selection" of motives and beliefs that result in the *intention* to initiate lrsp. (Quite a few organizations seem to have taken this step but have gotten no further.) If these persist and if the proponents have the power to do so:

Arrangements would be made to conduct lrsp-initiating activities aimed at realizing the lrsp-initiating intent. (For example, committees are appointed, titles assigned, money allocated, enabling memoranda are written.) With people now enjoined to do things, this would lead to:

Conducting lrsp-initiating activities (for example, future studies, goal-setting tasks, organizational development programs. Some organizations, including those in government, have begun this stage.) Eventually this would lead to efforts aimed at:

Elaboration and integration of lrsp-initiating activities into organizational norms and structures and functions for trying to conduct lrsp as such. (A very few organizations, such as the YMCA and General Electric, seem to have just begun this stage.) As the organization and its environment learned how to do these things, the organization—and society—would be becoming transformed into a:

Society operating according to the norms of frsl (which, presumably, would include the requirements in the Webber list given early in this chapter).

In real organizations things would not go this neatly. There will be much backing and filling, much personal pain and opportunity. Given the undesirability of rigidly controlling the people and processes involved, and our inability to do so, the phases certainly will not be clear-cut or the sources of movement singular and one-directional. Environmental characteristics may be more or less propitious at different times. So too, with the lrsp technology state of the art and philosophy. It will be very important who or what groups in the organization or its environment become interested in or antagonistic to lrsp, or some facet of it, and these also will vary over time. While conditions may converge felicitously to move the change-over process from phase to phase, a change in "input" may set back the effort or may wash out the whole thing.[40] At any point the costs of redoing

---

[40] For example, a very large corporation had put considerable effort into developing what was thought to be the most sophisticated strategic planning

or moving ahead may appear too high, and the uncertainty or risk too great. The intent to move toward lrsp may die, or be encapsulated as ritual, or become some other form of planning than lrsp. These counter-development processes seem to characterize most of the experience to date.

Since learning how to change toward lrsp will be long and difficult, even painful, certain needs felt strongly enough to sustain the experience will be necessary. Many of those working in organizational settings who have tried to initiate lrsp change-over efforts seem not to realize how difficult the task will be and also seem to lack the motives or needs that would sustain such efforts. When faced with the complexity and difficulty of the task, the effort bogs down or dies. It will be worthwhile, then, to review impressionistically some typical circumstances that presently lead to the first step in the phases of changing toward lrsp.[41]

A senior member of the organization becomes interested in long-range planning or social planning or a variant that uses some of the planning technology. He may simply be influenced by all the talk about planning in the management-oriented periodicals he reads or by the high-level seminars he attends (much as were many executives who invested their company's capital in computers because it was the thing to do) ; or he may feel that the image of corporation or agency efforts to do lrsp will be good public relations. At any rate, emulating others (but often lacking strong motivation), he initiates some activities. Perhaps he contracts for future studies, or sets up a small long-range planning group, or invests in a management information system (MIS) to give him the information he thinks he needs to plan or to shake up his organizational sub-sections so they will start to plan. Or he has a favorite long-range problem and he puts some people to work on it. Usually the effort is un-coordinated and spotty. "My research experience indicates that MIS is generally introduced through special task groups which are assigned to a small number of departments. In effect, MIS starts its test period in isolation from most of the company. In this setting, the MIS expert displays a combination of arrogant selling zeal and organizational defensiveness which does not make relations with suspicious managers any easier" (Argyris, 1970, p. 34). Note, too, that the superior initiating the activity

---

model in the industry. But a major reorganization of the corporation rendered the model inapplicable.

[41] In what follows, both Karl Marx's thesis that organizational change is forced or initiated from the outside, and Max Weber's thesis that change comes from within, are operative. In the societal situation we are concerned with, as often as not inside and outside will merge as members of organizations have an increasing portion of their role identity located outside the organization (see Chapter Nine). On the Marx versus Weber argument, see Bell and Mau (1968, p. 272).

may be outside a specific agency, as was the case when President Johnson ordered all civilian agencies to use PPBS in developing their future programs.

An organization faces a crisis or a deep sense of malaise or frustration with itself. With the help of outside consultants or using its own resources it tries to understand what organizational and environmental circumstances have changed or combined to produce the situation.[42] This leads then to questions about how it should operate in the future, which thereby introduces a self-conscious attention to the future as the context for making decisions. This then leads it to an intention to carry out the above steps—usually without an understanding of what it will be getting into if it follows through with that intention.

Under the influence of the professional fraternity's approval of lrsp, and with an eye to increasing their personal value to the organization, those responsible to the organization—they may be inside or outside of it—for short-range planning: begin to apply their techniques to longer-range problems and to encourage their clients to expand their time frame; and they try to convince their superiors that the organization should and can expand its time frame. In the same way, those responsible for solving small planning problems try to move their organization toward working on more comprehensive problems. Planning-oriented people in corporations and third-sector organizations (such as voluntary organizations, foundations, and colleges) try to move their superiors toward social planning in order to expand their "product lines" and to protect themselves from displacement by more encompassing organizations such as the federal agencies. Planning-oriented people in government agencies try to move their superiors toward social planning because, among other things, Congress and the Executive office keep adding activities and missions. Note that these moves toward lrsp are not necessarily approved or known about by senior executives. Sometimes they are the entrepreneurial or ideological moves of people with the skills, motives, organizational location, and legitimacy to push in these directions. Indeed, lack of senior

---

[42] The appreciation that there is "in fact" an organizational malaise that might be removed is in part a result of the idea, in increasingly good currency, that organizational development methods can help. Naturally, then, organizational development consultants are invited in. They in turn bring ideas with them that influence the organization to think about aspects of its relation to its environment which it had not thought about before. "Some researchers . . . suggest that external sources are the most important catalysts of change for administrators of formal organizations. Studies dealing with large-scale organizational change show that external sources, such as consultants, play a crucial role in developing awareness of needed changes in formal systems" (Rogers with Shoemaker, 1971, p. 307).

officer participation and support often leads to the demise or at least the stalemating of efforts to move toward lrsp.

At each phase of the evolution of the change-over process, an internal sequence of "collective innovation-decision steps" activities seems necessary, though some of them may be bypassed depending on what conditions precede arrival at a given stage of development. E. Rogers and F. Shoemaker (1971) offer the following sequence in describing decision-making in communities. Reviewing them will serve our purposes, especially since the environment would play an integral role in changing toward frsl. The sequence is: *stimulation* of interest in the need for the new idea (by stimulators); initiation of the new idea in the social system (by initiators); legitimation of the idea (by power-holders or legitimizers); decision to act (by members of the social system); action or execution of the new idea (p. 276). Rogers and Shoemaker stress that "these steps are not necessarily mutually exclusive, nor do they always occur in the exact chronological order" (p. 275). Here is how they summarize the characteristics of the stimulator, initiator, and legitimizer operating in a community:

Stimulators of collective innovation decisions are more cosmopolite than other members of the social system. This characteristic provides them with fairly easy access to innovations, and the ability to perceive needs and problems of the social system. The initiators of collective innovation decisions are unlikely to be the same individuals in a social system as the legitimizers. Initiators are noted for their favorable attitudes toward change and for their knowledge of the system.

Legitimizers are the high status power-holders of the system who sanction the change. Therefore, the rate of adoption of a collective innovation is positively related to the degree to which the legitimizers are involved in the decision-making process [p. 297].

In contrast, in organizations where efforts have been made to move toward lrsp, it seems to me that the stimulator and initiator are often the same person in a boundary-spanning role (see Chapter Seventeen). Occasionally the legitimizer, stimulator, and initiator are all the same person or group, but up to this time a lack of strong evidence of legitimation (beyond ritual pronouncements from the top) has usually thwarted the evolution of lrsp.

To apply their model of innovation decisions, Rogers and Shoemaker distinguish two means for diffusing innovations through the organization: a participative approach "in which there is a wide sharing of power, decisions about change being made in consultation with those affected by the change" (p. 316), which in our case would seem to mean just about everybody; and through "authority innovation-decisions." This approach involves five interrelated functions: "(1) knowledge about the need for change and the innovation on the part of the decision unit, (2) persuasion and evaluation of the innovation by the decision unit, (3) decision as to acceptance or rejection of the innovation by the decision unit, (4) communication of the decision to the adoption units in the organization, and (5) action or implementation of the decision by the adoption units" (pp. 315–316).[43] It is important to note that in the lrsp situation the kinds of groups and persons who would have to make such decisions at each stage and then carry them out, in order to evolve lrsp, may themselves be among those resisting the introduction of the changes required because they perceive lrsp as threatening their authority.

Some summary comments about related developmental processes aptly suggest the complex and painful sequencing tasks that will be involved in changing toward lrsp. In what follows, E. Miller and A. K. Rice (1967) are using, as their example, developmental problems in designing, building, and operating a new plant starting from scratch (on a "greenfield").

Our analysis suggests that, in most processes of institution-building, efforts to secure innovation will conflict with any attempt to secure commitment by involving the future members of the institution in design tasks. The only exception will be in the enterprise in which an individual or a small group, themselves the risk-taking entrepreneurs, can encompass the entire setting-up process. The setting-up task can then be contained within a simple system. If the task is large enough to require an internally differentiated organization, conflict will arise. Thus if the plant-design system does not include members of the future building system and the future operating system, first the builders and later the operators will be working to designs that they had no part in shaping. Predecessors' actions can then become alibis for current failures. Conversely, if the organization maximizes involvement in the design and building systems of members of the future operating system, innovation will be retarded.

The more general point is that conflict is inevitable in any setting-up process in which the task is to create a system with organized properties. Conflict and the attendant anxieties are likely to be stronger in the greenfield situation, where the heightened expectations at the beginning also exacerbate the ultimate feeling of let-down when—as must be so—the completed task does not live up to all the original expectations. The painful and destructive aspects of the creative process are perhaps easier to bear, however, if they can be anticipated and planned for [p. 156].

[43] See also Havelock and others (1971, especially Chapter 10, pp. 39, 53, 69, and 70).

The reader should take what has been proposed here only as an image, not as a model of what would or should be the phases and kinds of actors involved in the change-over process. Let Rogers and Shoemaker echo earlier caveats about the comparatively modest state of our understanding of our society or of the change processes operating in it: "Diffusion researchers have largely neglected the study of diffusion and adoption of innovations involving authority innovation-decisions; we know very little about the process by which authority decisions are made and organizational changes implemented" (p. 315).[44]

Is Lrsp Underway Outside the United States?

A frequent speculation suggests that the absence of extensive efforts to change toward lrsp in the United States is only trivially related to social psychological phenomena, and is better understood in terms of the inextricable snarl of statutes, prerogatives, and traditions that characterize our hyperpluralistic society. Often attached to this speculation is the presumption that lrsp *is* underway in other parts of the world, at least in the socialist or communist nations, or in the Third World, where economic planning has been a continuing activity for many years.

Clearly some countries, including Western European nations, are more deliberative about their development, at least over five-year time periods. How much more deliberative, how much more so in the spirit of frsl as emphasized here, is not clear.[45] G. Myrdal (1972), for example, has argued that Third World planning has been economic planning and that economic models are simply wrong in their emphasis and unresponsive to crucial social and psychological considerations, which is why they have failed as social planning technologies. It might well be that differences in attitudes toward expertise, authority and hierarchy, homogeneity of population, special historical experiences, and different levels of aspiration and expected standards of social services, would provide better grounds for beginning lrsp elsewhere if the attempt were made to do so.[46]

---

[44] Also see Havelock and others (1971) on the limits of understanding. A very amusing and very insightful "case study" of the processes by which information systems do and do not make their way in a corporate setting (and by easy extrapolation, in a government setting) is Strassmann (1969).

[45] An excellent overall review of recent government and corporate planning efforts in Europe—with a fascinating perspective on the United States included—is Shonfield (1965). Also see McNamara (1970b) and McNamara (1970, p. 10).

[46] In this regard, Dror (1968) writes, "Developments have been different, for instance, in the Netherlands, where the constant pressures of critical hydraulic, social, political, and economic problems have required very good public

A. Westin has speculated that "social psychological responses of the kind that inhibit efforts at long-range social planning are inevitable and natural consequences when human beings are set into the competitive and even combative relationships that the framers of the American Constitution saw as the way to inhibit the intensification of power in any one set of hands."[47] Also, until the environment elsewhere is perceived to be dangerously turbulent by local standards, other means of societal guidance may seem sufficient and the rigors of lrsp an unnecessary burden. All such factors would affect the social psychological setting since it is, by definition, the result of psychological processes interacting with social circumstance.

All things considered, what limited exposure I have had to other societies strongly inclines me to feel that *this is very much a book by an American reflecting and reflecting on the situation in the United States.* Beyond this, questions of comparative national capabilities for moving toward lrsp, as determined by the *product* of existential conditions and social psychological characteristics, and the extent to which nations are involved in lrsp as described here, are essentially unexplored.

---

policymaking merely for survival and have made much use of essential knowledge" (p. 249).

[47] Westin, in personal correspondence.

Sources of Individual Support
for Change Toward LRSP

ᕙᕙᕙᕙᕙᕙᕙᕙᕙᕙᕙᕙᕙᕙᕙᕪᕪᕪᕪᕪᕪᕪᕪᕪᕪᕪᕪᕪᕪᕪ

Since the resistances to efforts to change toward lrsp will be pervasive, strong, and interlocked, the reader may well wonder where the human pressures *for* lrsp come from. Even if there are societal circumstances that would appear to benefit from the application of lrsp, who and where are the human beings, operating as individuals or groups, who will provide the thrust that others will resist? This chapter looks at the perceptions, beliefs, and motives of those pushing for lrsp. We shall not be attending to them directly again until the Epilogue, where we will explore their chances, working in tandem with other social changes, of overcoming the resistances which have so far proved more powerful than any forces for change—imagery and good intentions not withstanding.

The importance of each of the factors to be discussed, to which groups and under what circumstances, is unclear. Nor is it clear how widespread these positive pressures are. At this point, the impression gained from a wide range of printed references to these issues is that these positive pressures are frequently expressed in sources as various as the technical-professional journals, house organs, and pop-culture magazines. Among those interviewed, these motives, beliefs, and concerns appeared to be pervasive (though this is hardly surprising since the respondents were expected to be concerned with planning). But it is also revealing that respondents often felt themselves fighting lonely battles, supported at most by few like-minded warriors. Let us look now at the perceptions, beliefs, and motives that infuse the literature and seem to sustain the proponents of lrsp.

Need to Anticipate the Societal Consequences of Whatever Is Underway Now

As thinking becomes sophisticated about the world scope and inter-dependence of all societal conditions, more professionals and laymen seem to be recognizing what has been called the "world macro problem," the "problematique," or the "problem of problems."[1] This is the most obvious indication of growing support for planning, and it is most evident in the areas of concern over the interactive impact of ecological degrada-tion, population size, and technology on both the social and natural en-vironments. Additional issues contributing to this awareness were men-tioned in Chapter One (and others are familiar to those reading this book by the very fact of their interest in planning). But there is a quality to this awareness that merits further mention here because of its psycho-logical implications.

For many of the familiar situations to which planning rhetoric is applied, the popular assumption, and often the professional one, is that a technical, legal, or educational "fix" will solve a problem over time and in the process will keep it from getting worse. (Indeed, for some, planning merely means finding such a fix and applying it to a present problem.) But, increasingly, some who look at the future worry about irreversible trends, trends which are already or may soon be so inextricably elaborated that no way out of the "traps" they represent is conceivable short of enor-mous reallocations of physical, social, financial, and psychological re-sources and commitments.[2] These observers doubt that this society has the will or the knowledge to make such shifts, and this doubt sometimes results in despair, or cynicism, or a blunting of sensitivity and awareness. Thus in some, a heightened sense of the need for planning also produces an intensified sense of being overwhelmed by the complexity of the task.

[1] See Markley, Curry, and Rink (1971); Peccei (1971); and Platt, (1969).

[2] Probably the best known example of "trap" delineation is Meadows, Meadows, Randers, and Behrens (1972). This is one of several studies sponsored by the Club of Rome. This international organization is dedicated to emphasiz-ing that we must learn how to perceive the nature and consequences of the multiple "problems" that engulf the world in a far more interactive way than we have yet managed to conceptualize. See Peccei (1971).

It seems, then, that persons who are deeply concerned have three options, and that all of them seem to be extensively and increasingly practiced. Some, to avoid facing the threat that would be posed to themselves, as competent and effective members of society, if they were to acknowledge that the issues are overwhelmingly complex, pretend that the issues are not there, or concentrate on bits and pieces (technological and social "fixes"), hoping that somehow they will all add up. There are some who press for more and more extensive long-range approaches and hope they will go well. (I am one of these.) And there are others who are unable to find grounds for unwavering commitment to either position. Clearly there are substantial differences, among those favoring long-range planning, regarding the meaning of planning and the proper approach to it; and there are differences in optimism or pessimism about its eventual effectiveness, to say nothing of the self-images held by those attached to one approach or the other. All are pushing for lrsp in one way or another, but they will not necessarily be allied or even compatible in their methods, goals, or constituencies. One thing seems clear: those who think we can "fix" things seem surer of themselves at this point than those who think only a comprehensive approach will work. (H. David speculates that this difference in mood may express the difference between those who know how to do the jobs they have and those who don't know what their jobs are.) It is important to keep in mind these differences in self image and problem perception, for they will affect the way those pushing for planning are perceived and received.

Hopes That Planning Can Undercut Dissidence

Here the motive seems to be to initiate activities intended to undercut anticipated dissidence, or to provide images of desirable and attainable futures that will undercut present dissidence. Corporations and government agencies are beginning to see more clearly that consumerism, environmentalism, political protests, advocate planning, and so forth can be better dealt with, possibly, by trying to change both the social and the natural environments before they produce these reactions, rather than by trying to respond to them only after they arise. And there is also a growing realization that the environment to be changed is inside as well as outside the organization: it is the inside environment that largely (but not completely) determines how the outside environment is perceived and responded to. This motive in support of planning has positive aspects, but it also encourages a manipulative and two-faced attitude toward the "planned-for" clientele. Moreover, it poses special social psychological problems integral to the differences between open and closed (social engineering) forms of lrsp. Open planning, as an integral aspect of its operations, invites environmental feedback and the open recognition of its errors so that all learn from the situation; closed planning tries to keep control of the environment by covertly scanning and manipulating it. This latter planning mode tends to fit the operating style of many engineers and corporations who are interested in getting into urban systems planning. They find it sensible and rewarding to try to "engineer" the natural environment and the "market place" so that both do what the engineers, or their clients, want them to do.

Hope That Professional Skills Can Facilitate Lrsp

Many kinds of social and physical engineers see planning as a new opportunity to contribute to social well-being, enhance their self-image, improve their incomes, stabilize their work environment, gain power, and be important. Some have demonstrated relevant competence in other areas, as in the aerospace industry or in university or think-tank research, or by contributing to the development, implementation, or evaluation of social welfare programs, management development, or administrative change. Some have demonstrated skill in teaching others how to plan, or at least how to use some of the technologies that could contribute to planning. But this heightened mood of opportunity for personal success and societal contribution carries with it a deepened mood of uncertainty. Sometimes the same person vacillates between moods; sometimes one or another dominates persons or groups. Together these moods will contribute to ambivalent pressures for more planning. Here are three kinds of ambivalences that will help us sense the social psychological context in which attempts to change toward lrsp will be embedded.

First, the growth of the "systems" perspective and the kind of "real world" problems that attract people using the systems approach have led some to recognize that traditional boundaries between parts of any social system are increasingly becoming blurred.[3] In consequence there is a growing feeling that a piecemeal approach to human problems just won't work, that it is shortsighted and probably counterproductive to think of housing without thinking of job location, transportation, and recreation, or to think of health delivery services without considerations for education, transportation, ethnic differences, nutrition patterns, and child raising approaches. With the appreciation of the need to shift to more synoptic approaches in time and space goes the hope that new planning technology will make the systems approach feasible.

---

[3] A deeply humanistic delineation of the systems approach is found in Churchman (1968). The dilemmas reasoning poses for reasoning, in a systems context, are explored in Churchman (1967).

A special hope inspires many professionals: the expectation that social science will provide the data base, and, gradually, the social theory based on the data, that will make better planning possible. Whatever else has impeded social planning, certainly a major obstacle has been the circumstance that little or no data existed or could be produced fast enough to describe the state of the society or the effects of particular programs. Some expect that computer-assisted processing of social indicator data and societal dynamics simulation will accomplish many things: force more attention to social indicators; provide a critical capability for planning what to do about their implications; provide data on how well a plan is operating; and force attention to the secondary and tertiary effects of both planned and unplanned activities. By doing these things, they will also require more planning.

But there is also much uncertainty about whether planning technology will mature soon enough and be supported well enough by social science theory to undertake the larger costs and risks of trying to do things on a more comprehensive scale. As a result, some planning proponents find themselves in a deep intellectual and ethical dilemma. They recognize that while systems approaches to social issues seems necessary, the consequent necessity of committing large amounts of resources over a long time period carries with it the potential for large disasters if the approach proves wrong. Their ambivalence is heightened by the appreciation that the technology and social theory needed for improving lrsp requires, to some unknown but substantial degree, testing and refining under conditions in which the systems approach is applied to real societal problems.

There is a second ambivalent wish to use one's professional skills to plan: the philosophical and engineering insights from cybernetics and systems analysis have heightened and legitimized appreciation among planners that social systems are open systems in which organized activities are mutually and invariably perturbable. To some degree, then, social systems are uncontrollable in the sense that they cannot be kept stable and predictable over long periods. For some professionals, especially those whose personal need for an orderly world has led them to seek it through planning, the open relationship between organization and environment is quite discouraging if they see the environment itself as turbulent, as they usually do. On the other hand, there are professionals who are increasingly hopeful that the planning technologies, including future studies, will make social change more plannable, more subject to direction and regulation. Some, though by no means all, of this hope (or indeed downright confidence in some cases) seems to be a psychological defense against feelings of role impotency. But that makes it no less important in the interplay of social psychological forces making for and against the change-over to lrsp.

There is yet a third ambivalent wish to use professional skills for planning: some persons concerned with social welfare development see in some parts of lrsp technology—such as program budgeting and planning, future studies, and the advocate planning approach—new opportunities for them to shift the attention of fellow professionals and service organizations away from input or output criteria, which redound to the organization's "productivity" image, toward impact measures which emphasize the environment's welfare. But those who see these possibilities as reasons to push for lrsp also recognize the new possibilities that lrsp provides for greater professional and organizational independence from the environment: the organization could get greater control over and preempt the skill required to use the complex information needed for lrsp.[4] This could lead to more manipulation of the environment. Hence in this wish, too, there is concern mixed with hope.

Academicians Seek Relevance by Contributing to Lrsp

Increasingly, academicians feel inadequate and immoral unless they involve themselves in "relevant" problems. Some discover that departmental discipline standards have insulated them from the "real" world. And some find that the very characterological needs which led them to choose the university life make them comparatively unfit for or uncomfortable in the outside world. For some, a popular resolution of both of these difficulties is to become engaged in interdisciplinary studies, to work at refining the conceptual and normative basis for coping with complex "real-world" problems. As a result, such persons become problem generators, solution proposers, and planning technology developers; they think about these in systems terms and view the situation in a longer time perspective, which is compatible with the academic perspective. Their activities thus enrich the recognition of problems in need of a planning approach and of planning means for approaching them. Writing about and advising on them further spreads and legitimates appreciation of the need for lrsp. It leads, too, to new subjects for research and teaching such as technology and social change, policy-making, and future studies.[5] These subjects fall between the territories claimed by one or another discipline into a no-discipline land, an area that appeals to the students and

[4] Two examples of this concern: Lowi (1972) and Michael (1968).

[5] For a survey of some such activities see de Hoghton and others (1971). Also see Huber (1968, Appendix, pp. 339–454.)

also to legislators who consider a large number of students per teacher a mark of well-husbanded academic funds.

Two consequences of academic involvement merit mention. To the extent that these new courses are influential, they will help to create a generation of long-time perspective, planning-oriented, social intervention-ists and voters supportive of frsl. Second, the steady output by academi-cians of planning-relevant materials in popular and professional publica-tions, and their consulting with and advising of non-government and government groups, stimulates public and organizational awareness. This in turn increases the pressures on planning-relevant members of organiza-tions, who see themselves as professionals, to attend to the ideas of their colleagues in academia and the think-tanks. As a result, the professional involved with planning activities is and will be faced with the difficult task of constructively exploiting two sets of role-defining messages which will often conflict.

Professionals Need to Be Needed

Like most people, experts have a deep need to create a human setting that needs them. Unlike many people, they have special opportu-nities to do so. Planning is being urged by its practitioners and would-be practitioners as a new social technology and as such it is getting a more careful hearing—in our society technology partakes of the Promethean mystique, and thereby wins both popular and serious attention. To be sure, the mystique is not as popular as it once was, but it is still strong and the very social messes that have tarnished technology's sheen also lead people to look for ways out of them via new technologies. The media still make the most of the gee-whiz-new-horizons-new-control-of-man-over-his-own-destiny message.

In some situations this promotion of planning technology, which is both praiseworthy and suspect, takes on a self-regenerating quality. For there are other persons—managers, administrators, executives—who see their recognition of the need for planning experts and planning technol-ogy as evidence of their own expertise. Whether they use the experts and technologies well is another matter: mostly they seem not to. What is im-portant here is that when managers, executives, and administrators speak about the potentialities of and need for planning experts and their tech-nologies—and their words are often published—they provide a special opportunity for the professionals also to speak, enlarging on the need for their skills. This encourages the managerial experts to begin another round of mutual reinforcement, resulting in growing mutual expectations that lrsp is or will be in operation.

This diffuse dialogue is increasingly facilitated by growing numbers of conferences, symposia, summer institutes, and formal and expensive training seminars for top-level executives and administrators. These also tend to reinforce the mutual support between the substantive experts and their potential employers, and they enlarge the technical understanding each has about the substantive skills of the other and about areas of potential problems and payoffs. But for the most part, these activities have a kind of social insularity about them. This results partly from naïvete about the depth of organizational and social change needed to make planning implementable; partly from a tendency to concentrate on planning technique and technology rather than on the problems of getting people and organizations into shape to use the techniques; and partly from emphasis on one or another special aspect of the whole task of planning, which results in ignoring its contingent and consequential aspects. All this gives a spurious sense of imminent, possibly easy, feasibility to the planning enterprise. When the larger picture is examined or when the organizational development tasks are explored, it turns out that the situation is not so exhilarating or payoffs so certain. Few participants find they can sustain the necessary psychological or operational opportunity costs. Thus, conscious and unconscious tacit agreement seems to predominate in this area of mutual support between experts and clients. In consequence, belief in one's capacity to deal with a situation in need of planning is sustained by splitting up the topic and by keeping it either at such a high level of abstraction or at such a low level of nuts-and-bolts tactical planning that the difficult issues of lrsp are avoided.[6] Nevertheless these activities seem to encourage an appreciation of the need for planning as such and are reflected in the following contribution to the thrust toward lrsp.

Increased Institutionalizing of Activities That Convey Intent or Capacity to Do Social Planning, Thereby Encouraging Others to Do Likewise

Note that the above says social planning, not *long-range* social planning; the deletion is deliberate because the activities in the process of being institutionalized are ambiguous as to comprehensiveness or time-scale perspective. But these activities do signal an intention to be more coordinated about and responsive to complex societal needs, and to be using or developing both physical and social technologies for doing so.

There are now more "planning" units in the federal government be-

---

[6] A rare admirable and partially successful attempt to deal with lrsp at the appropriate integrative level is found in the papers for and report of the Organization for Economic Cooperation and Development working symposium on Long Range Forecasting and Planning. See Jantsch, Ed. (1969a).

cause of pressures from what was the Bureau of the Budget (now significantly redesignated the Office of Management and Budget). Congressmen are promoting technology assessment and other legislation that encourages and depends on the application of planning philosophy and technology.[7] There is the quasi-private Urban Institute devoted to research and development on large-scale urban problems. In more communities there are advocate planning groups and, partially in response to them, city planning staffs have been augmented. Some states have begun to use program planning and budgeting systems (Schick 1971) and cities have established program management facilities, urban goals statements, and nonprofit think-tank adjuncts as in Los Angeles and New York City.[8]

Responding to these developments, more corporations and nonprofit organizations are seeking urban development contracts, and sometimes selling them on the promise of their urban systems design capabilities. Sales, of course, legitimize the strength of such aspiring groups in their parent organizations and also stimulate these groups to persist and expand. (Of course, it may also produce counterforces in the organization, and given the nascent state of much urban systems sales activity, those counterforces are often comparatively potent.)

Private organizations concerned with public service have also initiated efforts at planning activities, recognizing that their future functions are likely to be different from those in their successful past.

In addition to the more or less ad hoc academic courses in future studies, policy research on urban problems, and so on, which we referred to earlier, graduate student interests and those of some faculty and administrators are moving graduate departments in architecture, urban design,

[7] A few examples: "To Establish a Select Senate Committee on Technology and the Human Environment" (1967); *The Planning-Programing-Budgeting System* (1967); and *Full Opportunity and Social Accounting Act* (1967). More recent examples include Senator Mondale's effort to establish a National Commission on Health, Science, and Society (SS Res 75) and Senate efforts, following on Congressman Daddario's proposal, to establish an Office of Technological Assessment (S2302). See also Senator Mondale on the need for a Council of Social Advisors in the *Congressional Record,* August 5, 1971, *117,* 126.

[8] New York City is probably most notable for the program management facilities approach. As for preparing urban goals statements, several cities have moved in this direction, but very limited success in moving beyond capital improvement goals and in setting priorities among goals. Among cities that have tried are: Dallas, Texas; Dayton, Ohio; Seattle, Washington; and Los Angeles, California. Los Angeles's effort has been the most extensive and systematic by far. See *Concepts for Los Angeles* (1967), and *Discussion Paper: Planning Goals for the Los Angeles Metropolis* (1967). For nonprofit think-tank adjuncts, see the reports of the Los Angeles Technical Services Corporation and *The New York City Rand Institute,* January 1968–June 1970.

and urban and regional planning into areas that demand attention to human problems, social design, and planned social change techniques; the disciplinary fiefdoms are blurring and the blurring process is increasingly deliberate. Consequently, programs in social policy planning, whatever their particular titles, are being institutionalized at graduate levels through revisions in older more constricted programs and through new programs, departments, centers, and institutes. There is a growing output of people, ideas, and social technologies which, by their very existence, pressure for similar developments in the world outside academia. They legitimize planning concerns by their symbolic existence, and they provide the ideas and the agents for extending that concern and legitimacy. As more of those ideas and the people bearing them move into public organizations, they will contribute to further institutionalizing of activities that carry an intent to do social planning.

However, *longer-range* perspectives and recognition of the human and societal requirements for meeting longer-range developments are *not* central preoccupations in most of the institutionalizing now under way. They are sometimes present as subjects of intellectual and ideological concern, but the main emphasis is, as it always has been, on how to get things done better *now* by being more systematic and comprehensive. That is where the interests of administrators, executives, students, faculty, and fund sources are focused. Most of these institutionalizing trends are just that: they are not for the most part a suddenly new kind of social invention in the history of reformist America. They are important additional "inputs" in response to a growing appreciation that a bits-and-pieces approach, no matter how well run, is not enough: good-will and the hidden hand of pluralism won't do it. There is also the recognition that governments, especially the federal government, through its own agencies and through private organizations, will fund larger more comprehensive attacks on social problems and opportunities—which means that one way or the other they will fund planning. And there is also the infusion of new expertise, in which the "futurist" is of ambiguous significance.

Sources of Resistance to Lrsp

Taken together, the thrust of planning proponents in the direction of lrsp would seem irresistable. Why then the earlier assertions that there are deep, perhaps insuperable resistances to changing organizations toward lrsp? The answer is that the resistances are formidable because they are supported by conventional and widely imbedded societal norms that people subscribe to because they set the bases for reward and punishment. The resistances are supported by organizational structures that maintain and reinforce the norms. Indeed, as we shall see, these conventional norms and organizational structures operate so as to discourage interest in or practice of lrsp even among planners and planners-to-be, and among many others who want to be more comprehensive but only up to a "reasonable," "practical," point. So pervasive are these norms that, when people react to their adverse consequences by rejecting the organizations that operate according to them, they usually choose modes of reaction that reinforce the norms. As P. Slater (1970) argues, in seeking to break free of the hidden psychosocial costs with which the norm of individualism burdens middle class Americans, people seek even more individualism —for example, doing one's own thing—which only exacerbates the malaise it was supposed to remove. So too, in trying to break free of the social costs that result from organizational non-planning, groups seek "autonomy" and insularity from other groups, especially from established organizations. They want to be more "disjointed" if not more "incremental" than even the organizationally based incrementalists. They want to increase pluralism at just the period in history when the conventional tactics and values of pluralism seem to have become self-defeating or at least insufficient as means for dealing with systemic problems and processes and for discovering new solutions (Lowi, 1969).[9]

What provides the dialectic now, of course, is growth in this new set of intentions, aspirations, and resources to plan, a growth which is pushing at, invading, and threatening the conventional way of doing things and of being rewarded or punished for so doing. What, in the long run, will be the resolution or balance of this dialectic depends on what we understand about, and then what we want to do and are able to do about, the resistances to changing toward frsl. These subsequent choices require that we face up to what we want to do and are able to do about revising basic culture values which determine how we reward individuals and groups and what we reward them for. Both ideological resistances and the rationality of those ideological resistances, justified in terms of payoffs for maintaining those resistances, have to be dealt with.[10] If these resistances are to be overcome by those proposing lrsp, they will have to be overcome within the individual who finds meaning in his culturally

[9] The enormously difficult conceptual and operational tasks connected with necessary joint organization-environment involvement in planning will be explored in later chapters. The point here is that present responses to the consequences of non-planning—whether elitist or pluralist—tend to reinforce nonplanning as the means for trying to cope with social pains and opportunities.

[10] "Incoming messages are not admitted to the image gate free. At the gate of the image stands the value system demanding payment . . . we see the world the way we see it because it pays us and has paid us to see it that way" (Boulding, 1956, p. 50).

given and organizationally reinforced definitions of how to behave sensibly. This will be a very heavy task in individual and societal learning and relearning.

Summary

A major contribution to the difficulty of changing organizations toward lrsp will be a basic difference in philosophy and expectation within the pro-planning community, namely the difference between seeing planning as a social engineering type of activity and seeing it as societal learning process. As we shall see, the former viewpoint will exacerbate resistances to lrsp; the latter viewpoint could reduce them *if* the norm of society as a learning, experimenting state of affairs could come to the fore sufficiently to dominate in some quarters. But the norms of a learning society are profoundly different from those that organize our conventional ways of being and doing. The motives and the ambivalences held within pro-planning individuals and groups, and the different views of people and organizations associated with these motives and ambivalences, provide a critical context for understanding the social psychological issues I shall be exploring.

LRSP in Corporations

৯৯৯৯৯৯৯৯৯৯৯৯৯৯৯৯৯৯৯৬৬৬৬৬৬৬৬৬৬৬৬৬৬৬৬

*F*or some readers, this chapter will be an aside. Our concern in this book is with organizations that are legally or morally obliged to respond to the public interest, namely government and some third-sector organizations (though it is generally acknowledged that in coming years corporations will also be increasingly if ambiguously involved in the public interest). However, the widespread imagery about on-going long-range planning in corporations makes it desirable to review the corporate situation. Certainly, some readers are already familiar with the limits of corporate long-range planning and its insufficiency for long-range *social* planning. Other readers, however, do not know what in fact seems to be going on—or not going on—but do have strong impressions from the media and from speeches by corporate executives that a great deal is happening. This chapter, then, is for those in the latter group who may believe that the problems we will examine have already been solved in corporations.

What follows derives from the technical literature on what corporate planning should be, from the corporation-servicing media that reports what is happening in the corporate planning world, and from interviews with highly competent "insiders" and consultants to corporations.[1] Let me emphasize that what follows is based on more than a cursory look at the

---

[1] At their request, the names of some of those interviewed are not included in the List of Respondents at the end of this book.

corporation condition but on far less than a systematic examination. As with the rest of the book, my purpose is not to resolve the questions and conjectures raised by this exploration but to propose them as worthy of further study. What is more, as Shonfield (1965) has written:

The significant facts about the behavior of private enterprise are less readily established than about governments. This is partly because of the sheer volume of disparate elements, each pursuing its own separate interest, which make up the private sector; at best, one is dealing with statistical aggregates. The other factor which makes the study of the public sector easier is that even at its most secretive its actions in the conduct of economic policy are, in a democracy, subject to scrutiny, whereas private enterprise has often managed to escape it. That is not due merely to its talent for evasion; the observers themselves have been remarkably undemanding. Knowledge about such matters as how the typical business sets about pricing its goods or deciding how much to invest has only recently begun to be established by systematic empirical tests. Economic analysis, during most of the time that it has been practiced as an academic discipline, has been much less concerned with what businessmen actually do than with what they would *do on certain assumptions, including the major assumption that they are strictly rational men [p. 358].*

. . . there is a lack of systematic data on which to base precise and comprehensive generalizations in this field. Many of the changes which have occurred are in any case so recent that it would be surprising if much more were available at this stage than suggestive indications of underlying trends. The development of business planning is an obvious case in point. There is no way of measuring its significance [p. 362].

With due appreciation, then, that there may be more to the story, it appears that much that is claimed for and done in the name of corporate planning is only dimly related in practice and spirit to what is proposed in this book. Since the only research purpose for examining corporate planning efforts was to see if they might illuminate the problems and possibilities public organizations would face when attempting to change over to lrsp, there seemed no point in probing further. However, while the goals and conditions that set the conventional context for corporate planning are basically different from those we are concerned with, the developing societal situation is leading a very few corporations to try to move toward a mode of lrsp more akin in process and perhaps even in spirit to what I propose. As of this writing, to my knowledge only a very few corporations, most notably General Electric, have even described planning intentions that are in the direction proposed here. Whether these intentions can be implemented, whether the social psychological resistances can be overcome and the organization restructured and values and norms shifted, and whether the corporation could still operate as a profit-making entity, all remains to be learned. My strong impression is that many corporations will someday face the issues and social psychological processes to be described, but that not one has actually gone far enough in its lrsp development efforts to face them yet.

In what follows I will first very briefly review the conventional setting for corporate planning and then suggest some developing conditions that will put corporations in a context more akin to that of public agencies, with corresponding unfamiliar requirements which will both require lrsp and complicate its introduction.

The Conventional Corporate Situation Today

Many planning activities are said by corporate personnel to be underway, but there are proprietary and psychological defenses in depth that protect such assertions from careful evaluation. Executives associated with corporations where one might expect lrsp like to think of themselves as advanced and responsible planners. The aspirations that higher-level corporate management personnel hold about what they and their organizations should become are changing. These people are influenced by the imagery of the potency and potential of planning, systems approaches, computer simulations, and so on, and by the imagery that says that these are the things that advanced organizations are using and doing. (This influence by imagery, promulgated in the corporation-servicing media and by the organizations catering to corporate executives, seems similar to the earlier imagery that seduced many organizations to invest in computers without really knowing what to do with them.) Thus they tend to see whatever planning effort they have as in the vanguard and as influential throughout the organization—whether the planning activity is two people looking ahead twenty years at the state of society or twenty people doing sophisticated but comparatively narrow market or capital invest-ment planning. However, most senior personnel have little understanding of the processes of innovation and change in their own organization, being concerned with matters of money flow, market share, and so on:

Managers at the division level are likely to have spent much of their work-ing lives in their present or other divisions. Their "real world" is the people they see and work with every day, the products they manufacture, the physical facilities of the division, and the projects that are underway in the division. Customers and customer complaints are real; the products produced for them are tangible and are probably well understood. How well the product works and how efficiently it is produced are probably the result of innumerable personal challenges, successes, and failures. . . .

At the corporate level, in contrast, it is all too easy to feel that the real world consists of "the corporation" and those quantified abstractions which show how the corporation is doing with respect to the outside world—profit and loss statements, balance sheets, the market price of the stock, and so on. "What does it mean in earnings per share?" is often the all-important question with regard to division proposals or problems. The real world at the corporate level becomes the external and quantitative measure of corporate performance and health; divisions can all too easily be regarded as suppliers of financial statements which merely fit into the vast corporate totals [Ewing, 1969, pp. 50, 51].

Thus senior personnel tend to be naïve when assessing the alleged impact of planning on actual organizational behavior at lower levels.[2] However sincere, their responses to questions about the operational impact of planning cannot be accepted as valid.

Examination of the social psychological aspects of present and past corporate efforts to change toward long-range planning is complicated by other factors. First, much of what has been represented as advanced lrsp has been mere public relations.

It is unfortunately true that for the past five years or so, long-range planning and technological forecasting have been 'in' with corporations. Articles in the Wall Street Journal, *the* Harvard Business Review, *and* Fortune *have spoken glowingly of the virtues of technological forecasting as a component of corporate long-range planning. Hence, many corporations set up long-range planning groups more for the purpose of impressing the stockbrokers, or the public, or the executives of competing corporations, than for the purpose of making and implementing long-range plans. These groups were little more than window-dressing. Is it surprising, then, that when the crunch came many of them were disbanded? They were, after all, serving no useful purpose other than the advertising value gained from them, and when business is bad there are more effective ways to spend advertising money [Martino, 1971, p. 33].*

In the absence of studies in depth it is difficult to know whether one is dealing with naïvete or cynicism.

It is important to realize that many corporations which doubtless do

---

[2] For a detailed description of how resource allocation decisions at the top are very much an expression of many decisions made earlier far down in the corporation see Bower (1970).

some kind of long-range planning that includes a social component have the military as their chief client. This means that critical aspects of their planning are classified. Of even more significance for this study, the planning that has been done *so far* has been done in a situation where the organization-environment relationship and the goals of planning are profoundly different from those that characterize open systems confronted with changing and conflict-filled environments and social needs and wants.

Many corporations do plan, and probably all the large ones do. But, except for a handful, they do so in ways different from those proposed here, for different goals, usually for different reasons, and until very recently, in a different environmental context. Even then, on the whole, it appears that long-range planning in corporations seems for the most part to be far less practiced or perfected than its imagery implies. While there are exceptions, foresightedness usually extends from six months to two years, with five years usually being the extreme.[3] A recent survey by W. Hall (1972) of seventeen major banks, public utilities, and manufacturers, concludes: *"Most of the planning models which are being used are not significantly influencing the actual strategy formulation process within the firm.* In the words of one analyst: 'We run our planning model regularly, sending the output to a committee composed of our executive officers. Frankly we don't know what they do with the results —but we suspect nothing.' A senior executive in another firm who receives projections from a corporate financial model provides another perspective when he comments: 'All of the senior managers in our firm believe that these corporate models should be providing valuable information, but we just don't know what use to make of it' " [p. 3].[4]

Conventionally, the corporation's consumer environment was passive compared to today: it simply sold its products to those who wanted to buy and sometimes it created markets in its interest. Government regulations have usually been in the interest of, sometimes at the request of the corporation. Of course, corporations have battled mightily among themselves, but the purpose of the battle has always been the same—organizational survival and growth, never the public interest, and that also simplified the corporation's environment. Intrinsically, the chief organizationally shared goal was profit, or was profit-related, like the size of the share of the market. Thus goal choosing was chiefly instrumental: how to make a profit. Correspondingly, the most salient feedback from the environment were indicators of profit and loss, or share of the market, or some such profit-related measure. To be sure, there were other kinds of

---

[3] Surveys of the general status, time frame, and substance of corporate planning are found in Shonfield (1965, p. 221), and Steiner (1969, p. 23).

[4] Quoted with the author's permission.

feedback from the corporation's sub-environments (such as suppliers and distributers) but these sub-environments were comparatively easy to differentiate externally and matched internally through functionally specified activities (such as purchasing and marketing). Of great importance, the interpersonal and organizational relationships between the corporation and its sub-environments were understandable and essentially predictable. People played by the same rules: especially they shared the value of negotiating a reasonable profit for all concerned—most of the time.

The profit goal in typical corporate situations has meant that the time frame for planning has had to be short, given the rapid obsolescence of so many products. For some products like steel mills, aircraft, or computers, the time frame has been longer (as much as a decade) but the goal-setting task (will it contribute to profit) remained comparatively simple and the procedure for getting from here to there appeared clear. The tangible product requirements themselves defined the steps along the path.

Product development took place under conditions of proprietary secrecy, as well as it could be maintained. During the research and development stages the environment was ignorant of what was going on, or it was if informed at all the information was management-controlled. Hence what little environmental feedback there was, in addition to product purchases, began only after the product was marketed. Sometimes what was developed was influenced by market research, but consumer involvement was always at the wish and under the control of management. Deliberate creation of consumer markets has been an option open only to the largest corporations and has been a unilateral procedure chosen and implemented at the discretion of the corporation in *its* interests.

Typically, the corporate product has been a tangible physical product. The characteristics of the product itself impose a structure and direction on the planning of its development and dissemination. Commenting on the conditions that affect the usefulness of that basic tool and conceptual style of lrsp, systems analysis, C. DiBona (1967) has observed: "Some areas may be neater or inherently more tractable than others. The more the subjects of investigation are preplanned, the more they depend on the characteristics of large pieces of equipment with few operating modes and the more they are determined by early large events, then the more likely they are to be analytically tractable. These areas are less likely to be influenced by unpredictable behavior and states of training or to be dependent upon a myriad of small encounters" (p. 3). Physical things have to fit together; some things have to fit before other things; things have to have specific properties in time and space. The articulatedness inherent in properties of the product itself provides a scaffolding, a reference system, upon which to construct the instrumental goals, the time frame, the feedback requirements, and the means for assuring implementation of the feedback messages. Indeed all the requirements for long-range planning can be met, and sometimes have been met in practice, once the product specifications to be developed has been stated: they can be met because the properties of the product impose their requirements on the people seeking to realize those properties. The internal corporate environment is itself stabilized by the operations-structuring and information-specifying constraints of the hardware.

This same situation has been determinate in government programs that are typically pointed to as products of successful planning. The platitudinous question, "If we can put a man on the moon why can't we apply the same management and technological know-how to remaking our cities?" is in large part answered by the fact that Apollo was in effect directed by the properties of materials and the artifacts into which they were arranged, while city problems are directed by people and social processes: management and technological know-how cannot interlock nearly so well in this situation.[5]

The research and development corporation or the organization with an important research and development subsystem have more complex planning tasks and generally longer time perspectives. But since the research and development is almost invariably on physical products, the uncertainties that plague the social planning area are substantially absent. Nevertheless, as D. Schon (1967) has demonstrated, organizations are generally unable to deal with the uncertainty introduced by radically new research and development produced in their own organizations. They succumb to social psychological processes of the sort to be discussed later.

In essence, then, when conventional corporate planning was undertaken it was with a rather clear sense of knowing where the corporation

---

[5] Of the $15 billion Federal budget for "science," at least two-thirds is for development—that is, it is sharply focused on the time-bound achievement of certain specific end products or concrete certifiable objectives, such as landing a man on the moon. Clearly this part of "science" not only can but must be planned. In fact, one of the major achievements of the last ten years has consisted in advances in the state of the art for planned achievement of large, well-defined technical objectives in a rational and stepwise fashion. This art is most fully developed in areas where the limiting factors in the achievement of objectives are primarily technical, such as defense and space. In areas where social and economic factors are limiting, or at least a major component, and where large numbers of lay people have to be convinced of the validity of the specific steps of a plan, the planning art is much less well advanced, and the criteria of success much less clear-cut. We do not yet have the right tools for planning the attack on major "civil" problems such as environmental pollution. In fact, we do not know how to translate the global problem into a series of manageable technical problems, or realizable finite technical objectives, which is really the essence of good planning (Brooks, 1967, p. 200).

wanted to get and knowing how or what was likely to get it there. And the product could be tested in private, thus allowing careful assessment.[6] This kind of corporate planning is much more like scheduling than it is like lrsp. Indeed, moving ahead in the absence of that scheduling-like clarity has been deemed a poor risk, and when attempted at all it has been done in ways which hid that riskiness, or rather that uncertainty, from the environment—including that most relevant environment, the stockholder. Finally, product development and marketing choices were only constrained by the expectations of profit-loss risks and by legal restrictions, though good public relations were deemed an important concomitant of the profit-loss context. And legal restrictions often could be subverted, indefinitely ignored, diffused, or changed by the big corporations.

But even though the problems, perspectives, and organizational arrangements for corporate planning have been different in spirit and simpler than they would be for lrsp, corporations seem to have been burdened with some of the same social psychological problems that I shall conjecture will be involved in changing over to lrsp in public arena.

In sum, much is known about planning, but not enough corporate managers understand how to put it into practice and use sophisticated mathematical and computer tools. As a result, they are not equipped to direct the money spent on planning into the most effective channels. At the same time, executives frequently are unwilling to change existing organization structures and to give planners the tools they need to get the job done. As a result, the planner often works in a vacuum, acting as a sounding board for corporate management's futuristic thinking but isolated from the operating realities of the organization. Bolder and better directed experiments with planning techniques, organization, and administration are thus needed if this important function is to live up to expectations for it. We will, I believe, see many such experiments in the 1970's [Mockler, 1970, pp. 156–158].

D. Ewing (1969) argues that the very high failure rate in corporate planning is due at least as much to indifference to the human factor in doing and implementing planning as to anything else. "Planning has gone wrong because it has been defined too often in terms of economic analysis, production capacity projections, distribution schedules, acquisition formulas, forecasts of demand, and other bloodless criteria—in these terms almost to the exclusion of the 'people' aspects. As a result, there has been a tendency for the art and knowledge of planning to proceed in one

[6] Social technologies cannot be tested "inside" the organization. This enormously complicates evaluation and it changes, sometimes unpredictably, the relationship of organization and environment.

direction while the art of management and leadership has proceeded in another" (p. 42).

The Developing Corporate Situation Today

The evolving corporate situation is becoming much more like that of government agencies. The environment is active: both consumers and non-consumers, beneficiaries and victims of the corporation's products, are insisting that the corporation has responsibilities beyond making products available for purchase. The multifarious intricacies of natural-environment protection already confront them. Social indicator data will be used often by activist and advocate interests in the environment to confront and complicate the pursuit of corporate interests. Corporations will have to face the complex problem of who is to carry the burdens and reap the benefits of what have been "externalities": the secondary consequences of corporate activities will be demonstrable. This in turn means corporations will have to think and choose in terms of additional goals that may come to compete in priority with profit, and they will have to think farther ahead in societal terms.

In addition to dealing with an active external environment, corporations will have to face an increasingly active internal environment if they wish to recruit both workers and executives from the most thoughtful and competent of the younger generations—and, evidently, executives are getting younger (Butkis, 1971). Carrying their more complex self-images, job satisfaction requirements, and multiple roles into their work situation, they will disturb the organization's conventional perspectives about the proper conduct of the corporation. This means that corporations will be less able to plan in secrecy: there are almost certain to be more internal leaks—as in government agencies now—and there will be increasingly legitimated demands by external groups for representation in major corporate decisions that may affect their welfare through secondary long-term and short-term repercussions. The pressures for consumer representatives on corporate boards and the effects of laws and regulations that protect people from burdensome externalities will mean that corporations will be comparatively less able to go their own way. They will have to see their future and evaluate their present state in terms that attend to much wider societal considerations linked to corporate self-interest than just those that affect their market and the profits derived from it.

Finally, as corporations are now discovering, when they find they lack product-servicing personnel because of demographic and job skill changes in the society, and as corporations seeking to market services rather than goods have discovered, a totally different task is involved when the goal becomes the development of people and institutions instead of the development of things. In this case they start by not knowing how to get from here to there. Thus for some corporations, corporate goals and the means for reaching them will increasingly cease to be matters of risk calculation around tacitly agreed-upon goals. Instead they will become more matters for argument, rich in uncertainty, error production, and psychological discomfort. "As P. Drucker points out, 'the most common source of mistakes in management decisions is the emphasis on finding the right answer rather than the right question.' A primary job of management is to find the right problem and to define it. This, however, is not usually an easy thing to do. Very frequently as Gross points out, to ask the question, 'What is the problem?' of members of an organization will, if not summarily brushed aside, lead to acute internal discomfort. The reason is that it usually is a very difficult question to answer. Most organization problems, and all really important ones, turn out to be clusters of many interrelated problems" (Steiner, 1969, p. 337).[7]

By comparison, then, when conventional corporate planning has been done it has referred to and guided activities essentially unconstrained by or unresponsive to the very conditions that make lrsp necessary. In this newly developing situation, the extent to which corporations will have to plan in and for circumstances similar to those facing public agencies will depend on the extent to which the environment requires them to do so, through public pressures or laws and regulations, and on the extent to which corporations choose to become involved in activities that require them to do so. This situation is only beginning to unfold. Hence the capability of corporations to deal with the social psychological factors in order to change toward lrsp, in furtherance of either a changed or traditional corporate purpose, is only beginning to be a real question. "As for corporations themselves, there are still many that haven't succumbed to the notion that they're obliged to do anything but turn a profit. Others profess a social conscience but don't really mean it; they just recognize a public-relations fad when they see it. But behind the ballyhoo of anti-littering campaigns, self-congratulatory advertisements, and hot air from all sides, some major corporations are taking steps that they contend represent sincere efforts to gear social dimensions into their day-to-day operations. So far, the vast majority of these actions are in the realm of dealing with minorities" (Stabler, 1971, p. 1). It remains to be seen if these social dimensions will play a part in long range *social* planning in corporations. Given the difficulties most corporations have faced in doing any planning at all beyond the next fiscal year or the next product change,

---

[7] The reference to Drucker in the Steiner quotation is Drucker (1954, p. 351), and the reference to Gross is Gross (1964, p. 760).

there is every reason to expect them to have to struggle with the same psychological difficulties as those to be described here.

Corporate responses to the pressures to move toward lrsp take the form of buying future studies, particularly participating in Delphi-type forecasting exercises, sending their top executives to training seminars on lrsp and on the future, establishing in-house planning staffs (or more usually, planning persons), setting two to five year operational and developmental targets, and holding retreats and executive training programs aimed at improving interpersonal skills and team capabilities for doing and using lrsp. For each of these organization-initiated activities there is an increasing number of organizations and publications ready to service these desires—and to stimulate them by generating an imagery that everybody else is busily and innovatively doing even more of the same and that lrsp is the pragmatic and farsighted thing to do.

Results that go beyond such initial involvements seem meager for the most part. Certainly they fall far short of lrsp in the sense argued for here. While some corporations buy or do in-house future studies, there is usually no commitment to or effective means for using them. Generally the study ends with itself. If it is used it is because it is compatible with what the organization sees itself as doing now. In a few organizations a preferred vision of the future becomes doctrine.[8] Into it are pumped activities that reinforce it and screen out appreciation of its status as only one among several conjectures. Sometimes this preferred future is also used to screen out and select younger personnel according to their ability to contribute ideas and activities supportive of the accepted future. Some executives and planners in some corporations acknowledge that there are macroproblems at the societal level that their activities could exacerbate or ameliorate. But they see *doing* something about them as the government's responsibility. They still tend to pass on to government the ethical dilemmas around the societal consequences of their activities. At the same time, however, they seem to expect that it will be in the interest of the government to act on these dilemmas compatibly with the traditional interests of the corporations. Clearly, there is a knot of unresolved issues about the allocation of ethical responsibility, issues which were always

---

[8] Not surprisingly, the tendency is to emphasize those aspects of the conjectured future that can be faced within the existing social and structural context of the organization, rather than to pay attention to those aspects that an outsider (with a different bias) would see as part of their relevant future. By facing only a future compatible with their present, they avoid the pains of uncertainty over whether technological and social developments will in fact turn out to be compatible with their intentions. (One apparently widespread version of compatible future expectations: "We're not worried any about environmental protection chewing up our profits. New technologies will solve the pollution problem one way or another.")

complicated if not obfuscated but which are beginning to surface anew under the impact of the developing societal condition (Miller, 1966).[9]

In-house planning staffs are usually encapsulated, their outputs able to influence only the executives to whom they are responsible, executives who are usually much more influenced by the needs, actions, and purposes of their line management who in turn have little, if any, interest in future studies except those that further what they already are doing or want to do. After all, *their* futures are dependent on exploiting the rewarding characteristics of the present. "Reward systems generally favor the man who turns in a good *current* showing, whether measured in terms of profitability, sales volume, reduction of employee turnover, or some other way. Salary, bonus, and promotion rewards tend to be based on this month's, this season's, this year's performance—not contributions to goals three, four, or more years off" (Ewing, 1969, p. 47).[10] Most large organizations reward their middle management for extracting maximum present payoff because in divisionalized firms—85 percent of *Fortune's* 500—accounting data are the only means for judging division performance available to corporate officers who otherwise understand very little about the multiple businesses they are in. But rewarding *present* payoff makes it impossible by any known means to simultaneously reward concern with a future that would interfere with immediate payoff.

What few attempts there seem to be to move toward lrsp have produced multiple problems and possibilities. Issues arise around: what values are to take priority and how to reconcile them; what planning technologies to use; how to reorganize sub-units to meet corporate-level planning purposes; how to develop skills and motivations at the divisional or group level to plan compatibly with corporate planning; how to make the future rather than the past or present, the major input; what to do with people, especially senior people, who are unable or unwilling to move in these directions; how to establish feedback systems that truly evaluate programs undertaken in furtherance of planning objectives; and so on. Since the most advanced efforts at corporate lrsp are at most a year or two old, goal-setting and plan readjustment via feedback evaluation has been incomplete and itself inadequately evaluated. In sum, there are a very, very few corporations beginning to face themselves with the valuing, conceptualizing, operating, and evaluating issues that seem inherent in lrsp. At this very early date these corporations seem to show evidence that they will face the kinds of social psychological problems and opportunities conjectured about in subsequent chapters.

The eventual impact, on changing toward lrsp for the public

[9] On this matter the whole issue of the *Annals* (Charlesworth, 1966) is well worth reading.

[10] Also see Steiner (1969, p. 102).

interest, of these episodic, unarticulated, and new activities is unclear, especially given the changing roles of corporations and attitudes toward them. Corporations may yet experiment more quickly and effectively than government agencies with learning how to change toward lrsp. This possibility arises from the greater control that corporation executives can have over organizational boundaries and resources, as compared to government agencies; the growing corporate interest in and experiments with participative management and organizational development; and the opportunities for demonstrating successful new approaches to lrsp through successful market development in areas traditionally considered to be dependent on government services.

But the present role of private enterprise most certainly is not the protection and fulfillment of the public interest, and its norms and structures are decidedly different from those of government.[11] Whatever successes or failures corporations experience in trying to move toward long-range social planning—it does not follow that governments will experience the same. The important point of this chapter is that, as of now, corporations appear not to have overcome the social psychological resistances we shall be examining.

---

[11] A most revealing analysis of differences in federal and corporate executive experiences and roles, along with many illuminating anecdotes, is found in Bernstein (1958).

Part Two

The Burdens of Changing: Personal and Interpersonal

Changing toward lrsp will require changes in the way people see themselves, relate to others, and find their meaning within the structure of those relationships and associated expectancies that we call organizations. In the chapters to follow we will look at changes required of people and organizational structures, and we will look at them from a social psychological perspective, rather than from an economic, political, legal, or public administration perspective. Of course these several perspectives overlap, because all perspectives unavoidably reflect the social psychological properties of people and the structures within which they operate. Observers, examining the assests and limits of lrsp from these other vantage points, usually assume or ascribe, however casually or uncritically, social psychological properties to the human actors within their perspective. Each chapter that follows, then, deals with a kind of requirement that changing toward lrsp would place upon a person performing within organizational structures. These requirements are such that many people are likely to resist meeting them in a manner that would facilitate moves toward lrsp: consciously or unconsciously, those who resist will be those who feel threatened by the changes.

The sense that a situation is threatening results from what one has experienced with the norms, and the arrangements for expressing those norms, that comprise our culture. The contributions of those experiences may or may not be explicitly recognized: on the basis of past experiences, one may be able to "calculate" objectively the risks to self involved in a change, but that calculation may be only a rationalization for unconscious or intuitive messages of impending threat. Whether or not the change-over requirements would be threatening if those involved had been rewarded or punished for behaving in other ways, in keeping with different norms sustained by differently constituted organizations, is a very important question, and one which colors all the ensuing discussion. To some important but unknown degree, people will resist doing those things required by frsl—performing under high levels of uncertainty, acknowledging errors, trusting their colleagues, leaving socially supportive groups, tolerating high levels of role ambiguity and so on—if their experience has been such that, given their present situation, they would expect to suffer or at least lose rewards if they accepted these changes. So too, administrators will resist changing management procedures and reducing the barriers that protect the organization from its environment if their experiences lead them to expect they would suffer because of what would happen if they complied.

Generally speaking, we can discern three kinds of resistance-to-change behavior: avoiding awareness of the need to change; rejecting the proposed behavior or value change; and arranging things so that no supporting structure of sanctions and facilitators can develop to imbed the changed behavior and norms in the organizational processes. We will note all of these resistances operating in response to pressures for change toward lrsp.

Generally we expect an innovation to be "laid on" an existing organization. The typical experience associated with the introduction of an innovation into an organization is that the essential structure and norms legitimizing them do not change—or are not changed deliberately.[1] Minor readjustments are made, to be sure, but if the operational and managerial change requirements seem too large, most organizations will judge the innovation impracticable and reject it. Thus people tend to expect new technologies to affect their welfare by affecting them through conventional "rules of the game." Naturally, then, under these circumstances many people who would have to change if lrsp were introduced into their organization would perceive the changes as threatening.

But what if lrsp and the change toward it were treated not as the introduction of a technological innovation but, rather, as a learning pro-

[1] Exceptions, where norms and structures have been changed when planned organizational change has been instituted, will be discussed later. But this approach is still comparatively rare, and in government it is almost non-existent.

cedure and learning situation? And what if people expected their organizational and environmental norms and structures to be redesigned to reward that philosophy? Then they might not feel so threatened. Perhaps some threats would disappear all together. Of course some people would fear learning and relearning. Doubtless, many do as a result of their experiences as children and adolescents. At any rate, in what follows, the reader should not lose sight of the likely relationship between resistance to lrsp and what people expect of themselves and others, and of their organization, in the light of their previous experiences. I will try to emphasize this by suggesting from time to time possible ways of rearranging norms and structures so that the requirements need not be as threatening and hence engendering of resistance. These alternatives will derive from my position that lrsp can only be a learning procedure.

Since our appreciation here (appreciation in Vicker's sense, as explained in Chapter Two) is to be social psychological, I will be emphasizing the ways in which a person's meaning for himself and others is defined, supported, and expressed through the structure of an organization and through the norms that legitimize that structure. And I will emphasize how those structures and norms are reinforced by those people who find meaning by performing within them. While these reciprocal relationships are pervasive, and to be recognized as an expression of the human propensity to invent social reality (as discussed in Chapter One) they are by no means all that comprise a human's sense of self or all that holds together the structure of an organization. People have and find meaning outside their organizations, though often through other activities organized according to similar structures and norms. *"The properties of some groups might be defined in terms of a single organization, but an individual can be so defined only in terms of more than one organization.* This is putting it mildly. If any individual could be described in terms of one organization we would have 'organization man,' pure and simple. We do not think that he would be even humanoid. The individuals who carry the work of an organization are related as individuals and as groups to a multitude of other organizations. They cannot be defined as persons without reference to these varied interpenetrating relations" (Churchman and Emery, 1966, p. 82). And organizational arrangements are reinforced by laws and by economic and political circumstances, among other things. Certainly in these times when the relationship between people and organizations is increasingly unsatisfying, it would be foolish to assert a one-to-one correspondence between the expressions of people who are an organization and the expressions of an organization from those people who comprise it.

While I hope this will disabuse the reader of simplistic assumptions on my part, I must add, nevertheless, that people, perhaps especially those involved with government, find that much of the meaning in their lives is supplied by the norms and structures within which they work; and the norms and structures remain what they are or change because people, often unconsciously, wish them so. It is the preferences of people and organizations as they are conventionally expressed that I will emphasize, because these preferences are the social psychological source of resistances to changing over to lrsp. However, I shall also consider ways organizations and people might be changed. Clearly, more people are now finding their sense of self unrewarded enough within their present organizational arrangements to wish to change both organizations and themselves into something more meaningful.

In the following chapters most of the changes necessary to move toward lrsp, as well as the suggestions for change in appreciative settings necessary for perceiving lrsp as learning rather than engineering, will lead the reader to wonder about their implications for the attainment, retention, and use of power.[2] On first reading, much of what will be proposed may seem incompatible with what we believe about the pervasiveness of aspirations to power and incentives to use and keep it. The reader may feel that most social psychological sources of resistance to lrsp can be most easily explained as resistances to giving up power (or, at least, that other sources are secondary to this one), and that a person or organization would be foolish, irrational, or indifferent to survival to give up power or the quest for it.

I do not intend to explore the wellsprings of personal needs for power other than to note that while some people have a *compulsive* need to seek power, many cultures and many people within the United States culture are not driven by that motive or find ways to live so that it does not drive them.[3] While all organizations have to deal with personal needs for power, all organizations also have the instrumental need to accomplish the control Dahl describes. Often, though not necessarily, the two needs are expressed through the same individuals and some of the suggestions I will make are aimed at disentangling the two in favor of the instrumental. "If a person seeks power only for instrumental purposes, we can predict that his search will be bounded; he wishes to control other people

---

[2] While "power" continues to be a rather ambiguous term, I mean by it what most students of the topic also claim to mean by it, which is as R. Dahl (1957) defined it when he wrote: "A has power over B to the extent that he can get B to do something that B would not otherwise do" (pp. 202–203). As R. Bauer has pointed out in conversation, this would include such accomplishments as getting B to reperceive his situation so that B realizes his self-interest lies elsewhere than he previously believed.

[3] Lasswell (1948) is still a fundamental source of insights into power. Also see Lasswell (1968); George, (1968); and Etzioni (1968, pp. 300–386).

only insofar as that control will contribute to the attainment of other goals. If, on the other hand, he finds the experience of controlling others intrinsically rewarding, there may be few limitations on the number of people over whom he will strive for power, the magnitude of power to which he will aspire, or the kinds of activity over which power will be sought. The wider and deeper the search for power becomes, the more people and the more issues in conflict will be encountered. Conflict is maximized when the drive to power is neurotic, rather than pragmatic" (Kahn and Boulding, 1964, pp. 5, 6).

I will from time to time speculate on how some possible needs for power might be reduced or changed if lrsp were practiced. But my general position is that lrsp requirements do not remove the need for or practice of power: they would, however, change its modes of expression and performance. For example, R. Kahn has suggested that the basis for influence might move away from power based on legitimacy, or the ability to reward and punish, toward power based on expertise.[4] This statement makes sense in the light of the very environmental context that makes lrsp necessary. The pressures from the turbulent environment and the responses of that environment to organizational performance will be such, I believe, as to outmode some forms of power expression and introduce others.

For example, "embracing error" (Chapter Six) would remove those means of getting and keeping power that went with lying, hiding errors, or making others "take the rap." Power might go instead to those most skilled in discovering the nature of the errors they are responsible for, or to those who expose the incompetence of others who do a poor job of error detection or who try to hide their errors—perhaps even to the point of misrepresenting the nature of the information their opponent allegedly could have used to discover his own errors if he had been responsible in his role.[5] M. Crozier's (1964) analysis of power in conventional bureaucracies and the role of uncertainty in its distribution seems supportive of this argument when he writes:

Power can neither be suppressed nor ignored. It stems from the impossibility of eliminating uncertainty in the context of a bounded rationality which is ours.

In such a context, the power of A over B depends on A's ability to predict B's behavior and on the uncertainty of B and A's behavior. As long as the requirements of action create situations of uncertainty, the

[4] In conversation regarding the categorization of power types. See French and Raven (1968). Also see Barrett (1971).

[5] There may be some useful understanding to be gleaned about these possibilities by examining the Soviet and Chinese procedures of self-criticism.

*individuals who have to face them have power over those who are
affected by the results of their choice (p. 158).*

*We can thus envisage two complementary sorts of discretion within
an organization. The first one comes from the uncertainty of the task itself, and the second from the rules that have been devised to make it
more rational and more predictable. As long as some uncertainty remains
about carrying out the task, the most menial subordinate retains some
slight discretion. And, in a way, as long as a human being is preferred to
an automatic machine there will be some uncertainty. On the other
hand, the rules that limit the discretion of the subordinate to a minimum
can and will be used by the supervisor for preserving an area of discretion
and the possibility of bargaining (p. 160).*[6]

Two more brief examples of how power might be applied in the
context of changing toward frsl. One: instead of power depending on the
preemption of knowledge as it typically does now, it may devolve on persons and groups that can most effectively disseminate knowledge and get
it effectively used by their constituencies. (Nader's approach seems to
partake of this power.) Two: In some corporations, participative management procedures have increased the effectiveness of management over
what it was when the hierarchy assigned to it all decision-making power.
So, too, various forms of openness, trusting, and acknowledging uncertainty may provide new forms for the acquisition and use of power. My
general point is this:

*The argument for the essentiality of power to an organization is
not an argument for authoritarianism. To say that an organization must
be able to attain a certain level of power over the activities of its members
is not to specify the bases and sources of that power. The basis may be
punishment or identification with the organizational goal; the source may
be a formal leader or the entire peer group. The list of such possibilities
could be greatly extended; the crucial point is that the amount of power
which can be brought to bear within an organization must be differentiated from the basis of that power and the persons who wield it. It is es-*

[6] Crozier is subtle and insightful on bureaucratic processes. But his
bureaucrats seem to be more obsessed by rules and rigidities than those in many
United States federal bureaucracies, at least these days, when turbulence within
and without seems to have loosened up the kinds of organizations we are concerned with. For a somewhat contrasting view of bureaucratic social psychology,
see Blau (1963). Also see Kohn (1971). It is not clear from Kohn's report what
kinds of bureaucratic and non-bureaucratic situations he is comparing. Other
studies suggest that the number of levels in the hierarchy (which is his criterion
of degree of bureaucratization) does not of itself predict the social psychological
setting. For example, see Meyer (1968).

sential that an organization be able to exert power over the behavior of its members; it is not essential that such power be concentrated in a few hands or enforced by threats or penalties" [Kahn and Boulding, 1964, p. 4].

Research tends to corroborate this position as well as to reveal many subtle and complex issues relating control (or power) to organizational performance (Tannenbaum, 1968). Hopefully, then, the above will encourage the reader to imagine how power motives could operate under frsl change-over conditions rather than to imagine people and organizations abdicating power. It is possible, of course, that the approach proposed here would lead, in ways we cannot anticipate, simply to yet another arrangement of societal incapabilities to deal with the problems that I hope frsl would manage better than present methods do. And it is entirely possible—I think likely—that the old ways of seeking, using, and holding power, when combined with and when expressed through other sources of resistance, will make the introduction of lrsp impossible. Likely, that is, but not certain, because the changing relationships between organizations and their environments are making the conventional ways of doing things, including using power, less and less sufficient unto the day, to say nothing of the future.

On the Requirement for Living with Uncertainty

☙☙☙☙☙☙☙☙☙☙☙☙☙☙☙❧❧❧❧❧❧❧❧❧❧❧❧❧❧❧

*T*he very conditions that inform us that we live in a turbulent environment also tell us how little we understand about it. The perspective that leads us to want to cope with it by trying to institute lrsp emphasizes for us how presently inadequate are our techniques for quickly learning about that environment and doing something about it. "We want to eliminate poverty, crime, drug addiction and abuse; we want to improve education and strengthen family life, but we do not know how. Traditional measures are no longer good enough. Very different ones must be sought, invented, tried on a small scale, evaluated and brought closer to perfection. Many schemes will fail and the most profitable failures will be those that lead to the clarification of understanding of the problems. Many schemes will simply expose additional problems that social scientists will need to solve. Both design and evaluation are needed. . . . The overwhelming complexity of the nation's social problems and their immediacy, however, should not blind us to our ignorance of ways to solve them" (Social Science Research Council, 1968).[1]

---

[1] Quoted in Moynihan (1970). Moynihan's conjectures extend and are compatible with my own position on the likely consequences of our limited understanding of the processes of society and of the role of social science and the social scientist.

As our body of data increase so too will controversies about how to interpret them and indeed whether the really relevant data are in hand. All this will be especially true with regard to data used for designing and evaluating human development programs.[2] In a word, a state of mind of deep and continuing uncertainty will characterize those who choose to move toward frsl. Those who cannot live with high levels of uncertainty will try to avoid it, along with the conditions associated with changing toward lrsp that will necessarily emphasize uncertainty.

Everyone and every organization confronts many kinds of uncertainties; for most of the time they are bearable. There is, however, some level of uncertainty which is not, at least if some relatively unaltered state of the personality or organizational structures is to be maintained. When that level or threshold of uncertainty is reached, then passed, feelings of discomfort increase. At some point they reach sufficient intensity that persons and dominant coalitions suffer fears for survival. Long before this point is reached searches begin to reduce the uncertainty of important relationships.

We must add that the reduction of uncertainty (some would say tension) is not necessarily a linear phenomenon. Neither persons nor organizations necessarily attempt to extinguish uncertainty altogether. At low levels of uncertainty or absence of tension important relationships are quite predictable and unchanging. This state of organizational boredom seems to prompt active attempts to increase the degree of stimulation, surprise, and uncertainty. Search for uncertainty is probably associated with the capacity for risk-taking and very stable situations. But stability does not characterize the state of most contemporary organizations. Rather, organizations everywhere are experiencing considerable destabilizing pressure and many surprising conditions. If uncertainty is sought there is no end of situations available to satisfy this search. It is quite the other way around—how do persons and organizations respond to relatively high levels of perceived contingency, inadequate cause-effect beliefs, hence uncertainty in a turbulent environment [La Porte, 1971, pp. 7, 8]?[3]

[2] Complicating all this will be the need to develop theory and data that take into account the growing self-consciousness of both plan designers and plan users about their own involvement in the unfolding of programs and their evaluation. This will be especially true when plan designers and plan users—and in some cases, program evaluators—are overlapping groups.

[3] On the need for stimulus, some in the form of uncertainty, see Cohen, Stotland, and Wolfe (1959); Berlyne (1960); and Schroder and others (1967, Chapter 3, especially pp. 34f). On the non-linearity of tension reduction, see Sperlich (1971). (These references are cited with appreciation to La Porte.)

D. Schon, building on the work of F. Knight, makes an invaluable psychological distinction between the concept of risk and that of uncertainty.[4] Risk pertains when one believes that one knows what variables are involved in characterizing a situation. Hence one can assign probabilities to outcomes that depend on those variables. Uncertainty pertains when one believes one has either too much or too little information to feel confident about *what* variables define the situation. In this situation no probability of outcome can be honestly assigned.

Uncertainty as a Psychological State

Let me emphasize that throughout I shall be referring to the *psychological* state of uncertainty. This should not be confused with the economic or decision theory concepts of uncertainty. Aspects of behavior relevant for adequate logical responses to uncertainty, as defined in decision theory and economics, are quite different from the social psychological responses with which we will be concerned. We will be concerned with how people respond to the feelings, the anxiety, the fear, of knowing that they do not know. These feelings arise from the specter of losing control at least of the situation and perhaps of self, if the situation decays, and from fear of being caught out in a mistake. Anxiety about losing control is probably grounded in the very nature of an organism that depends for survival on learning rather than on instinct.[5] However, it is doubtlessly much intensified in cultures, and especially in ours, that seem to cope with existential anxiety about "who am I" through compulsive efforts to gain and keep control.

The enormous emphasis we place on control is evidenced by our preoccupation with technology and material possession, that is, with control of the natural environment; by our often gratuitous or ritual emphasis on rationality; and by the huge investments of ideas and dollars we make in "public relations" and advertising, which are aimed at controlling the directions of emotionality. The fear of being caught out in a mistake reflects the heavy emphasis our culture puts on the virtues and necessity of control of self and setting. Of course, the results of this preoccupation with control have been highly rewarding in many ways for most members of the society. This makes the possibility of loss of control and being caught out in mistakes all the more fearful and anxiety-provoking: without control and correct performance, the rewards could disappear.

Another way to understand this situation is to realize that anxiety produced by uncertainty results from the breakdown or anticipated breakdown of an established relationship between the individual and his human

---

[4] See Knight (1971); and Schon (1967).

[5] See Kaplan (1970). Through her historical perspective, Arendt (1958, pp. 155–224) illuminates this matter to unusual depth.

and natural environment. In this relationship the individual and the society in which he grows up "collude" to establish order and form, a pattern, that differentiates and integrates the environment so that the individual can attend selectively to aspects of that "blooming, buzzing, confusion." A person's perceptions and sense of self have an order and form that correspond in critical aspects to that in the outside world: the person's internal structure reflects the rewards and punishments experienced while learning to respond to and remake the external, societally given, order and form. To some extent, of course, the relevant external environment that rewards the person has been uniquely invented by that person, that is, ordered and formed by him. But for most people, the internal structure is very largely sustained by the external one: the external environment provides most persons with most of their sense of their own order and form.[6]

Among other things, Western societies differentiate the human and natural environments into those "things" and events toward which one takes a "rational" stance and those one is emotional about, and society also makes discriminations within these categories. (Of course, the societal definitions are not absolute and binding, as is increasingly evident in highly technologized societies among people moving away from conventional differentiations.) Once internalized, persons "know" those situations where one must be rational and not emotional or where one can love but not hate, laugh but not cry. This "categorized self" then reinforces and defines the categorized outside, and so on in a self-sustaining interaction. Self then comes to be defined and sustained in important part by the external differentiations and integrations. (I would expect this to be especially so for persons whose careers depend on an "accurate" assessment of the "realities": persons in planning offices, decision-making roles, or in engineering, for example.)

Now, if there are changes in the outside world there is likely to be a mismatch between the internal and external "reality" structures, and hence a loss of sustaining feedback. To the person, the shift in external structure means that the external world cannot be counted on to sustain the internal structure. To the extent the person depends on that external structure to keep self-organized, to keep the parts of the self separated and integrated, then there is anxiety about one's ability to keep the self in order. That is, there is felt uncertainty. There is a realization that one cannot keep the external environment under control in the same way that will, in turn, provide the input for keeping the self under control. There is fear that separations of emotions and rationality will break down; that one won't know how to act, that one won't know what is rewarding or

[6] The classic statement of this process of internalizing the external social environment, the "generalized other," is Mead (1934). Related versions are in Berger and Luckmann (1966) and in Riesman, Glazer, and Denney (1955).

punishing. Under such threatening conditions the tendency is to over-emphasize preferred order and form by becoming, for example, hyper-intellectual or hyper-emotional, whatever is in the direction of the previous match. In the extreme this becomes autistic behavior, reflexive behavior, essentially uninfluenced by what is going on outside the person.[7] Another kind of response under conditions of uncertainty is to project onto the external environment the sense of dissolution that is occurring in the self. Depending on how the environment is behaving, the feedback from it in response to the projected signals can further disrupt the sense of self—that is, the sense of ordered and formed beingness.[8]

The formal literature dealing with psychological uncertainty is small, though it has always been a subject for novels and occasionally it can be inferred in case-study accounts of decision-making in problematic situations. The formal literature is small because it is difficult in this society to get people to talk about their uncertainties, especially if their roles call for rational behavior and administrative skill—precisely the kinds of roles where uncertainty becomes critically important for efforts to change toward lrsp under conditions of societal turbulence. The literature is also small because chronic and deep uncertainty has not been an important organizational matter. The ways of dealing with uncertainty were usually sufficient for the operating and personal needs of those who faced it. Those who succumbed to it usually were "phased out" as individuals and organizations. Usually we do not research "failures." Finally, there has been little incentive to study psychological uncertainty in the laboratory. It was not seen as a problem in a competitive society where belief in the virtues of survival of the fittest made the behavior unimportant, therefore of low status as a research topic. Moreover, the kind of uncertainty we are going to deal with is deeply disturbing because it

---

[7] A dramatic example was the behavior of some Americans in combat in Korea. Faced with the psychological necessity to hate the enemy in order to kill him at close range, some Americans who, in keeping with conventional American standards, had learned *not* to feel their emotions strongly, especially hate, became terrified that they would be unable to control the "direction" of their hate and would turn it toward their comrades. Their resultant behavior, which in other settings had been called "combat fatigue" or "neurotic breakdown in battle," served their unconscious purpose to get out of combat; that is, to get away from their comrades, whom they feared they would kill. Treatment *near* the line resulted in a high rate of return to their platoons. Experiments demonstrated that to have taken them to the rear would merely have confirmed their fear that they couldn't control their hate. In Chapter Twelve we will note another version of such autistic behavior called "groupthink."

[8] I am indebted to Jody Ladio for the line of conjecture developed in these paragraphs, relating internal and external order and form to feelings of uncertainty.

threatens the very self-image, the ego defenses, of the unfortunate sufferer. It is both unethical to stress experimental subjects in this way and difficult to simulate a situation which would stress them to this degree.[9]

But this is not to say that uncertainty per se is a new problem for organizations or for those who study organizational behavior.

Most of our beliefs about complex organizations follow from one or the other of two distinct strategies. The closed-system strategy seeks certainty by incorporating only those variables positively associated with goal achievement and subjecting them to a monolithic control network. The open-system strategy shifts attention from goal achievement to survival, and incorporates uncertainty by recognizing organizational interdependence with environment. A newer tradition enables us to conceive of the organization as an open system, indeterminate and faced with uncertainty, but subject to criteria of rationality and hence needing certainty.

With this conception the central problem for complex organizations is one of coping with uncertainty. As a point of departure, we suggest that organizations cope with uncertainty by creating certain parts specifically to deal with it, specializing other parts in operating under conditions of certainty or near certainty. In this case, articulation of these specialized parts becomes significant.

We also suggest that technologies and environments are major sources of uncertainty for organizations, and that differences in those dimensions will result in differences in organizations.

Thus, in a broad effort to extend research and theories about organizational behavior, J. Thompson (1967) begins with major emphasis on the organizational task of coping with uncertainty, and with the assertion that uncertainty arises from the organization's internal technology and external environment. Thompson goes on to propose a number of ways that organizations reduce uncertainty. La Porte (1971) summarizes Thompson's proposals: "Internal strategies used in attempts to reduce un-

---

[9] There is related research on the General Incongruity Adaptation Level which merits attention, because incongruities in the environment and in the behavior of persons and groups will increase uncertainty. This concept postulates "that each person develops a general expectation concerning the amount of incongruity of all types (e.g., ambiguity, novelty, conflict, frustration, uncertainty, etc.) which he will normally encounter from day to day." The research problem is determining the conditions that affect the type of response to too little, too much, and optimum incongruity. "The degree and quality of emotion which accompanies and possibly amplifies or attenuates various degrees of incongruity are problems which have yet to be satisfactorily resolved. Experimental data on this topic are scarce and theory tends to be somewhat ambiguous" (Driver and Streufert, 1966). Also see Mumsinger and Kessen (1964).

certainty include the development of buffering units between the environment and the technical core, smoothing or leveling input and output transactions, and attempts to forecast or anticipate, then adapt to environmental change. When internal strategies are not sufficient to quell uncertainties and lower dependencies, organizations may pursue strategies which will decrease their dependence upon significant external elements resorting to contracting, co-opting, or coalescing with them" (p. 20).

However, the important limitation in Thompson's description of organizational means for reducing uncertainty is that it does not deal with the consequences of being *unable* to reduce uncertainty to a psychologically comfortable level and still deal with the issues characterizing our turbulent environment. By operating organizations, including conventional planning activities, so as to reduce the pain and impact of uncertainty by the conventional means Thompson delineates, societal crises and dilemmas have accumulated to the point that they now require lrsp. To change toward lrsp in turn requires people and organizations that will allow people to live constructively with uncertainty of the sort that can no longer be reduced to a comfortable level.

Recently there has been a growing suspicion that the categories of organizational theory do not take into account new and emerging sources of uncertainty. . . . Traditional conceptions of organization have great difficulty in handling qualitative changes in organizational environment.

As interdependent relationships increase in number and rate of change, the capacity of common or uncommon sense conceptions to comprehend them declines. Management and policy processes, apparently useful in the past for control, falter as conditions to which they are applied no longer meet the assumptions of traditional measures. To the degree this is the case for contemporary organizations, the importance of increased environmental dependence and perceived uncertainty is likely to mount [pp. 3–4].[10]

On the basis of their observations of many situations, Schon (1967) and La Porte (1971) argue that acknowledging high levels of uncertainty to self and to others is emotionally so painful, so anxiety-producing, particularly for members of organizations who see themselves as contributing to the rationality of the organization, that, in the absence of means for reducing uncertainty, people will repress their awareness that they know they do not know; or they will avoid situations which confront them with uncertainty; or they will treat them as if they were not uncertain situations.

Government policy making presently has . . . a tendency to delay

[10] Argyris criticizes much of organizational theory for its dependence on static, stable, or tranquil relationships with its environment in Argyris (1972).

for a long time the introduction of a new program because of uncertainties and then suddenly to jump in fully with a large commitment to a prescribed program, with no better knowledge base than before, when political pressures for doing something became strong. Once proposed or initiated, the program is then popularized among the public and in the Congress as a sure antidote, rather than as a promising probe of the environment.

This knowledge myth, which forces dedicated public servants to engage in charlatanism, seriously impedes the development of public policy. The channeling of large sums of money into programs predetermined on the basis of sketchy information narrows the range of alternatives that can be tried, and thus reduces the range of policy instruments that have to be tested. Further, it deters useful experimentation, since all programs are action programs. It places a high premium on actions likely to yield simple-minded quantitative indexes of immediate successes. . . . Conditions of great uncertainty call for imaginative and flexible probings, not vacillation between inaction and commitment [Nelson and others, 1964, pp. 173–174].

Contributing to this behavior is the expectation that members of the environment will demand certainty, and of course as members of the same culture as those in the organization, they often do expect it—or at least they fervently hope for it from organization spokesmen.

Sources of Psychological Uncertainty

Throughout this book, then, we will be contemplating people and organizations facing or avoiding ambiguity, confusion, and ignorance about who they are, what they are doing, and what difference it could make in the future or does make in the present. Those questions will arise in relation to more specific requirements that changing toward lrsp would impose on humans and on the organizational structures within which they operate, but in most cases there will also be a poignant and crucial conjoined source of resistance to meeting the other requirements—an exacerbated sense of uncertainty.

Uncertainty has been differentiated by J. Friend and W. Jessop (1969) into three classes:

Class UE: uncertainties in knowledge of the external planning environment including all uncertainties relating to the structure of the world external to the decision-making system—in the local government context this can be seen as including the entire physical, social, and economic environment of the local authority concerned—and also all uncertainties relating to expected patterns of future change in this environment,

*and to its expected responses to any possible future interventions by the
decision-making system.*

*Class UR: uncertainties as to future intentions in related fields of
choice including all uncertainties relating to the choices which might in
future be taken, within the decision-making system itself, in respect of
other fields of discretion beyond the limited problem which is currently
under consideration.*

*Class UV: uncertainties as to appropriate value judgments includ-
ing all uncertainties relating to the relative degrees of importance the
decision-makers ought to attach to any expected consequences of their
choice which cannot be related to each other through an unambiguous
common scale—either because the consequences are of a fundamentally
different nature, or because they affect different sections of the community, or because they concern different periods of future time [pp. 88–89].*[11]

Friend and Jessop found, in their study of the planning of the
rebuilding of Coventry, that attempts to reduce these uncertainties revolve
around felt needs for more research to reduce UE, more coordination to
reduce UR, and more policy guidance to reduce UV. In our situation,
these three means for reducing uncertainty will be interdependent most of
the time. Which receives emphasis when will depend on many considerations, including who or what organizational subsystem is feeling what
kinds of uncertainties most strongly and who has the power and resources
to do something about it. These problematic aspects will add their own
contribution to the mix and press of uncertainties. Friend and Jessop
report:

*It gradually came to be apparent to us that many of the stresses which
arose from time to time between the different parts of the decision-making
system in Coventry could be attributed to a failure to bring about some
reconciliation between such variations of perspective at a formative stage
of the decision process. Extreme emphasis on the need for research (in
our somewhat limited sense of resolving uncertainties in the external environment) could be seen to lead to an attenuation in time of the whole
decision process, and often to an undue preoccupation with some of the
more measurable variables; extreme emphasis on the need for coordination could often lead to the drawing together of more and more decisions
under the umbrella of a single grand design or master plan, making it
very difficult in the later stages for those concerned to review any alternative courses of action without calling the whole balance of the plan into*

[11] A related earlier and useful differentiation of kinds of uncertainties
distinguishes between uncertainties as to cause-effect relationships and uncertainties as to preferred outcomes. See Thompson (1964).

question; and extreme emphasis on the need for policy guidance could lead to resentment in some quarters—particularly among the less senior officers—because of a feeling that too many issues were being taken out of the hands of experts and resolved at a political rather than an analytical level [p. 96].

All information brought into the organization that carries messages of turbulence will generate uncertainty even though some feedback from the environment will, of course, reduce it in some places sometimes. (I am including feedback from the future, introduced via future studies, as well as from the present.) When values and feelings become strong considerations in decision-making and evaluation procedures, as they most certainly will, they too will generate uncertainty among the participants: we have so little experience with engaging our own feelings and those of others, especially when they conflict, as they often will, that we don't know what to expect of them.

New managerial and administrative arrangements to facilitate the introduction of specific activities intended to meet the requirements for lrsp will themselves generate uncertainty because we know we know so little about the organizational and environmental consequences of implementing those new arrangements. Organizational restructuring, aimed at coping with turbulence and at operationalizing frsl efforts, will generate uncertainty, just as uncertainty is generated by most more modest attempts at restructuring being made today in more conventional organizational settings. What is more novel and of greater importance, uncertainty will be acute for those doing the restructuring as well as for those being restructured, not only because they will be uncertain regarding the outcome but because their own roles and statuses will be altered as well. Uncertainty recognized within an organization will need to be shared with members of the environment so they can participate in the necessary societal learning rather than demanding or expecting certainty from organizations upon which their welfare depends. Their responses to uncertainty in turn will further complicate the characteristics of the environment. Finally, all these sources of uncertainty will emphasize uncertainty about how to deal constructively with uncertainty, how to live with it rather than trying to avoid it or reduce it at too great a cost to the very purpose of lrsp: societal learning.

Means for Avoiding Uncertainty

The circumstances just briefly summarized will be sources of uncertainty *if* they are faced squarely. But there are many ways to resist doing this, and we shall recognize later their contribution to resistances to other requirements that would need to be met in order to change toward lrsp. Describing them in more general terms here can sensitize the reader to their contribution in other settings.

The most direct way to avoid uncertainty is to avoid situations rich in uncertainty. In our case this would mean avoiding turbulence-manifesting information and avoiding role and structural changes that leave both the initiator of the changes and recipient of them uncertain about what to anticipate and how to perform. "The anxieties generated by the experience that one's knowledge is not always adequate for one's tasks can be calmed by making a ritual of conformity with those procedures with which one has become familiar" (Blau, 1963, p. 91). Another point (to be discussed in Chapter Six) is of profound importance; avoiding uncertainty would also require avoiding the recognition or the acknowledgment of error.

La Porte (1971) posits "ideological response" as another way used to cope with unwanted uncertainty. "Rather than withdrawing from the field, one engages with it on the basis of a cause-effect belief system which 'explains' past uncertainties. Often such explanations are accompanied by programs of action to change the objective situation so it will coincide with the images of a 'good' family, group, organizational structure or nation" (p. 8). As noted in Chapter One, any conscious theory of what is "really" going on "out there" is subject to this tendency whether or not it explicitly carries a particular political philosophy with it. Its social psychological utility is that it tells one what to pay attention to and why, thereby removing much from awareness that would otherwise be uncertainty-generating—including evidences that one's perceptual and normative boundaries need resetting. This means of uncertainty reduction by reification will seduce many a would-be social engineer who defines his reality in terms of what his technology can deal with or his theory emphasizes.

Apropos of this phenomenon, it is worth looking at the uncertainty-reducing virtues of an "idea in good currency" (Schon, 1971, pp. 123–128). Such ideas give aid and comfort because they are promulgated by professionals and then amplified until they seem reasonable and then valid in the reverberating circuit among professionals and their organizational clients. Such ideas have included disjointed incrementalism, the end of ideology, future shock, the impact of cybernation, urban renewal, Vietnamization, participant democracy, and the bag of strategic warfare tricks called controlled escalation, deterrence, and massive retaliation. (Of course, I hope that the idea of lrsp as frsl and the idea of error-embracing also become ideas in good currency.) My point is not that these ideas are useless or misguided but rather that they almost always become reified and influential far beyond their demonstrated utility.

Given their prestigious sources, the processes by which they become amplified, and their localized utility, they are grasped onto to reduce uncertainty much more strongly than the existential circumstances merit. Both promulgators and recipients grasp and evangelize the ideas with a fervor that, to those viewing the situation from other vantage points—usually ones where the burden of performing under uncertainty is not as heavy—smacks at least of proto-ideology.[12]

Schon demonstrates that a pervasive means for reducing uncertainty is to translate a situation of uncertainty into one of risk; that is, to act as if one knew what was *really* involved well enough to assign probabilities to outcomes. This gratuitous assignment of probabilities to situations that do not justify them is, in the United States, an endemic means for self-delusion and deluding others. Often the need to reduce uncertainty is so great that the person justifies the assignment of probabilities by that most tenuous and attractive of rationalizations—"It's the best we can do," or "It's better than nothing." The information recipient, in or outside the organization, in equal or greater need of uncertainty reduction, unconsciously, cynically, or naïvely, colludes, first in accepting the rationalization and then in forgetting that it underlies whatever arguments are put forth in support of the probabilities.[13] One of the most serious consequences of this behavior is that the resulting emotional relief encourages all involved to believe they really do know what is important, what is going on. Consequently, not only do they ignore input that challenges that belief but they entrap themselves in psycho-socio-political needs to repudiate the fact of error when their risk-based (in contrast to uncertainty-based) models and programs fail in action. Two very impor-

---

[12] Schick (1969) is especially illuminating on the ideological basis of disjointed incrementalism. Lowi (1969), in a scholarly polemic, has exposed the ideological basis of the political theory of pluralism that undergirds interest-group liberalism. This pervasive style of government depends on and reinforces disjointed incrementalism. See also the Dror (1964) symposium on "Muddling Through" cited in the Introduction to this book.

[13] In this regard it is enlightening and terrifying to recall the spasm of ritualized rationality that shook national strategic planning directed to deterring nuclear attack or, failing that, to recovering from it. Endless books, reports, and study groups acted as if enough were understood about the motivations of people under stress and the dynamics of democratic society to assign probabilities to the chances that the United States would recover given various levels of nuclear attack and material resources stockpiling. Other social psychological processes that we will examine contributed to that state of mind, but the need to avoid acknowledging deep uncertainty about the future of democratic America was certainly a heavy contributor. (Based on personal observations as a staff social scientist with the Weapons Systems Evaluation Group, Joint Chiefs of Staff; as a member of the staff of the Gaither Committee; and as a sometime "expert" on civilian behavior under warfare conditions. See Michael, 1955 and 1962).

tant opportunities to learn from a perspective of uncertainty are thereby reduced or obliterated.

Still another means for attempting to reduce uncertainty is by various managerial and administrative devices aimed at "tightening-up" the organization. The ends sought in this way include increasing internal incisive action, controlling what goes in and out of the organization that could rebound as more turbulence, and reemphasizing the role and ability of management to reduce uncertainty by resort to the traditional tightening-up ritual.

When individuals are frustrated in their attempts to get their own work successfully completed, when they are worried by the successful rivalry of others, when they feel insecure or under attack—these situations provoke an urge for the clarity, the no-nonsense atmosphere, of a mechanistic organization. It promises so many other dividends too. It is not only quicker to divide tasks into parcels, label them "responsibilities," and post them to subordinates or other parts of the structure; this kind of procedure has the connotations of visibly controlling others, and the appearance of knowing one's own mind, which are valued aspects of executive authority. Conversely, one has the security of unquestioned power through orders to subordinates, the security of knowing the limits of one's responsibility and of the demands and orders of superiors. . . .

. . . Necessarily, when the environment or technical base of a concern is changing rapidly, the situation is alive with opportunities for advancement and transfer, alive also with actual or potential threats to the status, power, chances of success, or actual livelihood of some of the members of it. . . .

Under such threats there is bound to be latent or overt conflict between individuals or groups; and, as anthropologists have pointed out, hostility against persons in authority and aggressive action against rivals is often sanctioned by an appeal to traditional or other familiar values and modes of behavior [Burns and Stalker, 1961, p. 132].

One observed all too often controls being imposed not to protect the task system from interference but to protect management against anxiety. Parameters are controlled not because they are relevant but because they are measurable. Their function is to create an illusion of certainty as a means of coping with intolerable uncertainty [Miller and Rice, 1967, p. 263].

Schon (1967) refers to some of these procedures as "propose-dispose" management schemes for channeling sources of uncertainty to them, there either to be squelched or transformed into risk. Like the previous method, this one is comforting for all involved. It gives the feeling that those who know what to do are doing it. For a while it seems to work—until the manifestations of turbulence inside and out surface again.[14]

These essentially counter-productive means for reducing uncertainty will be amply evident as they are used to deal with efforts to introduce those changes toward lrsp that will increase uncertainty. It should be noted, however, that some people do and will see components of lrsp as uncertainty *reducers* and will encourage their application for that reason. Management information systems and social indicators, among other lrsp technologies, will from time to time really reduce uncertainty. At other times they will only appear to reduce uncertainty. Nevertheless they will comfort those unable to live exposed to turbulence and its concomitant high levels of uncertainty.

There is then a dialectic to be expected and it will be noted throughout this book. While lrsp efforts, far more often than not, will increase psychological uncertainty, there will be times when knowledge and circumstances will converge propitiously with lrsp efforts to reduce objective uncertainty, times when things go as planned, when understanding increases faster than awareness of how little is understood, and when the exhilaration of frsl-inspired collaboration gives new feelings of social potency. This variable reinforcement, familiar to golfers, slot-machine players, and even social engineers, will be a continuing stimulus to efforts to initiate lrsp and an encouragement to others to join the effort.

Three types of responses to uncertainty are much more promising than those just reviewed, though at least two of them are subject to decline into the counter-productive forms described. The third type we know too little about, as yet, to know its strengths and weaknesses well.

The first type, which is really a class of organizational responses, is that which organizations typically use to deal rationally with uncertainty.[15] Undoubtedly these will be used and modified to try to make lrsp feasible. But in their conventional forms they apply to a simpler world, in par-

---

[14] Corresponding to organizational tightening up under conditions of uncertainty may be personal tightening up in disasters. Studies of disaster behavior show that unless one's competence is such as to be functional in disaster (as expected of a doctor or clergyman), people and organizations tend to rigidify and perform in ways that are unresponsive to the environmental situation. Even some people with disaster-relevant competences cease to adapt to the situation and instead rigidly perform in ways that are counter-productive or irrelevant. A disaster can be understood as a situation in which there is no supporting environment, the environment which gave the feedback that guided, energized, or informed the matched internalized sense of self and the world. It is a situation of acute uncertainty.

[15] These are mentioned early in this chapter in La Porte's summary of Thompson's (1967) analysis.

ticular to one where uncertainty about value judgments played a far smaller part than it would when changing over to lrsp. In their present form these means apply where first priority goes to organizational survival— to protection of the "technological core" of the organization (in Thompson's term), rather than to environmental reconstruction for social growth, for self-actualization. In their conventional forms these responses set organizational well-being ahead of environmental well-being by constraining both organizations and environment in ways inadequate for societal learning through lrsp. These uncertainty-coping means are probably too self-protective— "probably," because it is unclear where the balance should be between organizational survival and environmental development. In the past, belief in the beneficent operation of the hidden hand prevailed and was translated into doctrines to the effect that what is good for a large organization is good for its environment. Contemporary experience asserts this just isn't necessarily so, and it is now quite acceptable to propose everything from radical organizational self-renewal to self-destruct institutions.[16] Clearly, protection of "the technological core" will not do for lrsp if that protection is at the expense of the uncertainty-acknowledging required for the growth of lrsp. Yet there must be "technological cores" if the environment is to have the much-needed organizational resources lrsp could help us learn how to get and to use. Where and how the balance will be struck would be one of those things to be discovered through the learning context lrsp is intended to provide.

The second response is a special and increasingly used version of the "Thompson-class" of responses: greater use of professionals to discover, define, and to solve problems that otherwise would contribute to uncertainty. The professional has special abilities for defining and solving problems relevant to and appropriate for his trained skill and his occupational allegiance.[17] Here we will look at the ways in which professionals play an important part in uncertainty reduction.

The skills of professionals bring understanding and control where little existed before through their perceptions of aspects of the environment which are different from those derived from historical perspectives and conventional organizational expertise. To this extent they provide a valid basis for uncertainty reduction. Indeed, it is in large part this

[16] For example, see Gardner (1968).

[17] "Professional" is used here in its vernacular meaning: as a specialist with credentials. I do not mean professional in its original meaning: a person who, by virtue of skills, autonomy, and ethics, is responsible to the client in certain carefully specified ways. On the absence of necessary professional-client standards, see Chapter Six, "The Need for New Managerial Values," in Gross (1970).

capability that gives hope that the technology of lrsp can be used for societal learning purposes. Such skills are fundamental for discovering what aspects of the turbulent environment can be understood, transformed, and guided by scientific knowlege. The challenge, of course, is to prevent these important uncertainty-reducing capabilities from becoming either ritual or defensive—two counter-productive, uncertainty-reducing characteristics of professionals described next.

The professionals' skill training, along with the definition of reality encouraged by the appreciative setting (in Vickers' sense) of their collegial community (into which they have been socialized through their skill-training experience), typically results in a trained incapacity to recognize the enormity of the problems characterizing a turbulent environment. Their selective perceiving of the world leads them to see order and discriminability where others, not so professionally embedded, see complexity and problems linked into other problems, ad infinitum. This trained incapacity varies, of course, from person to person and profession to profession. Also, developments in some schools that train public and private administrators and planners are enlarging the perspectives and tolerance for ambiguity among professionals-to-be. But as of now and for some years to come, the consensus of observers seems to be that many professionals—whether they be urban planners, systems analysts, or social workers—will strongly tend to hold professionally reinforced definitions of reality that help them filter out much uncertainty. In particular, it seems that older professionals, self-recruited for and trained in the "management sciences" and the more analytic sectors of the behavioral sciences, are inclined to be more rigid about, what constitutes reality, or more intolerant of or uninterested in ambiguous and uncertain definitions of it. For these professionals, the "other problems" are other professionals' problems. Most professionals seem to work well within a philosophy of disjointed incrementalism.

The emphasis on personal legitimacy associated with some professions also encourages strong identification with the special view of the world that characterizes the learned values, competences, and activities of the profession. Whatever challenges that world view necessarily challenges the criteria that bolster certainty about who one is. By perceiving the world in their professional way they reduce their own uncertainty to acceptable levels. This increases their willingness to involve themselves in situations which others try to avoid. But it also increases the chances of generating pseudo-problems and pseudo-solutions which, while they respond to the reality as perceived by the professional, do not respond to that as perceived by the environment.[18] What is more, the professional's

---

[18] Moynihan (1970) is illuminating on this.

special aura of legitimacy itself seems to reduce the uncertainty felt by his clients—which leads to another way the professional reduces uncertainty.

The attitudes and beliefs held by professionals about causes and effects and what can be done about them help reduce uncertainty for many of those who use their services. Their clients believe that professionals "know something" and that if one knows something one has the power to control something, to bring about order where there was none before. Then, too, the self-assurance that some professionals project, implying that they are bearers of a legitimized world view, gives some clients a feeling that things aren't so uncertain after all, that they really have the situation under control, or soon will. La Porte summarizes the contributions professionals make to uncertainty reduction in themselves and in others:

The rigors of professional education result in a relatively well articulated system, which is often internally consistent and generally captive of a technical language available only to other professionals. Such a situation makes weaknesses of a theory invisible to outsiders and largely unassailable by managers who are not professionally trained.

Second, a professional in good standing (i.e., one who is thought well of by professionals of similar stripe) is supported in his professing of cause-effect beliefs and implied action by others holding similar views. His authority is validated by those who could effectively refute it. The community-at-large, having no alternative explanation for the same phenomenon, is also likely to sanction professional authority. Furthermore, professionals generally give explicit attention to maintaining the quality and exclusiveness of their skills in interpreting a particular cause-effect belief system. Insofar as they are successful, this enhances their monopoly of skill held by their profession.

Finally, uncertainty reduction capacities of professionals are directly related to how intensely potential clients perceive their own need for specific expertise. If they have learned, or are taught by professionals, the utility of "professional assistance," then the salience of cause-effect beliefs and the professional group's monopoly in interpreting them is very conducive to uncertainty reduction [pp. 27–28].

A third constructive means for coping with uncertainty may be to openly acknowledge and share that state of mind. This is the most radical and most necessary approach if lrsp is to be a learning process. All of the means for coping with uncertainty, with the exception of the professional approach properly applied, encourage and sustain unconscious, or deliberate hiding, usually from oneself almost always from others, of one's sense of uncertainty. Indeed, the rules of the game and the rewards that go with playing it usually require that participants act toward each other as if they were certain or at least knew the risks. The conventional definition of what constitutes effective human conduct, that says competent people know what they are doing, makes those dependent on the competence of others prefer, and often insist, that those they depend on do not face them with expressions of uncertainty. As one federal executive put it: "Part of my job is to *look like* I know what I'm doing. Otherwise morale would go to hell here. *Somebody's* got to look like they know where the end of the tunnel is in this mad-house!" But such hiding would be fundamentally self-defeating of any serious attempt to change toward lrsp. Because lrsp will be valuable in an open society only if it is used as a means of learning how to guide that society, and because one of the things we will need to learn is how to introduce and use lrsp as a learning device, it is critical that those involved do not act as if they *already* had learned, as if they really knew what to do and how to do it. They cannot be models for others if they do not model the appropriate behaviors in themselves and in the organizational expressions of themselves.[19]

Advantages of Acknowledging Uncertainty

To learn requires recognizing what one wants to learn, and that means recognizing what one doesn't know. Otherwise one cannot choose ways to learn or evaluate whether one has learned. Since lrsp requires both organizational resources and close, responsive linkages with the relevant environments, that recognition of ignorance must be shared among and contributed to by many persons; it cannot be secretive.

Sharing uncertainty can help ease the pain of carrying it alone, uncertain about who else feels uncertain and even if uncertainty is appropriate to the situation. The emotional support that sharing could provide also would discourage repressing the uncertainty by raising the level at which the anxiety becomes too great to bear constructively.

To be able to acknowledge uncertainty openly would make three

---

[19] P. Ratoosh has pointed out to me that some people might be moved at least to tolerate an uncertainty-acknowledging style in leaders they want to depend on if those leaders assert with certainty that the only way for them to be effective is to acknowledge their uncertainty. The seeming paradoxical nature of this position is resolvable according to the generally accepted position in symbolic logic that a statement about a statement is not bound by the constraints asserted in the latter statement. Nevertheless, those not trained in the niceties of symbolic logic may not see it that way. More important is the question of whether a leader's own statements can change a popularly held definition of what constitutes leadership. Perhaps if enough leaders took the same position, then their role redefinition would be accepted. But we know very little about the process by which redefined role characteristics come to be accepted.

critical contributions to the conduct of frsl. First, it would reduce the chances of undertaking planning in the mistaken belief that one knows what one needs to know, whether this belief is held by the planning body or its environment. Hence it would increase the chances for the tentative, exploratory mood necessary for societal learning. Rather than judge the effort as successful or unsuccessful in terms of predefinitions and precommitments, whether phrased in the rhetoric of certainty, of calculated risk, or of prudent investment, all would know that they were participating in social experiments. All would share in the costs and benefits of the experiment because it would be recognized that it is not really clear what should be done or how to do it, and that the only thing to do is to experiment to find out.

It is rather well recognized that under present conditions poor people are increasingly opposed to being "experimented on." Aside from the fact that the situation we face requires experiments at all social and economic levels of the society, indeed of the world, the situation we are envisioning is fundamentally different from the present one in two ways: the environment would consist of people who would be involved in the design and evaluation of the experiment in which they take part; and by acknowledging uncertainty and embracing errors those in organizations associated with the experiment would themselves demonstrate that they were part of the experiment as well as being numbered among the experimenters. Whatever else offends those now "experimented on," they are certainly offended because the risks of failure or unanticipated consequences are not shared by the experimenters.

Second, acknowledging the limitations in the available facts and theory would encourage a setting of trust and an attitude of permissiveness toward restructuring the problem at hand. This in turn would encourage creative approaches drawn from intuition, feeling, and hunch, sources usually ignored in order to "stay with the facts." By ignoring these sources we are too often saddled with pedestrian and inadequate approaches.

Third, acknowledging uncertainty would reduce the chances of people remaining committed to a single definition of reality. Typically, during the reign of an idea in good currency, failures in programs are taken to be a consequence of the program choice or its implementation rather than a result of an inadequate model of reality (Caplan, 1971).

What Is Required to Acknowledge Uncertainty

Open sharing of uncertainty is, I believe, a necessary condition to be met if efforts to change toward lrsp are to be effective. It is in no sense a sufficient condition. Moreover, there are presently no tested arrangements in organizations for doing or using such sharing, with the partial and very constrained exception of some research and development organizations. Indeed, under present operating conditions open acknowledgement of uncertainty within an organization is considered foolhardy at the very least, and sharing uncertainty between organization and environment would be decisively punished. Neither the custodians of the image of organizational competence as now defined nor many of those in the environment who equate competence with certainty would stand for it.

Such an approach would require not only learning to trust but also learning to transfer some of the potential "blame" for "failure" from others to self. This transfer will be refused so long as the situation is defined as one in which failure results in someone (group) getting blamed —that is, someone running the risk of being punished and losing self-respect. This suggests that the norms and circumstances under which we reward and punish uncertainty must be altered, not only in that reflection and justification of home and school, the organization, but in homes and schools as well.

Acknowledging uncertainty and acting on it also requires skills in interpersonal behavior that most of us lack as members of task groups. To acknowledge that "I don't know" is to acknowledge that one's information or control are inadequate, or that one has been unable to make available to others the bases for control which one had been employed to provide. Under normal operating conditions this alone would be threatening enough. But there are additional threats to conventional definitions of what it is to be competent as a decision-maker or planner: if the formal data are acknowledged as insufficient for decision-making, then hunch, intuition, and feelings would become irrepressible contributors to the planning process and these are just what the "rational" approach in conventional organizations tries to eliminate.[20] Having succeeded well in repressing if not eliminating them, we have not learned how to use them and thereby we mostly fear them—again in part because they seem uncontrollable, especially in ourselves.[21]

Acknowledging that "I don't know" is dangerous enough, but acknowledging that *"we* don't know" would, in our present scheme of

[20] Dror (1968) deplores the rejection of the "extra-rational" and insists it must be a part of the policymaking process; see pp. 149–153 and pp. 157–159.

[21] To the extent that members of the environment are not constrained by role requirements that stress "rational considerations," environmental feedback will be rich in such extra-rational information. This, plus a cultural shift toward more expressive behavior, may facilitate the incorporation of "extra-rational" inputs into planning. This in turn may make it easier to cope with feelings and ideas that arise under uncertainty. Brainstorming, sensitivity training, and such proprietary schemes as Synectics, Inc. (Gordon, 1961) encourage expressing the extra-rational. However, such expressiveness may be best sustained in organizations that are not burdened with a heavy sense of uncertainty.

things, apparently leave little to keep one's world together, little for one to count on. What is more, expressing the intuitions and feelings that would well up in a "we don't know" situation runs counter to all canons of rational behavior set by and for professionals operating in formal organizations, particularly in government agencies. To support others in doing so would take much unlearning of interpersonal styles that have previously been highly rewarding—or have seemed to be. Learning to support such behavior in others depends on learning to support feelings and hunches in oneself. To do this requires a willingness to risk sharing these with others. This kind of learning does occur under appropriate conditions, but it is painful, takes time, and atrophies unless the learner's working context is supportive and rewarding of these new skills. But so upsetting is this unlearning and new learning, and so fraught with fantasied and occasionally real psychological danger, that people will tolerate conventional behavior to the point of not noticing gross organizational malfunctions, or of rationalizing them as "natural" human negotiating behavior. If uncertainty were routinely acknowledged, the content, processes, and procedures would be quite different for the conduct of programming, evaluation, goal-setting, changing organizational design, and handling relationships with the environment. Obviously, there will be heavy burdens involved in learning what the new substantive, interpersonal, and structural conditions should be. Reluctance to assume these burdens will add to resistances to changing over to lrsp.

Haven't People Always Acted Under Uncertainty?

We shall continue to note the interplay of these reluctances, along with the rewards of repressing uncertainty, in connection with other change-over requirements. But some response is needed at this point to the counterargument that "people have always acted under conditions of uncertainty." My response is tentative. We need to know systematically much more than we do about how people act under conditions of uncertainty, and more about the arrangements they contrive to protect themselves from knowing that the situation is uncertain. But I hope that what follows will help to differentiate the familiar situations for which this argument probably holds from the conditions associated with trying to change toward lrsp.

The argument goes that people in responsible administrative and executive roles have always acted under conditions of uncertainty: whether or not they showed it, or acknowledged it, they knew it. The role of leadership, so the argument goes, requires that this burden and its dissimulation be accepted as part of the role. My position is that it makes a profound difference whether one *shares* one's uncertainty or whether one acts in ways that mislead people into believing that one really knows the risks involved. It affects what is expected, how arguments are conducted, what is concentrated on, and what feedback can be tolerated. It makes a difference in the trust that can be called upon, and it makes a difference in the image which the denier of uncertainty has of himself and of the competences and response options he bestows on those he deceives. G. Vickers has speculated that one can stand a great deal more uncertainty when one can trust oneself and one's friends.[22] Indeed, under such high-morale circumstances uncertainty may be sought as a challenge, as La Porte noted earlier. In the present and in the years ahead, those we are concerned with will be less certain of themselves and of their work associates or friends (Chapter Twelve), and this will make uncertainty about the environment less tolerable.

Additionally, trying to include in present actions the implications of future environments seems to be a psychologically new situation, thereby changing the content of the uncertainty for the man who knows that is his state of mind. In describing the implications of management information systems (MIS), which is a part of the technology required for lrsp, Argyris (1970) observes: "MIS requires managers with higher levels of intellectual and conceptual competence. They must be able to deal with the interrelationships among the facts. Typically, this is not a skill possessed by many executives. In the past, when data were incomplete a manager used intuition to fill in the many blanks with possibly valid data. Managers immersed themselves 'in the facts' of their past experience. A sophisticated MIS is able to develop a much richer set of facts with past and present quickly summarized" (p. 34).

In the past, a person's experience often told enough about the relevant variables so that even if, in some objective sense, the decision-maker didn't know what was going on, his experiences afforded a good basis for feeling that he really could deal with the situation. In the turbulent environment, past experiences, even those that were successful, will be less and less adequate for anticipating consequences: "there will be a greater mismatch between the degree of the world's predictability and controllability and the degree which [he] has come to expect.[23] In the past, information about the actual state of the society was so lacking that leaders felt no real challenge to their definition of what "really" was going on. The very fact that a leader had been successful enough to get to a place of leadership "proved" that he knew what was going on. With moves toward lrsp and the concomitant use of data banks, social indicators, and simulation, competent administrators, planners, and executives will have to consider "counter-intuitive" alternative interpretations of

---

[22] In personal correspondence.
[23] G. Vickers, in correspondence.

complexity (to use J. W. Forrester's term) and will have to know that they have insufficient knowledge at a given time to choose between them. This will emphasize to them uncertainty in the situation at least as often as the technology provides them with a better basis for assigning risk. It will be much harder to avoid recognizing, or being told, that one "doesn't know."

In addition to these "in-house" indicators of uncertainty there will be those from outside that will undermine the conventional means people have used to deal with uncertainty. The persisting challenge to legitimacy, the growth of competent advocate groups and volunteer organizations representing different definitions and appreciations of reality, and the persistence of distrust of government and corporations will mean that the practitioner of conventional means for coping with uncertainty will not have the rewards available that tell him his means of coping are working. In the future he will not be nearly as well protected from turbulence or from evaluations of his responses to it.

On the Requirement
for Embracing Error

᚛᚛᚛᚛᚛᚛᚛᚛᚛᚛᚛᚛᚛᚛᚜᚜᚜᚜᚜᚜᚜᚜᚜᚜᚜᚜᚜᚜

"We are in increasing danger of acting as if we knew what we were doing, when we don't: and then not being able to bear the consequences of having erred" (Biller, 1969).

Avoiding and Repudiating Error

Frsl requires acknowledging openly the sources of uncertainty and risk inherent in fulfilling one prerequisite for societal survival: preparing for the future through present actions that take their directions from systematic conjectures about the future. Changing toward lrsp requires that, instead of avoiding exposure to and acknowledgement of error, it is necessary to expect it, to seek out its manifestations, and to use information derived from the failure as the basis for learning through further societal experiment. More bluntly, frsl makes it necessary for individuals and organizations to embrace error. It is the only way to insure a shared self-consciousness about limited theory as to the nature of social dynamics, about limited data for testing theory, and hence about our limited ability to control our situation well enough to expect to be successful more often than not. Under such conditions it is the only way to insure that members of the environment will be responsibly involved in specifying objectives and goals to be sought, in participating in the experiments to be undertaken in their pursuit, and in determining the characteristics of the evaluative feedback necessary for learning from the errors detected.[1]

In our society errors made by members of an organization are presumed to be the consequence of miscalculation, incompetence, bad luck, stupidity, or impotence in the face of social challenge. One way or another, error seems to carry with it an aura of failure, of "unelectedness" in the Calvinist sense, and hence a taint of sinfulness. Failure is punished and success rewarded. We begin to learn this early in school when we suffer the consequences of erring on tests or misjudging the teacher's ability to cope supportively with our error-acknowledging confusion or error-prone whimsy, imagination, and exuberance. "He learns that to be wrong, uncertain, confused, is a crime. Right Answers are what the school wants, and he learns, as I described in *How Children Fail*, countless strategies for prying these answers out of the teacher, for conning her into thinking he knows what he doesn't know. He learns to dodge, bluff, fake, cheat. . . . What the children really learn is . . . [how] to keep out of trouble, and get other people in. . . . [and] mean-spirited competition against other children. . . . [and] that every man is a natural enemy of every other man" (Holt, 1970, p 19).[2] This error-avoiding and error-denying behavior is reinforced by parental approval of good grades, which mostly depend on learning the Right Answers. When the norms of school and home which emphasize that error-making and error-acknowledging are reprehensible are incorporated into the superego (or conscience), it is very difficult to expunge them in adulthood.

So important is it to be right that, when a person or organization is allegedly in error, it is considered within the bounds of the ethic which sets the highest priority on organizational survival to assert that no error

---

[1] In our traditional attitude toward error, the incentives all rewarded organization members for denying the environment access to program planning or evaluation. Thus when errors did occur, the organization was able to avoid being punished by an environment which did not know about them or could not evaluate them, because it did not know what really was expected to be accomplished, or how well or poorly it had been done (except, of course, on an immediate experiential level). Coopting members of the environment can be seen as a device for playing on *their* reluctance to embrace error. Those who join the organization's activities reap the rewards of affiliation and generally can be counted on to respond to organizational errors the same way other members "naturally" do—by suppressing or repudiating them.

[2] On adult learning and relearning, its problems and potentials, see McClusky (1971). At the Ontario Institute for Studies in Education, teachers learning permissive "open classroom" techniques are asked to note what they have learned from their "most successful failure." My informants tell me that it is very difficult for the teacher-students to see themselves as learning in this way.

occurred, or that if it did it was unimportant, or that if it was important it was someone else's fault. Succeeding by any one of these gambits brings rewards, at least to the extent that punishment is avoided. To the extent that the capabilities of an organization are judged by the competence of its leadership, things are arranged if possible so that a leader's error is not verified by actually punishing him for it—or at least not publicly, or at the time, or heavily. To do so would threaten the organization and undermine confidence in the much depended-on role of leadership per se.

The assumption of responsibility becomes vital in a world that is impossible to understand or control, but the manner in which leaders are held 'responsible' is highly revealing. It is expected of the top executive of every large organization that he will periodically proclaim his willingness, even eagerness, to take personal responsibility for the acts, and especially the mistakes, of his subordinates. Each time this stylized manifesto appears everyone involved experiences a warm glow of satisfaction and relief that responsibility has been assumed and can be pin-pointed. It once again conveys the message that the incumbent is the leader, that he knows he is able to cope, and that he should be followed.

In practice, however, it turns out that the message is the only one such ritualistic assumption of 'responsibility' conveys. It emphatically does not mean that the chief executive will be penalized for the mistakes of subordinates or that the latter will not be penalized. On the contrary, it is ordinarily only the subordinates who suffer for mistakes. It is they who are fired, denied promotion or demoted, or haled before a congressional committee to explain and be publicly castigated. So clear is the general understanding that the hierarchical chief benefits rather than suffers from the assumption of 'responsibility' that his political opponents are outraged when, in a specific incident, he refuses to allow a subordinate to be identified and says he will shoulder responsibility himself. All concerned then understand that no one will in fact suffer at all and that the chief executive has scored heavily [Edelman, 1964, p. 79].[3]

Adversaries, whether they be political parties, investigatory commissions, crusading news reporters, or Nader's Raiders, try to place blame

[3] There is a traditional saying that confession is good for the soul, and there are occasions where, in all honesty, error is publicly acknowledged. But the acknowledgement is usually made in a stylized context which emphasizes that the acknowledgment is an exception to the rule. Importantly, the "confessor" cannot be sure how his error-embracing will be received. There is no clear norm or organizational structure that indicates when he will be rewarded for this exceptional behavior the way there is for conventional error-avoiding or error-denying behavior that succeeds. Thus, idiosyncratic error-embracing does not of itself encourage others to do the same under present conditions.

and to extract punishment for errors, but it is noteworthy how seldom the leadership really suffers when exposed and how blurred the issue becomes. In part this is because often, in complex interdependent organizations, the old concept of personal blame for error simply does not make sense. In part it is because of the ambivalence the above quotation suggests: we don't want to believe that our leaders are error-prone; we don't want to undermine our institutions by seeing them as error-prone. At least many of us don't.

In situations where societal learning could be undeliberate, even unconscious, and often seemingly unnecessary, given how well things were perceived to be going, and given how little information or few effective advocates were available to make a legitimate case to the contrary, error-repudiating responses could certainly be "natural" considering there were also rewards for making them. But when societal learning must be self-conscious and as rapid as possible, and when there will be increasing amounts of data purportedly clarifying the nature and source of error, it would seem that the "natural" response would have to be one of error-embracing. To better appreciate the problem of overcoming typical error-avoiding responses, we will here return to a further examination of the heavy emphasis our society places on control.

In yesterday's world, characterized by scarcity and less interdependence, those personalities who could increase the likelihood of predictableness could increase the likelihood of controlling access to survival resources and vice versa. Those skills that lead to control could be found most frequently and vigorously practiced by those described as "compulsive" characters; persons who display a strong need to have things under control.[4] An often compulsive need to control, and possession of the skills for maintaining and extending control, seem to characterize members of such pertinent occupations as inventor, engineer, manager, executive, elementary school teacher, and bureaucrat.[5] Organizations have evolved into structures that support and reward those who have the skill and the will to control, to make the internal and external environment predictable, to arrange things so that the outcome is as intended—that is, successful. As a result, even when the situation is one where less compulsive performance is preferable in order to deal constructively with less predictable, less con-

---

[4] There are fundamental differences between a compulsive character, which is what we are discussing, and an obsessive-compulsive neurotic personality. Generally speaking, the obsessive-compulsive neurotic personality would be too preoccupied with struggles inside himself to be effective and adaptive in controlling his environment, although personality needs and environmental control requirements occasionally do match.

[5] I am indebted to P. Ratoosh for pointing out the extent to which this society produces compulsive characters and rewards this style of performance.

trollable situations, there is still a strong tendency to maintain the structures and norms that encourage recruitment of and accommodation to compulsively controlled styles of performance. Persons attach themselves to potential outcomes that are so hedged or so incremental that one is unlikely to be caught out in an error: that is, one plans so as to expect to end up in control of one's own situation, at the very least. R. Millward (1968) points out that planning, programing, and budgeting systems, which ought to encourage more pragmatic approaches to planning, are more likely to encourage safe rather than high-risk alternatives because PPBS makes it easier to trace back wrong choices.[6] W. Pounds (1965), reporting on planning behavior in a large and presumably typical corporation, observes: "Planning models represented the minimum performance the manager could reasonably expect if several of his plans failed or were based on the minimum organizational expectations of managerial performance, whichever was higher. Planning models were in general very conservatively biased historical models" (p. 17). David Birch (1966) quotes an engineer in an aerospace firm doing advanced research and development: "One thing you find out around here very quickly is that you can't make a mistake. . . . So everyone sort of walks around delicately trying to get through the system without stepping in a hole" (p. 88).[7]

[6] Some appreciation of the influence of personality on risk taking can be gained from Scodel, Ratoosh, and Minas (1960).

[7] This contradicts the prevailing belief that research and development organizations can only survive by taking innovative risks, which in the nature of the situation means that they must fail often and, so the belief goes, be able to absorb their errors constructively. Sometimes they do, but the internal culture is different from the one we are speaking about in ways which emphasize the social psychological difficulties that would be involved in error-embracing in public agencies. In "hardware" R and D failures, the project outcome usually cannot be faulted as to research technique, the validated theory applied at the time decisions were made as to what projects to pursue, or the data base subsequently used. Failure can be attributed to nature being different from what man expected it to be or to a *calculated risk* on research strategy not panning out. But if the calculated risk was taken on good rational grounds, then failure is seen as the result of nature having different properties rather than as the result of man's incompetence in applying what he *had* known. It is accepted that there are limits to our knowledge about natural reality. In the social area any decision is seen as questionable because theory, data, and research techniques are all seen as challengeable. Thus, failure can be blamed on people rather than on a misunderstanding of social nature. In part this is because people tend strongly to believe they *know* the reality of social nature. They argue about it and challenge others' social theories, but the assumption is that I am more right and you are more wrong. Seldom do both acknowledge that they may indeed be wrong. Thus failure in R and D need not reflect on technical competence, which is where the self-image and self-respect of the technologist is located. In the social situation,

This is not to say that all persons intensely committed to hard work or to a vision have a compulsive need to control or to work in settings that encourage such compulsiveness, though many probably do if descriptions of their private and public lives are to be believed. Nor is it to say that those with a compulsive need to control are not creative and socially valuable: obviously they can be. Nor are they psychologically "strange" or dangerous by conventional standards. On the contrary, we have praised them just because they excell in intensive commitment, hard work, and skill and will to control: in traditional terms they are the epitome of a culture norm. But it is to say that positions of control are likely to be more vigorously sought, more frequently filled, and by conventional standards more successfully operated by people whose strong compulsion draws them to such positions. And these people more than others would have an especially difficult time relinquishing control of a situation or accepting the fact that a situation in which they feel compelled to act is probably beyond their control and, as a consequence, the outcome is likely to be failure. While there are of course exceptions (which thereby add plausibility to these conjectures) arising from the mix of personalities and the press of events, it seems eminently reasonable to propose that most men of power and status, as well as those seeking

---

failure reflects on everything about the self-image of those involved. For these reasons a modest amount of error-embracing is *sometimes* feasible in R and D where it is not in social planning. But only a modest amount of error-embracing is acceptable, because in the long run technical competence becomes equated with overall ability to outguess nature. R and D organizations are designed to measure success on the average rather than each time around. Such a standard of effectiveness would, under present norms, be extremely difficult for public agencies to claim in the face of multiple and conflicting environmental demands and in the absence of adequate evaluations.

Moreover, while this kind of error-embracing is provisionally acceptable at the technological level, it is almost invariably abjured by spokesmen who link the organization with the environment (except under the ritual circumstances Edelman describes). Publicly, the organization still has to look like it really doesn't make mistakes or that it has learned from the last ones and next time everything will most assuredly work. Thus, an R and D organization is grudgingly allowed by its environment the opportunity to learn from its mistakes, but in turn it must give reassurances that it has indeed learned enough to eliminate error the next time. In the social policy and program areas this assurance could not be given. By avoiding error-embracing the policy-maker avoids acknowledging that he may not learn enough from his mistakes to eliminate them next time. Aside from its political inexpediency, error-embracing would be a confession of technical incompetence as well, and thereby of personal inadequacy. (I am indebted to Kai Lee, whose conversation with me regarding his research on R and D firms provided the substance for this footnote. I am of course solely responsible for what I have chosen to abstract from his observations, and for my interpretations.)

power and status, have a deep need to avoid becoming involved in situations that they believe are likely to reveal them to have been in error. The prevailing "sensible" norm is epitomized by Lindblom (1969) when he supports the political and logical reasonableness of disjointed incrementalism by warning that "nonincremental policy proposals are typically unpredictable in their consequences" (p. 33). Such people, then, represent a serious source of resistance to undertaking the required changes needed to try to move toward lrsp, because they are likely to be found at the organizational levels where initiating decisions are made, and because many professionals who now think they want to promote planning will find they have the same strong need to control if lrsp is actually attempted.

Leaders and members of organizations try to avoid acknowledging error not only because it serves to sustain a view of self as able to control but also because it elicits the support of members of the relevant environment, who, belonging to the same tradition, evaluate persons and organizations in the same way. For most people leaders are not leaders, nor are organizations effective, unless they commit few errors and act as if they do not intend to make any. "It can rarely be known what concrete future effects public laws and acts will bring. Economic interactions, psychological responses, the actions of foreign governments and of domestic groupings all contribute to uncertainty. Because men are anxious about impersonal, uncontrollable, or unknowable events, however, they constantly substitute personality for impersonality in interpreting political events. They attribute wider maneuverability to leaders than the latter enjoy. They want to believe that officials have the power and knowledge to produce particular results" (Edelman, 1964, p. 193).[8]

If lrsp is to be for societal learning, those in the environment must also be able to learn how to be part of a societal learning system by condoning error-embracing. To do so, persons and groups in the environment would have to give up the reassuring belief that there really are extant solutions to existing problems, a belief that would be sustained in part by excluding members of the environment from participation in and responsibility for those activities that constitute lrsp. If they were part of an

---

[8] Lewis Long (Center for Studies of Metropolitan Problems, National Institute of Mental Health) suggests a related reason that members of organizations and environments prefer their leaders or supervisors to avoid error-embracing. Error-embracing would revive painful feelings in their followers or subordinates associated with those childhood experiences in which they suffered as the result of parental errors. One of the advantages of believing oneself to be an autonomous adult is freedom from the threat of suffering further from misguided parental behavior. Leaders who acknowledge errors or who make errors that cannot be denied remind adults of their dependence upon those they choose to follow or work for. Hence they remind them that they can suffer again as they did in childhood through the actions of these surrogate parents.

error-embracing, frsl system, the environment would not be able to sustain such expectations or routinely punish for error. Instead they would be *part* of the experiment, part of the error-embracing societal learning structure, rather than outside of it. This kind of participation would deny the environment some of the comforts of ignorance and the satisfactions of blaming others for not protecting it from turbulence and uncertainty.

Could Error-Embracing Have Social Psychological Rewards?

However, there could be social psychological advantages too. By subscribing to error-embracing, polarization around goals or choice of means could be reduced when it results from the assertion of advocates that their position is right and would work if implemented. An understanding that failure is possible, indeed likely, either way, given our ignorance, could ease some of the demand for commitment to the exclusion of other commitments because it could be recognized that all means and ends are likely to need change as their weaknesses are discovered. Foreknowledge that in the event of error, there would be no pressure to pronounce a goal or program successful, or to persist in it if it were unsuccessful in order to avoid acknowledging error, could sometimes make it easier to take a wait-and-see approach, deferring the competing approach, knowing that it would get its chance later if the one being tried did not work.

If neither party are willing to wait, it might sometimes be politically, economically, and operationally easier to attempt both approaches on an experimental basis since neither approach would have to be "sold" on the grounds that it would most certainly work. Acknowledging the likelihood of error before error occurs would make it easier to abandon the rhetoric that anticipates no error and then requires further rhetoric and action to hide the errors, rather than to learn from them. As a result, it would be easier to set clear and meaningful goals; a norm of error-embracing would make it acceptable to revise goals and to evaluate programs undertaken in their pursuit without fear of being caught up in an error. Certainly a chief contributor to our proclivity to substitute means for goals is fear of failing to reach the goals or of discovering that they are inappropriate.

Such a shift in perspective and style may not be impossible for some persons and groups: there is a growing pressure to "tell it like it is." Science rewards error-embracing. Major religious traditions emphasize that human control is fallible and mostly a chimera and that acknowledgment of error is not only praiseworthy but necessary for enlightenment. "This above all: to thine ownself be true" is not questioned in principle. Moreover, the cultural norm that emphasizes and rewards compulsive control seems to be weakening among some of the more articulate young, and even here and there among older persons holding positions that traditionally were filled with the most aggressive controllers. But given the "naturalness" and the rewards of error-avoiding and error-denying, such a shift across a wide spectrum of environments will be difficult—so difficult that only the increasing inability to hide errors may supply the sufficient condition for coming to place a positive value on error-embracing.

Consider, too, that while acknowledging uncertainty requires error-embracing in order to cope and to learn, error-embracing requires acknowledging uncertainty. The loop is painful either way one goes around it. The incentive to avoid engagement with both conditions is multiplied and sustained by the unrelieved pain. However, if people could bring themselves to embrace error then perhaps uncertainty and the turbulence that produces it would themselves become less painful conditions to bear. Part of the pain results from anxiety and apprehension about the great likelihood of making errors in a turbulent and uncertain world and of being punished for them. If error-embracing were sanctioned it should be easier to live with the presumed *consequences* of uncertainty and, thereby, easier to accept uncertainty as a personal and organizational condition of life.

Accountability Under Conditions of Error-Embracing

Although error-embracing appears to be supported by the logic of learning, and the experimental method in science and group process training experiences provide evidence that error-embracing is not a psychological impossibility, there remains the question of accountability. The argument goes that if people are not threatened with punishment for making mistakes, errors will be made out of indifference, gratuitous distraction, or even maliciousness. In short, people won't work hard to avoid making errors.

I know of no complete or invariably convincing answer to this argument and its implicit assumptions about what it takes to get humans to do things right, but I do have some comments that may encourage a view that appropriate accountability may not be impossible. I offer them in the spirit that, if this view could be promulgated, it could reduce resistance to trying to change toward lrsp, because some resistances will derive from and be sustained by beliefs about what it is "natural" for humans to do about making and avoiding errors.

In the first place, there is growing evidence that men need not be controlled like machines to get accurate, efficient output from them when this is in fact possible. Slothfulness, nastiness, and irresponsibility are not necessarily built-in tendencies. The assault on hierarchical management systems and the demonstrable utility of shared goal-setting between worker and supervisor and of participative-management systems give evidence that the rewards of self-guidance and self-respect produce responsibility, attention, and positive involvement.[9] The threats of punishment implicit in the present meaning of "accountabilty" for errors need not be the incentive for encouraging minimum gratuitous errors.

A somewhat less insulting image of man than that just dealt with poses the question in the form, "What is the incentive to take risks if you get rewarded whether you fail or succeed?" Implicit in this "reasonable" formulation is the assumption that failure is more likely to be the result of doing things differently rather than continuing to do what one or one's organization is already doing. The argument for lrsp assumes that continuing to do the conventional is also an invitation to disaster in the situations we are concerned with. Also implicit in the question is an assumption about human nature—that, things being equal, men will take the easy way out. Put that way, its falsity is obvious. But there is something positive to be noted, too, if error-embracing were valued. With efforts involving lrsp, the "success" of a program is only likely to be evident well off in time: the rewards of succeeding will be delayed. But there will be frequent opportunities to be successful as a "teacher" or "learner" as error-embracing efforts reveal new knowledge, allow new understanding, and advance societal learning during the unfolding of the program.

How to reward error-embracing and punish error-avoiding so that appropriate accountability is maintained would be one of the many things to be learned by trying out different norms and procedures. We did not begin this age with our present norms about punishing errors full blown: indeed, they are still in the process of evolution as we learn the costs and benefits of punishment within the present social and organizational structure. We have learned to distinguish many kinds of errors of omission and commission and to allocate punishments according to subtle or gross distinctions between them. An obvious example has to do with the distinctions between degrees of homicide. Note, too, the present efforts to avoid gratuitous damage to children's self-images by removing the grade of "failure" from the lexicon of measures of learning accomplishment. Note the shift in allocation of "punishment" costs from the worker to the employer when the worker's error results in physical harm to himself that can be avoided by a safety device. No-fault auto insurance, no-fault divorce, and legalized abortion all represent shifts in the definition of error or, more important, changes in the perceived utility of assigning accountability for errors for the purposes of punishment. Con-

9 As one example of the large literature in this area, see Gooding (1970). See also the works of Likert, and almost any issue of the *Harvard Business Review* and the *Journal of Applied Behavioral Science*.

sider too the implications of attempts to legislate compensation for manufacturers whose products (such as cyclamates) cannot meet evolving
FDA standards.[10]

A few directions in which a norm of error-embracing could be
rewarded without encouraging gratuitous error can be imagined. First,
there would be a need to distinguish between those errors that result from
deliberately undertaking uncertain goals, objectives, and programs for
the purpose of lrsp, with the intent of learning from them for the social
good, and those errors produced in situations lacking such intent, such
as routine actions. An essential aspect of accountability would be the
requirement that a person or organization demonstrate that appropriate
actions were taken to seek out errors and openly report them. Under this
norm, what would be punished would be the *failure* to embrace error.
Technical competence would be partially measured by the ability to
detect error and the ability to use the information gained for learning
more about where to head and how to get there. This competence would
in part be demonstrated by the capability to get the error-relevant information to the people who could most effectively do the learning and
revising—whether they were in the organization or its environment.
Such behavior would be rewarded because it would help make possible
societal learning by enriching the data base and reinforcing those conditions of trust needed to live creatively with turbulence and uncertainty.

But how *much* error-embracing? If *everything* were exposed to
everybody, wouldn't it present a set of operational and interpersonal
problems as intractable as error-denying? There are two parts to my response to this question: in principle, and in the practice associated with
change-over efforts.

First, "in principle." In a later chapter we will examine the interpersonal skill requirements necessary for lrsp. These include capacities for
trust, expressions of feeling, interpersonal support, and so forth. These are

[10] H. David has pointed out that we do not expect ballplayers to bat
1000, though we reward most highly those who come closest. And we admire
skilled sportsmen who try to break records even if they fail; we admire them for
their conscientious *attempt*. It is this sort of appreciation that would have to
pertain in order to meet the error-embracing prerequisite for moving toward
lrsp. It seems to me that this observation also emphasizes another prerequisite
for frsl—access to and participation in lrsp by members of the environment. I
suspect that players are not expected to bat 1000 because fans can observe the
workings of the game and of the players, and most of the viewers have tried to
excell at baseball or some other sport. There are no secrets about what is involved
in failing or in succeeding. Because they understand the requirements for successful ball-playing or record breaking and the problems of meeting them, fans
content themselves with applauding skilled and systematic efforts to do so that
come off comparatively well. The same exposure and experiencing philosophy
might work for legitimizing error-embracing in the areas of societal development.

skills that most of us lack throughout our interpersonal lives, not just on the job, so to speak. Consequently we have developed interpersonal styles that allow us to "make do" by keeping our defenses up, thickening our skins, and withdrawing from ourselves and others. However, the plethora of books and training programs aimed at helping people become skilled in intimacy, group processes, self-knowledge, and in better relations between spouses, between parents and children, and between supervisors and supervised, are symptoms of a growing awareness that the traditional means of coping with one another are increasingly unrewarding.[11] If we were to become a society that valued open and supportive interpersonal relationships, and was skilled at creating them, then it might well be that error-embracing would be valued as a way of learning more about self and others as well as about society.[12] If error-embracing were valued, then the social psychological rewards from sharing the problem and learning from it would positively encourage error-embracing whenever appropriate. If it were accepted that lrsp is prerequisite for self-conscious societal development, then error-embracing in some situations would seem to be a "natural" prerequisite for learning. But in a turbulent environment, organizational structures will be altering, as will organizational-environmental arrangements. Under these circumstances, restricting error-embracing to some situations would not seem feasible, and I conjecture that that norm would diffuse throughout the system if it were established at all.

Of course, we are not now such a society, and we are not going to become one during the period immediately ahead, when we must be trying to change in that direction. What then "in practice"? The time period just ahead will be one in which more people will be learning interpersonal skills. In addition to the widespread and growing appreciation of the need for them, the repertory of skills that can be learned, and the opportunity to learn them, are growing too. Of course, many people will not learn them. Yet the evidences of error in public programs may become so irrepressible that it may well become politically expedient to acknowledge the likelihood of error beforehand and certainly at the time of the fact. What could be anticipated, then, is a situation in which some people and organizations, some of the time, will try error-embracing and will be variously rewarded or punished for doing so. This, after all, is what we have done for a few decades with fiscal and monetary policy. It is what we do with international negotiations, shifting from open to secret activities and back. There is no reason to argue for or suppose that an approach to societal learning as radical in its way as were Keynesian

---

[11] In part, these activities are also the result of attempts to exploit dissatisfaction from whatever source by "locating" *the* source in interpersonal relations.

[12] For related arguments, see the last paragraphs of Argyris (1969).

economics, bail for the poor, or Medicare will be perfected or applied full-blown and consistently from the beginning. But even as these examples represent once radical responses to societal needs, and just as their practice inevitably shifted the definition of what is "natural" and right for society to be and to do, so too might error-embracing come to play its "natural" part in lrsp.[13]

[13] Cognitive dissonance, a theory formulated by Leon Festinger and the subject of extensive research and conjecture, is sometimes proposed as the explanation for why a person, once having made a choice between options, resists acknowledging that the choice was in error and instead seeks evidence to bolster his belief in the rightness of his choice. Very likely some such psychological process, which serves to reduce the tension after a choice has been made between equally attractive but exclusive alternatives, operates for some people in some circumstances. Unfortunately, the operational ambiguities regarding the motivations, perceived options, and outcomes, the relative attractiveness of options, and the decision contexts make it extremely difficult if not impossible to apply the concept to real-life situations as complex as those we are dealing with. See Aronson (1969).

With regard to the general thesis of this chapter, it would be well worth the reader's attention to absorb H. Arendt's argument that the only interpersonal "transaction" that is sufficient to cope with the essential irreversibility of human action that "goes wrong" is forgiveness, forgiveness in the sense initially promulgated by Christ—with all that implies for changes in norms and social structures. See her "Irreversibility and the Power to Forgive" (1958), pp. 212–218. This concept deserves much more attention when speculating further on the matters discussed here. (I came upon her idea too late in the preparation of this manuscript to do justice to it here.) Also see my footnote 6, Chapter Seven.

On the Requirement for
Future-Responsive Goal-Setting

☙☙☙☙☙☙☙☙☙☙☙☙☙☙☙☙☙☙☙☙☙☙☙☙☙☙☙☙☙

*T*here is a substantial literature, reflecting the state of mind of many planners and policy-makers, which contends that goals for public policy cannot, or need not, or should not be specified. The argument goes that people cannot often reconcile value differences but they can agree on means that serve their different goals; that people cannot rationally grasp enough of the issue at hand to set goals that are neither too broad to be guides to action nor too narrow to be other than program targets; and that the inherent requirements for carrying out functionally differentiated tasks raise goal conflicts that cannot be resolved even if values are similar.[1] Thus the incrementalists conclude that, "instead of simply adjusting means to ends, ends are [and should be] chosen that are appropriate to available or nearly available means." (Hirshman and Lindblom, 1962, p. 218).

The Meaning and Purposes of Goal-Setting in Frsl

There is no denying the descriptive validity of this argument under many conditions, especially in government. Yet, there are truly limited

[1] On the functional inevitability of goal conflicts between organizational components, see Simon (1964). Also see Haberstroh (1968).

144

though vast human and material resources that must be applied to complex problems, and there are social purposes that must necessarily have their realization in the future (with its different social context). There must be, then, some basis, especially in government, for the selection of direction, commitment of effort, and allocation of resources beyond the expedient and inertial motives that respond to the present, which itself has accumulated out of past incremental actions. Nor, in a long-range perspective, is it sufficient to argue that ends should be chosen which are appropriate to available means, because future means could be made to be different than those available now and because "availability" will be a function of commitments made and actions taken earlier in pursuit of a long-range goal. Finally, in the light of the accumulating mass of societal problems, those who feel that planning is crucial for felicitous societal growth reject as a sufficient alternative to goal-setting the processes that have dominated government actions: "Through various specific types of partisan mutual adjustment among the large number of individuals and groups among which analysis and policy making is fragmented . . . what is ignored at one point in policy making becomes central at another point. . . . Similarly, errors that would attend overly ambitious attempts at comprehensive understanding are often avoided by the remedial and incremental character of problem solving. And those not avoided can be mopped up or attended to as they appear, because analysis and policy making are serial or successive" (Hirschman and Lindblom, 1962, p. 216).[2]

That there is both need for and great difficulty in setting meaningful future-oriented goals is evidenced by contrast between the growing number of attempts to do so by cities, a presidential commission, voluntary organizations, and agencies trying to meet PPBS goal specifications and their comparatively feeble results.[3] For many reasons they end up as ritual statements or just fade away. These experiences, combined with relevant theory, provide a basis for anticipating some social psychological sources of resistance to goal-setting when its purposes would be to facilitate social planning for the future. The very reasons that make goal-setting necessary provide sources of personal and organizational threats that will result in resistance to efforts to change toward lrsp.

Before continuing along this line of inquiry, and as a contribution to it, it is useful to note that there have indeed been occasions when goals have been set that could be evaluated. We need to know much more about

---

[2] For an elaboration of this argument, see Wildavsky (1964), especially the last chapter.

[3] On the need for and difficulties besetting goal specification, see Colm and Gulick (1968). On reactions to the National Goals Research Staff report, see Abelson (1970), and "What Goals?" (1970).

the conditions that permit this to happen, but two examples will suggest some contributing social psychological aspects and will emphasize, in the process, how difficult it will be to learn to set evaluatable, future-responsive, goals. The existence of a clear threat to an organization's survival, combined with an acknowledged leadership that has control of the resources needed to implement the changes required to meet new goals, may be one such combination of circumstances. An example was the transformation of personnel and structure of New York University from a "School of Opportunity," for those unprepared for universities with high academic admission standards, into a high standards university but with an urban emphasis. Specific goals were set by the top administrators with no real participation from staff or environment. The characteristics of the (near) future university were specified and actions taken to realize them —with, apparently, considerable success but at the cost of considerable trauma within the organization (Buldridge, 1971).

A second example is the Employment Act of 1946, which set as a national goal, "maximum employment, production, and purchasing power." While the actual statute left matters rather less incisive than these words suggest, employment and income measurements were developed that gave some basis for assessing the extent to which the goals were being pursued. Of course "maximum" continues to be the sticky concept here. The point is, that such a goal was completely compatible with a variety of values held then about conditions at that time. The question of whether that goal was appropriate in the light of anticipated alternative future conditions was not examined. Only now, with the advent of ecological considerations, is the meaning of that phrase beginning to be examined in the light of alternative conjectures. One conjecture that seems quite safe is that, next time around, that phrase would not be compatible with all value systems—particularly with those anticipating various longer-range futures.

In contrast to these examples, changing toward lrsp would require goal-setting where values conflict, and where goals will need to be recognized as crucially important but potentially temporary, and evaluations designed accordingly. Moreover, it would be desirable if goals could be developed in other than crisis situations. Lastly, overriding leadership and resource control probably will be lacking.

It is desirable to note in this context another type of goal-setting, which at first glance seems to refute the expectation that it will be difficult to do in ways that are appropriate for changing toward lrsp. Several cities have undertaken goal-setting efforts, describing them in ways that might be measured. However, attendent circumstances emphasize rather than contradict the position being taken here. Sometimes goals have been set, but because of disagreements between the groups involved no priorities have been assigned. Sometimes priorities have been set, but then the group setting the goals has been homogenous and "establishment." Some goals that have been set and are being carried out have been capital improvement activities not explicitly related to *social* planning as such. Seldom if ever has attention to the longer-range future been the context for setting these goals or priorities.[4]

Goal-setting as I mean it here is necessary in order that societal learning can occur: it is both a way of stating what is to be learned and it is a necessary condition for discovering whether we are learning. It is not done to commit us to getting from A to B but as a means of discovering where we are and where we think we want to go given our understanding of A and B, an understanding which is in part the result of committing ourself to the task of goal-setting. We cannot evaluate whether we are approaching a desired future condition without having specified how that condition is to be recognized. Nor can we evaluate the continuing relevance of chosen future conditions unless there is a previous choice to compare with our changing appreciation of what is important to avoid or attain in the future. A goal can refer to an end state, or a desirable future condition that is not in itself an end state, or it can refer to establishing a norm.[5] These different types of goals would be represented by asking for ten million new houses by a given date, for housing of a stated quality for all within a given period, or for the application by a given date of a regulatory process for monitoring and revising housing standards. Goals are necessary because long-range planning activities extend over a long enough time to require means and ends reevaluation as we move into that future and because the future is likely to appear different enough from the present to allow and require choices among options only attainable in the future. Goal-setting stimulates and provides the reference for scanning the future beyond and aside from the goal, thereby exposing costs as well as benefits that may be associated with the goal. It makes possible explicit

[4] These observations derive from interviews in Dayton, Ohio, and Los Angeles, California, as well as from a paper prepared by Del Guidice (1970), in the form of a memo to Executive Director, Bicentennial Commission, and R. Bauer, Executive Director, National Goals Research Staff.

[5] G. Vickers (1965, pp. 31–35) emphasizes that much of life is not aimed at end-point attainment but rather at norm maintaining, and that the task of coping with the contradictory functions of balancing and optimizing organizational behavior by setting norms is more important and more realistic a preoccupation than end point goal-setting for the purpose of getting from here to there. I agree, especially for organizations dealing with a comparatively familiar band of internally and externally varying conditions responding to a comparatively short-future time frame. And I am sure that norm-setting will be an important type of future responsive goal-setting, as I am using the term. But it also seems to me that in the public policy area many of the goals to be set smack more of end-point targets and direction-setting than of norm-setting.

appreciation of the undesirable features that will accompany a preferred future. As such it sensitizes and emphasizes the evaluation and goal-resetting processes that would become operative once goals were chosen.

Finally, long-range goals provide a kind of myth to which hopes and commitment can be attached.[6] Thereby, goals provide a symbolism for creating the future. Goals can become a statement of what we can be and an injunction to try and, if societal learning is the mode, they carry with them the obligation to evaluate and revise them over time. F. Polak (1961) has much to say about the way images of the future provide a guiding quality to the present. Goals, as used here, necessarily derive from images of the future and encapsulate the meanings of that image. Of images of the future Polak says: "While mirroring man, they also hold up another mirror which shows him how he could and should be. To the extent that they can move man to look at the changing image reflected in this other mirror, they can help him grow into this new image. Positive images of the future create an active type of man, possessed of influence-optimism, indirect or direct, with regard to the future. Their dynamic power to compel the dramatic movement of cultural events through time lies in the human intermediary, in the man moved to action by his vision of the future. *History does not unfold of itself, but evolves through man's evolving*" (p. 117).

Resistances to Effective Goal-Setting for Lrsp

When future-responsive goal-setting is attempted in conventional organizational settings it is and will be upsetting, so much so that the activity usually dies aborning or ends as a ritual statement, too specific or too overblown to be useful for guiding and inspiring movement into the future, and disconnected from goal evaluation and goal revision processes. Misplaced expectations about the purposes and consequences of goal-setting, which derive from social engineering assumptions and from the norms and behavior-defining competence in conventional organizations, result either in avoidance of goal-setting or in so much anxiety and frustration that the activity is truncated and self-defeating.

Typically, when goal-setting is attempted, it is done largely to

[6] See Wieland (1969). This research does not prove this speculation, but it offers interesting support and does strengthen the general argument made in this chapter. In regard to this position, see H. Arendt's argument that the only interpersonal "transaction" that is sufficient to cope with the essential unpredictability of human action and its consequences is the relationship embodied in a promise. See her "Unpredicability and the Power of Promise" (1958), pp. 219–224. As with her concept of forgiveness, the function of promise deserves much more attention when speculating further on the matters discussed herein. Also see footnote 13, Chapter Six.

avoid, or to gain a sense of avoiding, uncertainty. Goal-setting is attempted as a psychological means for reducing uncertainty, and when participants succeed in stating and agreeing on goals, it symbolizes a reduction in uncertainty. It is, in this case, an agreement, usually tacit, on a prediction: "This is what can be made to work out." Thus, implicit in the wish or expectation that goals can be set is the hope that a consensus will be forthcoming on what constitutes reality and what legitimates selecting aspects of that reality that merit attainment or avoidance. In this state of mind, if agreement on goals could really be reached it would imply a greater likelihood of order, and this anticipated reduction in uncertainty is comforting to contemplate. The hope or belief that the act of goal setting would reveal an attainable future, and encourage tranquil participation in its attainment, comes through clearly in this comment of a staff member of a voluntary organization concerned with community action: "There's no reason why we can't get agreement on where we want to be in the future. Everybody really wants the same things out of life. And in this country we've got the means to get those things if we get clear on them. All we've got to do is get together and stay together."

But effective goal-setting for the longer range turns out in fact to confront those involved with new uncertainties. In the absence of a validated theory of social change, future conjectures are only future conjectures, no matter how artful, systematic, and rational the means of deriving them. While users have more information than they had, they have no reliable way of knowing whether they have the information they need for choosing among these conjectures in order to set goals for the purpose of attaining one or another aspect of the futures emphasized in the conjectures.

Attempts to translate this uncertainty into the more comfortable form of risk would require additional efforts to better assess the state of the present and the dynamics of change. But in the light of our inadequate understanding of social change (in spite of competing serious and pop sociology models proporting to describe it), and in the absence of enough data about any complex aspect of social process, examination of the present to get a better purchase on the probable future is far more likely to increase uncertainty than to reduce it.[7] Thompson and Tuden (1959) have proposed a typology of decision-making (which presumably would include decision-making about goals) that emphasizes the uncer-

---

[7] Of course there are occasions when the exercise of goal-setting in a long-range perspective does clearly seem to provide a better basis for choosing among present actions. Then there is an accompanying sense of uncertainty reduction. These occasions reinforce further efforts on behalf of lrsp. So far, these occasions are most likely to arise around comparatively narrow and technological decision choices. When the task perspective is broadened, the uncertainty increases again, as we see when technological assessment methods are enlarged to include the societal context.

tainty which infuses that act. The typology is built around beliefs about causation and preferences for possible outcomes. When there is agreement on both causation and preferences, the decision-making process is one of computation. When there is agreement about causation but disagreement about preferred outcomes, the process is compromise. When there is disagreement about causation but agreement about preferences, decisions are based on judgment. But when there is disagreement about both causes and outcomes, decision-making is by "inspiration." Inspiration would seem to be the most likely process for many future-oriented goal-setting decisions.

If those involved in goal-setting acknowledge to themselves and to their peers this fragmented and unvalidated theoretical and factual basis for setting goals with regard to the longer range future, then restricting those goal choices to purely "rational" data and models would become ridiculous or fraudulent. But if goal choices are not restricted to criteria based solely on data, theory, and so forth, then the door opens for preferences, values, ideologies, and the feelings that underlie them, to become a major and *explicit* part of the goal-setting process.

The problems this presents will be greater than they would have been in the past. Even if values may have differed among members of a goal-setting group in the past, the differences probably were far less than those expected in the future. A major condition that makes planning necessary for guiding societal development is the absence of an agreed-upon value system with shared goal priorities and approved means for attaining them or for resolving conflicts over their rank. Sharply differing values will characterize the people filling the overlapping and sometimes conflicting ensemble of roles through which planning-relevant tasks will be performed. This will be especially so because members of the environment must play an integral part in frsl.

In a brilliant and unique analysis of policy analysts and their work, M. Rein (1971) has emphasized the ineluctable role of beliefs in such activities, whether they be goal-setting, program choosing, or evaluation. He argues that the research for policy-making and program development, and the application or non-application of the research, as well as the choice of what is to be implemented, depends finally on professional and political creeds. But while the contributions of these creeds to the definition of problems, policies, and programs is evident, when illuminated as in Rein's analysis, the contribution of beliefs is not attended to explicitly in the interpersonal setting in which planning-relevant activities are invented or decided upon. What I am suggesting here is that one reason the central role of beliefs is not dealt with directly and constructively is because the idea of deliberately dealing with strong emotions is so threatening to those involved that planning-relevant activities, in this case goal-setting, are waffled so that the issues do not have to be faced and worked through.[8]

Two social psychological conditions intertwine here. The first is that serious attention to a more distant future will raise questions, holding a likely range of value positions in a goal-setting group, about social priority, moral stance, and utilitarian justification for organizational survival. "Who am I, and what am I doing here as a person, and what is this organization doing here in the light of these possible futures?" have already become very uncomfortable questions for some members of some organizations. Future conjectures examined for goal-setting guidance will often be mirrors reflecting ethical, personal, and operational obsolescence. Of course other people with other values and other organizations or components will see instead new potentials and purposes. But for those who don't like what they see, or are fearful of it, goal-setting for guidance into alternative futures will be an emotionally loaded activity and as such one to be avoided, particularly when another part of the group is perceived to like what it sees.

The second condition results from the multiply-reinforced norm that personal feelings have no place in decision-making that is supposed to be rational in its methods and purposes. There is the real-politik injunction to "play it sensibly." There is the widely subscribed-to position that argues the efficacy of rationality per se, especially as enhanced by the techniques of management science. Both positions argue that feelings distort organizational goal-setting efficiencies and clarity. One important consequence of the pervasiveness of these viewpoints is that people seeking and attaining high-level decision-making policy positions do and will tend to discount to others, and often to themselves as well, the contribution their feelings make to their choices. (While some will credit hunches or intuition in private, they will not acknowledge this in their public role performance.)

By assuming the cloak of rationality and being rewarded for it with successively more powerful and central decision-making roles, those responsible for goal-setting (if and when it is undertaken) will often be reinforced in a culturally approved and occupationally trained inability to deal constructively with their own feelings and those of people who would be involved with them in such decisions. This trained incapacity to engage feelings constructively will not be limited to those at the top. They will model the approved behavior for junior aspirants, and what is more, they will evaluate the performance of their subordinates. So the superior's style of avoiding exposing or exposure to strong feelings has and will

---

[8] Attention to beliefs also undermines the authority of "science" by emphasizing the insufficiency of quantitative data. This undermining contributes its own modicum of emotions and compounds the threat.

·

heavily influence the norm. Thus, the strong tendency, as has been commented on, and demonstrated often enough, will be to repress feelings and avoid situations that might elicit them. (See Chapter Ten.) Since during the changing-over period those involved would have to assume that in seeking to set goals there would be strong value and ideological differences—perhaps among members of the organization and certainly between the organization and the environment—and since these differences will be expected to be unresolvable by "rational" means of adjudication, goal-setting will be avoided if possible as too disruptive to be a part of decision processes. Thus, a major reason for resisting purposive (as contrasted to ritual) long-range goal-setting would seem to be the fear of facing and of being unable to cope constructively with intense feelings in oneself and among participants, feelings arising from value conflicts and ideological differences that would be expected to accompany such future-derived and future-oriented goal-setting.

In addition to the fear of facing open emotional conflict, those involved in change-over efforts would recognize that if goal commitments were made, actions to implement them should follow. Since these actions would take place in a turbulent environment, feedback intended to assess goal-approaching would often indicate that the actions are not succeeding or that there is no way to know whether they are. There will be fear, then, that feedback generated as a result of and dependent on goal specification will make it easier to be identified with erroneous decisions. Also, when the goals are set well into the future, anticipations about the characteristics of that future are very likely to change over time; then goal-specifying tasks would have to be undertaken anew, and the criteria for program evaluation altered. The reluctance to experience renewed exposure to intense feelings in renegotiating goals will also encourage resistances to future-responsive goal-setting.

These uncomfortable threats to status, values, and interpersonal relationships that would arise or would be expected to arise if goal-setting for lrsp were undertaken, will encourage members of organizations to use a number of readily available structural and interpersonal devices for resisting serious goal-setting.

Means Used to Resist Serious Goal-Setting

The most familiar device is to set goals in such global or ambiguous terms that value differences are not engaged and ostensibly goal-related activities are impossible to evaluate on their face. Nor need upsetting feedback from the present or the future be solicited. A second means is to encapsulate the goal-setting activity within a small group at the top who share mythologies and who then disseminate a goal's statement for its ritual utility and public relations value. A third means is to set the future that is attended to close enough to the present so that future scenarios do not contain societal situations that require any shift from present goals or instrumentalities, accumulated out of past experience, according to which the organization believes it operates. In conducting an informal survey of Federal agencies during the preparation of the National Goals Research Staff study, the staff director had this experience: "We simply would go in and sit down with people [in Federal offices] around the table and in a very quiet way say: Let's assume that we did everything that you say that we should do. What would that have contributed to the quality of life in the nation by 1980? What would have been the cumulative effects of our following your advice in 1980? And how would that fit in to what other people, in and out of government, are doing with respect to the general climate in which you operate, by 1980? I can only report that no one answered the questions. No one answered *any* of those questions."[9] Corporations that assess the future in terms of product-oriented markets and government agencies that assess their relevant future as the duration of the present administration both have a realistic reason for short-term future perspectives and a good rationalization for avoiding the potential pain of longer range future-relevant goal-setting.

A fourth device is to reject longer-range future studies on the grounds that "they are not specific predictions and anybody's guess is as good as anyone else's"—especially if "anyone else's" conjectures require no goal readjustment.[10] Fifth, if goals are clearly stated the subsequent uncertainty and the need to revise the goals can be avoided by avoiding relevant feedback, that is, by structuring the organization so that it does not get or cannot use goal-checking information. A sixth device for avoiding goal-setting is to base organizational and personal evaluations on comparisons of the present with the past, or with other on-going analogous activities. A seventh means is to limit goal-setting to situations which can be treated *as if* the needed data and theory were in hand, so that the decision can be "rational" and feelings, values, and ideologies need not, indeed shall not, play a part—or more correctly, shall not be acknowledged by the participants as playing a part. By excluding feelings and values, the situation is transformed into a ritual. Participants recognize that it does not face up to implicit conflicts: as a result they lose interest

[9] Comments of C. Williams to an informal interagency committee on futures research, September 1970. Quoted with his kind permission.

[10] By deprecating future studies, agencies also reduce the occasions for improving them, so that even though they are not able to predict, they still could be compelling stimuli to goal-setting and program choices. Persistent feebleness of future conjectures is of course desirable if the intent is to resist serious goal-setting.

and commitment and are indifferent to implementing the goals settled on. (However, some of the participants may accept the myth of knowledge sufficiency so completely that they are unaware of the essentially uncertain situation they are dealing with.) Eighth, people avoid goal-setting by subscribing to the rationality and moral rightness of disjointed incrementalism, thereby also reducing their fear of making errors—in the short term. They also reap the rewards of reducing uncertainty by moving away from an unsatisfactory and clearly defined situation in the present rather than toward a chosen but problematic future.

Are There Ways to Reduce Resistance to Serious Goal-Setting?

It appears, then, that the social psychological resistances to the kind of goal-setting required for moving toward lrsp will be formidable. Again, however, it is worth speculating about the possibilities of removing or at least reducing the social psychological resistances by emphasizing the necessity of goal-setting for societal learning. We have seen that, whatever else impedes serious goal-setting, the following social psychological contributions are important: inability to acknowledge great uncertainty, fear that one's errors will more easily be detected if goals are set, and fear of dealing with intense feelings in self and others over beliefs as to what constitutes the present and the future and what priorities should pertain. In earlier chapters we examined possible means of ameliorating the fear and anxiety attached to acknowledging uncertainty and embracing error. In later chapters we will examine other ways in which lrsp makes heavy demands for interpersonal competence to deal with feelings and we will look at possible means for enhancing these competences. Perhaps, then, these means can facilitate the acceptance of a definition of goal-setting that interprets it as a procedure for becoming clearer about what we need to do in order to learn how to move toward societal conditions that may be preferable to those of the present. If we can stop thinking of goal-setting as establishing once-and-for-all commitments to a specific future, then perhaps people may be able to expose themselves enough to the activity to begin to learn if it can be done in ways that facilitate learning how to change toward a future-responsive learning society.

What about conflict of interests or confrontations that leave no room for mutual exploration and learning? Such confrontations simply are beyond the capabilities, as I envision them, of future responsive planning. As for conflicts of interest, many of them may be lessened by joint seeking of longer-range goals which, by that shift in appreciation, encompass the present conflict and put it in a new perspective. Emphasizing an experimental approach that allows more than one goal or approach to be tried simultaneously or sequentially may also ameliorate the conflict for reasons discussed in our examination of error embracing. In general, it is not clear what kinds of irreconcilable conflicts of interest would arise if organizations were trying to change toward performing according to the characteristics of lrsp—which would mean that their environment was also involved. Probably there would be new conflicts of interest, just as there were when the poor became involved in urban resource allocation decisions. Certainly the expression of feelings and beliefs will intensify working them out. But these expressions might also make it possible to work out some conflicts that otherwise would remain intransigent or subversive just because goals were not faced squarely.[11] Dealing with conflicts of interests when goal-setting in a planning context will be a learning process, as it has been all along in circumstances devoid of planning or goal-setting.[12]

D. Moynihan (1970) has emphasized another difficulty in seriously setting goals. His proposed means for easing the difficulty fits the position being developed here:

The difficulty with national goals is that they too quickly become standards by which to judge not the future but the present. In a sense, they institutionalize the creation of discontent. The setting of future goals, no matter how distant, drains legitimacy from present conditions. Once it is established and agreed upon that the future will have to be very different from the present, it becomes absurd to be content with the present. The past is annihilated. The most extraordinary progress counts for little if it has brought society only to a middling point in an uncompleted journey.

Yet the creation of discontent is in part the object of goal setting. Discontent is commonly a condition of creativity in an individual or a society: it is at all events an immensely useful spur to progress. The art of

[11] D. Campbell has drawn my attention to an argument that asserts that it might be more socially constructive to leave human-produced events to chance rather than face the potentially destructive consequences of making it clear who could be blamed for failures resulting from a goal choice. I agree that this would be so if policy and decision-makers had the responsibility for planning *for* an environment that had no part in the policy formulation or decisions. The environment could then blame the decision-maker for the failure. But in the frsl approach, those who are the recipients of the consequences are also involved in the goal-setting and are learning the consequences of what they have tried to do as they are trying to do it. It seems to me the risk Campbell refers to is much more of a risk in an error-denying, planner-planned-for arrangement, than in the kind we are looking at.

[12] One of the most useful analyses of levels and kinds of conflict applicable to the matter at hand is Vickers (1972). Also see Stagner (1971).

national goal setting, then, is to be realistic about what can be attained, and to use social data in such a way as to enable both the expert and lay publics to understand that progress toward any seriously difficult goal is going to take place by increments, and to measure that progress as it occurs (or fails to occur, which is often the case) [p. 11].

Of course there would be risks in dealing openly with these strong value issues and questions of priority. But the risks seem to me to be different than and probably no greater (whatever that may mean) than those attached to continuing to stumble backward into the future, the result of, among other things, not trying to set goals in the spirit of frsl. I emphasize, *in the spirit* of frsl, because in its absence, openness about these things would be disastrous, as numerous observers have pointed out in justifying or explaining secrecy, ambiguousness, and value avoidance in conventional planning situations.

VIII

Social Psychological Burdens
in Coping with the Future

Goal-setting puts particular emphasis on the future as an unavoidable criterion for choice. But all lrsp change-over activities will be more or less infused with an awareness of the future and all decisions will be influenced by that awareness. Most of the effects which emphasizing the future will have on social psychological reactions to efforts to change toward lrsp are dealt with in other chapters, but a few pervasive aspects can be more usefully explored by themselves.

Beliefs About the Future as a Function of Beliefs About the Past

When interviewed, those who were sanguine about the future invariably justified their expectations that conventional public and corporate governance processes could deal with the future by refering to the past successes of these processes under conditions of crisis and change. In personal conversation, the historian and public administrator H. David suggested that men probably project at least their mood regarding the future from their personal interpretation of history.[1] Some implications of

[1] Fraisse (1963, p. 177) lends support when he writes: "The temporal horizon of each individual is the result of a true creation. We construct our past as well as our future. It is evident that adaptation is a characteristic of this

such a probable relationship merit further conjecture here. The past, as experienced directly and as absorbed vicariously, must be a part of our self-image; it helps us explain to ourselves our successes, failures, and how we arrived at where we are. Moreover, our self-image is the fundamental reference by which we project ourselves into the future, and it partially shapes our images of the rest of the world, images which are also partially the product of our historically derived image of ourselves.[2] One body of research, although requiring cautious extrapolation, strongly suggests that those who value achieving and who have achieved feel more potent with regard to their capacity to deal with the future than those who do not value achieving so highly. "If past-present connections are made through the sense of personal efficacy, control of activity or, more simply, autonomy, then present-future connections become the inferred extension of this autonomy. Inference gives life and meaning to the future. Prior achievement, therefore, breeds possibility and reinforces credible planning" (Cottle, 1969, p. 549). In contrast, as T. Cottle observes in summarizing the research of others, "Anxiety, on the other hand, has been shown to deflect individuals away from the future and increase sentiments that success in personal action has a low probability of occurrence. . . . Thus, if anxiety causes an exaggeration of the future's dangers, achievement values reinforce an exaggerated sense of man's ability to control these dangers" (p. 541). He warns, however, that "for the most part, definitions of past, present, and future remain unstudied. . . . Can one meaningfully discuss a future orientation, for example, if for some the future commences seconds from now, while for others an expanse literally of years appertains to what they themselves call present?" How expectations about the future vary as a function of beliefs held about the past is only beginning to be studied as a topic in behavioral science.[3] Such studies would further help us understand reactions to attempts to change over toward lrsp.

Here, I must speculate in proposing a typology of relationships between past organizational experience and expectations about the future. First, the group sufficiently comforted by the organization's past competence to be able to look at futures. This group divides into those who

---

activity. Man must somehow free himself from the state of change which carries him through life, by keeping the past available through memory and conquering the future in advance through anticipation. This control over time is essentially an individual achievement conditioned by everything which determines personality: age, environment, temperament, experience."

[2] These processes are extensively described in Mead (1934) and Berger and Luckmann (1966).

[3] One of the few deliberate attempts in this direction is Bell and Mau (1968), especially Part One. Also see the seminal volumes Experimental Symposia on Cultural Futurology, 1970 and 1971.

expect the future to be like the past and those who expect it to be different from the past. The latter group can be divided into those who feel
their organization will be able to operate more or less as it has just because it has been successful and those who foresee a need for radical revision if the organization is to continue to be successful. This latter group
seems to be very small, but if lrsp is to gain support, it will come from
these people. We need to understand better the source of such ego strength,
of such a broad appreciative setting. Second, those who are sufficiently
discomforted by the past performance of the organization to be apprehensive about the future. These people either will avoid attending to the
future or will attend to futures that are sufficiently like the present to keep
their apprehensions at a level that allows them to go on doing essentially
what they have done. Probably a few people who are discomforted by
the past performance of the organization can nevertheless look at radically
different futures and recognize that their organization is obsolete or will
die. But they do not publicly acknowledge this awareness, except occasionally as a prophetic incitement to radical self-renewal. Certainly such
predictions are not expressed by members of government agencies.

The degree to which identification with selected aspects of the
organization's past affects the capacity to seriously consider really different
futures would seem likely to be more highly correlated among successful
than among unsuccessful senior personnel. For one thing, they are more
likely to have a longer history with the government agency, and because
of their success in rising toward the top, their self-images are more closely
bound to the agency's history as they construe it. For another, a successful
career has usually also required learning to hew to the agency line. "Overall, careerism probably is an important discourager of creativity, innovation, and risk taking because of the perceived or imagined dangers of
stepping out of line. And insofar as it assures that the older officers within
the system will hold the top positions of the agency, it assures continuity,
stability, and conservatism in agency policy" (Mosher, 1971, p. 58).[4]
Crudely put, most senior personnel will tend either to perceive that the
future will be like the context in which they succeeded (else their sense
of continuing to be successful would be threatened), or they will believe
that the future will be different but the means for organizational success
will be the same. For such people the idea of changing over to lrsp from
the mode in which they were and are successful would probably be repressed or ignored. In this light I would expect encouragement to move
toward lrsp to come mostly from outside the organization via consultants

---

[4] This article argues for and specifies major changes in public service,
training, and rewards that derive from a view of what is happening and what
needs to be done that is thoroughly compatible with what is proposed here.

or newly arrived members in the bureaucracy, from its political super-structure, or from legislative or executive directives. And this is the way the process seems to have operated.

Those senior members who can face the threats to their organization and themselves that the future seems to hold, and who can appreciate the need to move away from conventional operations toward lrsp, will be an innovative stimulus. So far, these people have been far more evident in private organizations than in government. To what degree being innovatively future-oriented though senior in the organization is a matter of personality and to what degree it is a matter of organizational structure and history are unknown, though both doubtless play a part.

The Consequences of Future-Thinking as a Threat to Competence

Trying to think seriously about the future poses another challenge to one's sense of competence: additional complex and unfamiliar information must be absorbed and incorporated. As I emphasized earlier, this information will be ambiguous, intricate, and incomplete in contrast with the articulated construction about one's personal and organizational past that most people probably hold (at least if we accept the memoirs of successful people). A future different enough from the past to require a different way of dealing with it by that very fact requires a shift in one's appreciative setting. Thinking oneself into the future requires the ability to think dialectically and cybernetically; that is, to think not only about trends but also about counter-trends and about the trends that grow out of the contrasts between these. My experience, and it is shared by others who try to help people think about institutional and social change, is that very few people are able to think this way. Recognizing one's limits, especially if one has been successful thinking in a linear and disjointed manner, is most disconcerting. As a result, in order to avoid recognizing their incompetencies most people probably avoid exposing themselves to situations in which they need to think dialectically.[5] And all this competence-challenging input from the future must be dealt with in the midst of an already information-overloaded situation. "Each schema derives its meaning both from the experiences which it subsumes and from its relation to other concepts similarly developed. Changes which would shake

---

[5] That people attend seminars and lectures on the future is not incompatible with this conjecture. Listening to someone else do the thinking is not the same as trying to do it oneself. Nor is participating in a workship on how to think about the future, which is likely to consist of the blind leading the blind. And too, as mentioned earlier, many presentations about the future emphasize bits and pieces so there is no need for the participants to think dialectically and cybernetically about social trends.

this conceptual system are resisted with vehemence proportionate to the extent of the threat; and the extent of the threat varies . . . with the nature of the change involved. It is minimal when the change is by differentiation within an established concept; greater when it comes through the recognition of a wider category under which several established concepts can be subsumed; and greatest when it involves the dissolution of a concept and the distribution of its contexts among others" (Vickers, 1965, p. 68).

But not only does attention to a future that is not a projection of the characteristics of the past and its present (including the relationship of the organization to the past) increase information overload. This information, by its incompleteness, differentness, and inherently conjectural nature, must, if paid attention to, increase the recipient's uncertainty about what it means, about what to do, and inevitably about who one "is." While it is this very uncertainty that makes planning necessary, it also makes many people tend to avoid recognizing it or to do so in ways that autistically attempt to reduce it. As R. Wohlstetter (1962, p. 397) observes: "There is a good deal of evidence, some of it quantitative, that in conditions of great uncertainty people tend to predict that an event that they want to happen actually will happen."[6]

One could argue that such autism occurs only under conditions of great uncertainty. However, in the experience of a number of observers, persons usually attend to those forecasts in future studies which are compatible with what they want to happen or which they believe they can cope with because of experience with past situations. Perhaps this is because it is organizations which are already sensing increasing uncertainty that commission such studies—which then add too much to their uncertainty for adaptive responses. A typical example emphasizes this important point. I was present at a long, detailed presentation, based on sophisticated and extensive data about the present and past, that was the basis for what was to be a long-range planning effort by one of the largest and most technologically sophisticated American firms. After this semipublic briefing I commented (in private) to the chief of the project that if he considered some alternative plausible intervening events over the next years, his picture would come out drastically different. Expressing both annoyance and astonishment at my misunderstanding of his situation, he pointed out that if his company took those possibilities seriously, it would be out of business. (And so, I dare say, would he, if he pushed such alternatives.)

Future studies can thus expose latent uncertainties. This exposure can and occasionally does encourage a reallocation of effort in the light of

[6] Also see Webb (1969, pp. 39–40).

those previously unrecognized contingencies. But more often the exposure of latent uncertainties is resisted or ignored simply because they add too much to be attended to; often they expose plausible future weaknesses in present arrangements, weaknesses that would require more pain and effort to correct than anyone wants to invest, especially if things are going well. The social costs are seen as too great and the view of the future as subject to change anyhow. "I say let my successor worry about it if these things happen. I've got problems enough putting out our stuff today. Besides, 'today' is what my boss is worried about—spending *this* year's dollars." Fear of exposure of latent uncertainties helps generate resistance to paying serious attention to future studies.

Future Studies as a Source for Myths

Whether feedback from studies about the future will contribute deliberately or unintentionally to the creation of new and compelling mythologies remains to be seen. And I am not using myth in a deprecatory sense here. All coherent systems of belief are self-validating: they provide their members with directions and inspiration about what to pay attention to and why it is important to do so.[7] "The process of myth-forming is essential to mental health. Since myth is man's way of constructing interpretations of reality which carry the values he sees in a way of life, and since it is through myth that he gets his sense of identity, a society which disparages myth is bound to be one in which mental disorientation is relatively widespread" (May, 1969, p. 192). The social psychological pressures to create new myths are already strong. Contributing to them will be the tension between the need to appreciate alternative futures as a basis for lrsp and the inability of future studies to give assurances about what the future will be. One plausible way to resolve this tension, to fulfill the intense wish to reduce uncertainty under conditions that are likely instead to increase uncertainty, is to become committed to a myth about what can be, and, inspired by that vision, to make a commitment to actions that increase the likelihood of realization. (In a sense, this is D. Gabor's 1964 thesis, emphasized in his book title, *Inventing the Future*.) F. Polak (1961, p. 124) offers historical support for this position:

There is little doubt, to my mind, that the creative images of the future of Zoroaster, Isaiah, and Jesus, of Plato, Paul, Augustine, and Joachim, of Bacon, More, and Marx, etc., have through the centuries made the cul-

[7] On the function and unavoidability of myths, see Novak (1970); May (1959 and 1953); and Campbell (1968 and 1969), especially Parts II and VI.

tural history of the future. The Greek poets, thinkers, and dramatists, as well as those who rediscovered and revived them in the times of the Renaissance, ushered in a new time, just as the English and French philosophers of the Enlightenment foreshadowed and helped to bring about a revolutionary epoch, the German chiliastic-idealistic philosophers an evolutionary epoch, and Nietzsche and Spengler a reactionary epoch—all through their images of the future. . . . The spirit of their own time spoke through these visionaries, it is true. But the goal-directed energy potential which they generate also determined to a significant extent which future out of a number of possibilities in a situation still open and fluid would become a part of the actual historical chain of events. They were not only prophets, but also agents who assisted in bringing about that which they predicted. Themselves under the influence of that which they envisioned, they transformed the non-existent into the existent, and shattered the reality of their own time with their imaginary images of the future. Thus the open future already operates in the present, shaping itself in advance, through these image-makers and their images—and they, conversely, focus and enclose the future in advance, for good or for ill.

While subscribing to a myth about the future would to some degree be unintentional, it need not be exclusively so. "We do not make myths or symbols; we rather experience them—mainly unconsciously as the source of the images of the charter of the culture, such as the values, the goals, and the identity. By becoming conscious of the processes we can, however, mold our myths and symbols" (May, 1969, p. 193). Traditionally, and to some extent today, we deliberately expose ourselves to great theatrical and literary myth-derived drama to be inspired and informed and in some sense changed in our appreciative setting. We might choose to do so with conjectures about the future, themselves an art form with their own dramatic trappings of complex and impressive rationalistic methodology. The problem is to encourage the inspiring, committing, and informing contributions of myth without loosing our capability to reexamine it and revise it. I do not know how this might be done. Perhaps it cannot be done. Perhaps the important thing is trying, for the effort should change both thought and behavior. Or perhaps we would not need to revise the myth that should grow from concern with the future—the myth that a future in which future-responsive societal learning would be the norm is both desirable and attainable.

IX

How Changing Toward LRSP Intensifies Role Conflict and Role Ambiguity

As turbulence flows into the organization via feedback from the present and the conjectured future, it will upset the definition and compatibility of the roles in which people perform their organizational functions and find an important part of their definition of self.

Social process [can be regarded] as an interaction of positions patterned in terms of these complementary expectations [about rights and duties] which are themselves called roles. Thus, role and its personalistic correlate, identity, represent the implications of social position incumbency and can be comprehensively described only with reference to other roles which bear a complementary relation to the focal role.

. . . since persons occupy multiple positions in life and are only partly involved in any single position they occupy, they have multiple identities that combine in various ways to affect their views and the enactments of their singular roles. And, whatever else may be involved, the modes of a man's participation in structured social intercourse will be reflected in his concept of himself and in the fabric of his personality.

. . . Roles are social phenomena—no doubt of that. However they are not only external 'demands,' they are dynamic interactional processes carried out by individuals who color their performances personal. By way of reciprocity, however, through their identity implications roles become operationally integral to individual personality. Thus, roles more than link the individual and the social (or structural), they unite them [Lichtman and Hunt, 1971, p. 51].

The Significance of Role Conflict and Role Ambiguity for Lrsp

Relatively stable organizational situations supply many psychoogical rewards for most people through the security they find in knowing who they are, which results from knowing what they are supposed to do and vice versa. The sources of this satisfaction run deep indeed. A predictable place in which to be a predictable person among predictable persons, offering comparatively predictable access to survival resources of money and friends, is the antithesis of the precarious condition of fighting to survive individually in an unpredictable, hence dangerous, world of scarce supplies. Of course, vigorous organizations, including government agencies, are not completely tranquil and life in them and the roles in which it is played out are by no means totally stable. Some activities, such as those in the Secretary's office of a federal agency are comparatively transient, often in turmoil, and roles may be full of conflict and highly ambiguous. Indeed, the role stresses and strains of that working situation exemplify what lower levels in the bureaucracy might be like if faced with the requirements for changing over to lrsp. And changing toward lrsp would, of course, add greatly to the role performance complexities in offices that now operate like those at the Secretary's level. We need to look, then, at the kinds of role conflict and role ambiguity with which the requirements for lrsp would additionally burden organization members. For the personal strains thus produced among people with no stomach for the hustle and hassle of a "political" office—and often, eventually, among those who do seek such activities—would absorb energies needed for substantive tasks and could sap loyalties and commitment, stimulate painful self-searching and questions of identity, confuse communication, and lower trust. Therefore role conflict and role ambiguity will exacerbate other threats to self and organization such as those that arise from increased uncertainty, increased error, and increased organizational and environmental turbulence. Such consequences from excessive role conflict and role ambiguity would inhibit changing over to lrsp.

Role *conflict* exists when the role incumbent tries to carry out role-performance directives, from persons he perceives as legitimate role-definers, that require what he believes to be incompatible behavior—the two-boss phenomenon is an example. Role conflict also arises when carrying out one's role in fact conflicts with the role performance of others. Role *ambiguity* "is conceived as the degree to which required information is available to a given organizational position. To the extent that such information is communicated clearly and consistently to a focal person [the role incumbent], it will tend to induce in him an experience of certainty with respect to his role requirements and his place in the organization. To the extent that such information is lacking, he will experience ambiguity. The relationship between the objective condition of ambiguity and the intensity of the ambiguity experience for a certain person will be modified by various properties of personality" (Kahn and others, 1964, pp. 25–26).

Role conflict and role ambiguity produce serious personal stresses and their reflections in performance have serious organizational consequences:

[*Role conflicts*] *generally have the following effects on the emotional experience of the focal person: intensified internal conflicts, increased tension associated with various aspects of the job, reduced satisfaction with the job and its various components, and decreased confidence in superiors and in the organization as a whole.*

The strain experienced by those in conflict situations leads to various coping responses—social and psychological withdrawal (reduction in communication and attributed influence) among them [pp. 70–71].

The ambiguity experience is predictably associated with tensions and anxiety . . . and with a reduction in the extent to which the demands and requirements of the role are successfully met by the role occupant [pp. 25–26].

. . . the presence of conflict in one's role tends to undermine his relations with his role senders, to produce weaker bonds of trust, respect, and attraction. It is quite clear that role conflicts are costly for the person in emotional and interpersonal terms. They may also be costly to the organization, which depends on effective coordination and collaboration within and among its parts [p. 71].

What is more, studies conducted at the Institute for Social Research have demonstrated that management and administrative job stress, in part the product of role conflict and ambiguity intensified by responsibility for other people (who themselves are struggling with role conflict and ambiguity), "are primarily responsible for many of the chronic diseases that have been hitting American males hard in middle age, notably the big one, heart disease" (McQuade, 1972, p. 102).[1] And hardest hit are those hard-driving "compulsive" organizers and controllers commented on earlier.

In all, the stresses and consequences would seem most serious for precisely those kinds of people who would be involved in initiating and innovating the change-over toward lrsp:

Of the various forms in which role conflict is encountered, two emerge as characteristic of the high-conflict, innovative roles: interpersonal conflict and intra-role conflict. Each of these takes a special guise in such cases. The interpersonal conflicts of the innovator are fought out around his proposals for innovation, a kind of continuing battle of new guard versus old. The intra-role conflicts of the innovator stem from his engagement and commitment to the creative, nonroutine aspects of his job and his corresponding disinterest and disdain for the routine or uncreative demands placed upon him; as a result he experiences a conflict between these two categories of role requirements, both legitimate and unavoidable, but only one truly ego-satisfying [Kahn, 1964, p. 127].

. . . role conflict is greatest where the prevailing expectations in role set emphasize low rules orientation, low closeness of supervision, and low universalism—that is, in groups which deviate from the general organizational norms in the direction of permissiveness, autonomy, and a willingness to deal with people in individualized, personal terms. Moreover, the tension scores of focal persons are significantly higher in role sets which deprecate orientation to rules and closeness of supervision [Kahn and others, 1964, p. 161].[2]

In view of these unpleasant consequences we can expect people to try to avoid the stresses of role conflict and ambiguity by resisting those changes that produce them or are expected to produce them—in our case, changes associated with changing toward frsl. But those who would be asked or compelled to change will not be the only ones who may come to resist in order to avoid more role stress: those who seek to move toward lrsp will find themselves caught up in unexpected role stresses which may well undermine their enthusiasm. Most of the roles in organizations that attempt to change over will be subject to alterations. How to reconstitute them and how to relate them one to another in less conflicting, less ambiguous, ways will be a major learning task for organizations trying to move toward lrsp.

[1] Also see French and Caplan (1970).
[2] On this general topic, also see Hunt (1967).

In this chapter we will not look at specific role changes. Instead we will look at some special contributions to role conflict and ambiguity, contributions made by the turbulent environment on the one hand and the requirements for lrsp on the other, that will have an impact on many roles. We will look at conflicts and ambiguities engendered by arguments about what constitutes role legitimacy, role competency, and role responsibility under such circumstances. In what follows I will conjecture about situations that will probably arise from the conflicting and ambiguous messages role incumbents receive from relevant role-information "senders," including themselves. These ambiguities and conflicts will express themselves within the receiver, who perceives or anticipates them as conflicting or ambiguous messages, and at the performance level when interaction with others performing their roles is experienced as ambiguity and conflict. Both anticipated and experienced role conflict and ambiguity will be stressful. Moreover, at this stage when there is so little experience with actual efforts to change toward lrsp, it is more useful to anticipate logical or social psychological conflicts or ambiguity than to anticipate specific operational ones. Then, too, in other chapters, many of the generalized situations to be discussed here will be recognizable as more specific operational situations in which role conflict and role ambiguity (also to be called "role stress") will be rife. A purpose of this chapter is to aid in that recognition.

Role Stress from Challenges to Legitimacy

There is a widening challenge to the legitimacy of any established organization's purposes, priorities, and procedures that seems to be a concomitant of our contentious, complex, and intensely communicating society. Who has the right to do what (including planning and making demands) about what, and for or to whom, is increasingly an open question. While some challenges derive from generational differences, increasing challenges to legitimacy that are not at all generation-bound come from within and without organizations.[3]

Since people live both overlapping and conflicting roles, at least in their larger lives, questions of legitimacy will challenge them in their organizational roles as well as in their roles outside of the organization. Some people will face new problems in justifying their organizational roles to those outside; some will have an increasing problem justifying their organizational role to themselves, when they see themselves from the vantage point of their other roles.[4] This does not mean that people are

---

[3] See Slater (1970) and Bell (1970).
[4] A little studied but often commented on example of this may be seen

unable to reconcile roles or that all members will recognize themselves to be in conflict situations. But it probably does mean that the broader the educating experiences of the role incumbent (and those involved will have increasingly broad experience), the greater likelihood there will be of being in conflict or the more difficult the task will be of legitimizing oneself to oneself.[5] That is, some of the very kinds of people who will seek to facilitate changing toward lrsp are those who are complex enough in character and intellectual attainment to be unable to aviod self-doubt and self-searching regarding their own efforts to cope with difficult and inter-dependent ethical, operational, and interpersonal problems. Of course, others seeking to implement lrsp will not be so burdened. Those whose personality or skills tend to make them indifferent to or obtuse about questions of legitimacy will be indifferent to or resentful of such challenges. (Those who find their rewards in designing and applying highly quantitative, logical, and technological approaches to social problems seem more prone to this reaction. But not all of them are, of course, nor do such professionals have a monopoly on indifference or obtuseness.) And some who by training or temperament could be susceptible to challenges to their legitimacy may find the additional uncertainty about self and situation others introduce too much to bear to pay attention to them.

An inability to see one's own legitimacy as properly open to question will distort the use of feedback from the environment. A self-image that is so self-protective that it cannot seriously attend to self-questioning about legitimacy is too defensive to work in ambigous situations in the trusting, feeling-laden, and supportive manner necessary to understand and constructively live with questions of legitimacy. Rather than becoming learners about legitimacy issues, they are likely to blame others for raising or responding to legitimacy issues while they pursue more rigid planning styles. Between the responders to and the rejectors of legitimacy challenges will arise some of the most difficult and divisive interpersonal issues that will complicate role definitions within and between organizations. We have already seen this in the anguished and embittered divisions in some universities that are the result of different faculty members siding differently with student demands, demands that often repudiated the legitimacy of the faculty and administration to make certain decisions or to maintain decision-making arrangements that excluded students. And student groups have been chronically split over what constitutes legitimate means of representation for their group.

---

in those administrators, executives, and professionals who have become disen-chanted with "the system" to which they contribute by exposure to criticism from their children experienced in their role as fathers.

[5] On education for these experiences, see Erber (1970), especially Part III.

W. Rein (1969) has reviewed some dilemmas of legitimacy associated with planning, that is, with the legitimation of roles performed in furtherance of particular planning strategies:

[There are] three strategies that reformers and planners rely on to legitimate their actions. Each appeals to a different aspect of the democratic process: the need for consensus among elite institutional interests; the reverence for science and fact; and the validation of pluralism, diversity, and conflict on which democracy depends for its vitality. The dilemma seems to be that reform that works with the establishment, searching for a consensus, tends to lose its soul and its purpose. It abandons its real feeling and commitment for the poor as it sacrifices innovation and reform for survival and growth. Yet, any program that is based solely on a fight for the rights of the poor and that fails to work with established institutions not only is likely to create conflict, but also may fail to generate any constructive accommodation that can lead to real reform. Organizing the poor on a neighborhood basis cannot achieve very much fundamental change. Vision is limited to issues around which local initiative can be mobilized; most typically there is failure to give attention to broad social and economic policy. Research can interfere with both functions, for it can be used, in Gouldner's graphic term, as a "hamletic strategy" or delay and procrastination, responsive to political realities, while avoiding action that will provide authentic services for the poor. Research can compete with reform for resources, and it may pursue competing aims. The documentation of social injustice, which seeks action by confrontation, may embarrass the bureaucracies and make cooperation with the reformers more difficult. But without research, without some kind of objective analysis of the consequences of action, social policy moves from fashion to fashion without ever learning anything. It is, after all, useless to continue to create innovations and to spread new ideas if one never checks to see whether the new ideas and innovations are mere fads or whether they do indeed produce any kind of demonstrable change.

How then can these dilemmas be resolved? The answer, I believe, is that they cannot, for the contradictions are inherent in the nature of American social life.

. . . The search for a welfare monism that rejects pluralism and conflict only fosters utopian illusions. When all three strategies are pursued simultaneously in the same organization, internal conflict develops over time.

. . . Fragmentation of function does not, however, resolve the dilemma; it serves only to exacerbate the problem of interorganizational relationships as lack of coordination becomes a perpetual crisis [p. 242].

Another kind of dilemma will arise for members of an organization who are loyal to it because it is trying to move toward lrsp, but who voice questions about legitimacy of the sort Rein delineates. They may weaken motivations in others to persist in the effort or they may find themselves rejected or muffled for offering unwanted "internal" feedback:

It must be realized that loyalty-promoting institutions and devices are not only uninterested in stimulating voice at the expense of exit: indeed they are often meant to repress voice alongside exit. While feedback through exit or voice is in the long-run interest of organization managers, their short-run interest is to entrench themselves and to enhance their freedom to act as they wish, unmolested as far as possible by either desertions or complaints of members. Hence management can be relied on to think of a variety of institutional devices aiming at anything but the combination of exit and voice which may be ideal from the point of view of society [Hirschman, 1970, pp. 92–93].[6]

To leave the organization removes the possibility of eventual influence from inside (though, perhaps one might be more influential outside). Yet to remain quiet and let the legitimacy dilemmas remain unappreciated would undermine the very purposes which make the effort to try to move toward lrsp worthwhile in the first place. If there is a way to cope effectively with these dilemmas it is apparently in some other normative context than the conventional one. Perhaps it is a context that emphasizes future-responsive societal learnings. Certainly it will take much societal learning to find out.

Thus, at the very time lrsp could become important as a way of evolving new, legitimate organizations and activities, those espousing such developments will have to cope with a heavy psychological burden of challenges to *their* legitimacy from themselves and from others in their organizations and environments. One's sense of competence in one's role probably decreases with a sense of increased uncertainty. One's sense of satisfaction with one's competence probably decreases with challenges to one's legitimacy if one is responsive to those challenges. But legitimacy helps reduce uncertainty about who one is and what one is doing. So questions of legitimacy, added to other sources of uncertainty that result from opening the organization to feedback as required by lrsp, will increase role ambiguity. But role incumbents become defensive and rigid in order to avoid feelings of increased uncertainty. As rigidity increases, so

---

[6] This is a unique and seminal exploration of the dilemmas and trade-offs arising from emphasizing or combining ways of expressing dissatisfaction with an organization from within and without. In the same spirit, see Flacks (1969).

too would resistance to assuming the learning mode required to learn new roles. If those espousing lrsp cannot feel legitimate, or cannot believe they are seen as legitimate, they will suffer a grave deficit in the motivation needed to undertake the role relearning they will need to do. And since legitimacy carries with it definitions of accountability, questions of legitimacy will raise questions about who and what is accountable. This, too, will increase role ambiguity and uncertainty and the likelihood of the counterproductive consequences associated with that anxious state of mind. The interdependent personal costs and benefits of role ambiguity and role conflict are usefully described in the following observations about their effects on personnel in a corporation undergoing major changes:

> *Moreover, and equally important, the insecurity attached to ill-defined functions and responsibilities and status, by increasing the emotional charge of anxiety attached to the holding of a position, increased also the feeling of commitment and dependency on others. By this means the detachment and depletion of concern usual when people are at, or closely approaching, the top of their occupational ladder, the tendency to develop stable commitments, to become a nine-to-fiver, was counteracted. All this happened at the cost of personal satisfactions and adjustment—the difference in the personal tension of people in the top management positions and those of the same age who had reached a settled position was fairly marked. Such a cost seems, in the present state of knowledge about the effective operation of working organizations, to be an inescapable element of successful adaptation to growth and change [Burns and Stalker, 1961, p. 135].*

Role Stress from Challenges Concerning What Constitutes Competent and Responsible Performance

At least some of the issues discussed below about what constitutes competent and responsible role performance are perennial arguments unsolved or variously solved in conventional organizations. They are reiterated here because they will be intensified under conditions of trying to introduce lrsp. This will be due partially to the state of the environment and partially to difficulties in shifting appreciative settings from anticipating lrsp as social engineering to anticipating it as a means for societal learning. These circumstances will make roles even more conflict-laden and ambiguous, thus generating more internal and external upset. This will increase the threat to the sense of competence held by those required to change, and also by those seeking to induce change, who will thereby have responsibility for the managerial confusion their change efforts will generate.

First, these different definitions of what constitutes competence and responsibility will come from philosophical differences, ambiguous research findings, and contending normative theories, rampant among one's professionally connected role senders, as these are reflected in journal articles, graduate school curricula, training seminars, job specifications, conference speeches, and so on.[7]

A second source of differing definitions of role competence will be pressed by special interests in the organization's environment: protest groups, consumer groups, advocate planning groups, and other volunteer organizations.

Third, conflicting and ambiguous role definitions will arise *within* some of the role incumbents themselves as a result of contending definitions of competency and responsibility that cross the boundaries between their work situation and their environment "outside." Many professionals who will be drawn to or are presently engaged in trying to encourage change toward lrsp will, out of those very motives, identify themselves with an overlapping, intertwining world in which role distinctions will be increasingly blurred as between work and color, work and gender, work and religion, and work and community. Persons become persons by combining their perceptions of other people's perceptions of who they are with their own definitions of who they are. Therefore, these other role definitions will often be in conflict for priority and emphasis with those definitions conventionally operating in the more narrowly defined work situation. In earlier times, when there were fewer socializing agents that strongly influenced one's sense of self and when there was more consistency between the self-definitions signaled to the young person by his or her socializing agents (parents, ministers, teachers, and heros), there probably was more compatibility between roles in and outside the work situation, even though there was usually some conflict. But with the multiplication of socializing agents to include the media, especially television, and peer groups, and with the multiplication of contending value systems and legitimacy criteria, the conflicts are likely to increase, the more so for the people involved in efforts to forward frsl, given the likelihood that they will have been exposed to richer and more various socializing experiences.

Fourth, conflicts and ambiguities about responsibility and competence in role performance will arise from contending definitions pro-

---

[7] A most perceptive exercise in delineating different definitions of role competence is in Archibald (1970). Also see Gans (1970, pp. 239–245).

vided by the political structure. This will be a crucial source of stress for
public agencies and for organizations that are dependent on government
for funds or legitimation. There are certain to be contradictory messages
from political superiors, constituencies, and from professional colleagues
about the utility or disutility of risk-taking, error-embracing, and uncertainty-acknowledging in a political setting which itself will be changing.
There will be an abundance of conflicting messages about whether the
competent and responsible participant in efforts to move toward lrsp
should emphasize political savvy or technical competence, along with injunctions to excell at both. Also central will be conflicting messages regarding the primacy of loyalty to the president's administration or the
government agency versus loyalty to the problem or to the constituency.[8]
Issues of legitimacy, competence, and responsibility will converge around
the balance between what needs to be done on the basis of professional
beliefs and knowledge and what needs to be done on the basis of political
beliefs and knowledge.

While it is widely recognized that planning cannot be divorced
from politics, that appreciation does not now provide the roles, norms, or
structures for felicitously combining planning and politics (as Rein's
article, referred to earlier, makes abundantly clear). These questions of
role competency and responsibility in a political setting have been informatively explored by others.[9] Our task here is to recognize that under
the conditions we are examining, this source of role stress will be especially upsetting and will probably be avoided, insofar as possible, by conventional obscurantist tactics. To overcome the tendency to resort to such
tactics will require that those who fill the politician's role, whether in the
legislature or appointed by the incumbent administration to run a government agency, must themselves be participants in learning how to change
over to frsl and must be strong proponents for doing so. Since the relationship is by no means invariably dominated by the politicians—they are
dependent on agency expertise for guidance and ideas (and sometimes on
the support of agency constituencies)—the possibility of bringing politicians
into the learning mode need not depend on their unilaterally initiating
decisions to do so.[10]

R. Burco (1971), a young consultant planner, has studied and personally experimented with the differences between the conventional role
characteristics of the competent and responsible "expert" in planning-re-
lated activities and what seem to him to be the requirements for experts

[8] See Hirschman (1970), especially Chapters 7–9.
[9] For a look at the past, see Marris and Rein (1967). For conjectures
about the future, see Marini (1971).
[10] See Peabody and Rourke (1965); also Wildavsky (1964).

who want to try to facilitate movement toward lrsp. His summary of these characteristics helps emphasize the variety of role stresses that will be involved. (As with all such categorizations, the impression of polarized extremes is conveyed too strongly. In reality, neither the old or the new expert is so completely differentiated. Nevertheless the direction of emphasis seems appropriate.)

Old Expert	*New Expert*

Solution Oriented
  (defines a problem in
  terms of a solution)
  bounded
  emphasis on primary effects
  simplifying
  assumption accepting
	Problem Oriented
	  (explores a situation to
	  find the problem)
	  unbounded
	  secondary and tertiary effects
	  complexifying
	  assumption challenging

Question *Answering* Expertise
  professional
  error denying
  surprise-free
	Question *Asking* Expertise
	  extra-professional
	  error embracing
	  surprise embracing

System *Closing*
  elitist
  technocratic
  comforting
  conflict masking
  product oriented
	System *Opening*
	  democratic
	  public
	  threatening
	  conflict exposing
	  process oriented

Organization *Captive*
  protected
  "hired gun"
  institutional
  client-oriented
	Boundary *Spanning*
	  exposed
	  free floating
	  personal
	  issue-opportunistic

Politically *Explicit*
  late in political process
  choice related
  well-defined expectations
	Politically *Ambiguous*
	  early in political process
	  issue formulating
	  uncertain expectations

Three more substantive issues can be discerned in which role stress over the appropriate demonstration of competence and responsibility will intensify:

1. The balance the role incumbent is to set between using and emphasizing, on the one hand, the technical skills of rationalized plan-

ning, and on the other the intuitive skills that transcend or give perspective to the findings and directions forwarded by the techniques and the technologists.

2. The degree to which the role incumbent is expected to attend to ethical aspects of the planning activities he is involved in, beyond and aside from ethical positions forwarded and supported by the ignorant, the naïve, or the practitioners of the conventional wisdom in the organization and its environment.

3. The extent to which the incumbent is expected to be skilled at and encouraging of the use of techniques for facilitating group task competences if these techniques can be expected to result in management processes and interpersonal relationships different from those in conventional operation.

These issues are not new sources of role conflict—organizations pay endless lip service to the obligation to attend to them—but the issues and the correlative challenges to self-images and organizational structure, interlocked through role behavior, will be much more intense than in the past in the setting with which we are concerned.

Consider the first item above. The very nature, variety, and complexity of formal planning technology and the high professional identification of the practitioner-proponent with that technology—an identification established through his intensive training in its use and legitimized by his value commitment to rationality—will strongly tend to make many technologists vigorous advocates, but with a comparatively narrow view of what constitutes a social problem or a social answer. His own advocacy —that he perform his technologist role and that others perform theirs so as not to produce role conflict or generate role ambiguity—will be supported by a general organizational culture bias toward ever greater rationality. This thrust toward greater rationality will be reflected in role definition messages sent to policy-makers by others besides the technologists involved in planning. At the same time, other experts, including that most important and rare expert, the generalist, will be drawing vociferous attention to the very important limits of the technologies, telling executives, planners, and administrators, that competent and responsible role performance requires that they not depend too much on the technology, that they should define role competences in broader or different terms. And various groups in the environment will deprecate those technologies as too rationalized to be responsive to human needs and human aspirations, too confining of the definition of a social problem or its solution. The blends of technique and intuition that role senders will define as acceptable for specifying various decision-making and planning roles will be in

continuing ferment, and those filling the relevant roles will find themselves confused and in conflict.[11]

The question of what level of ethical understanding will be deemed
appropriate for the roles we are examining will be perplexing and abra-
sive. The issue not only revolves around questions of legitimacy but arises
from an appreciation of the growing power humans have to intervene in
their societal processes, even though we are essentially ignorant about how
to anticipate the consequences of our actions; it also arises from a growing awareness that decisions regarding the longer-range future must be
made with full awareness of our ignorance. To be sure, socio-historical
conceptual systems like Marxism and religion make anticipated futures
the basis for present action and for the ethics that justify it. But in the
United States we believed that the future would take care of us, that destiny was on our side.[12] Now that image of the future is changing, and
future conjectures, by presenting us with alternative images of the future,
require that we choose between them. We will no longer be able to act as
if we were ignorant of our options, or as if we expect the future to work
itself out to our benefit. Thus, explicit valuing and choosing between
values will have to become self-conscious acts surrounded by ethical controversy, frought with complexity and emotionality.

The pressures to plan, along with exhilarating and devastating experiences trying to learn to plan, will begin to change our sense of human
priorities and trade-offs, and this will change the ethical bases for choosing one approach or problem rather than another. The very idea of an
experimenting society is rich in ethical dilemmas, at least within the present cultural setting, and those dilemmas would have to be faced and
learned from as attempts are made to change toward frsl (Rivlin, 1971,
pp. 108–119). Which persons or groups are to get which resources for
what ends? Under what circumstances do unborn generations have rights
to survival and amenities that override our own "rights" to alter ourselves
and our natural environment? Differing definitions, arising from self and
from professional, environmental, and managerial role senders, will assert
that decisions should be based on one or another ethic, as we see in the
present controversies over legalized abortion and marijuana. There will be
role competence definitions that stress pragmatic skill over ethics (or
require the capacity to blur ethical distinctions), definitions that stress
action rather than reflection, and so on. Whereas workable ethical systems
have slowly evolved through trial and error, infused with the power and

[11] See Moynihan (1970) for excellent speculations on this; also Archibald
(1970).

[12] An excellent description of United States optimism in this regard is
Heilbroner (1959).

insights of wise people, what some involved in changing over to lrsp will face is the burden of deliberately trying to discover viable ethical principles. This will be a heavy burden indeed for people who have been protected from that obligation by working within large organizations. For some, then, the obligation to be especially enlightened about ethical theory and practice will be a role requirement that is certain to bring them into conflict with others who assiduously try to avoid the introduction of that kind of complication in the performance of their roles.[13]

Accepting a role definition that highly regards the abilities and obligations to encourage and to use interpersonal skills (Chapter Ten) and to sustain the opportunity costs and personal stress involved in using them will be a problem more for those at the top, but it will also be a problem at the middle levels of government organizations. Middle-level managers and administrators will increasingly be exposed to definitions of role competence that emphasize these skills. Some are learning and more will learn these skills as part of their professional training and during their exposure to other professionals in the applied behavioral and management sciences. But for years to come, many effective managers will reject these techniques and will fear exposing themselves to the experiences through which they can be learned.

But to the extent that senior people in an organization are older people, secure in a self-image evolved in conventional organizational-environment settings, they will have more trouble changing their role definitions to include such competences—if they take notice of the conflicting messages at all. Their own role-definition messages tell them that they are where they are because they "get things done" by intellectual superiority, or charismatic domination, or finesse at interpersonal manipulation, or by ruthlessness. A large part of the self-image of their role has to do with their "poker playing" skills and their belief in and ability to capitalize on the organizational norms that made success dependent on such role-performance definitions. Seldom if ever have they been rewarded for sharing power, being open, trusting or engendering trust, or being honest. But interpersonal skills necessary for supporting a learning norm require these competences. And successful development of such group task skills requires allocation of substantial opportunity costs, extending over several years, to learning those skills and restructuring the organization to use them.

Most important, it takes explicit commitment from the top to provide the supportive atmosphere farther down that is needed if the training is to be more than ritual or is not to fade out all together. What little evidence there is makes it clear that the same kind of commitment is

13 See Boulding (1966); also Tead (1962). Indeed, the whole volume and its companion (Lasswell and Cleveland, 1962), are most relevant.

necessary for any serious effort at planning to make any headway.[14] That support means the participation of top personnel in such training or planning efforts. Otherwise the unavoidable message is that those below need it, but those at the top do not. This defeats the very intent of the training because it is always clear to those below that those at the top need the training at least as much as they do. If the top avoids such involvement, then the whole effort becomes defined as ritual, and no one will take the political risks, time, or make the psychological effort involved to learn about themselves and others working in groups in order to gain the greater group task competences such learning can provide. If such training is made obligatory by top management (as it sometimes has been) the purpose is also foiled, because coercion is not compatible with learning the conditions for openness and trust that the training is supposed to provide.

Thus the role definitions which many people at the top accept as applying to them, and which they and their peers apply to each other, will conflict with role definitions advocated by growing numbers of people that top administrators and executives also pay attention to: professionals, clients, some other top executives, highly competent junior executives, consumer spokesmen, and writers for the prestigious media. These will more frequently insist that top people are truly skilled and competent only if they develop interpersonal skills. But the role conflict will become even more poignant and pressing. In all large organizations, and certainly in government, conventional executive role performance requires repressing feelings of uncertainty, to say nothing of not sharing those feelings with others; it requires repressing acknowledgment of error; and it requires discouraging the expression of strong feelings about values. Thus role style will conflict with the psychological need executives will feel to share their distress over environmental and organizational conditions that appear, in their way, to threaten the viability of conventional top management roles.

The Advocate Planner as Exemplar of Some Relevant Role Stresses

These various sources of role conflict and role ambiguity can be more concretely exemplified by summarizing the role stresses confronting the advocate planner working with the poor. (As H. Gans has pointed out, the city planner has always been the advocate planner for the affluent.) The advocate planner, in his exposure to his environment, better exemplifies some potential role stresses for those involved in changing toward lrsp than does the typical conventional planner. (In other ways,

---

[14] See Steiner (1969, p. 94), and the books of Argyris, Bennis, and Likert listed in the References.

of course, his situation is very different.) The advocate planning role is likely to be an important "input" to lrsp in all its phases, and it might well encourage its development by pressuring established organizations to be more comprehensive in their planning. It could, however, also over-load government offices to the point that no longer-range planning would be possible, much as congressional hearings can keep an agency so busy preparing for them and responding to them that nothing else innovative can get done. Either way, the advocate planner, and reciprocally his colleagues within the establishment, will face the following role conflicts.[15]

1. Whereas the planner is trained for using rationalized planning techniques, the advocate planner often has to compromise these skills in order to enable the adequate participation of the poor. This may create conflict between his image of self as a professional and the high salience of his commitment to the "participation ethic."

2. The professional training of the advocate planner (as a planner), and therefore the standards by which he will usually evaluate his competence, involves technical skills, while his work as an advocate planner often involves skills emphasizing group organization and interpersonal skills—that is, skills as an organizer, liaison, or middleman. A related conflict for the advocate planner is between his training, which emphasizes the apolitical and cooperative nature of planning, and his work, which emphasizes the politics and conflict involved in attempting to help his clients.

3. The advocate planner, because he is an advocate, must represent his client's interests even when he knows, from his professional training and orientation, that his client is wrong. This is a particularly acute problem because his refusal to support his client's views would probably jeopardize the trusting relationship he has tried so hard to develop.

4. The perspective of the planner typically involves the larger issues related to communities and the city as a whole, whereas the work of the advocate planner concerns the immediate self-interests of his clients, which may be at odds with his perception of what would promote city-wide betterment and to be the ultimate benefit of his client.

5. While most advocate planners are intellectually oriented and have considerable commitment to the poor, the continuous demands of the poor for evidence of this commitment and the almost total lack of intellectual stimulation from the client may bring about considerable strain for the advocate planner. This strain may foreclose the practice of full-time advocacy planning or the practice of advocacy planning for more than short periods of time (such as a year or two), and either of

[15] This section on advocate planning derives from Guskin, Michael, and Crowfoot (1970, pp. 24–26). See also Kaplan (1968).

these results will exacerbate the potential reference-group conflict discussed below. This may also be true for the advocate planner who is a member of the same ethnic or racial group as his client.

6. At least for the time being, there are considerable potential reference-group conflicts between the advocate planner's planning colleagues and his client. One aspect of this conflict is that long-term rewards for the advocate planner will probably tend to come more from his colleagues than from any specific client. Secondly, the development of his skills as a planner will come as much or more from sharing knowledge with other planners as from working with his clients. Third, the continuing norms of his profession are established by his colleagues, not by his clients. Thus, if there is any difference between the norms, values, and perspectives of his clients (or himself) and his colleagues, the advocate planner who wishes to consider himself as a planner is in considerable intra-psychic (and potentially interpersonal) conflict.

7. A problem related to the reference-group conflict, and probably one of the most difficult problems for the advocate planner, is his client's mistrust of professionals. Since the advocate planner often identifies with his client, he himself may begin to mistrust professionals. This causes conflict for him because he may still simultaneously consider himself a professional and because most of his personal friends (and his major reference groups) are professionals.

8. A gnawing conflict for many an advocate planner would seem to be the growing realization that his actions may not solve the pressing social crises, that the problems are too big to be affected by his commitment and work and that of his clients. This kind of realization is not limited to advocate planners, but it becomes particularly difficult for them to handle because of their strong personal, professional, and ideological commitments to their work.

On the Necessity for Greater
Interpersonal Competence

猫猫猫猫猫猫猫猫猫猫猫猫猫猫猫猫猫猫猫猫猫猫猫猫猫

*A*cknowledging uncertainty, embracing error, and changing roles are not only individual acts calling for intrapersonal strengths and skills. They are, in the context of changing over to lrsp, interpersonal transactions. They depend on reciprocal competence. Feedback from present society and problematic futures will always carry potential threats to preferred programs and to the deeply held beliefs they at least partly incorporate. This ever-present potential for goal and program changes will threaten the survival of socially supportive groupings which are attached to potentially disruptable tasks. Resistance to accepting the conditions that will produce these threats can be lowered only if people have others with whom to share their fear and anxiety and with whom to find the imagination and support to risk experimenting in order to learn anew. But sharing to promote creativeness and learning under such conditions of stress and conflict will depend on trust and emotional support, and these in turn will depend on interpersonal openness. Openness requires the occasion and the ability to express strong feelings: feelings of commitment, fear, enthusiasm, and anxiety; feelings of rejection, anger, hostility, and affection; and feelings attached to ideas, actions, persons, and personal styles of expression. In this chapter I shall emphasize how changing toward lrsp will depend on the ability of people and organizations to sustain far more trust, openness, emotional support, and expression of strong feelings than is conventionally accomplished. Unless people substantially increase their interpersonal competence in these areas, and unless there are changes in organizational structures that will support and encourage such competence, the resistances to meeting the requirements for lrsp will be invincible.

Evidences of Interpersonal Incompetence

In order to better appreciate why interpersonal incompetence will result in resistance to changing toward lrsp, let us look at some research findings in this area. In spite of ritual protest or honest disagreement from people so unaccustomed to interpersonal effectiveness that they do not notice its absence, evidence points one way: to endemic interpersonal incompetence and organizational structures that sustain it when it comes to giving and accepting trust, openness, support, and feelings.

Americans, in general, pay fulsome lip service to all forms of co-operation, teamwork, togetherness, etc. The problem is that there is no social translation of this ethic. Indeed, many observers of the American cultural scene point to the discrepancy between individualism, as expressed in Jeffersonian democracy, and cooperation, as expressed in the original confederation of states. The resultant dilution of both ethics is what David Reisman calls 'antagonistic cooperation': we feign harmony and act autonomy.

This is no easy conflict to resolve. There is a necessary dialectic between the individual and the group, identity and community. . . .

The problem of [horizontal] collaboration presses. As professional workers join large-scale organizations in increasing numbers, as tasks become more complex and interdependent, as diverse specialists come together for relatively short periods of time to solve problems, as responsibilities become too complex for one man's comprehension, new social inventions of collaboration are imperative. . . .

The problems of vertical collaboration stem from qualitatively different stresses than the horizontal type. Predominantly, a superior controls the means to the need satisfaction of his subordinates. From this basic structural fact springs all the difficulties which separate bosses from employees, fathers from sons. Experience and research demonstrate conclusively that subordinates tend to withdraw and/or suppress views that are at variance with those of the boss, invent political solutions rather than engage in joint problem solving, allow their superiors to make mistakes, even when they, the subordinates, know better. For their part, superiors desire an atmosphere of trust in order to encourage authentic communication, but they rarely understand how to create and maintain— or even trust—this atmosphere. Read's (1962) research demonstrates that upward communication depends on three factors: (1) trust between superior and subordinate, (2) the perceived power of the superior from the point of view of the subordinate, and (3) the ambition of the subordinate. To the extent that the superior and subordinate do not trust each other, to the extent that the subordinate sees the superior as having higher power, and to the extent that the subordinate is highly ambitious, upward communication is restricted. In short, power without trust is the main condition of poor communication between ranks [Bennis, 1966, pp. 199–202].

Argyris's (1969) summary of several of his field studies supports and extends Bennis's observations about horizontal and vertical sources of interpersonal incompetence:

Small groups were studied in 10 organizations; 4 of which represented business and industry; 2 represented research and development laboratories; 2 represented consulting firms; 1, a large governmental bureau; and 1, a university executive development program. Twenty-eight groups were studied over time periods ranging from two months to two years. The number of meetings studied for every group ranged from 3 through 20 with the total number being 163. The groups, when studied, were accomplishing a wide variety of tasks such as: discussion and solution of investment decisions, production planning, quality control, engineering, new pricing, personnel problems, foreign policy, long-range planning, new product development, sales promotion, marketing, organizational changes, executive promotions, relationships with the White House, and the development and introduction of mathematical models to the management of business problems. . . . A total of 45,802 units of behavior were recorded [pp. 893–894].

From these studies Argyris infers that:

The interpersonal world of the individuals in the groups studied is one in which individuals tended to express their ideas in such a way that they supported the norms of concern for, or conformity to, ideas. They were significantly less open to ideas and expressed (slightly less so) their ideas in such a way that supported the norms of individuality or antagonism.
       Individuals did not, nor did group norms, support their owning up to their feelings, being open to their own and others' feelings. There was almost no experimenting with ideas and feelings and also no trust existing in the groups. Rarely did individuals help others to own up to, be open with, and experiment with ideas and feelings. People rarely said

what they believed about the important issues if they perceived them to be potentially threatening to any member. They preferred to be "diplomatic," "careful," "not to make waves." Under these conditions, valid information about unimportant *issues (task or interpersonal) was easy to obtain. It was very difficult to obtain valid information regarding* important *issues (task or interpersonal). It was very difficult to problem solve effectively about these important issues since people tended to cover up important information. Also, individuals rarely received valid information about threatening issues. For example, in a study of 199 important influence attempts (among a group of 20 executives over a period of a year), 134 failed and 65 succeeded. In only two cases was honest feedback given about the failures. In all other cases the individual attempting to have the influence was assured that he had succeeded when, in fact, he had not. Of successes, 54 represented influence attempts made by the president. The observers reported that the influence attempts succeeded in that the president got the message across that he wanted. However, in 48 cases the subordinates felt hostile toward him. None of them communicated these feelings to the president.*

The game of telling people what they "should" hear and the consequent lack of valid information understandably led individuals to be blind about their impact upon others [pp. 895–896].

These typical behavior characteristics are sustained by the typical beliefs about organizational efficacy held by people who behave that way:

These data suggest that individuals tend to hold three basic values about effective interpersonal relations. They are:

1. In any given interpersonal relationship or group, the important behavior is that behavior that is related to the accomplishment of the purpose or task of the relationship or of the group.

2. Human effectiveness increases as people are rational and intellective. Human effectiveness decreases as people focus on interpersonal feelings and/or behave emotionally.

3. The most effective way to tap human energy and gain human commitment is through leadership that controls, rewards, and penalizes, and coordinates human behavior.

Individuals "programmed" with these values may be expected to focus on the rational and intellective, to suppress the emotional and interpersonal, and to employ norms that sanction conformity [p. 899].

Argyris, echoing Bennis, further observes:

It is important to note that these values can be shown to be similar to the values implicit in formal organizational design. Apparently any organization that is structured in a pyramidal form, that uses the typical budgetary and accounting controls, that adheres to the concept of specialization, will tend to create a system whose values are identical to the ones described above. Thus the organizations in our society support those values. . . .

We may tentatively infer, therefore, that the "typical" interpersonal universe tends to be populated with individuals, groups, and organizations that tend to create an interpersonal world in which the conditions facilitating effective interpersonal relationships tend to be infrequent. Effective interpersonal relationships tend to be conceived in terms similar to the superior-subordinate relationship. At any given moment, A, if he is effective, is carefully and covertly diagnosing B (since openness is not sanctioned) and is acting on his unilaterally determined attributions about B. The individuals also tend to be blind to the negative impact of their relatively low degree of openness, expression of feelings, risk taking, and the low potency of the norms of individuality and trust. Indeed, they tend to see these concomitants as "natural" [p. 900].

So much for some devastating evidence about the way people typically behave toward one another and the beliefs about appropriate interpersonal behavior: the literature is replete with substantiating research.[1]

It remains to emphasize that it is demonstrably within the realm of normal human behavior for people in groups to be able to be more trusting, open, supportive, self-knowledgeable, and to be able to expose themselves to strong feelings and strong interpersonal conflicts. Argyris reports on some of his research findings as follows:

In 13 T groups that were studied, feelings were expressed in all meetings ranging from 20 to 50 percent of the total observed behavior. Trust f scores represented up to 1 percent of the behavior in 76 percent of the sessions and up to 2 percent of the behavior in 8 percent of the sessions. In 23 percent of the sessions, 1 percent of the behavior was experimenting with ideas. The meaning of these scores is best indicated if it is recalled that no trust f scores and only .001 percent of experimenting with ideas were observed from nearly 35,000 units in the 112 task sessions.

It is also interesting to note that the only mistrust i or f scores were observed in T groups. These data suggest that T groups can produce much more "negative" behavior than regular task sessions. Finally, help-

---

[1] See, for example, any of the works of Argyris, Bennis, Schein, or Rice, or any issue of the *Journal of Applied Behavioral Science.*

ing others to own up to, to be open with, and to experiment with feelings were only observed in the T groups. The T groups began with the typical [interpersonally incompetent] pattern and after several sessions, if successful, developed the atypical pattern . . . in which feelings are expressed and risks are taken; in which helping others to own, to be open, and to experiment occurs; and in which the norms of conformity and antagonism become less potent while the norms of individuality and trust become more potent [i.e., Pattern B behavior].

. . . The phrase "if successful" is emphasized because not all T groups become effective; indeed by our scoring methods a minority develop into Pattern B. Task-oriented groups have also been changed to produce B interaction patterns. The development of Pattern B therefore is not limited to T groups [p. 878].

Such findings are not limited to Argyris's work or to T-group techniques. Other approaches used by other practitioners and researchers have also been effective.[2] Too few definitive tests of these procedures have yet been made and there has been very, very little application undertaken within government. The facilitating organizational structures to reinforce and effectively use the training are for the most part undeveloped, and the conventional rewards under conventional arrangements have discouraged frequent and necessarily risky and uncomfortable experiment.

Argyris's observations emphasize that interpersonal incompetence is sustained by the structures within which men express or repress themselves. People need other kinds of interpersonal skill training than they conventionally receive in this society, but organizational structures must be changed to use and sustain that training.

New developments for rational decision-making often produce intense resentment in men who ordinarily view themselves as realistic, flexible, definitely rational. Managers and executives who place a premium on rationality, and work hard to subdue emotionality, become resistant and combative in the back-alley ways of bureaucratic politics when such new technologies are introduced.

These reactions sound paradoxical. Yet they stem from ingrained, almost unconscious processes in American organizational life. Waves of fear, insecurity, and tenacious resistance arise unbidden from the bowels of the organization. Strange but true.

It's also understandable in human terms. It does not happen be-

[2] Recent issues of the *Journal of Applied Behavioral Science* are illustrative. See also Rice (1965).

cause men are stupid. It happens because of their long and successful education in organizational survival, where they learn deceit, manipulation, rivalry, and mistrust—qualities endemic to our present organizational structures [Argyris, 1970, p. 29].

Bennis (1966) elaborates:

Information and understanding are necessary but not sufficient components for inducing change. More is required if the change is to affect important human responses. For human changes are bound up in self-image and its maintenance and the complicated context of the social life and groupings which help to define and give meaning to the individual's existence. If intended change is perceived to threaten (or enhance) the self-image, then we can expect differential effects. If an intended change is perceived as threatening the social life space of the individual, then safeguards must be undertaken which ensure new forms of gratification and evaluation.

In short, I am saying that human changes affect not only the individual but also the social fabric and norms from which he gains his evaluation and definition of self. It means, quite probably, that thinking solely about the individual's understanding of the change and its consequences is not enough [pp. 175–176].

T. Burns's and G. Stalker's (1961) studies of organizations lead them to the following comments, which emphasize the links between interpersonal incompetence and organizational structure—and in passing emphasize the special stress these contribute when an organization is trying to change itself to respond to a changing environment:

The translation of organizational difficulties surrounding the person into charges which can be made against others, or a technical problem of relationships into an emotional one, is a characteristic human process familiar enough when it is worked out in terms of national or international politics or inter-class or inter-racial conflicts. This is not to say, of course, that the reverse is true, that all emotional difficulties are resolvable into technical problems. Nor does it permit the emotional charges engendered by the process to be written off as irrelevant or superficial. People are often unfair to subordinates and others, ignorant where they assume knowledge, prone to see dangers or hostility in situations where none threatens, or clumsy and insensitive, or selfish, or lazy, and the people with whom they deal will dislike them for it. Yet what we have described was a general process repeated in a number of different firms, with very different casts performing very similar sets of parts. The recurrent ap-

pearance of a number of similar difficulties which were construed by in-
formants in terms of the personal characters of other people suggested
very strongly that the cause lay in what was observably common—the
situation and the organizational vicissitudes of the concern. The origins of
the trouble, also, dated from the introduction of the development group
into the concerns, when, we must assume, there was a general willingness
on the part of top management and the newcomers, to make the new
venture succeed, and at least a chance of gaining the support of the other
members of the concern for an effort aimed at improving its chances of
survival [p. 143].

It is important to reemphasize the effect of organizational structure on interpersonal behavior lest the needed perspective be lopsided. It
must also be emphasized that while there is evidence that people can become interpersonally competent, there is no theory for deliberately designing organizational structures so that, when combined with the operating
requirements for using the organization's technology, members can opti-
mally use their improved interpersonal skills. There are organizations that
have invented arrangements that have led to improvements in their performance and there are others trying to do so.[3] Out of these experiments
and others, informed by the requirements for changing over to lrsp,
should come, slowly, some tolerable theory for designing better systems.
With these should come better chances for the acceptance of the requirements for changing toward lrsp—to the extent that it is interpersonal
incompetence that creates resistance to doing so.

Before examining the implications for organizational structure, it
will be useful to look briefly at specific examples of situations that will
necessitate much greater interpersonal competence if the requirements for
changing toward lrsp are to be met.

Expressing and Coping with Expressed Feelings

Almost all aspects of the requirements for doing lrsp are bound to
elicit strong feelings; this is especially true of goal-setting, evaluation, and
program changes. If there is no opportunity to express feelings in connection with the circumstances that elicit them, they will be displaced into
other activities, thereby complicating and obstructing them.[4] Strongly felt
differences over goals or means which are transformed instead into "logi-

[3] Among these are Thompson Ramo Wooldridge (TRW); Teledyne
Castings; and the National Office of the YMCA.
[4] At his untimely death, A. K. Rice's research at the Tavistock Institute,
London, was emphasizing this phenomenon. For an earlier formulation of the
process, see Rice (1965).

cal" or "political" matters, or which are simply ignored or left vague or unsettled, seem inevitably to rise, wrapped in circumstantial camouflage, to corrode and destroy subsequent programatic efforts and evaluation. Societal learning will not occur under such conditions because, if feelings are treated as if they wern't part of the message or shouldn't be, positive feelings will not be engaged and negative feelings will not be explicitly and constructively included as part of the information needed for choosing alternatives and trading priorities. If feelings are not directly included the activity becomes a charade, a ritual, a game, a means to other ends. Whatever the choices made or actions taken, people will impute intentions that cannot be validated and the occasions for distrust will therefore multiply.

This is and will be especially so in the public arena, where subcultural differences of age, color, education, life style, and income will contribute to different valuings, different feelings about those values, and often different styles of expressing those feelings. The insistence by nonprofessional lay persons that their feelings get into the activities in which they participate with professionals exasperates and threatens the professionals. The professionals' transparently unsupportive or misdirected responses generate hostility and distrust among the lay people. Usually neither group is trained in the skills needed to use feelings constructively. Without such training *either* the expression of feelings or the repression of feelings, as part of the dialogue and issue, tends to increase rather than reduce turbulence and complexity.[5] When professionals—particularly bureaucrats, administrators, managers, and technical consultants—meet among themselves, the problem arises differently. Inside the organization, feelings simply are not verbally expressed, or if they are it is assumed that the person is acting, not "really" feeling. There is no easy way to tell if it is "an act" because the participants are too unskilled at working in group situations involving feelings, too unwilling to trust themselves or others with real feelings, and too anxious to probe more deeply in a situation

[5] Consider the gratuitous complications produced when expressive people impose arguments containing feelings on "establishment" types without also working on the problems raised by the inability of these more conventional persons to deal effectively with emotionally laden messages. However, training *can* help. An extraordinary and so far an apparently successful attempt to facilitate task skills among various representatives of the environment and the guiding organization, by exposing all participants to group process skill training (including the guiding organization's members), has been the Hartford Development Project, under the guidance of the American City Corporation, Columbia, Maryland, 1972. M. Hoppenfeld tells me that the training vastly facilitated working on touchy issues openly and effectively, and as a result generated great commitment to the tasks.

where the probers would not know what they were getting into. "It just isn't done and it's not the way to get things done."

When feelings are excluded consciously or unconsciously, self-respect withers and along with it commitment, willingness, and eagerness to risk the self in learning how to plan in a turbulent society. When strong feelings go unexpressed or remain unengaged because they are successfully (though perhaps inadvertently) ignored by those who should respond to them, they turn back upon their source and enfeeble it. In our culture, emotional depression that destroys vitality and creativity seems to be the usual consequence of not expressing or acting on what one feels strongly. Those feelings of depression arise from the self-disparagement, the self-hate we feel toward ourselves for not respecting our own feelings, for our feelings are the very core of our sense of self.[6] In many people the feeling of self-disrespect is projected outward into feelings of hostility toward the person and circumstances that ignored those feelings. Whatever way, creativity and learning are frustrated and distrust and interpersonal ambiguity are increased—so that changing toward lrsp is further resisted or avoided altogether.

Feelings associated with conflict cannot be eliminated by repressing, obscuring, or ignoring them. But they can be managed productively by making them part of the activity in which they arise. Otherwise they generate further feelings of distrust, self-hate, hostility, or cynicism, and they encourage short-sighted manipulativeness.

Basically, conflict originates from two structural sources: (1) vertical, between ranks; (2) horizontal or between various groups and departments. Bureaucratic strategy for resolving vertical conflicts depends solely on a vague "law of hierarchy," and an unvague implication: when in doubt, the boss decides. The bureaucratic strategy for horizontal disputes depends on the equally vague "law of coordination," with an assist from the "rule of hierarchy" when the former fails. In other words, the boss arbitrates and then rules. There is a third, more informal, rule that is typically practiced as a last resort. The boss calls the disputants together and invokes the "rule of loyalty" for the general good. The "rule of loyalty" is a curious one, for more often than not its effects are undesirable and tensions are aggravated, rather than relieved. One of the basic, but often unrecognized, paradoxes of organizational life is that its chief device of integration tends to induce excessive in-group cohesiveness at the price of intergroup cooperation [Bennis, 1966, p. 199].

[6] This is standard clinical psychology, agreed upon across doctrinaire boundaries. As a starter, see the classic Horney (1937).

When conflicts in feelings are openly acknowledged they become part of information-defining options, expectations, operating styles, and understanding of the valuing and cognitive content of the task. Often they can stimulate new ideas that reconcile the conflict. But whether they do so or not, open recognition of feelings strongly held increases trust and reduces what would otherwise be gratuitous ambiguity and confusion in already enormously complex and uncertain situations.

I am not arguing that because a person feels thus and so those feelings must be the only basis for engaging in the activities comprising lrsp. Far from it. I am arguing that if feelings cannot be openly expressed and effectively included among the factors, contingencies, and circumstances that go into those activities, then two things will happen: those activities will be far weaker in their genesis and effectiveness than they need be; and acknowledging uncertainty, embracing error, setting goals, evaluating programs and so on, as required for social planning, will be impossible because each of these activities would require the inclusion and often the expression of strong feelings.

Offering Support

Interpersonal skills are also necessary to supply the emotional support people need to risk the changes in role that changing over to lrsp requires and to live meaningfully in the midst of the inevitable role conflict and role ambiguity that will accompany change-over efforts. Changing one's roles in the directions required for lrsp means more or less risking reconstruction of one's self-image, and often that is a frightening reconstruction to undertake. The crucial and protean function of boundary spanner (Chapter Thirteen) is bound to be an ambiguous and conflict-laden role, certain to generate strong feelings in both the boundary spanner and in his constituencies, who depend heavily on him for information but fear his comparative autonomy and the potential power he wields through his real or fantasied understanding of what is really going on across the contending and collaborating groups in the organization and outside of it. Effectuating that role will call especially for high levels of interpersonal skill, both by boundary spanners and by those they span. It will take support from others, support that can be trusted to be honest and perceptive in its evaluation of what is happening to the persons who are changing their roles amidst conflict and ambiguity. Honesty and perception require both self-understanding and understanding of others, as well as the skill to combine these into supportive and relevant interpersonal transactions.

Help is another form of support that people in this society manage very poorly. Giving help without patronizing or depreciating the recipient

is difficult for us to do. Receiving help without resisting or feeling sub-
missive in accepting it is equally difficult. People giving help are anxious
about being rejected and people accepting help are anxious about being
dominated. This form of interpersonal incompetence is regularly displayed in almost any group setting when members try to "be helpful" by
introducing an idea or suggestion for advancing the task at hand. Unless
the group has learned how to give and accept help or unless the group
has worked together long enough for its members to have learned how
much they can trust each other at the level of the group activity, a new
idea will be "shot down" by being ignored, attacked, or transformed into
something else without checking with the originator as to what was really
meant. On the other side, the person proffering the idea will do so diffi-
dently, aggressively, or loquaciously, for example, depending on his or her
learned style for trying to overwhelm the anticipated reactions. Indeed,
many persons will not risk offering help or responding to it in order to
avoid the experiences that go with giving or receiving help. More effective giving and receiving of help can be learned by using the techniques
for overcoming the various contributing forms of interpersonal incompetence described here.[7]

In the society envisioned here, and in the face of our very modest
understanding of its dynamics, we shall have to depend on highly imaginative ideas that have little if any support in "hard" data and reliable
theory. Necessarily, these will have to derive from feelings, intuition, and
hunch more than from "logic." A willingness and desire to help by sharing and by urging "way out" ideas, especially those based on intuition,
hunch, and feelings, unprotected by a shield of logic, will depend on the
proposer's estimate of how far he can trust his audience to respond supportively. Putting one's intuitions on the table almost anywhere, and certainly in a government agency, takes courage, trust, commitment, and
high hope. Therefore intuitions are usually presented in disguised form,
as results of logical analysis, or as implications for policy decisions. Thus
disguised they loose some of the stimulation they might otherwise provide
to the intuition of others by appearing to be more solid, less "hunchy,"
than they really are. To offer an intuition or a hunch "raw," so to speak,
would be an invitation to subtle or openly derisive undermining by colleagues who are threatened or offended by the "illogical" source of the
ideas and the emotionally expressive style of presenting them. Indeed,

[7] One of the most striking and effective learning devices available in this
area is a "game" called "The Helping Hand Strikes Again." Invented by
Prof. F. Goodman, School of Education, University of Michigan, it has been used
to teach school children and social workers, among others, how badly people give
and receive help and how to do it well.

under present conditions a person operating in a conventional setting would not even be likely to conceive of a new idea, especially a "wild" one. We will have to learn how to support and encourage those intuitive ideas in formal organizational contexts even though, at the same time, these contexts will be necessarily and increasingly pervaded and legitimized by the techniques and values of professionals who define themselves by their skills in explicit, data-based, logical thought.[8]

Self-Understanding

Self-understanding is a prerequisite for relearning about society and about self and organization as both try to learn *how* to change over to lrsp in order to learn about society. The critical function of self-understanding as a prerequisite for undertaking other personal and interpersonal activities aimed at changing toward lrsp is further emphasized by C. Sofer (1962). His numerous field studies of efforts at organizational change, and his own involvement in them, have led him to propose that, in general, "One of the key events that discourage a group attempting to change is the discovery that significant changes can rarely be made merely by persuading other people to act differently. *Sooner or later one must alter that last sacred object, oneself. Whatever has been said before, or acknowledged at the intellectual level, the impact of this depresses and retards the group*" (p. 156).[9] But that self-understanding can only be learned in relationships with other people. Or more precisely, usually it can only be verified and refined by practicing it in transactions with others. Interpersonal skills are needed to improve self-understanding and self-understanding is needed to improve interpersonal skills. This is not a chicken-and-egg dilemma. Rather it is a dialectical process that requires the opportunity for people to develop both skills through cycles of self-consciously working alone and together to do so. This opportunity requires growing levels of interpersonal trust and the openness of relationships that verify that trust.

The greater A's defensiveness, the less the probability that he will create conditions where he can receive helpful (descriptive nonevaluative) feedback [about his behavior]. However, the greater the defensiveness of B, the greater the probability that he will give distorted feedback to A.

---

[8] This is not a new requirement, of course, but we shall have to meet it much better than in the past if we are to move toward lrsp. For an elegant description of the relationship between logical and non-logical thinking, in connection with decision-making, see Barnard (1938, Appendix, "Mind in Everyday Affairs," pp. 301–322). Also see Gore (1966).

[9] See also Jung (1956, especially pp. 204, 237–238, and 276).

Thus, A is in a human bind. He will not learn unless he is willing and capable of learning and unless B is willing and capable of helping him learn. He will not tend to be willing and capable unless A helps create the conditions in which B will not be highly, defensive. The opposite is also the case. A cannot decrease B's sense of self-acceptance without hurting his own. If A hurts B, B will respond defensively, and the feedback A will receive will either be designed to hurt him or it will be distorted, which may have a negative effect on it [Argyris, 1962, p. 20].

Greater self-understanding is imperative if one is to increase one's ability to recognize and live with uncertainty, through exposure to turbulence and complexity, and to embrace error. Inherent value contradictions and ethical dilemmas that could be hidden from oneself by avoiding uncertainty, denying error, and repressing conflicts about values, goals, and organizational arrangements become all too evident when efforts are made to meet the requirements for lrsp. Struggling inside oneself with value conflicts and ethical dilemmas, and shifting one's appreciative setting and behavior toward self and the world will be a difficult and anxious experience. Without interpersonal support, most will lack the will and strength to risk going along with change-over efforts: they will resist relearning "outside" because they will sense that it will cost them too much "inside."

Subgroup Affiliation

In situations where turbulent environments were mostly shut out and where knowledge was sufficient to maintain a stable relationship between organization and environment, that stability was reflected in the general stability of task groups within the organization. These task groups invariably evolve into sentient groups—groups which provide their members with the social rewards of membership. So great have been these rewards that any reorganization to meet changed tasks has usually been so personally disruptive that person, task, and organization have suffered accordingly. In the situation we are attending to, regrouping will become the norm rather than the exception, and those who participate in change-over efforts will have to learn how to depend less on relatively permanent sentient groups and learn instead how to establish and participate in transient groups that provide the needed social support (Chapter Twelve). W. Bennis and P. Slater (1968) emphasize this and related aspects of this chapter as follows:

As routine tasks become automated, those requiring human participation will increasingly relate to the boundaries of current experience—to inven-

tion, ambiguity, unusual synthesis, catastrophic changes, and so on. This means that the skills required will include larger quantities of creativity, imagination, social perception, and personal insight, and will hence draw upon all layers of the personality with maximum involvement and commitment. Such involvement will tend to drive other social affiliations out —temporary systems will inherently be what Lewis Coser calls "greedy organizations"—but only temporarily so. Instead of partial commitment to a relatively large number of groups over a relatively long period of time, we will see relatively total commitment to a single group over a short time period—the organizational equivalent of 'serial monogamy' (in which a person may have several spouses but only one at a time) replacing a kind of organizational polygamy [pp. 92–93].

This, too, will call for interpersonal skills at quickly establishing trust, openness, and support for and help with feelings and ideas in new or transient group affiliations. A very few research and development firms (which Miller and Rice consider the prototype of this kind of relationship) are already investing in trying to develop such skills.

Trust

In Chapter Fourteen we shall look at the sources of resistance that may arise over changes in the management of the information resources of an organization that would be required to facilitate moving toward lrsp. The resistances have to do with who is to have access to what data and what programs for using the data. This is already a chronic problem, especially with urban data banks. Data give power, and those who have data do not trust those who do not to use data in ways that would protect the interest and aspirations of those who do. Those who do not have the data distrust the interests and aspirations of those who do, and they distrust the motives the data-possessors have toward them. The result, so far, is just what might be predicted in hierarchical, closed, environment-avoiding, error-avoiding systems, which by those very structural and interpersonal conditions discourage trust and openness. The trusting relationships needed to overcome this and related counterproductive conditions cannot be imposed by fiat, and they cannot be created simply by imposing "experiments" in data sharing. Such experiments are being made, but the fundamental distrust apparently continues. The openness and trusting required for changing toward lrsp will have to come about as a general consequence of improved interpersonal skills along with organizational restructuring that would reinforce new norms based on more trust.

Collaboration not only for data sharing but at all stages of lrsp requires what R. Walton (1966) calls "a problem-solving decision process" in contrast to the more familiar "bargaining decision process": "A problem-solving decision process is a joint decision activity that involves full sharing between the units of all mental processes at every stage of the decision process. A bargaining decision process is joint decision activity that involves only sharing of one unit's preferred solution or some overstatement of it" (p. 414).

Walton reviews an array of research and theory and arrives at a number of propositions suggesting that a collaboration which, as a trusting condition, produces flexibility, experimentation, interaction, supportiveness, and positive affect, also further enhances trust. Bargaining produces the opposite situation.[10] As a result, he concludes that "Under conditions of hostility and low trust, persons will adopt competitive behavior strategies in the decision process. For example, one adopts decision patterns which involve furnishing another with less information and less accurate information when one dislikes or distrusts the other. . . . Negative attitudes lead to perceptual distortions, which in turn lead to competitive decision-making. . . . Strong negative affect often leads one unit to interfere with the other unit's activities, just to frustrate the latter's goal achievement" (pp. 423–424).

Nevertheless, distrust is an endemic operative assumption in government processes, as was knowingly delineated by A. Wildavsky (1964) in his description of the various styles by which agencies go politicking for their budgets.[11] There is good evidence that distrust grew in the United States between 1964 and 1969, especially towards politics, peacekeeping, and communications (Rotter, 1971). And whatever other factors lead to confrontation politics, persistent mutual distrust is certainly one of them. Whether distrust *must* always be part of confrontation is unclear. Need different appreciations of a situation invariably engender distrust or could they be the basis for joint learning through societal experimenting? There seems to be no good reason why conflict, if not confrontation, must breed distrust if the conflict is dealt with openly for the purpose of resolving it, of learning from it. To what extent can organizational experiments aimed at generating increased internal trusting be sustained if distrust comes into the organization via those members of the environment involved in the lrsp process? Indeed, to what extent can trust be extended within the organization as more of its members bring into the organizational setting their values and roles rooted in their environmental al-

[10] See, for example, Friedlander (1970), and Deutsch (1949 and 1960).
[11] See Wildavsky (1964). Chapter III, especially, is a fascinating recounting of the various devices by which those in the budgeting process trust each other to misrepresent facts, interests, and needs according to agreed-upon procedures, trusting to "process politics" to come out with the best solution on the average. See Schick (1969) for an incisive dissection of this fallacy.

legiances? These are questions that can only be answered by deliberate efforts to learn how to do lrsp. The problem, of course, is that learning how to do societal learning depends on improving the level of trust in order to undertake that precarious activity. Fortunately, improvements in ability to trust are not impossible to attain. Whether the improvements would be sufficient to permit and encourage moving toward lrsp remains to be seen.

The methods of organizational development alluded to earlier have already demonstrated their usefulness for improving interpersonal competence in a number of corporations and third-sector organizations. However, they have not been used, except for a very few short-lived experiments, in government. If the thesis of this book is correct, the rewards of conventional interpersonally incompetent behavior will become fewer for more people while the pressures to try changing to lrsp will increase. Therefore I expect there to be increased incentives for discovering how to design person-structure-technology systems that reward interpersonal competence, and more incentives for organizations, especially government agencies, to try them out.

Part Three

The Burdens of Changing: Structural and Organizational

Preceding chapters have emphasized social psychological processes that operate within the person, so to speak, or between persons, recognizing that these processes are in important part a reflection of the organizational structures within which these processes are expressed. In subsequent chapters we will deal with changes in the relationships between parts of the organization, and between the organization and its environment, which seem to be required if attempts to change toward lrsp are to be successful. These relationships I refer to as "structural"; they are "systems of specialization, authority relations, and communications patterns" that give coherence to the social processes we abstract as "organizational" (Simon, 1968). There will be social psychological implications for those involved if the requisite structural changes are attempted, and what is accomplished or resisted will depend on how people react to the proposed changes. It will be helpful to begin with a preview of the more direct relationships between the next several chapters.

Since the purpose of lrsp is to serve the environment, not to protect the organization from its environment (though it can help do this, too), we shall look in Chapter Eleven at aspects of the relationship between the organization and its environment. For, even if the primary mission of an organization in the public sector were to become service to the environment rather than organizational survival, as is now the case, the structural relationships between organization and environment would still have to be rewarding for the members of the organization. But there will be problems here. Environmental characteristics should fundamentally affect the structure of the serving organizations, if the situation is to be one of changing toward frsl. Yet efforts to redifferentiate and reintegrate the organization in order to match changes in environmental structure and needs are certain to stimulate resistances.

The following three chapters are especially interdependent conceptually and with regard to the social psychological problems of restructuring organizations for changing over toward lrsp. The chapters deal respectively with three circumstances: the unavoidable existence of both task-oriented groups and personal-need-fullfilling groups (sentient groups) within any organization; the requirement for differentiation and integration of subgroupings (subsystems, divisions, departments) within an organization so that effective responses are made to the environment; and the need for boundary-spanning activities in order to link subgroups within the organization and to link the organization and its subgroups to different parts of the environment. These three circumstances are especially interdependent from the perspective of our concern with social psychological reactions to efforts to change toward lrsp because the turbulent environment and the learning perspective required to try to cope with it will mean that: organizations will have to experiment continuously with changes in subgroup boundaries and functions in response to changes in the organization's relations to its environment; shifts in boundaries and functions will disrupt both task-groups and sentient groups; and boundary-spanning, in order to integrate subgroups and to link organization and environment, will be especially important. But under conditions of uncertainty, turbulence, and role ambiguity, sentient groups become an especially important source of personal security; and boundary-spanning becomes especially threatening for those who are linked, and anxiety-provoking for those who are the spanners. In other words, the structural and task requirements for changing over to lrsp become especially threatening to the means by which people, including administrators and planners, protect themselves from disruption and upset. In response to these threats, a number of sources of resistance to changing over to lrsp are generated. While I shall examine the three topics sequentially, it should be clear that the resistances to lrsp *might* only be coped with through overall personal and structural rearrangements.

Present management systems in government bureaucracies are partially based on statutory and other regulations. These regulations reflect assumptions about the kinds of accountability that are deemed necessary, and they assume that accountability is chiefly ascertainable and demonstrable through conventional control structures. But the requirements to be met, if there are to be changes toward lrsp, will depend on substantially different management styles, styles that forego conventional hierarchical means of control in favor of more self-regulating, self-organizing processes. While this change in management philosophy and structure will be prerequisite for all efforts to change toward lrsp, it will especially require changes in the management of access to information and the input of information. These will be particularly discomforting. The changes in management philosophy and structure needed to facilitate information sharing for lrsp will require the introduction and continuing application of organizational development techniques.

Organizational servicing of the environment will depend crucially on effective arrangements for feeding back information from the environment, as an on-going reciprocal basis for organizational-environmental learning. Environment participation in the solicitation and application of feedback from the environment would, I believe, be prerequisite for establishing a commitment and responsibility to frsl by members of the environment. Present organizational norms, and the structures that sustain and are sustained by them, discourage feedback; hence they make it close to impossible for either the organization or its environment to learn how to plan and what to plan.

Since all the requirements for lrsp imply major structural changes which will increase internal turbulence and uncertainty more than they will reduce it, they will be resisted unless there are changes in the norms sustaining the structures and large improvements in interpersonal competence, so as to make the consequences rewarding or at least acceptable.

XI

Why the Social Environment
and Changing Toward LRSP
Require Organizational Restructuring

Part of the environment may be represented by organizations that act more or less as boundary spanners to the target government organizations. Part may be diffuse, being a collectivity of people who are the deliberate or inadvertent beneficiaries or victims of the organization's activities. This collectivity from time to time may organize into specific interest groups and sometimes into competing groups with the same interests.[1] Here we will limit our attention to conjectures about structural requirements for linking publics and servicing organizations and the implications of these requirements for social psychological resistances to changing over toward lrsp. The primary emphasis will be on how these affect organizations, but I will note, too, some complications for the environment. There is at least another book to

---

[1] I will not review here the large literature on how, to what degree, and how effectively publics make known their needs and wants or respond to the activities or inactivities of the servicing agencies. Nor will I review the large literature on how organizations act so as to protect themselves from control by the environment or act to control the environment. Etzioni (1968) discusses these matters at length and provides a substantial bibliography.

be written on the task of changing over to frsl primarily from the perspective of the environment instead of from the perspective of the organizations related to it. The magnitude of the linking requirement and the need for it are summarized in terms compatible with the approach we are examining by D. and A. Wilson (1970):

> *We live in a culture that focuses on decisions and decision makers. Our status ladder's top rung is for the executive; our highest rewards are for those who make our choices. In emphasizing the opting, we too frequently ignore the options. We relegate to a subsidiary role the generating of the alternatives among which the choice must lie and the testing of whether the candidate options adequately exhaust the possibilities open to us or do justice to our creative powers. In emphasizing the optors, we also too frequently ignore the criteria by which the choices are made. We tend to leave unexamined the unprogrammed pressures that intrude into the decision making process. The spotlighting of the most dramatic part of the action—the decision itself—serves to render less visible the rest of the action; the decision maker, the decisions already existing in the decision making process, and in the yardsticks or pressures by which the choice is made.*
>
> *In order to bring into perspective these overlooked but vital components of choice governing our movement into the future, we must bring before our citizenry the germinal ideas, the research programs, the unfolding trends, the prospective opportunities, the incipient threats, possibilities, probabilities, forecasts—all of the ingredients that go together to generate our options. We must view these ingredients and their implications not when the newspapers tell us that they have arrived as options on the decision makers' desks, but as long beforehand as is possible in order that they may be understood, discussed, assessed, and given appropriate support or opposition according to our preferences. Participation in the generation and assessment of options is the citizen's responsibility in a democracy. Citizen participation cannot be secured only through expression of choice after options are printed on a ballot. By then, the future has to a large degree already been shaped. In an age of rapid change a way must be found for the citizen to participate in the generation and selection of the options [p. 23].*

Certain social trends and circumstances seem especially important as the context for environmental relations with the servicing organization. More educated people, the persistence of differential exposure to the costs and benefits of the society, which are made more evident to more people by increased communications, mean that social protest, consumerism, and other active, organized, and spontaneously acted-out demands by more subgroups in the environment will persist and probably grow. These demands will be intensified by the availability of increased amounts of social indicator data on who is getting, or not getting, what. This expressiveness will be aided by new laws facilitating citizen criticism and demands on government agencies and corporations. Challenges regarding the commitment, legitimacy, and competency of government agencies and corporations will partly be the legacy of endemic distrust of government and large organizations in general. Efforts to avoid changing norms and structures in government and the continuing exposure of incompetence and duplicity will sustain that distrust. The growth in the number of professionals eager to assume advocacy roles means that the public will be able to draw upon a pool of skilled advocates who know what information and services to demand on behalf of their clients and what to do with the information when they get it. Such skilled, activist professionals will stimulate demand as well as represent it.[2]

Both evanescent publics represented by skilled professionals and the more permanent groupings usually represented by organizations, especially voluntary organizations with their component of skilled professionals, will increasingly demand access to public agency planning activities and information about their intentions, on-going programs, and their evaluation. And they will increasingly supply their own data to the dialogue and propose their own plans, as is already happening through such means as advocate planning for the poor and public service investigations à la Ralph Nader.

Some groups will make short-run demands while others will be demanding organizational responses that are long range (though they may not be recognized as such). Meeting demands for immediate actions may really require lrsp, and some allegedly long-range issues may not be long range at all. Certain demands by the poor for immediate remedies and certain demands by the affluent for environmental renewal are contrasting examples. Part of the structuring task will be to arrange organizational-environment relationships so they encourage shifts in time perspectives appropriate to goals, means, and knowledge.

Organizations can respond to these demands by refusing to acknowledge them, by pretending to acknowledge them, or by collaborating with the demanders to cope with the situation.[3] On the face of it, it

---

[2] See Arnstein (1969). On the general question of participation of the environment in determining its future, see Cahn and Cahn (1968); Clark (1965); Clark (1967); Coser (1956 and 1967); Edelston and Kolodner (1968); Gamson (1968); Pickering (1970).

[3] Collaboration could include aiding (or at least not obstructing) the establishment of contending organizations. Contending organizations probably are prerequisite for carrying out a learning approach to understanding and improving our society.

doesn't appear that organizations can pursue the first course indefinitely and still survive. As to the second course, no government agency will be able to secure its internal workings and its data base sufficiently to protect itself against exposure, as congressional efforts to increase public access to information, the Pentagon Papers, and the chronic dribble of exposés and leaked reports amply demonstrates. Organizations will be less able to prevent leaks so long as there is an increase in the number of professionals who are inside the organization but who do not rigidly separate their bureaucratic roles (including their loyalties) from their roles as members of groups in the environment. Indeed, in a crunch, their loyalty will be more likely to go to the "consumer" than to the agency.[4]

The third option, then, would seem to be the one that organizations will have to *learn* to live with, painful as that learning will be, if they are not to suffer the pains of being exposed or displaced by more effective agencies. If they do try to respond, their effectiveness will depend on the capabilities to increase their boundary-spanning resources, to disseminate data, ideas, and plans, internally and externally, and to make the internal shifts in organization needed to respond to changes in present and anticipated clientele, service mixes, and evaluation approaches. This shift will not come easily for most planning staffs, which are already burdened with the overloads that are the result of insufficient financial or statutory support and of outmoded styles of planning. (The director of city planning in one large city expressed the mood of a number of his compeers this way: "There are too many people around to meddle in too many city issues to get anything really in place.") Whatever other organizational functions these capabilities would facilitate, clearly they would be needed to meet the requirements for changing over to frsl.

An example of the structural and associated social psychological transformations involved: In response to advocate planning pressures to do thus-and-so, an agency, an administration, or a political party trying out an frsl approach might state publicly: "We don't know the answers and you can't prove that you do either. The task for both of us is to acknowledge our uncertainties and then design *together* experiments to resolve them." Confrontation and loss of face might be avoided and societal learning advanced thereby. A variation on this position was expressed by C. Argyris: "I wouldn't collect data from a group without

[4] There is a plausible future in which the conservative forces of law and order, catalyzed through people's limited ability to tolerate uncertainty and turbulence, produce a dictatorial system in which the first two alternatives above, are the operative ones. We will not explore that future here, not because I think it impossible or even highly unlikely, but because the purpose of this book is to see if lrsp is possible in some kind of open society, given the resistances to it that will arise from social psychological sources even in an open society.

teaching them how to use the data [including its meaning]. Otherwise they may exploit the data or be exploited by it."[5] Under such circumstances planning groups within organizations or organizations trying to move toward lrsp might gain power, compared to organizations that did not try to move toward lrsp norms, because their relevant environments might see them as repositories of flexibility, open to alternatives and helpful in proposing alternatives.

But reducing public distrust, inventing effective means for members of the environment to participate in societal learning by planning, and overcoming their inabilities and resistances to accepting a learning perspective regarding societal development, especially when the learning delays what is wanted right away, will be very difficult requirements to realize. These environmental change requirements seem even more difficult to accomplish than overcoming organizational resistances to changing toward lrsp. If they cannot be met, it seems to me that the whole enterprise of frsl would be infeasible. It is not possible to say whether society could evolve quickly in this direction. Organizations have not made this their mission because it has not been a purpose of society to adopt or implement a goal of future-responsive societal learning. If organizations adopted an uncertainty-acknowledging, error-embracing stance, some members of other organizations in the environment would probably find it easier and more worthwhile to wait out the evolution of programs while still supporting and being involved in serious evaluation of those programs and their goals. Also, if an organization were trying to change toward lrsp, those organization members who also had strong roles in the environment could urge a supportive stance and help shift environmental appreciation to the need for frsl without appearing to have been co-opted. Obviously, the whole of society could not change over at once, but it is not clear that parts of it could not change enough to begin to find it rewarding to continue to do so, and hence find themselves in a positive feedback mode that would accelerate the acceptance of frsl. (See the Epilogue.)[6]

The other component of the environment that will require new structures if lrsp is to be attempted is the one comprised of other organizations: other government agencies, voluntary organizations, legislatures, and non-governmental providers of funds. In examining this component

[5] Informal lecture at the Institute for Social Research, University of Michigan, 1971.

[6] On changes needed in structure and in the performance of the environment in order to allow more effective policy-making, see Chapters 19 and 21 in Dror (1968). Note that the changes Dror proposes would require a shift to a learning norm. Otherwise they are too threatening to undertake. Moreover, of themselves, they require lrsp to accomplish. Also see Friend and Jessop (1969, pp. 129–188) and Smelser (1972).

it should be emphasized that useful theory (to say nothing of generaliz-able research) on inter-organizational processes is woefully inadequate. The conceptual problems are as basic as how to think about an organiza-tional "boundary," especially in complexly interactive situations like government.[7]

With this caveat in mind, let us consider two important observa-tions. All organizations in the public sector will be faced with internal and external pressures for and against lrsp, but these will not come all at the same time or degree. Nor will efforts to try to move toward lrsp, the re-sults of which will, in turn, influence the direction of further efforts, happen in the same sequence in different organizations. Second, all orga-nizations will face, even more than they do now, uncertainty about what other organizations will be doing. (UE, in Friend and Jessop's terminol-ogy described in Chapter Five.) In particular, they will be unclear about the degree to which they will collaborate or compete in anticipated future situations. This uncertainty will be the residue of traditional relationships between agencies, modified and complicated by shifts in norms and struc-tures produced by attempts to introduce lrsp. Their source of uncertainty will increase because even without the intent to try to do lrsp, organiza-tions will find themselves increasingly applying the systems philosophy (in part because they will be increasingly dependent on skilled persons who think in these terms). As a result, organizational mandates and the boun-daries of their relevant environments, functions, and programs will be-come less clear regardless of how they have been specified by legislative statute or directive.

Both collaboration and competition can be expected and either can be constructive or destructive to changing-over efforts. To the extent that working with environmental groups means opening up data and program

[7] "Most organization theorists concede that environment of an organization is an important determinant of its behavior and functioning. Yet, it is true that environment has entered into the equation of organizational functioning only tangentially, often as a constant or a 'given' but not as a variable" (Tripathi, 1971). Statutory distinctions look good on the books, but they do not help, especially under changing conditions of the sort we are assuming. What is more, as A. Weston has emphasized (in conversation), directives from legislatures to government agencies are sometimes deliberately, and usually inadvertently, con-tradictory or ambiguous. This further obscures and complicates systematic under-standing of the way organizational structures and norms, combined with the mix of bureaucratic and free-swinging interaction among their members, interact at the interorganizational level. Also see Lowi (1969). Some admirable tussles with interorganizational processes are exemplified by: Evan (1966); Halperin (1971); Levine, White, and Paul (1963); Levine and White (1961); Litwak and Hylton (1962); and Long (1958). On the insufficiency of theory or practice for dealing with interorganizational arrangements at the federal level, see Mansfield (1969); Warren (1968).

information, one of the chief means for competition—differential access to information—will be eliminated or at least reduced. To the extent that specific environmental demands affect more than one agency, as will often be the case, given both present overlaps and newly developing task definitions derived from the systems perspective, agencies will find it worthwhile at least under some circumstances to learn to collaborate in order to meet the demands.

There is an interesting organizational autonomy dilemma to be noted here. Each organization will need more information about its environment, either to serve it effectively or to try to control it in the interests of organizational survival. More information will be more economically available if agencies pool information. But pooling will reduce organizational autonomy as the organization becomes increasingly dependent on more and more information and to get it trades information about itself for information about other agencies, corporations, and third-sector organizations. As turbulence increases inside the organization, and with it uncertainty and the risk of error, organization members are likely to become less inclined to try holding to conventional mandates and more inclined to share the social psychological burdens of coping with error, turbulence, and uncertainty with other organizations while they learn to embrace error and try to anticipate it through lrsp. One consequence could be that, as more organizations collaborate, UE (uncertainty about the intentions of other organizations) would be reduced. One result of that rewarding state of affairs could be a strengthening of incentives to move toward lrsp.

Increased collaboration would require the rewriting of legislation and the reallocation of the perogatives of congressional overseeing, but the loss in control this would represent for some congressmen, who now jealously impose and protect that control, could turn out to be in their interest as well. It would redistribute *their* burdens of coping with error and uncertainty in a world where it will be increasingly difficult to hide either one. Moreover, as older legislators are replaced by persons more deeply educated and experienced, and as legislative intentions to arm Congress with systems-analysis staffs bear fruit, congressional shifts in perspective should open up possibilities for statuatory and procedural innovations that are not now possible.

But obviously this shift, this redistribution of power, this redefinition of what constitutes power, will not come about quickly or easily for many reasons, including the social psychological reasons. Therefore, we can expect the conventional attractions of competition and efforts at organizational aggrandizement to persist. To a point, this can be helpful to change-over efforts toward lrsp. In the first place, if members of an organization see lrsp as a means for advancing their own interests, it will give impetus to internal efforts to change in that direction. There seems to be much to be done *within* organizations, by way of trying to initiate lrsp, that may not be contingent on very much more cooperation from other organizations than is usually available. To be sure, in the absence of collaboration, uncertainty about the intentions of other organizations will increase, but when lrsp is for the purpose of societal learning, one of the things learned about would be the costs of competition versus the costs of collaboration. Also, just because lrsp is a means for societal learning, competition between agencies or programs within agencies for the purposes of "proving" that one approach to a problem is more effective than another (or that both approaches together are more effective than either separately) could be a desirable aspect of lrsp *if* the learning purpose were truly kept as the first priority.[8]

The structural implications and their social psychological concomitants for interorganizational lrsp arrangements seem to be like those required for effective relationships with the non-organizational parts of the environment: much more boundary-spanning capability, shifts in organizational differentiation and integration, shifts in "products," and changes in management processes. We turn now to some of these specific requirements.

[8] We have regularly used synthetic competition procedures in the weapon systems area. An aerospace firm is often declared the "winner" of a developmental or prototype contract in order to keep it alive. For years the putative evils of monopoly or oligopoly in the automobile industry were avoided by a not so tacit government-industry agreement not to wipe out American Motors. The same kind of philosophy might be made to operate among government agencies for the purpose of stimulating future responsive societal learning.

XII

On the Requirement for Changes in the Use, Duration, and Significance of Sentient Groups

*T*here is a body of experience and research going back at least to the work of E. Mayo (1933), F. Roethlisberger (1941), and W. J. Dickson (1946) that distinguishes between and explores the implications of the worker as a task-oriented person related to a task-oriented group, contrasted with the worker as a person oriented to other persons within their psychologically defined work space—oriented, that is, to "the group to which individuals are prepared to commit themselves and on which they depend for emotional support" (Miller and Rice, 1967, p. 253).

The Functions of Sentient Groups

All stable task groups develop a sentient component. It is often suppressed or repressed in the performance of the task, but it nevertheless influences the group in many ways: how it goes about its task; how it rewards its members for performing task-oriented or sentient-oriented roles in the group; how it incorporates new members into the norms and performance styles of the group; and what strengths and weaknesses the group displays in handling conflicts between sentient and task demands (Bion, 1961, and Rice, 1965). In the situation we are contemplating, organization members will deeply need the emotional support and sense of commitment that sentient groups provide. In the face of turbulence and uncertainty, anxiety will need to be allayed and a sense of personal "location" provided when change-over efforts are instituted. The strains of role ambiguity and role conflict will also need easing. Those initiating such change-over efforts and those who are asked to make the changes will find themselves turning to others for support as they try to cope with the changing world that impinges from the outside and the one that changes inside the organization. Under these insecure conditions people will turn to their sentient groups to gain the psychological strength to resist change, or to accept change, or to try to institute change. For some people sentient groups will be within the organization; for others, the sentient group will be outside. Or, lacking such affiliations, individuals may turn in upon themselves, isolating themselves from others in an attempt to isolate themselves from turbulence and uncertainty, and the anxiety they produce. The former response is far more typical, but the latter is not an infrequent response among men in high places. One way or the other, the functions served by the sentient group will be especially important in determining reactions to efforts to change toward lrsp under the organizational circumstances with which we are concerned.

Effective task performance depends heavily on the relationship between the person's task group and the person's sentient group.[1] "Forms of organization in which task and sentient groups coincide may have relatively high short-term effectiveness; in the longer term, such groups can inhibit change and hence can lead eventually to deterioration of performance, and in consequence to social and psychological deprivation rather than to satisfaction" (Miller and Rice, 1967, p. 253).

Within this observation lie some critical dilemmas, both real and false, for changing over to lrsp. As defined herein, both lrsp and the processes of changing organizations toward a lrsp philosophical and operational mode will themselves be learning activities, research and development activities. All these arrangements and activities will thereby be subject to change. Sentient groups that operate to discourage change are inimicable to learning and to implementing what is learned. And strong sentient groups, melded with task groups, will reduce the credibility and usefulness of the boundary spanner: sentient subgroups would tend to be

---

[1] How the group "socializes" its new members is well described, in terms compatible with this study, in Warwick (1971, Chapter 13, especially pp. 386–393).

more resistant to the potential for change inherent in boundary-spanning activities.

One of the chief social psychological purposes that sentient groups serve is to provide people with a feeling of security, of imbeddedness and continuity.

A professional orientation makes officials concerned with impediments to efficient operations and directs them to attempt adjustments, but it also engenders anxiety. The greater their interest in professional objectives and the fewer the external restraints on their method of achieving them, the more likely it is that they will experience anxiety. The bureaucratic officials observed found themselves in this predicament, although perhaps not to the same extent as do independent professionals. Anxieties that persevered, whether among interviewers or department heads, agents or reviewers, led to maladaptation, rigidity, and poor performance. Adaptation to the organization in general and the ability to reorganize procedures when necessary in particular depend on relatively cohesive work groups, which relieve such anxiety. [Blau, 1963, pp. 258–259].

Sentient groups are also the locus of a person's sense of commitment. Thus, anything then that threatens to break up a person's sentient group will be strongly resisted: one's very sense of self is threatened because the group helps define and sustain that sense of self. Conventional management will also see as in its interest the melding of task and sentient group.[2] When task and sentient group are identical, then loyalty to the task is heightened and things get done with less external coercion and managerial intervention than would be required otherwise.

"Analysis confirmed the impression that one of the ways the high-producing managers are achieving better communication and more accurate perceptions is by building greater peer-group loyalty. The results also show that the greater the peer-group loyalty, the greater is the agreement between the foremen and the men as to what constitutes a reason-

---

[2] Note that usually not all members of groups that are a mix of task and sentient functions are equally "in," either in their own eyes or those of other members of the group. The degree to which the member is "acceptable" will affect how autonomous the member's response is to innovations that the group as a whole seeks to reject or accept. A. Guskin, reviewing the literature on conformity and social support, concludes: "In short, conformity to the norms of a group is curvilinearly related to the acceptance that individuals feel within the group as well as the attraction they feel towards each other. Generally, a very high degree of acceptance leads to independence, moderate degrees of acceptance tend to lead to conformity and a very low degree of acceptance leads to a lack of conformity to group norms" (Guskin, 1971, p. 7).

able figure or standard" (Likert, 1961, p. 55). While this quotation refers to R. Likert's studies in industry, the same circumstances pertain in office situations.[3]

When task group and sentient group can be kept separate, it would appear easier to introduce task change but harder to generate organizational loyalty. This is especially likely in the days ahead when more will work in government agency activities because they see their government work as having special potential for advancing their sentient commitment to groups outside the organization. To "consumer" groups, and to many younger professionals moving into government and corporations, it is immoral to hold different values in one's "inside" compared to one's "outside" sentient group affiliations. Under this arrangement, if the work situation is frustrating or unproductive from the standpoint of task accomplishment, or if other jobs look more attractive from the perspective of fulfilling sentient group commitments, or if a person finds the efforts to change his situation in the direction of frsl too threatening, he may be more inclined to "exit" than he has in the past.[4] Leaving may disrupt ongoing activities, especially if the person is a professional or administrator, and he may take with him information the agency wants to keep secure. In the absence of sentient group affiliations located within the organization, the conflict-resolving utility of appeals to loyalty noted earlier would be seriously reduced. Management that needs to feel in control would find such a situation extremely threatening. Thus, management will also resist breaking up sentient groupings for the purpose of changing toward lrsp if management fears the threat of loss of loyalty or feels unable or unwilling to undertake a different style of management to compensate for anticipated losses in sentient group control. Of course this would be especially true if the sentient groups to be disbanded were those with which managers identified.

On the other hand, sentient groups seem necessary as the buffers and sustainers for those who take on the task of innovating in the direction of lrsp. In theorizing about the implications of successful efforts to introduce new weaving technology into a textile manufacturing organization, Miller and Rice (1967) observe that, as a rule, "what is important is the relative balance of sentience of groups committed to the status quo and groups committed to change. Efforts by other workers to replicate elsewhere the experimental changes in weaving cited above often foundered through a failure to create initially a strong sentient group com-

[3] See Etzioni (1968) on the prevalence and utility of what he calls "normative compliance" in professional situations.
[4] Hirschman (1970) speculates elegantly and usefully on the various mixes and intensities of factors that influence leaving ("exiting") an organization in decline.

mitted to experimentation. It was only such a group that could provide the necessary protective boundary within which innovation could be encouraged to take place. In the case of the loom-sheds already referred to, however, once the new autonomous groups had established themselves, they acquired their own valency and froze into a new status quo, and the group committed to experimentation disappeared." They add: "To maintain adaptiveness, the greatest sentience must remain vested in a group committed to change" (p. 260). And at least with regard to some changes, particularly those generated within the group, sentient groups can provide the emotional support to risk change.

"Recurrent co-operative and congenial interaction with most co-workers, and not merely with a few friends, gives officials a feeling of security in the work situation. This promotes assimilation in the bureaucratic structure and efficient performance of strenuous tasks, such as complex negotiations. The social support of the group also makes it easier for officials to adopt new practices, since it lessens their need to find emotional security in familiar routines. Social cohesion, therefore, paves the way for the development of new adjustments. In addition, it furnishes the group with instruments for instituting them" (Blau, 1963, p. 259).

Three relevant examples of the application of this property of sentient groups were noted during interviews for this study. In Los Angeles, Chief City Planner Calvin Hamilton was making large changes in the composition and functions of the planning staff. He deliberately introduced schemes that built sentient group support for undertaking new means for establishing and maintaining new programatic activities. Among other things, he used organizational development techniques to teach the interpersonal competences needed for creating working groups that could both risk and develop organizational changes.

Within the Bureau of Research of the Office of Education, David Bushnell established a highly innovative curriculum change program, ES '70, in seventeen school districts around the country. A number of activities were developed deliberately to bring the involved superintendents together to share their experiences and innovations in ways that effectively made them into a strong sentient group. Part of Bushnell's reason for emphasizing sentient group-building was to increase the likelihood that these superintendents would find enough strength from their sentient group participation to continue to risk innovations in the event federal funding dried up—which is what happened.

Thompson Ramo Wooldridge (TRW) has frequent occasions to establish temporary task groups around aerospace engineering development activities. These groups must work together intensively and must be careful not to develop sentient group attachments that isolate them from other groups involved in the same project. Effective interaction is critical. Therefore, before these teams begin work, they spend time under the guidance of an in-house organizational development staff becoming sensitized to each others' work style and social support needs. They also learn what sentient group tendencies are likely to interfere with their working relations with other involved teams in the particular work context they face. (For example, two such teams might be a rocket engine test team working in the field miles away from the analysis and development team back at the computers.) [5] They also learn techniques for dealing with such tendencies, and these are used—usually with the help of the organizational development staff—when the danger signs are noted in the intense working situation that follows.

An early and major component of many organizational development techniques is improving interpersonal competence so that sentient groups can realistically and openly support their membership in the risks of changing.[6] It may well be that a major source of a sentient group's resistance to innovations from outside the group is its inability to move *beyond* conventional interpersonal support to the support required to understand and face up to what each needs from, and needs to give to, the others in order to share the fears, and hopes, and actions therefrom that go with the occasion to change.

In sum, it appears that many sentient groups are likely to resist efforts to change toward lrsp, but that sentient groups skilled in interpersonal competences, groups that participate in planning change-over efforts, and groups specifically designed for introducing lrsp attempts are likely to facilitate change attempts. Thus change-over seems to require the simultaneous dissolution of sentient groups built around routines and values that resist lrsp, the establishment of others that favor the proposed changes, and the establishment of *temporary* sentient groups to support those most directly involved in designing and implementing lrsp-directed innovation. A lrsp goal for the organization would be to learn how to institute a structure and norm of intense but changable group identifications of the sort described in the earlier quotation from Bennis and Slater.[7]

---

[5] An analogous task, which is chronically badly managed and which it would be crucial to manage well if an organization were trying to move toward lrsp, is that of developing a supportive working relationship between field and office, especially between program development people in the office and evaluation groups in the field.

[6] An excellent review of organizational development technique and philosophy in their relation to the changing environmental setting of organizations is Katz and Georgopoulos (1971). Also see Mead and Byers (1968). The photographs and text in this book are invaluable for elucidating the interplay between task and sentient group needs and the kinds of competences necessary to meet both.

[7] Bennis and Slater (1968) are most imaginative and perceptive on the

Clearly the task of restructuring sentient groups will be time-consuming, difficult, and complex. It will be a learning process in itself.

Sentient-Group Characteristics of Professionals, and Their Influence on Efforts to Change Toward Lrsp

Some further appreciation of how sentient group responses will aid or hinder change-over efforts can be gained by looking more closely at sentient group characteristics of professionals. Some of these people will be the innovators of lrsp change-over efforts, and others will be the resisters. It is important to have some of their social psychological attributes in mind, as these are reflected by sentient group needs. Their resistance to or support of efforts to change toward frsl will be a function of what happens to their sentient groups, since redifferentiation and reintegration of organizational structure and revisions of programs would alter or eliminate sentient groups of which they are members.

When their task situation is frustrating or their role ambiguous, or when professionals need more assurances about their social usefulness than their organization provides, some will find their sentient groups outside, perhaps exclusively outside, their agency. An important sentient group for the professional has been his professional association. "The sentient groups to which professional men and women commit themselves and from which they draw their support are the professional associations and their related learned societies. Membership is a qualification to practice. And the sanction to practice those professions that are concerned with the lives, liberties, and property of their clients has, in our society, the force of law. Society, in effect, not only defines the boundaries of the task system and of the sentient system, and separates them, but also, through the sentient system, controls professional conduct in the task system" (Miller and Rice, 1967, p. 254). But the big professional associations are also victims of the turbulent society. They are racked with internal dissension over purpose and means: splintering or threats to splinter are the order of the day.[8] In consequence, the traditional legitimized basis for controlling professional conduct is in jeopardy, along with the feeling

---

personality requirements for temporary affiliations. These conjectures are well based in social, anthropological, and psychological research. There is also a large body of research and theory on "reference groups" that is complementary to the subject of this chapter. For a review and bibliography in this area, see Hyman (1968).

[8] For an example, see Shapley (1972). A particularly good example of the redefining of a profession is Dumont (1968). He explores, sensitively and informatively, the changing professional criteria for performance and relevance in the "mental health" area.

that one has a collegial and value-shared professional association to turn to for a sense of commitment and emotional support.

One emerging result seems to be the growth of splinter associations that provide their members with strong sentient group rewards, certainly stronger rewards than the parent organizations have provided in the recent past. Over the years ahead the need for a sense of commitment and for emotional support in a turbulent world may well encourage the pro- liferation of doctrinaire distinctions and organizational activities akin to the intense sentient and task group subsect differentiation that character- ized sixteenth-century Protestantism.[9] This could happen because the splintering is a reflection of increasing specialization and the desire of those practicing new specialties for the status and support that a profes- sional organization provides. Correlative with this process, splintering in professional associations also seems related to differing membership views on the association's relevance for social issues—the same issues which give impetus to lrsp. That is, professional skill *plus* a particular viewpoint about its appropriate application to societal problems become the basis for new professional organization. Relocation of the professional's sentient group will increase the problems of sustaining organizational loyalty to agencies or corporations. At the same time it could increase professional support for efforts to change toward lrsp.

Particularly disconcerting for control-oriented and security-oriented senior personnel will be that sentient group composed of a sub rosa net- work of like-minded "guerrilla" bureaucrats who set commitment to prob- lem ahead of loyalty to agency. Such persons are described in more detail in Chapter Fourteen; I mention them here to remind the reader that some "bureaucrats" who seem innovative, risk-taking, and devoted to the public interest increasingly seem to be part of this sentient group, which not only spans the government but reaches into the professional com- munity outside.

What about sentient group in relation to task group for top-man- agement and executive levels of the organizations with which we are concerned? How will their sentient groups affect the response of such persons to efforts to move toward lrsp? Our knowledge here is murky. We have little systematic knowledge of these matters, though much has been reported more or less anecdotally in novels and in case studies. These are the people who see themselves as "successes"; in their own eyes at least, they would not hold the positions they do if they were not "suc- cesses." Their self-image tells them they *know* what they are doing and how to do it. But these are the people who will have the ultimate respon- sibility for dealing with the inpouring of the turbulent environment across

[9] For a fascinating description of that period see Brinton (1953, p. 79).

their organizational boundaries, bearing its threats to their self-images. And from these people will have to come the necessary if not the sufficient stimulus and continuity of support for efforts to change toward lrsp. It is important, therefore, to speculate upon how their sentient groups will help sustain their self-image of success, their emotional needs, and the location of their commitment, and, in so helping, hinder or advance efforts to change toward lrsp.

Sentient-Group Characteristics of Top Decision-Makers: Groupthink

In times of crisis, sentient group and task group coalesce. (Probably this is not unique to the upper levels of administration and decision-making, but it is more apparent and more important there.) To a degree, this coalescence seems to be the case for everyday deliberations also, but under normal conditions an effective operating distinction between sentient and task group demands seems more maintainable by those involved and by the executive or manager in charge. However, in crises or under stress the distinction seems to get lost and usually (but not invariably) the interpersonal processes operative in sentient groups come to dominate even though the task is still the ostensible objective of the group. Since the turbulent environment outside the organization and the efforts to change or resist change inside the organization, with all that implies about uncertainty and error, mean that the situation will be frequently and perhaps chronically stressful, it is important to keep in mind some special characteristics of high-level deliberative groups when sentience and task purposes fuse.

Under conditions of high stress, these sentient groups often resist change in perspective and performance by resorting to what I. Janis (1971), who has studied a number of such events in government, calls "groupthink."

In each case study, I was surprised to discover the extent to which each group displayed the typical phenomena of social conformity that are regularly encountered in studies of group dynamics among ordinary citizens. For example, some of the phenomena appear to be completely in line with findings from social-psychological experiments showing that powerful social pressures are brought to bear by the members of a cohesive group whenever a dissident begins to voice his objections to a group consensus. Other phenomena are reminiscent of the shared illusions observed in encounter groups and friendship cliques when the members simultaneously reach a peak of "groupy" feelings.

Above all, there are numerous indications pointing to the develop-

ment of group norms that bolster morale at the expense of critical thinking. One of the most common norms appears to be that of remaining loyal to the group by sticking with the policies to which the group has already committed itself, even when those policies are obviously working out badly and have unintended consequences that disturb the conscience of each member. This is one of the key characteristics of groupthink [p. 43].

Janis proposes as the "main principle of groupthink": *"The more amiability and esprit de corps there is among the members of a policy-making ingroup, the greater the danger that independent critical thinking will be replaced by groupthink, which is likely to result in irrational and dehumanizing actions directed against outgroups"* (p. 44).[10] He concludes: "While I have limited my study to decision-making bodies in Government, groupthink symptoms appear in business, industry, and any other field where small, cohesive groups make the decisions" (p. 76).

Miller and Rice (1967), drawing on their field research experience with corporations and other non-governmental organizations, have a similar message with further insights.

Disasters are fortunately rare, but they serve to emphasize the importance of defined boundaries and of boundary control functions. We have seen that any transaction across enterprise boundaries, an essential process for any living system, involves the drawing, temporarily at least, of new boundaries. And the drawing of new boundaries contains the possibility that the new boundaries will prove stronger than the old. Any transaction across enterprise boundaries has in it, therefore, the elements of incipient disaster, in which not only are essential tasks undone, but sentient systems are destroyed as well.

We can learn something more from the examination of disaster. So far as is known, the actual occurrence of mass panic is rare; but the myth of panic in disaster is strong. The myth, and belief in it, is a mechanism by which stress is discharged and control restored. The destruction of boundaries is so stressful that somebody has to go, or has to be believed to go, to pieces—somebody or some group has to carry the role of panic leader. In more normal situations, religious sects, immigrants, racial groups, delinquents, or other socially condemned minorities can threaten, or be perceived to threaten, the integrity of group boundaries. The preservation and protection of adequate sentient boundaries often depend,

[10] Janis enunciates a number of more specific characteristics of groupthink. None seem incompatible with or essentially different from what we have been examining and hypothesizing throughout. (Also see Janis, 1971a).

therefore, on finding or inventing other groups on whom can be pro-
jected the feelings and behavior that, if retained within the sentient
group, would destroy its sentience [p. 268].

These independent findings suggest that when faced with crises
and stress from the turbulent environment, we can expect to find that
executive group members, unless trained to act otherwise, are likely to use
the sentient group qualities of their work situation to "push away" the
uncertainty and threat of making errors that a learning posture in fact
requires. The effective resistance from the executive's sentient group to
changing toward lrsp may be among the most formidable if the members
respond in a groupthink manner to the crises that would usually be pre-
cipitated if the organization were opened to environmental feedback
needed to learn how to change toward lrsp.

Resistances to change by sentient groups perform a valuable stab-
ilizing function in smoothing over disruptive inputs to organizations. That
function is appropriate in organizations doing routine operations and
facing routine stresses. It is much more likely to be deeply counterproductive in the lrsp change-over situation, with its occasions of novel and
heavy stress. This is especially so because the aura of expertness and the
inaccessibleness that surrounds senior groups further protect them from
accusations of incompetence, even though under stress they are very likely
to be operating by groupthink norms. What is more, those who are dependent on the senior group for their status or resources, or those who
identify with them, usually do not want to believe that their superiors are
so psychologically vulnerable: it is less upsetting to blame events or other
groups than to use them as sources of information needed for facilitating
efforts at social planning.

Other Sentient-Group Characteristics of Top Decision-Makers

We turn next to examining some sentient group needs of senior
managers and executives for what they may tell us about other sources of
resistance to lrsp or support for change-over efforts. Let us divide these
persons into those who will choose to face turbulence and uncertainty, and
all that follows from that, and those who will avoid such impacts if they
can. The first group includes those who will be responsive to changes toward lrsp, or will even be pushing for such changes. The second group
represents those who prefer to operate by short term, incremental, and
other conventional means for relating organization to environment; this
group can be divided into those who are "loners" and those who will
have their sentient groups to support them in anti-lrsp organizational
responses.

As for the loners, in the nature of the situation, what evidence there is is mostly impressionistic. It suggests that some persons at the highest organizational levels manage to isolate themselves from the organization and its environment, and to cut themselves off from sustaining sentient group affiliations within the organization (Grinspoon, 1964). In the future, such isolation will be feasible only in organizations with routine activities operating in a placid environment. Since organizations in need of lrsp will engage a turbulent environment, isolated executives will be screened out over the years ahead, probably through crises or disasters that expose their inadequacies, inadequacies which arise partly because they are unprotected and unsupported by a sentient group that could also be their task group working on change-over efforts.

The more typical situations will be those in which senior executives or administrators create their sentient groups by surrounding themselves with like minds and values, with the sycophants and entourages that insulate them from enough of the turbulent environment inside and outside the organization to produce a chronic state of at least mild groupthink.[11] The sentient group can be as small as the executive and one close friend. And of course many such people have their sentient-group affiliation with others like themselves outside their own organization. Organizational folklore is replete with examples. It is enough here to note that this kind of sentient group contributes much to the inability to cope with uncertainty or embrace error, and thereby sustains resistance to moving toward frsl.

It is worth noting again, however, that a sentient group is by no means necessarily comprised of open, trusting, deeply supportive members. Interpersonal incompetence seems as great in such groups as elsewhere. In fact, such groups of executives or administrators may be particularly careful not to test the depth of mutual understanding, commitment, and willingness to risk on behalf of the other. When task and sentient groups overlap, a number of devices ostensibly directed to task accomplishment are often used to avoid testing the availability of mutual support. Often a group will agree without testing its assumptions about its "client"—its beliefs, for example, about what "Congress," or "the public," would "never buy." "Getting on with the job" or meeting a deadline (which often is not as immovable as it is accepted to be) are often used as ways to avoid the kind of exploration of values, goals, priorities, and feelings that usually inhere in the task. In these ways sentient-group members avoid exposing differences that might very well go beyond the group's experienced ability to support its members. Indeed, the dynamics of groupthink can in part be understood as a partially unconscious collusion

---

[11] A recounting of such, rich in detail and understanding, is found throughout Hoopes (1969).

by the members of the group to avoid testing each other's comradeship and emotional supportiveness by not acknowledging that the situation is in fact a "moment of truth."

Those senior executives and managers who innovate in the direction of lrsp can also be divided into two groups for our purposes: those who are naïve about the personal changes that will be required of them and their group, and those who are knowledgeable about this requirement. Consider the first category. By their very appreciation of the need to attempt and to risk change-over toward lrsp, members are likely to be a part of an overlapping task and sentient group that has been more exposed to the turbulent environment, hence better able to deal with crises and stress innovatively, or at least under less influence from groupthink tendencies. As these executives and their sentient groups attempt to innovate toward lrsp, exposure to organizational resistance and to information from boundary spanners within and without the organization will emphasize that profound structural changes are necessary, with consequent interpersonal changes required of themselves as well as elsewhere in the organization, if lrsp is to be used to facilitate learning. Previously arrived-at "definitions" of one another's competences and usefulness to the group and to the organization will have to be reviewed, and shifts in appreciation, self-image, and status will be inevitable. Without special preparation most groups cannot face this kind of reassessment. This is especially so for well-mannered people who have worked together for the rewards of mutual esteem. Whether, during this period, the innovator-executive's sentient group finds that it has the will to face these interpersonal readjustments, or whether it reverts to more familiar avoidance responses, will depend on the confluence of many factors, including those discussed here. The point to be made is that the executive's sentient group, whether inside or outside his organization, can provide critically necessary emotional support for him if he is to sustain the risk and discomfort of moving his organization toward lrsp, but whether the group will in fact support him in such moves is problematic.

The knowledgeable executive or manager, by the nature of that knowledge, will already have begun the interpersonal competence training and the structural reorganization that must precede effective movements toward lrsp. Janis points out that there are structural means for reducing the tendency to groupthink and that they have worked successfully.[12] While very little has been done by way of linking these personal and structural changes with regard to sentient group affiliations, there are a few organizations, mostly non-governmental, that have moved rather

---

[12] See both of his works cited earlier in this chapter. Other recomendations are found in Wilensky (1967), and Webb (1969).

well toward fulfilling these necessary preconditions for introducing change toward lrsp. One consequence is that the executive's sentient group becomes less than typically hierarchical and status-bound in these settings. As a result, more information is infused into the sentient group from the organization and the environment. This type of sentient group is, of course, better able to handle the emotional charge implicit in the task of introducing lrsp activities, without the counterproductive consequences we have examined elsewhere.

However, groupthink persists and the structural and interpersonal changes that Janis, Likert, Miller, Rice, and others have recommended for improving organizational responsiveness continue to go unimplemented for the most part. Some who could make such changes are ignorant of the existence of organizational development technology. More often, however, the recommended procedures remain unimplemented because the changes demanded of the innovating officer and his overlapping sentient and task group are too threatening to the self-images of task and interpersonal competence built up in earlier days; older senior people feel a special need to maintain these images in the face of the threats of societal turbulence. This need probably will be especially strong in government agencies, where trying to move toward lrsp will create greater uncertainty than in typical non-governmental settings (though the situation will change in those circumstances too). Under these conditions, sentient group support will remain much more important evidence of personal success and accomplishment than evidence from the environment. Unambiguous evidence in the environment will be hard to find, and if it is there, many others will contend for it.

In this regard, it is important to note that there is evidence that under ambiguous conditions or when rewarding feedback from the environment is a long time in coming—both characteristics of the lrsp situation—people tend to seek more immediate sentient group feedback as evidence of competence or acceptability. "The planner's dilemma is thus a complicated one; how does he get meaningful feedback which enables him to evaluate his performance when the realization of his plans [lies] in the distant future? And, how does he avoid on over-dependence on those who do provide satisfying interpersonal feedback?" (Guskin, 1971, p. 25). This dilemma is often resolved so as to sustain the morale of the planner or planning staff and to contribute to the image of much planning activity, but resolved at a cost: insufficient effort is made trying to assure a significant planning impact on the organization. The planning-oriented people get their assurances of competence and value from other planning-oriented people—their local and extended sentient group—not from the people who should be using their planning efforts. Indeed, this is a major reason why they are so dependent on their sentient group. Thus planners, frustrated because their efforts do not result in action, compensate by exchanging expressions of support with other frustrated planners and would-be plan-users, instead of leaving the organization or seeking other means to begin to make a difference within the organization. To be sure, this behavior is by no means limited to the planning fraternity, but it is especially important from our perspective.

Sentient-Group Characteristics of Middle-Level Administrators

The influence of sentient-group membership on efforts to move toward lrsp seem not to differ from those already described for professionals and senior personnel. As management and administration becomes more professionalized, they too will look to their associations or splinters thereof for sentient support. Others will find their sentient groups among their immediate staff and among associates attached to the office's programs or administrative activities. Some will be old-line bureaucrats who have been successful in the hierarchy and its sentient groups and are unable to relate themselves to others in different kinds of working relationships. Increasing numbers of young managers will be the products of the sort of education and experience which, when combined with the turbulence that spreads across the boundaries of government bureaucracies, will result in neither respect for nor belief in the criteria said to define the bureaucratic ideal: "hierarchy, jurisdiction, specialization, professional training, fixed compensation, and permanence" (Marx, 1957, p. 22). As noted earlier, some of these people will have strong involvements of commitment and support with groups in the bureaucracy's environment.

Some middle-level people will have received training in organizational development skills, and they will not be upset by the loosening of controls that follow when stable and loyal sentient groups dissolve. Indeed, in the interest of organizational learning they may encourage dissolution. Others, lacking such training or values, will be made anxious and will resist changes that encourage dissolution of stable and reliable sentient groups. Those who happen to be responsible for the performance and morale of organization members, and who fear efforts to change toward lrsp (because they fear dissolution of their sentient group), will carry a heavier burden coping constructively with these fears. If those responsible are among the managers who fear or want to avoid the loss of control over subordinates that conventional sentient groups provided, they will be especially resentful of efforts to move toward lrsp and especially intent on sabotaging them. Or they may transfer to another more traditional organization. Organizations such as those described earlier, which have moved toward less structured organizational settings, have lost personnel at all levels who could not deal with the greater ambiguity and changes in their sentient group's openness. If sentient groups are often altered in their duration and membership, as moving toward lrsp would require, managers will have to deal with this source of internal turbulence as well.

A General Electric future study ("Our Future Business Environment," 1968) nicely highlights a number of matters we have dwelt upon. It is attending to the anticipated corporate situation, which in itself is worth noting, in the light of Chapter Four, but it would seem to apply as well to government in the years to come:

Compounding the problems caused by an organization in a virtually constant state of flux will be the greater mobility of managerial, professional, and technical personnel. In a fluid organization setting, and in an economy of tight labor markets, it will become progressively easier for an individual to consider his prime commitment to be to his profession and/ or his self development, not to a single organization. Predictably, therefore, a key problem will be that of motivating individual commitment to organizational goals: predictably, too, however successful an organization may be in this regard, it will also (in a sense) fail, for the turnover of this type of personnel is almost certain to increase, even under the best of circumstances [p. 41].

Either the General Electric authors have overlooked the need which "managerial, professional, and technical personnel" will have for sentient associations—as if these persons were archetypal American "loners," latter-day cowboys or private eyes—or they have assumed that professional commitment will fill that need. Certainly it will for some people, but for those who are unsatisfied by that option the attractions of mobility will be in conflict with those of more lasting interpersonal associations. And others will move in the direction that Bennis and Slater suggest: toward intense short-lived sequential associations. The point is not that everyone will need the same kind of sentient arrangements. Quite the contrary. The point is that the requirements for changing toward lrsp would change the sentient group arrangements that are available. In the process, many people would be required to change the ways in which they expect to find interpersonal support and commitment. Those structural changes will be resisted and welcomed: either way, learning how to make the changes in ways that encourage frsl will be a long and difficult learning task.

XIII

On the Requirement for a
Frequent Restructuring Capability

Changing toward lrsp will require a capability for frequent organizational restructuring. On the basis of their several studies, Lawrence and Lorsch (1967) conclude that an organization is more effective if the differentiation and integration of its internal structure tends to match the characteristics of its relevant environment: "We have found that the state of differentiation in the effective organization was consistent with the diversity of the parts of the environment, while the state of integration achieved was consistent with the environmental demand for interdependence. But our findings have also indicated that the states of differentiation and integration are inversely related. The more differentiated an organization, the more difficult it is to achieve integration. To overcome this problem, the effective organization has integrating devices consistent with the diversity of the environment. The more diverse the environment, and the more differentiated the organization, the more elaborate the integrating devices" (p. 157).

Why a Restructuring Capability Is Necessary

The empirical evidence they provide and the conceptual model in which they imbed it is supported by cybernetic theory as expounded in

226

Eric Ashby's (1956) fundamental "law of requisite variety."[1] This law states, in effect, that the repertory of responses an entity can make to its changing environment is determined by the degree to which its complexity mirrors the complexity of the environment. Ideally, an organization would be differentiated and integrated to the same degree as those aspects of the environment to which it is supposed to be responsive.

As defined by Lawrence and Lorsch, differentiation refers to "the difference in cognitive and emotional orientation among managers in different functional departments, including differences in time orientation and interpersonal orientation" (p. 10). Integration refers to "the quality of the state of collaboration that exists among departments that are required to achieve unity of effort by the demands of the environment" (p. 11). In other words, for there to be requisite variety in an organization to meet environmental obligations, its sub-component managers should have cognitive and emotional orientations (including time and interpersonal orientations) and collaborative arrangements that permit the activities for which they are responsible to match the demands the environment places on those activities.

Because it would enlarge both information input from the environment and the variety of participants engaged in planning efforts, changing toward lrsp would heavily accentuate the requirements for effective matching of the organization to its environment through internal differentiation and integration of its activities. Of the utmost importance, with more exposure to the environment the environment would be perceived as itself differentiated and integrated into a variety of patterns according to the appreciative settings in the organization and among members and groups in the environment that influence the organization.

Anyone familiar with organizational life can multiply examples . . . where different problems will come to attention in different parts of the organization, or where different solutions will be generated for a problem, depending on where it arises in the organization. The important point to be noted here is that we do not have to postulate conflict in personal goals or motivations in order to explain such conflicts or discrepancies.

[1] See Ashby (1956). See also Wilkins and Gitchoff (1969). "Change makes prediction difficult because the utility of past experience is reduced. In particular, bureaucracies require predictability, and the simplest means to obtain predictability is to reduce variety. Thus, conformity facilitates predictability. . . . To achieve predictability in a high variable system, the information available to the subsystem concerned with social control must match that variety. But information can never fully match the variety of human existence. Therefore we are concerned inevitably with decision processes under uncertainty" (pp. 126, 129).

*They could, and would, equally well arise if each of the organizational
decision-making roles were being enacted by digital computers, where the
usual sorts of personal limits on the acceptance of organizational roles
would be entirely absent. The discrepancies arise out of the cognitive
inability of the decision makers to deal with the entire problem as a set
of simultaneous relations, each to be treated symmetrically with the
others"* [Simon, 1964, p. 17].

The task here is not to propose a best way to differentiate and integrate
the organization but rather to show that, in the nature of frsl, these appreciative settings will be changing: the organization will have to redifferentiate and reintegrate itself accordingly, accepting this as the *normal*
state of affairs. But there will be strong resistance to doing this and,
hence, to changing toward frsl.

Redifferentiation and reintegration appropriate for frsl would
mean more than the typical organizational "shake-up." It would mean
changing the communication patterns, authority relationships, and systems of specializations not only as they occur within the organization but
as they interact with the environment. And it would mean changing appreciative settings with regard to tasks goals and means and with regard
to relationships with the environment. There would be consequences,
then, for members' sense of self and relationships with others. Since the
outcome of the changes must necessarily be problematic—this too would
be a learning situation—many will resist giving up the comparative cer-
tainties they enjoy in the existing structures. Role conflicts and ambiguities would be accentuated, questions about a person's usefulness would
arise, and sentient groups would be broken up. Uncertainty would increase not only because more and different information would be flowing
in from the environment, but because the redifferentiation and reintegration would itself introduce new operational and interpersonal uncertainties. To the extent that people would have to undertake revising their
appreciative setting, intrapersonal anxieties and uncertainties would be
increased as well. And of course the chances for error would multiply. All
these consequences or the anticipation of them would generate resistances
to redesigning the structure and norms of the organization so it could
learn how to have a capability to restructure itself continuously, as appropriate for frsl.

Whatever the prevailing appreciative setting, the environment will
be differentiated and integrated in terms of what products (things, services,
ideas, imagery, events) its various members need and want, and also in
terms of the consequences resulting from what they do with these products. As we are beginning to understand, consumption has consequences
that extend far beyond the consumer, and it is to this probably larger

domain of consumption consequences, compared to consumer needs, that lrsp must be additionally attentive and responsive. Of course no perceived pattern of differentiation or integration can structure the environment completely: turbulence, in the sense in which Emery and Trist define it, means that at all times the environment will have undifferentiated and unintegrated properties which, under some conditions, may quite overwhelm those aspects of the environment which at other times are recognizable as structured and regulatable, if not precisely predictable. (How this turbulence might come to overwhelm the structured and regulatable, and how often, are among the key questions, of course.)

In order to try to change toward lrsp, organizations will have to be structured differently and certainly more elaborately than conventional organizations have been. In particular, lrsp-tending organizations will need extensive capabilities for scanning the present and future environment, for interpreting information so obtained, and for applying it to the evaluation, transformation, and design of programs, policies, and organizational structure. All agencies claim to do this, but if they do so at all, they do not direct the kind of attention to these tasks that moving toward lrsp requires. That is to say, they do not differentiate tasks to make them match the environment's differentiability into information generators that express needs and wants, and give feedback on the consequences of their being met or unmet. Even more glaringly absent are integrative means within organizations to insure that useful information is gathered and applied.

Conditions That Will Stimulate Restructuring

Social indicator data and the computer will heighten the pressures for redifferentiation and reintegration by facilitating disaggregation of the environment into whatever categories seem relevant for providing more refined and targeted services and for evaluating their consequences. And the environment may also redifferentiate itself, for whatever its reasons. Especially, it may redifferentiate itself in response (possibly in reaction) to the categories suggested by the social indicator data, either as these are interpreted by the relevant agency or by advocate interpreters in the environment. The agency will have to redifferentiate itself and then reintegrate accordingly or deal with the internal and external operational, ethical, and role stress consequences of not responding as well as it could.

How often and to what extent organizations will need to redifferentiate is not at all clear, though it seems reasonable to speculate that it will be more rather than less often if an lrsp-tending mode is rewarding.

In addition to the influence of disaggregated social indicator data, two other stimuli to restructuring merit mention. One source will be theoretical reformulations about the nature of society and the services it requires. In an extraordinarily perceptive and stimulating paper, N. Caplan and S. Nelson (1973) argue that a strong tendency of psychological research and theory is to blame the person rather than the system for deficiencies, inabilities, and inadequacies. They argue the need to understand that behavior is also the product of the system, and that "solutions" to social problems are as likely to require system change as person change. To this end, they quote a major speech by Judge D. Bazelon (1972), long a world leader in introducing sophisticated psychology and psychiatry into the interpretation of criminal law: "Why should we even consider fundamental social changes or massive income redistribution if the entire problem can be solved by having scientists teach the criminal class—like a group of laboratory rats—to march successfully through the maze of our society? In short, before you [correctional psychologists] respond with enthusiasm to our [society's] pleas for help, you must ask yourselves whether your help is really needed, or whether you are merely engaged as magicians to perform an intriguing sideshow so that the spectators will not notice the crisis in the center ring. In considering our motives for offering you a role, I think you would do well to consider how much less expensive it is to hire a thousand psychologists than to make even a miniscule change in the social and economic structure" (p. 6).

If Caplan, Nelson, and Bazelon are correct, and I think they are, then as more system-blame theories develop along with new person-blame theories, there will be revisions, for example, in concepts about the sources and consequences of crime, drug abuse, pollution, and education. As these become ideas in good currency they will lead, in an lrsp mode, to organizational restructurings of programs, functions, and procedures appropriate to the newly invented image of reality.[2]

Information forced into the organization from the environment will be the other increasingly strong stimulus to restructuring. Urban riots, loss of motivation in the younger blue collar work force, professional and public service unionization, and environmental disasters are examples of environmental stimuli that will lead to restructuring.

Restructuring, as with other requirements imposed by lrsp, would not be an experience completely new to organizations. Restructuring of sorts—though chiefly cosmetic—happens in government organizations with every change of administration. And corporations restructure: there

[2] In this regard, D. Waldo, Editor in Chief of the Public Administration Review, conjectures (in correspondence) that the questions of productivity in the public sector will be increasingly salient.

is a body of evidence that as organizations become larger and more complex they become more horizontal in structure and use committees more than hierarchical command for decision-making.[3] The resistances generated by such restructuring efforts provide insights into what to expect if efforts were made to change toward lrsp.

Sources of Resistance to Restructuring

Conventional restructurings help make clear the differences in both degree and kind involved in differentiation and integration for lrsp. Some of the resistances to conventional restructuring can be understood as resulting from expectancies that the norms of the organization will remain what they have been even if the table of organization is different, and that restructuring is an exceptional state of affairs rather than a normal one. Restructuring is not expected to be or *designed* to be a normal state of affairs, as it would have to be to meet the requirements for changing toward frsl.[4] Also, it is clear from successful restructurings, accomplished through the techniques of planned change, that resistance is heightened by inadequate attention to the social psychological circumstances at work at such times. Some of the procedures designed for continuing redifferentiation and reintegration will have to emphasize attention to these circumstances if the restructuring is to occur more easily and the consequences to be effective.

Restructuring of functions and activities would result in reallocations or dissolutions of authority, authority formally prescribed by regulations and informally achieved through demonstrated task competence and interpersonal qualities in sentient groups. The satisfactions that accompany one's command of predictable patterns of influence, the satisfactions of power, could be jeopardized. Others would see new opportunities to attain power. Again, as with sentient groups, restructuring would have

---

[3] A very good summary is found in Tripathi (1971).

[4] In some research and development organizations restructuring is understood to be a continuing process to the degree that project teams expect to be broken up as their projects are completed. There clearly are social psychological costs as well as benefits for those involved, even though they are self-recruited for the jobs (Glatt and Shelly, 1969). We need to know much more about this kind of arrangement and its implications for people and organizations in the public sector. The Secretary's office in a federal agency can be thought of as a temporary system and a very fluid one. But it is not designed to be a component of a larger learning system that includes the rest of the agency. But perhaps the kinds of people who comprise a Secretary's office, who seem to enjoy a fluid and hectic work setting, represent an important resource for moving toward lrsp. Schon (1971, Chapter 5) is enlightening on government as a learning, and a non-learning, system.

an impact on those who have the authority to initiate such changes as well as on their subordinates: there will be situations in which superiors would have to alter substantially their own span and expressions of authority. For example, "The locus of influence to resolve conflict is at a level where the required knowledge about the environment is available. The more unpredictable and uncertain the parts of the environment, the lower in the organizational hierarchy this tends to be. Similarly, the relative influence of the various functional departments varies, depending on which of them is vitally involved in the dominant issues posed by the environment. These are the ways in which the determinants of effective conflict resolution are contingent on variations in the environment" (Lawrence and Lorsch, 1967, pp. 157–158). Shifting the definition and location of relevant information will threaten extant autonomies and will be resisted. In a large government agency or corporation, components are organizations in themselves. Conventionally, "every organization with any drive towards autonomy is concerned with achieving control over the information it needs for decisional independence. Control over the communication of information requisite to key decisions is to an important degree control over the decisions themselves. This fact often plunges the most seemingly harmless fact-gathering enterprise into the storms of politics" (Long, 1962, pp. 145–146). In conventional bureaucracies the tendency would be to resolve conflicts hierarchically (as Bennis observed in an earlier chapter). But that form of conflict resolution is inadequate if the intent is to change toward frsl, and so it is inadequate as the means for establishing the conditions and criteria for redifferentiation and reintegration.

Attempting to reintegrate the differentiated components will generate similar social psychological problems and sources of resistance. First, there will be the difficult and continuing task of reperceiving both environment and organization so that what is freshly perceived about environment components and their interrelationships will be used as a "template" for redesigning organization components and their interrelationships.

Second, there will be the task of designing operational processes for establishing, maintaining, and evolving integrated components. Those who have the power to establish and maintain relations between components will have the power to adjudicate conflicts and to alter relationships between components. Thus, new integrative arrangements will mean new allocations and distributions of authority: those threatened by loss of their power and sense of usefulness will resist the changes.

Ignorance About How to Restructure Humanely

In government, the task of accomplishing successful inter-organizational redifferentiation and reintegration is at least as difficult as at the intra-organizational level. The combination of psychological and statutory resistances to restructuring are so great that the only effective recourse seems to be to differentiate by establishing a new independent agency. The task of integration with other agencies is left to the uncertain, slow, and usually errosive processes of committees, congressional pressures, and the like (even though, written into the enabling legislation, there are injunctions to coordinate with other agencies). Indeed, observers and legislators alike agree that legislators, at least at the federal level, usually don't want effective autonomous integration among agencies, preferring to oversee that task themselves. Effective autonomous integration would necessarily require redifferentiation of legislative committee fiefdom boundaries and hence reallocations of authority, status, and other perogatives, among congressmen. In effect, there are no established reliable integrative procedures presently available that can be counted on to provide an interagency equivalent of an effective intra-organization integration—which is rare enough within organizations. One response to this situation, which reflects other changing self-images of professionalism, legitimacy, and a shift in appreciative setting toward the systems philosooophy, has been the aforementioned development across agencies of an informal, sub rosa, integrative mechanism consisting mostly of young bureaucrats exchanging information for the purposes of problem-solving rather than agency survival (see Chapter Fourteen).

In Chapter Fourteen we will examine a potentially potent integrative mechanism called boundary-spanning, and the resistances it is likely to elicit. But the fact is that we know very little about designing effective integrative mechanisms, much less systems of integrated components that are alterable in response to changes in the environment. "Although reorganization [or the pretense thereof] is a frequent phenomenon in complex organizations in modern societies, our social-scientific understanding of it is meager and largely derived as a by-product" (Thompson, 1967, p. 79).

"Specialization of technology and product in sub-enterprises or separate enterprises can no doubt increase the efficiency of the parts, but until new forms of organization are invented, with activity system, task group, and sentiment group adequately differentiated and their interrelations controlled, it is not certain that greater efficiency of the parts will necessarily add up to greater efficiency of the whole" (Miller and Rice, 1967, p. 266). Since there is neither a shared body of comparable experience about procedures for establishing integration mechanisms in complex, changing organizations nor a theory of integration derived from research, there exists no established repertory of skills sufficient to tie together the multiple aspects of person, structure, and planning technology.[5] Especially skilled and knowledgeable persons have helped some organizations redesign themselves using a combination of art and behavioral science knowledge.[6] But designing an organization so that it has the capability for continuing redesign would result in an organization vastly different—in design, membership, and norms—from a *redesigned* organization per se. It is the former that changing over to lrsp requires.

In all, frequent redifferentiation and reintegration as the mode of organizational behavior, while changing toward lrsp, would have unsettling social psychological effects, producing its own internal turbulence and threatening status, belongingness, autonomy, and certainty. Occasions for conflict would increase, and by the very fact of frequent structural revisions the legitimacy of formal authority would decrease. This would place much heavier demands on the organization's ability to manage conflict by non-authoritarian means, means which also allowed the kind of learning that would enhance the organization's abilities to restructure itself in conformity with the requirements of frsl.

Lawrence and Lorch propose that

the possibility of more systematically planning and implementing conflict resolution procedures hinges on establishing a baseline in terms of the required and actual patterns of differentiation in an organization. This baseline establishes the frame of reference for tackling the conflict resolution problem in an orderly fashion. This clarifies what the conflict is all about, what creates the differences of judgment, and what knowledge is

---

[5] Lorsch has emphasized to me that his research compares organizations as they are. He has not studied the ways in which organizations come to be differentiated or integrated and why they stop at the point they do. Excellent criticisms of and reservations about the present capability of organizational development theory and practice to specify structure design and core technology requirements are found in Argyris (1972); Bennis (1969); and Bowers (1971). A sense of the difficult conceptual problems involved in fusing person change, structure change, and technology change can be gained from Georgopoulos (1970); Leavitt (1965, pp. 1144–1170); and from Hunt (1970). An excellent description of research needed in this area is offered by Bennis (1966, pp. 181–211), and by Mohr (1969).

[6] See Bennis, Benne, and Chin (1962 and 1969); Blake and Mouton (1968 and 1967). Also Beckhard (1969); this book and the next four are in the Addison-Wesley series entitled *Organization Development,* edited by E. Schein, W. Bennis, and R. Beckhard. Bennis (1969), Schein (1969), Walton (1969), and Zimbardo and Eabesen(1969). Examples of integrative mechanisms that have worked, but under much stabler conditions than envisioned here, are R. Likert's "link pin" approach to participative management; and various matrix schemes which in effect assign a man two "bosses" (he is evaluated both as a team member and as a member of a professional pool). See Likert (1961).

relevant to its resolution. From this vantage point we can see why conflict must be accepted as a continuing result of living in a complex civilization. Resolution is not then put up as some final Utopian answer, but simply as a sensible solution to today's issue—with awareness that basic and legitimate differences will generate new conflicts to be resolved tomorrow. From this baseline managers can move more directly toward designing procedures and devices that are adequate for processing the flow of conflicted issues that will surely arise [p. 224].[7]

Note, however, that this approach assumes agreement on what the "required" patterns of differentiation should be. In our situation, instead of knowing these, government organizations will have to discover them, in part by assessing the impact of services rendered as determined and allocated according to a particular model of environmental differentiation and integration. Thus, as usual, the only way lrsp requirements for organizational differentiation and integration could be met would be if those involved saw it as a learning procedure. In this case, as with goal-setting, they would agree for the time being to experiment with *a* model of environmental structure against which to match an internal structure. Means for arriving at such temporary agreements to experiment and revise would be among the things to be discovered via lrsp. Certainly it would involve appreciation of and attention to other matters described here, and it would take a willingness to shift to a norm of societal learning. Lawrence and Lorsch conjecture on some aspects of how this learning might be facilitated:

The viable organization of the future will need to establish and integrate the work of organization units that can cope with even more varied subenvironments. The differentiation of these units will be more extreme. Concurrently, the problems of integration will be more complex. Great ingenuity will be needed to evolve new kinds of integrative methods. The viable organizations will be the ones that master the science and art of organization design to achieve both high differentiation and high integration. . . . To conceive new organizational forms and to develop the managerial behavior needed in these viable organizations, managements will rely increasingly on formally designated organizational development departments. These departments, staffed by trained specialists in the be-

[7] An important statement regarding conflict management is found in Cleveland (1972). He argues that whereas executives (including the last three Presidents of the U.S.) typically try to reduce organizational tensions, the future executive will see his task as maintaining a "web of tensions" as the driving force for creativity and response.

havioral and administrative sciences, will be involved in planning new organizational forms for the effective utilization of human resources and in training managers to operate effectively in these settings. . . . As the demands for both differentiation and integration become more acute, top management will also find it necessary to devote more and more of its explicit attention to the achievement of these organizational states [pp. 238–239].

On the Requirement for
More Boundary-Spanning

*T*he following quotation serves to introduce the critical role of boundary-spanning, for meeting the differentiation and especially the integration requirements for changing toward lrsp, by summarizing the organizational mood that creates more rather than less resistance to restructuring:

The adaptive function . . . move[s] in the direction of preserving constancy and predictability in the conditions of organizational life. The maintenance function moves toward a constant set of internal structures. The adaptive function tends to achieve environmental constancy by bringing the external world under control. . . .

The adaptive function can move, however, in both directions. It can strive to attain control over external forces and maintain predictability for its operations in this fashion, or it can seek internal modification of its own organizational structures to meet the needs of a changing world. . . . The hypothesis seems tenable that the dominant tendency in the powerful organization will be to seek control over the environment rather than to modify internal structures to accord with external changes. The organization thus will proceed on the principle that it is easier to make the world adjust than it is to adjust to the organization, and the

latter alternative will be adopted only if the first offers small hope of
success.

> *. . . A change of internal structure is a threat to the organization.*
To resolve an organizational problem by changing the environment con-
stitutes no such threat. Indeed, if it can be brought off successfully, it
affirms the power and rightness of existing organizational structure.

> *The limiting variable is the relative openness of the system to ex-*
ternal influence. . . .

> *The choice between internal and external change does not only*
depend upon degree of openness; it also depends upon the extent of the
needed modification. Sometimes the modification requires changing both
people and organizational structure (the multi-determined patterns of
interaction), and sometimes just people, or certain of their specific prac-
tices and ideas . . . if an organization is confronted with the alternative
of changing some preferences in its clientele or changing its own struc-
ture and personnel, it will take the former path. If, however, it must
change outside structures and personal habits, as against a limited internal
change in practice, it is more likely to seek the latter solution. In general,
structural change means radical change in what is considered legitimate
and proper; it implies new role prescriptions, new roles, and the task of
getting people to accept their new roles and even to like them [Katz and
Kahn, 1966, pp. 91–93].

Boundary-Spanning as Integral to Lrsp

In terms of our exploration, these quotations from Katz and Kahn
direct us to two underlying aspects of the social psychological challenge
posed by boundary-spanning undertaken to encourage the changing over
to lrsp. On the other hand, conventional organizations do what they can
to reduce the need for boundary-spanning, and its internal turbulence-
generating consequences, by trying to control their environments. On the
other hand, the very societal conditions that create the need for lrsp mean
that the potential for controlling the environment will be low.[1]

---

[1] Throughout this chapter we will be looking at boundary-spanning as
an activity that occurs across the boundaries of components *within* an organization and across the boundary *between* the organization and the relevant environment. Boundary-spanning may be between organization components and
their relevant environments or between the environment and what T. Parsons
(1960) has described as the "institutional" subsystem—that organizational subsystem which has the "most critical supportive task of relating to the larger
society and of legitimizing the part played by the organization" (Katz and
Kahn, 1966, p. 456). In large organizations the same sources of resistance seem

Partially because more information technology will be used by both the organization and its environment, there will be an increase in information that clarifies the distribution of several consequences: consequences of the organization's activities; of the interaction of activities between organizations; and of the interaction of those activities and the turbulent properties of the environment which are independent of the organization's activities. This increase in information will press organizations to pay more attention to who it is that they burden with social costs or bless with benefits. In turn, this will increase the need for them to connect themselves, by boundary spanners, with other organizations in order to enhance the rewards and reduce the costs to the environment, both of which will become clearer with more social indicator data. Anticipating environmental demands will encourage attention to the future, and once an organization begins to try to anticipate relevant futures and evaluate programs in terms of future impacts, its internal and external linkage needs will change and grow.

With social indicators and computer-facilitated disaggregation of clientele, there will be pressures to differentiate the environment into many more special clienteles and situations. Differentiation of clienteles means dealing with more demands, including more coalitions and volatile groups, and this will require more highly skilled boundary spanners. That some new heavy organizational costs must be sustained in order to provide more discriminating services has already been demonstrated, though in less sophisticated form, through client-differentiating feedback supplied by boundary spanners in citizen-participation and advocate-planning situations.[2]

---

to arise whether the threats and opportunities are from another subsystem or from a consumer group, Congress, a city council, or another agency. I will not usually distinguish between organization and subsystems in the organization in discussing their boundary-spanning relations.

[2] In their classic study of the dilemmas of eliminating poverty through community action, Marris and Rein (1967) emphasize that because "the administrative and political structure of the United States explicitly intends that no power, at any level of government, shall claim an authority broad enough to control all the social institutions of a community—concerted social policy [must] rest on a consensus, and the creation of a consensus involves, like any compromise, conflict, intrigue, and ambiguous accommodation" (p. 137). The question for us is whether the conflict, intrigue, and ambiguous accommodations, need be so great that concerted social policy must always founder, that frsl must be impossible. Some of the difficulties encountered could be ascribed to the absence of *effective* boundary-spanning. Fears of being coopted by the spanner, spanner fears of being coopted, distrust, misunderstanding, subversion of the spanner, disagreement on representativeness, all are evidences of the inability of those involved to cope with the threats and ambivalences that boundary-spanning contains and will contain until we learn how to use it appropriately. Also see Moynihan (1969) and Arnstein (1970).

As a result, an organization will need more boundary-spanning in order to relate itself usefully to its environment; and it will have to cope with the internal consequences of new boundary-spanning activities. These consequences will result from the importation of turbulence and uncertainty, introduced by more boundary-spanning, and from the requirement of coping with the input more by internal reorganization than by the conventionally preferred means of environmental control. As we have seen, changes in the environment will require restructuring of the organization if it is to provide adequate functional responses. This redifferentiation must then be integrated internally if the organization is to allocate its resources effectively and evaluate its programs in terms of overall organizational goals. All this will require increased efforts at internal, as well as more external, boundary-spanning to the relevant and changing subenvironments. Inside and outside the organization, those who feel that more boundary-spanning is needed will have to seek the competences and the structures to support this crucial activity.

The social psychological situation pertaining to the use of these competences and the resistances to them, on the one hand, and the organizational structures required to use them, on the other, will further complicate coping with information feedback in general. Organizations and their members will have to cope not only with the information produced from boundary-spanning but with the circumstance that the information is borne by, and frequently generated by, human beings performing that function.[3] Thus interpersonal and personal matters will be ensnarled in this form of feedback more than in dealing, say, with social indicator data. The boundary spanner function will be protean: scanning, stimulating data-generating activity, monitoring, evaluating data relevance, transmitting information, and facilitating interpersonal intercourse. The spanner is in one way or another a carrier of information between systems of activity, and as carrier he is both an information feedback system and an information-generating system. He is often a feedback vehicle for information generated in consequence of his interventions to get information. As a human he will be fallible in what he observes and reports; and activities he initiates for the purposes of generating information may not turn out to be the ones he intended. He is thus especially vulnerable to error, and because of ambivalence toward him, his messages will often be ignored, repressed, rejected, or distorted. Inevitably, the boundary-spanner function will be ambiguous, conflict-laden, ambivalently performed and re-

---

[3] I will write mostly as if the boundary spanner were a single person, and often that will be so. But sometimes the function will be performed by a group or an office. Either way, the problems posed by the function seem very much alike.

sponded to, and thus precarious. Boundary spanners will often be distrusted and resented by all parties they span between. Yet they will also be depended on by those pushing for lrsp, or pushed toward it, for without the boundary spanner's commitment and skill, lrsp will be impossible even to initiate, much less to institutionalize. These ambivalences and confusions will generate additional resistances to changing over toward lrsp. But they will also facilitate inadvertent moves in that direction.

Types of Boundary Spanners

Before looking in more detail at the social psychological sources of resistance to boundary-spanning, two kinds of boundary-spanning merit mention. First, there will be those activities that are responsive to each "stage" of the change-over process itself. Recall that there will be five cognitive-affective boundary-spanning tasks that would be associated with each stage of change-over: stimulating interest in the possibility of lrsp as such or of some facet of it; initiation; legitimation; action decisions; and implementation or routinization (described in Chapter Two, under "Phases and Actors in Change-over Processes"). Second, there will be the structural boundary-spanning tasks stretching across organizational subsystems, functions, or offices to the environment. H. Wilensky (1967) provides useful descriptions of three important types of boundary spanners that emphasize these two kinds of tasks.

The more an organization is in conflict with its social environment or depends on it for the achievement of its central goals, the more resources it will allocate to the intelligence function . . . [to] experts whom we might call "contact men." The contact man supplies political and ideological intelligence the leader needs in order in find his way around modern society; he mediates the relations of the organization and the outside world. His primary concern and skill is with facts about the techniques of changing the thoughts, feelings, and conduct of men through persuasion and manipulation [p. 10].

The more an organization depends on the unity and support of persons, groups, factions, or parties within its membership for the achievement of its central goals, the more resources it will devote to the intelligence function . . . [to] experts whom we might call "internal communications specialists."

The internal communications specialist supplies political and ideological intelligence the leader needs in order to maintain his authority. He transmits policies downwards or reports on membership sentiments and opinion, or both; he helps induct new members and train activists and leaders. His primary concern and skill is with facts about and tech-

*niques of changing the thoughts, feelings, and conduct of members
through persuasion and manipulation [p. 13].*

*The more an organization sees its external environment and in-
ternal operations as rationalized—that is, as subject to discernible, predictable uniformities in relationships among significant objects—the more
resources it will devote to the intelligence function . . . [to] experts whom
we might call "facts-and-figures men." The facts-and-figures man supplies
technical economic, legal, or scientific intelligence that helps the leader
build his case in dealing with outsiders and members, fend off attacks,
and compete with rival organizations for markets, power, and prestige.
His primary concern and skill is with data, records, arguments; he is expected to produce quick simple answers to complex technical questions
as well as judgments of the power and intent of competitors and enemies
[p. 14].*

However, these descriptions need modifications to meet our perspective.
Wilensky's description refers to people performing in conventional organizations subject to conventional norms and definitions, including the
overriding priority of organizational survival through aggrandizement.
As we shall see, much of the resistance to and ambivalence about boundary-spanning arises because of the perceived costs as well as the advantages it embodies for organizations engaged in survival-aggrandizement
efforts. Boundary spanners appropriate for changing over to lrsp would
have to work within and try to encourage the establishment of norms appropriate for frsl. Wilensky's terminology, as abstracted here, gives the
impression that spanners work only for organization leaders, and even
then in the essentially passive role of information provider. In our situation, there would be boundary spanning at many levels to serve and stimulate many activities. And, in the nature of boundary spanning to facilitate
changing over to lrsp, boundary spanners would often be advocates, trying to influence their peers and superiors as well as providing them with
information with which to influence others.

R. Havelock's (1971) encyclopedic review of innovation methods
has led him to propose several categories of "knowledge linking roles,"
which overlap and expand Wilensky's categories, and are valuable to have
in mind (Chapter 7, pp. 4–5).

Role Type	*Function*
Conveyor	To transfer knowledge from producers (scientists, experts, scholars, developers, researchers, manufacturers) to users (receivers, clients, consumers).

Consultant	To assist users in identification of problems and resources, to assist in linkage to appropriate resources; to assist in adaptation to use: facilitator, objective observer, process analyst.
Trainer	To transfer by instilling in the user an understanding of an entire area of knowledge or practice.
Leader	To effect linkage through power or influence in one's own group, to transfer by example or direction.
Innovator	To transfer by initiating diffusion in the user system.
Defender	To sensitize the user to the pitfalls of innovations, to mobilize public opinion, public selectivity, and public demand for adequate applications of scientific knowledge.
Knowledge-builders as linkers	To transfer through gatekeeping for the knowledge storehouse and through defining the goals of knowledge utilization. To transfer through maintenance of a dual orientation: scientific soundness and usefulness.
Practitioner as linker	To transfer to clients and consumers through practices and services which incorporate the latest scientific knowledge.
The User as linker	To link by taking initiative on one's own behalf to seek out scientific knowledge and derive useful learnings therefrom.

A boundary spanner effective at stimulating interest in moving to a particular stage of lrsp may not be the same person who can legitimize that interest. This is one example of the more general observation that the style, substance, and circumstance of boundary-spanning will vary, and that different persons and groups will be more or less appropriate for particular tasks. However, in the very few cases so far where persons have either been assigned the task of developing a lrsp capability or have in-

vented the task out of their own inclinations, the multifarious spanning tasks
have been done by one or a very few people in each organization. Consequently there have been heavy personal and organizational costs, for social
psychological reasons we shall examine.

The boundary spanner who is committed to change-over to lrsp
will have to try to arrange his activities so that he can make the interpersonal and informational contacts, and arrange the interrelationships between them, so that they sustain him personally; do not threaten those he
seeks to link so greatly that they extinguish him; and allow him to gain
and use influentially the information and ideas needed to move others to
act in support of rather than against the implementation of lrsp. This
means he must seek out and bring together people concerned with, and
information about, several matters: the future; what different groups that
should be integrated are doing about that future and about each other,
including shared or differing goals; what other organizations are doing
regarding lrsp; and the nature of the relationship of the organization to
its environment and vice versa.

All of these linkage efforts will require the boundary spanner to
relate to the outside with understanding and skill as carefully as he
relates to the inside of his organization. Otherwise, in the turbulent environment he will quickly be seen by his external links as exploitative,
imperialistic, manipulative, and not to be trusted.

Reactions to Boundary-Spanning That Result in Resistance

By pursuing activities necessary for changing over to lrsp the
boundary spanner will seem threatening to other members of the organization and its environment; he will carry sensitive information to others
outside a given subgroup in the organization or outside of the organization itself. In general, the boundary spanner will facilitate feedback from
the environment and between subgroups in the organization. He will be
the experiencer of turbulence, reporting and interpreting his own experiences to those who only hear about turbulence. Because it is crucial, this
information-diffusion process is an almost certain source of disturbance.
By his very presence or his deliberate actions, he encourages the environment to produce information it might not otherwise recognize that it
possessed, and from which it can benefit by supplying. Thus he may be
able to enlarge the range of demands on his organization, and perhaps
also the sources of support for it. Boundary spanners perforate subsystem
boundaries and thereby threaten their autonomy, their secrets, their security, their unexamined raison d'etre. The boundary spanner who is pushing
for lrsp will be spanning, in part, in order specifically to encourage the

joint use of lrsp technology, which itself threatens conventional subsystem autonomy.

There will be strong inclinations to resist such "invasions" even if it means abjuring information available from the spanner's "invasion" of the subsystem at the other end of the link. The most direct resistance will be to activities introduced by the boundary spanner in order to facilitate one or another aspect of changing toward lrsp.

Resistance to the boundary spanner can be effectuated by so constraining the person that he is recognized and recognizes himself as playing a ritualistic role, in which he is not to be trusted or taken seriously. Organizations regularly ritualize their boundary-spanning activities in order to appear "in touch" while exposing themselves to a minimum of uncertainty, error recognition, or reorganization pains. Advertising is often the agent for this ritual boundary-spanning (consider expressions of "shared" concern for the environment, and puffery about new arrangements that will insure a direct response to a customer's complaint). Ritual is sometimes the intent of the legitimizers of Presidential Commissions, White House Conferences, and special advisory panels. Assigning boundary spanners to the morass of inter- and intra-organizational committees is a standard method for undermining effective boundary-spanning, though sometimes this backfires.

Tavistock Institute research on group processes has illuminated another means for resisting disturbing input, including feedback supplied by human carriers: people are frequently chosen for boundary-spanning roles—though the motivation for the choice made by other members of the group is often unconscious—as a means for getting the person "away" from core activities of the subsystem which other members feel are upset by the presence of the spanner-to-be.[4] Also, members of the sentient group associated with a task feel the group strengthened if they partially eject one who is not so committed. Finally, it usually appears to such groups that there may be some benefit in linking themselves to the environment and thereby gaining more information about it. Often, however, this is a rationalization, since members of organizations who would find changing toward lrsp uncomfortable would prefer to minimize the amount of non-routine information they must deal with. One who believes in the need for lrsp and seeks to implement it in a situation where that belief is not widely shared—which would characterize most bureaucratic activities—would create just such a disturbance. There would be a strong tendency, then, to move him away from the core of the activity by linking him to the outside. But removing this source of internal turbulence would be gained at the cost of heightening uncertainty and anxiety.

---

[4] In conversation with A. K. Rice. Also see Rice (1965).

On the one hand, the boundary spanner may come to identify more with the organization or persons spanned to than with the organization spanned from. Then he could subvert or desert the original organization, or at least discard its norms and purposes.[5] During the effort to change an organization toward lrsp there will indeed be occasions for the spanner to be seduced away from his organization. To date, the frustrations and the sense of marginality associated with the boundary-spanning roles related to lrsp initiation have been so punishing that people in these roles usually find their cognitive and affective support, and therefore their allegiances, outside of the organizations they are trying to change.[6] This situation will persist even if change-over attempts are made. Outside his organization the boundary spanner is likely to find more people supportive of his efforts to introduce lrsp. They will be involved in activities that provide the input for lrsp: designing the technology, holding the seminars, and doing the studies. For some boundary spanners these will be both cognitively and affectively attractive activities. Carried on without embroilment in the enormously difficult and frustrating tasks of organizational change we are attending to herein, these groups will be intellectually wide-ranging and imaginative, and the people involved will often offer each other more emotional support and shared commitment than the boundary spanner will find in his "home" organization. Moreover, these people will not be ambivalent toward him or subject him to the institutional and personal pressures he must live with in his own organization (because of role conflicts and ambiguities), as he tries to move it toward lrsp. Other agencies may also appear seductive, if only because "the grass is greener" syndrome is especially operative when frustration and a sense of only partial organizational attachment are chronic, as they are likely to be for many boundary spanners.

On the other hand, some boundary spanners will have enough task-group and sentient-group support within their own organizations to find the challenge of facilitating change-over efforts deeply rewarding. This is especially likely to be so for boundary spanners skilled in organizational development techniques. They will be better able to anticipate and understand what is or is not happening, and they will be better able to

[5] This, of course, is well known to organizations like the State Department, which regularly rotates its foreign service officers and brings them home for reindoctrination. R. Kahn suggests that for boundary spanners associated with frsl, the purpose of removing them from that role from time to time would be twofold: through them, to better indoctrinate other organizational personnel with *outside* perspectives; and to relieve them of the role strain attached to the boundary-spanning function.

[6] Based on numerous interviews. Also see L. Duhl's paper (1966) prepared for the American Academy of Arts and Sciences, Commission on the Year 2000, not yet published. It is in Vol. III of the Commission's Working Papers.

see the slings and arrows they suffer as expressions of the situation rather than as personal attacks.

But for the less fortunate boundary spanners, the threat of defection will create uncertainty and hence anxiety in those who commissioned the boundary spanner, whether they did so to enhance linkages with the environment outside their boundaries, or as a means of reducing internal turbulence. By rejecting the spanner they now must also worry about persisting turbulence within the organization and its ability to assure allegiance, as well as about what threats to organizational survival or status may result from information revealed or public positions taken by the ex-boundary spanner that would expose organization weaknesses and, hence, those of its members—especially those that created the opportunity that lead to defection.

All top-level officials (and many others) are frequently in danger of being embarrassed by revelations of their illegal acts, failures, lack of control over their subordinates, and sheer incompetence. . . .

Even the most brilliant and impeccably ethical leader of any large organization will eventually develop some skeletons in the closet because of the nature of large organizations. This is particularly likely if his organization's functions involve great uncertainty, rapidly changing environments, large expenditures, and heavy pressures from external agents.

. . . No leader of any large organization can avoid undertaking acts he does not want made public. Therefore, the desire for personal loyalty among subordinates is a universal phenomenon among such leaders" [Downs, 1966, pp. 71–72].

This threat will be very real in a turbulent society where roles outside the organization will often heavily interact with roles performed inside the organization.

This diffusion of allegiance associated both with the boundary-spanning role and with the strong inter-linking of organizational and environmental roles, helps, I think, explain the increasing difficulty government agencies face in keeping what used to be "in-house" information within the agency. It also accounts for some of the recent truculence of staffs and members of official commissions. They are more frequently disinclined to accept a problem as it is defined for them by the official sponsors, and they have a tendency to make "indiscreet" reports. Obviously not all of those holding such extra-organization perspectives are imbued with the philosophy of lrsp. But those with a lrsp perspective often have competences growing out of that perspective that are increasingly in demand. At the same time, their perspectives and their corresponding feelings of urgency about getting on with lrsp make them more indifferent to parochial values about organizational prerogatives and public relations images. This deritualization of committees, commissions, and conferences set up to link public interest with political policy epitomizes the defection threat that even "leashed" boundary spanners will carry. It will be a growing threat to error-denying, uncertainty-resisting organizations and environments, because in the very nature of their activities, many who seek the boundary-spanning role see themselves as expendable. They come from environments and carry self-images that value problem solution over organizational stability, even over organizational survival, and there seem to be more such people produced in our changing, multi-valued environment.

"Characteristically, there develop among federal agencies informal networks that can realistically be called 'undergrounds.' These are groups of individuals attracted to the idea of change in agency policy and practice, and committed to the use of the informal system to effect that change. Such undergrounds may be used . . . to preserve continuity of effort underneath a changing pattern of agency heads. They may also represent guerrilla movements aimed at changing agency policy and, sometimes, at subverting official policy to other ends" (Schon, 1971, p. 171). Indeed, these "guerrilla" bureaucrats hope that the uncomfortable information they help produce will perform the feedback and crises-generating functions that encourage organizational revisions and thereby open up possibilities for changing in the direction of lrsp.[7]

Finally, the boundary spanner's special opportunities to discover more rewarding affiliations will stir the embers of discontent and frustration that always warm the yearnings of persons struggling to be meaningful in upsetting, uncertain situations. Coping with perhaps unsought but nevertheless self-generated pressures to look farther afield, like the bound-

---

[7] This kind of behavior draws our attention to a historical circumstance that contributes to the complexity and depth of ambivalence that will accompany new boundary-spanning activities related to changing toward lrsp. To date, it has been boundary-spanning for another purpose that has contributed to the frustration and demoralization of some governmental bureaucratic attempts *to* plan (albeit in a more limited way and in more "engineering" spirit). Members of bureaucracies who have wished to resist proposed programs or procedures have been able to span across their organizational boundaries to seek support from their own program constituencies, including legislators. In that way they have introduced turbulence and uncertainty into those parts of their bureaucracy that threatened them. Given the vested interests in their environment, this boundary-spanning supported the entrenched programs and undermined attempts to redesign activities. Most government civilan bureaucracy boundaries are far more permeable than those of corporations, which is one of the reasons why corporations much more than federal, state, or local governments have been able to manage organizational development and, in some senses of the word, occasionally to plan.

ary spanner does, will add to one's personal burdens. These stirrings, transformed through the ubiquitous psychological process of projection, will lead one to be more questioning of the organizational loyalty of one's colleagues. Unconscious desires to avoid these uncomfortable states of mind will provide yet another incentive to restrain the boundary spanner, and in the process to resist efforts to change toward lrsp.

Ambivalence toward the boundary-spanning function when applied to lrsp activities is evidenced by the reluctance of top executives to commit sufficient resources to develop this function even when they assign it. The rationale offered is that they want to see what will develop before they invest heavily. But investing so meagerly practically assures that those who are given the lrsp-initiating, boundary-spanning roles will have too few resources of authority, time, information-generating and synthesizing capabilities, and legitimacy to do an adequate initial job. Usually the assignment fails; either the spanner is worn down by frustration and antagonism toward him, or he is reassigned by higher authority because his activities bring too little payoff or too much actual or potential disruption to the organization.

Within this situation lies another source of ambivalence toward the boundary spanner intent on furthering the change toward lrsp. It resides in executives and managers, from those at the top down through those responsible for the various functionally differentiated subsystems that must be linked to meet the requirements for lrsp. The boundary spanner (especially if he is performing in the role of long-range planner) comes to understand the ramifications of the interactions between the subsystems better than the subsystem administrators do. The spanner sees the picture broadly, "from above," whereas the subsystem administrator is rewarded for seeing his activities narrowly, from the vantage point of what most benefits his subsystem. The executives at the top rarely see the detailed interactions of their own organization; their perspective and rewards come from looking outward at the relationship of their organization to its environment. These executives really have little control over or understanding of the interactions between their subsystems that affect the character of the output. Information coming up to them is deliberately filtered and distorted to protect the senders, and interaction between subsystems is supposed to be managed by their subordinates. The role of the boundary spanner, however, frees him from the reward structure that constrains the actions and perspectives of those middle-level executives. Thus he is able to obtain information, and to derive implications from it which he can apply to understanding what is going on in the organization, that is different from the information available to top-level or middle-level management. The boundary spanner learns things and puts them together in ways that are potentially threatening to the autonomy and au-

thority of executives and middle-level administrators, threatening to their
feeling of competence and control.[8]

The uncertainty and anxiety attached to the establishment of
boundary-spanning activities, whether the activity is to gain environmental contact or to reduce the impact of an internal source of disturbance, is
succinctly summarized by Miller and Rice (1967):

> *In general, the setting up of any intergroup relationships involves
> the drawing, temporarily at least, of new boundaries. And the drawing of
> new boundaries contains the possibility that the new boundaries will prove
> stronger than the old—that the new boundaries will enjoy a greater senti-
> ence than the old.*
>
> *Potentially, therefore, the setting up of any intergroup transactions
> has destructive characteristics since the relationships involved may destroy,
> or at least weaken, familiar boundaries. But any open system, in order to
> live, has to engage in intergroup transactions. The members of any group
> are thus inevitably in a dilemma: on the one hand, safety lies in the
> preservation of its own boundary at all costs and the avoidance of trans-
> actions across it; on the other hand, survival depends upon the conduct of
> transactions with the environment and the risk of destruction.*
>
> *. . . Clearly, the more numerous the members who 'represent' an
> enterprise to its environment, the greater the chance of inconsistency; and
> hence, as we have postulated, of reducing investment in the enterprise
> boundary [pp. 23–24].*

Burdens and Incentives Experienced by the Boundary Spanner

In Chapter Nine we examined the psychological burdens produced
by ambiguous or conflicting roles. I will not review these here, but will
note only that boundary spanners will necessarily be subject to heavy role
stress.

Another burden will often be added to those already described. A
decision to try to influence an organization or parts of it to change toward
lrsp involves additional overloads on already overloaded persons. At

---

[8] This is not to say that the boundary spanner would be more competent
or should be in more control than the administrator or executive. While the
spanner's perspective is likely to be broader, it will be different from theirs
partially because, not being in their roles, the spanner will not understand their
perspective completely—just as those inside the organization will have trouble
getting the "feel" of the turbulence outside that the spanner has. These mutual
inadequacies of understanding and response to each other's needs can only be
reduced if time, resources, and self-conscious efforts are committed to acknowledging them and working on them. (An observation by R. Bauer.)

whatever level or source the initiative comes from in the organization, a person who thinks in terms of lrsp must already have been formally or informally in touch and inter-linked with many trends and activities beyond those that occupy him in his job. Otherwise one would hardly appreciate the need for lrsp, much less be motivated to initiate it, especially given the rewards that go with conventional organizational perspectives. Such persons are almost certainly already overloaded by organizational and extra-organizational activities. But initiating lrsp requires spanning beyond one's conventional organizational boundaries and activities to garner the conceptual and operational ideas and resources needed to encourage internal lrsp-oriented activities. And this boundary-spanning means further overloading, with concomitant additional exhaustion and emotional discomfort.

Most boundary spanners will perform that function by virtue of some specialized competence which they or their superiors believe legitimizes the linking function. As a result, for years to come the boundary spanner can be expected to provide his own contribution to the resistances to changing over to lrsp. These will derive from his trained incapacities associated with his special competences. These incapacities are not inevitable correlates of specialized training; but so far, the professional socializing experiences of many who would fill these roles, or who would attempt to establish them, have produced personal styles of behavior that have militated against their easy acceptance by others not similarly socialized. More specifically, since many aspects of lrsp technology will depend on mathematical-logical styles of thinking, persons with these skills are likely to find themselves by choice or assignment bridging the proposed lrsp activity and the conventional organizational activity they hope to influence to use the new techniques. By training, and sometimes by temperament, persons who use these cognitive styles are often obtuse to the point of being, or appearing to be, downright arrogant about the priority and rightness of their expertise.[9]

In contrast, there is the boundary spanner who is "all heart," who

[9] It is generally acknowledged that the Pentagon experts brought over to indoctrinate the civilian agencies in PPBS, in the wake of President Johnson's executive order that civilian agencies use PPBS, did a first-rate job of alienating almost everyone by their "arrogant, insufferable, know-it-all" attitude toward the civilian innocents. Doubtless, some "civilians" saw them this way as a rationalization for their resistance to these upsetting changes. As D. Campbell has observed, "It required some who had previously written vacuous program statements now to write dishonest ones." But the retrospective impression seems so widely shared that there is no reason to doubt that arrogance was evident. I have seen it in operation elsewhere, though the arrogance can often be more usefully understood as a style of interpersonal incompetence rather than as the expression of a self-conscious know-it-all self-image.

has analogous trained incapacities to recognize the need for or possibility of rationalizing organization-environment learning relationships in the spirit of lrsp. For these spanners, that which ought to get planning attention may seem to be ineffable, transcending all efforts to embed it in a systematic societal learning system, or it may seem to be a matter that can only be dealt with by those in the environment who have *lived* the situation.[10]

Therefore, there will be the task of structuring the organization and its organizational interfaces so that certain cognitive and interpersonal inadequacies can be dealt with openly and constructively in order that boundary spanners can learn to enlarge their interpersonal skills and substantive knowledge. This again emphasizes the reciprocal aspects of building a trusting, open, uncertainty-acknowledging, error-embracing organization by improving the interpersonal competences of its members and changing the norms and structures that sustain them.

In view of the conflict-laden, ambiguous, and potentially frustrating role that will be inherent in boundary spanning, why would anyone choose to perform it? There seem to be several rewards. For one intent on pushing for changes toward lrsp, the role could be particularly potent. The incumbent has the opportunity to define new realities and opportunities among groups that need to collaborate if lrsp-oriented changes are to be tried out. His access to information beyond that known within the boundaries of any subsystem and his comparative freedom to interpret and embellish the implications of that information afford him special opportunities and resources to be influential. As boundary spanner with the aim of moving toward lrsp, his monitoring activities could afford him and his sponsors special opportunities to channel and regulate developments to facilitate their movement in that direction. Whether these fantasies are fulfilled is another question. So far they haven't been, and most of those with whom I am familiar have sooner or later given up the role—or have been forced out of it. But for those aspirants yet to come these can be potent enticements—especially if they are naïve about the matters discussed herein.

Motives like the above will also be boosted by other psychologically rewarding aspects of the role: a sense of omniscience and an expectation and sometimes the realization of influence (sometimes as a response to his omniscience).

The boundary spanner knows more than the groups he spans between because he has access to more sources of information, and because, given these multiple inputs and given his role, he has the incentives and resources to make more interpretations. The added facts and interpreta-

[10] See Cottrell and Sheldon (1963); also Moynihan (1970).

tions are what makes him valuable (as well as what makes him threatening). The feeling of knowing more and of being valuable because one
knows more is heady stuff indeed. It has kept more than one boundary
spanner going in the face of hostility, rebuff, and only occasional influence.

For some, there is the satisfaction of feeling powerful by virtue of
their omniscience. Not only may they influence but they can defect—with
all the potential for upset that implies. Sometimes they do both, but even
when they don't, the belief that they could influence by defecting compen-
sates some for frustrations and rebuffs.

Related to the satisfactions of feeling powerful is the satisfaction of
operating clandestinely. Boundary spanners know that efforts to introduce
lrsp activities are bound to be resisted, at least by superiors who have
reached that status by commitment to bureaucratic routines, or who are
political appointees for whom the requirements for lrsp would jeopardize
their ambitions or operating styles. Hence there are special satisfactions
for some in the opportunity to transform conventional roles into boundary-spanning activities, to establish alliances outside the formal lines of
authority, to beat the system while operating within it.

And finally there is the feeling of mobility that such spanning tasks
inspires, as well as the experience of wider horizons and exposure to more
people and situations and alternative career opportunities.[11] This, too,
helps compensate for inadequate or unreliable in-house recognition.

Of course in addition to those who seek such a role, there will be
persons and groups who are assigned to boundary-spanning activities
whether they like it or not, because in the eyes of their superiors their
present roles or organizational titles seem right for the job. But they may
not be at all right for the job, and they may not want it either, although
some may come to like it for the feelings of power and omniscience it
provides. However, for others, including some members of in-house planning staffs, the psychological burdens may well be intolerable. Many persons, who from their location in the table of organization would seem to
be "naturals" to forward lrsp, in fact will sabotage such efforts because
they are unable to operate effectively under conditions of high role
ambiguity, role conflict, and vacillating, ambivalent support. This will be
true for many who recruited themselves for and trained in the more rigid
conventional skills and professional standards of city planning, land-use
planning, operations research, computerized data processing and simulation, and other such areas of quantitative expertise.[12]

---

[11] In his first year on the job, making over and opening up the Los
Angeles City Planning Department to the Los Angeles community, the Director
made 180 speeches. While this is exceptional by conventional standards it
probably represents the future direction of this type of boundary spanning role.

[12] Some administrators, recognizing this fact of life, have made humane

Note that a number of compensations associated with boundary-spanning have to do with real or fantasied behavior by the role incumbent of precisely the kind that would generate hostility and anxiety in his clientele: those who fill the role may find in it compensations that are truly threatening to those dependent on them. Thus those who need the services of boundary spanners may have valid reasons for their fears. These fears would be less valid if the boundary-spanning role were valued enough by the organization to provide direct rewards instead of fantasied omniscience and power. But as long as users are ambivalent, the role is unlikely to be positively valued with any consistency. The dilemma is unreal, however: making boundary-spanning more acceptable organizationally and more rewarding personally requires the personal, interpersonal, and structural changes mentioned throughout these chapters. What seems clear is that boundary-spanning cannot be incorporated as an essential part of changing toward lrsp merely by imposing or overlaying that activity on conventional organizational norms and structures.

---

use of it. When reorganizing their planning activities to make them more flexible and open to the environment, those people who are unable to deal with "turbulence at the interface" have been deliberately shifted to jobs that emphasize routine.

How Conventional Organization Structures Resist the Requirement for Information-Sharing

The intimate and reciprocal relationship between the person and the organizational structure is sharply exemplified in the resistances put up to requests to share information garnered and used by sub-units in the pursuit of their missions.

The Present Status of Information-Sharing

There are many types of information that persons and organizations resist sharing. The forms of resistance and circumstances for resisting can be expected to vary to some degree depending on the kind of information involved, but I will not attempt such an elaborated description here: that is more appropriate for later systematic studies. Nevertheless, it is worth noting some of the types of information which those possessing it will resist sharing. To do so will help explain why information sharing is so crucial a requirement if efforts are to be made to change toward societal learning through long-range planning. Information-sharing would include sharing information about: data, data sources, and data collecting methods; program instructions for processing, combining, disaggregating, and summarizing the data; interpretations of the data and the theories or assumptions upon which interpretations are made; and decisions about who has access to any of the above, including who is obligated to use what data, programs, or interpretive concepts as a basis for organizational action.

Today a person's or a sub-unit's power in an organization is often a function of the capability to preempt information. There are several advantages in preempting information, though no one advantage is exclusively determined by information control. Nor is information control usually the only determinant of relative power, influence, and invulnerability. But information control can be a formidable asset, often well worth protecting under present norms. By controlling access to information, persons or sub-units can protect themselves somewhat from invasions of authority because others lack the information they would need or could use to dislodge them. To some extent they can protect themselves from accusations of inefficiency or unimaginativeness, because they have control of the information others would need to prove their case. They can protect their appreciative setting about what constitutes the relevant reality in their environment by the kind of information they collect. This self-serving image of reality gives them a measure of value in their own eyes. They can define their situation much more as they choose to because they have information about it others lack. Indeed, others may also judge their significance through their image of reality because others have less information about the environment—except possibly the people who comprise it. And they can bargain with information for power and status and for other information they need to improve their control capability and status.

Resistance to sharing information often also benefits those who ought to use the preempted information if they could get it. By not having more information of the sort that would expand the considerations they should apply to their interpretations and decisions, uncertainty is not increased and the risks of errors from decisions made in an unfamiliar larger context are lessened. A person or his unit remain responsible only for what can be done in the face of constraints on the information available to them. In other words, the rule "live and let live" often supports information preemption.

Yet moving toward lrsp will fundamentally depend on the degree to which resistances can be overcome to giving up these advantages gained from information preemption. Every aspect of the conduct of lrsp will depend on the sharing of information available in units of an organization. Moreover, this sharing will have to extend to constituencies in the environment and to other organizations involved in overlapping service areas. Unless the data base and the assumptions used for interpreting and applying it are shared with the environment, societal learning will be impossible.[1] Also, the very legitimacy, utility, and viability of servicing organizations will depend in part on their ability to respond positively to demands for information from constituency representatives skilled in data interpretation and utilization.[2]

The experience to date clearly supports theoretically based conjectures that would predict that conventional organizational structures and norms will encourage strong resistance to this requirement for changing toward lrsp. For one, there is the repeated experience (including my own) of those who have interviewed in agencies where efforts have been made to push for data bank utilization, management information systems, and other data-sharing technologies. Reports on the status of urban data banks make it clear that their planning and policy-making limitations are by no means exclusively the result of inability to get the needed data or inadequate models for applying it.[3] Internal resistances to sharing data play an important part. "What I'm finding as I study the impact of information systems on organizations is that some valid knowledge is considered bad—bad because it is threatening. In many companies, valid data on important problems would reveal a maze of cover-ups, elaborate fictions, incompetence, missed opportunities, and distrust. All these things can impede an organization from reaching its goals, or even keep it from

---

[1] There is, of course, endemic resistance in federal agencies to sharing information with the public. At the time of this writing the Justice Department has helped and encouraged agencies to resist even in the face of the Freedom of Information Act (Wade, 1972). By the time this is read, no doubt other public actions will have been taken by various public officials to emphasize to the public that things will be more open from now on. Perhaps they will, partially because the growing sophistication of various publics makes it politically sensible to look, even to act, in support of this public demand. But there is every reason to believe that the directives to "open up" will speak much louder than the acts of those who should do the opening. However, the direction is favorable to lrsp even if the distance moved is likely to be comparatively short.

[2] An example of things to come: after the State Highway Department strongly suggested to disapproving members of the university faculty of a midwest city that it would bring pressure to bear to get its preferred highway location approved, and that it could prove the correctness of its choice on the basis of computer analyses, it had second thoughts; the faculty members threatened to demand through Washington (federal funds were involved) that the Highway Department make available to the faculty members the computer *programs* it used for deriving its conclusions—not just the comparative results for alternative locations. Elsewhere I have proposed an on-line citizen-used computer system for access to and manipulation of the same data the servicing agencies use. My purpose was to stimulate appreciation of the necessity for and possibility of such a system, and to demonstrate the enormous political and personal changes required to realize it. See Michael (1968). Also see Friedmann (1972).

[3] For example, see the evaluation reports in the last section of *Urban and Regional Information Systems* (1968).

rationally defining its goals. Valid data from an MIS [Management Information System] would reveal to many managements how much has been hidden from it all these years" (Argyris, 1970, p. 29).

Those familiar with on-going efforts to use information-sharing systems such as urban data banks and management information systems (MIS) conjecture that resistance will continue.

Within city governments, those who actually control automated data systems gain in power at the expense of those who do not. Most city officials are acutely aware of this potential power shift. Each operating department naturally wants to retain as much power as possible over its own behavior and its traditional sphere of activity. Its members are especially anxious to prevent "outsiders" from having detailed knowledge about every aspect of the department's operations. Hence nearly every department with operations susceptible to computerized management will at least initially fight for its own computer and data system controlled by its own members [Downs, 1967, p. 208].

The manager's reactions to threats and arrogance [from MIS-connected personnel] can be predicted. His feelings of mistrust, suspicion, and fears of inadequacy find ways to influence other managers to let the MIS group atrophy or be disbanded. For example, not enough company departments will be persuaded to pay for the MIS services. Or management will find that people don't understand the value of the new systems and can't use an operations research group effectively [Argyris, 1970, p. 34].

Structural Sources of Information Preemption

If there are ways to overcome these resistances to information-sharing they will depend upon changing structural arrangements that reinforce personal and interpersonal behavior and self-images that are rewarded for resisting changing them. We need to look, then, at what seem to be the structural sources that encourage resistance to information-sharing. Wilensky serves our purposes well when he explains them as the result of hierarchy, specialization, and centralization. With regard to hierarchy, he writes:

Information is a resource that symbolizes status, enhances authority, and shapes careers. In reporting at every level, hierarchy is conducive to concealment and misrepresentation. Subordinates are asked to transmit information that can be used to evaluate their performance. Their motive for "making it look good," for "playing it safe," is obvious. A study of 52

*middle managers (mean age 37) found a correlation of +.41 (p. 01)
between upward work-life mobility and holding back "problem" information from the boss; the men on their way up were prone to restrict information about such issues as lack of authority to meet responsibilities, fights
with other units, unforeseen costs, rapid changes in production, scheduling or work flow, fruitless progress reports, constant interruptions, insufficient time or budget to train subordinates, insufficient equipment or supplies, and so on. Restriction of such problem information is motivated by
the desire not only to please but also to preserve comfortable routines of
work: if the subordinate alerts the boss to pending trouble, the former is
apt to find himself on a committee to solve the problem. . . .[4] Hierarchy
blocks communication; blockages lead to indoctrination; indoctrination
narrows the range of communication [Wilensky, 1967, pp. 43, 45].*

*At the upper levels, subordinates tend to "think positive" (remain
within the tolerance limits arbitrarily set at the top); they react primarily
to crises; they tend to create win-lose competitions between groups for
resources and esteem; they hide information; and they create "just-in-
case-the-president asks" files [Argyris, 1970, p. 30].*

Specialization, as a source of resistance from those rewarded by the
norms that are designed around particular functions or competences, has
two aspects for us. First,

*As a source of information blockage and distortion, specialization
may be more powerful than hierarchy. . . . Each service, each division,
indeed every sub-unit, becomes a guardian of its own mission, standards,
and skills; lines of organization become lines of loyalty and secrecy. . . .
Top men . . . are reluctant to let their subordinates "take on" rivals by
asking for information for fear that their unit will betray weakness, invite
counter-inquiries, or incur debt. While information can also be used to
persuade potential allies and to facilitate accommodation with rivals . . .
it is more commonly hoarded for selective use in less collaborative struggles for power and position [Wilensky, 1967, p. 48].*

*Because organizations foster competitiveness, lack of trust, and
win-lose dynamics, the subordinate tends to build walls around his department to protect it from competing departments or arbitrary superiors.
Thus interdependence becomes only partially effective and primarily
through constant monitoring by the superior [Argyris, 1970, p. 33].*

A second source of resistance from specialized sub-units will be
their reluctance to risk present operating styles and rewards in order to

---

[4] The research referred to is Read (1959).

use the existing immature and untested information-sharing technology. As specialists, their "objective" estimates of the high economic, political, and operational costs of shifting to an information-sharing system based on new information technologies has a valid rational component. "In the long run, the biggest technical payoffs from improved urban data will probably arise from better knowledge of underlying causal relationships in the urban environment now shrouded by ignorance. But developing theories about these causal relationships, and then testing those theories, requires an enormous stockpile of data about how each factor varies under a wide diversity of conditions. Hence this important technical payoff may not become available for something like a decade after massive urban data systems are installed and working. This situation will further discourage many urban governments from initially purchasing comprehensive urban data systems" (Downs, 1967, p. 206). However, their estimates are also likely to be a rationalization, in many cases, for continuing to do things the familiar way, that is, in ways that are less uncertain, hence less prone to error, and less likely to require personally upsetting restructuring. Negative estimates will confront lrsp advocates with a particularly sticky kind of argument to overcome, especially since many executives and managers will prefer the rationalization offered by their conservative experts rather than face the consequences of information-sharing.

There is a deeper reason for executive resistance. It's rarely discussed because executives themselves are rarely aware of it. This basic, unspoken reason usually surfaces after lengthy discussion about the probable long-range effects of MIS.

At this point managers slowly begin to realize that fundamental changes will be required in their personal styles of managerial thought and behavior. That's when the danger signals start. Those other stated objections—lack of knowledge and the primitive state of the art—are important, but only temporary. Eventually they will be overcome by research and dissemination of knowledge. But concern and fear about what MIS will do to managers—what it will reveal about the way they've been operating all this time—is what creates the basic resistance [Argyris, 1970, p. 30].

Wilensky's third structural contributor to resistances to information sharing is centralization.

Related to the information pathologies of hierarchy and specialization is the dilemma of centralizatoin: if intelligence is lodged at the top, too few officials and experts with too little accurate and relevant information are too far out of touch and too over-loaded to function effectively;

on the other hand, if intelligence is scattered throughout many subordinate units, too many officials and experts with too much specialized information may engage in dysfunctional competition, may delay decisions while they warily consult each other, and may distort information as they pass it up. More simply, plans are manageable only if we delegate; plans are coordinated in relation to organizational goals only if we centralize.

. . . In the minds of political, military, and industrial elites the advantages of centralized intelligence have apparently tended to outweigh these dangers. Most executives have been less concerned about preserving the independence and objectivity of their experts than about controlling them. For their part, the experts, seeing a chance for greater influence, have not been loath to secure guidance from the top [Wilensky, 1967, p. 58].

As the informal modes become explicit, information comes increasingly under the control of top management. The top level starts to see things it never saw before. Middle managers feel increasingly hemmed in. In psychological language, they will experience a great restriction of their space of free movement, resulting in feelings of lack of choice, pressure, psychological failure. These feelings in turn can lead to increasing feelings of helplessness and decreasing feelings of responsibility. Result: a tendency to withdraw or to become dependent upon those who created or approved the restriction of space of free movement.

Sound familiar? MIS can do to middle and near-top management exactly what the job specialization itself does to lower-level employees [Argyris, 1970, p. 32].

There are ways to reduce these oppressive, adverse effects, as demonstrated by the evolution of divisionalized large corporations. To achieve this in government would require a radical design of bureaucratic structures and of the relationship between executive and congressional control of the agencies. This would also be true at the state and local levels. More basically, it is unclear that the suboptimizing philosophy inherent in corporate decentralization is appropriate for defending or pursuing the public interest. The reconciliation of intra-agency and inter-agency conflicts, and of the purposes of congress and the executive office, does seem to require some kind of top management that knows more and more even as it requires the same down the line—which brings us back to Wilensky's dilemma, just quoted.

In a conventional bureaucracy the contribution of these structural stimuli to resistance will be compounded by another characteristic of the context for change-over attempts. As I have repeatedly emphasized, attempts at changing toward lrsp will have to be *learned* from if the effort toward frsl is to advance or at least have a chance of persisting in the face of the failures and the many sources of resistance we have examined. But learning will itself require an information-sharing system to facilitate just that purpose. An additional organization function would have to be integrated: an information-sharing system for applying the learning to further efforts at lrsp. A general observation of Wilensky's (1967) emphasizes the additional organizational redesign task implicit in the requirement for a learning-system, information-sharing, structure:

> Other things being equal, the larger the size, the greater is the public impact, the more intense is the problem of internal control, and the more resources are available for the intelligence function. The more specialization, the more interdependent are the specialized parts, the greater the cost of failure of any one part, and, therefore, the more resources devoted by each to keep track of the others, and the more staff at the center to coordinate the whole. Moreover, greater specialization increases the difficulty of recruitment and training and the amount of effort needed to secure information about morale and performance. Finally, the more heterogeneous the membership or constituents of an organization, the more ambiguous, diffuse, diversified, and numerous its purposes or products; this more complex structure of goals means more variables to consider and a more urgent problem of coordination [pp. 38–39].

If organizations try to meet these requirements by the conventional means of hierarchy, specialization, and centralization, organizational learning for changing to lrsp will not be possible: information will not be shared enough.

Some Unresolved Dilemmas

If there is a way out of the auto-regenerative set of resistances to sharing information, it will certainly require a willingness to acknowledge uncertainty and embrace error. Information-sharing could be disastrous for the donor if the recipient uses it to further those organizational and self needs that are rewarded by the same norms that make it worthwhile to resist information-sharing. Discreet sabotage, deceit, and duplicity are usually rewarded by the conventional structures if they serve organizational survival or, sometimes, sub-unit aggrandizement; and there is no reason to believe that such well-learned performance styles will be given up easily by people who have found them rewarding and thus expect the same behavior from others. On the other hand, there will be the environment of clamorous constituencies and advocates insisting on access to information. Once some information, and the premises regarding its applicability, are partially shared with the environment, it will be difficult to know what is still worth jealously guarding or can be guarded outside or inside—especially if other persons and other agencies are advancing themselves by sharing even more with their environments.

However, there is an important dilemma here, one that would need to be worked through. One advantage in controlling data access is that it reduces outside pressures. There is less distraction and interference because there is less basis for queries, questions, challenges, and arguments. All systems, including biological systems, control the information they allow to influence them, in part by what information they put into the environment. Even as congressional demands for information do at times claim most of the creative and top administrative resources of an agency under fire, unlimited access to information could immobilize the agency, leaving it too little time, energy, and ideas to do more than provide information. Societies, especially their repositories of power and information, have vacillated between being relatively inaccessible and relatively accessible to information, though inaccessibility has been the more frequent and elaborated response. Nevertheless, if we wish to move toward frsl it can only be by increasing the access to information. What the rules of the game would have to be, if we want to provide access to information but also protect the capability of the information-sharing organization to accomplish its other functions, would be one of the many new kinds of norms and procedures to be discovered, to be learned, through attempts to move toward lrsp.

But while pressures from the environment will tend to force data-sharing within an organization, they will not of themselves provide the directions for effective and humane changes in the structure, supportive norms, and interpersonal behavior that have traditionally sought to gain advantages from information preemption. Directions for these changes are to be found, I believe, among considerations of the kind we have attended to in other chapters. Additional directions for structural changes appropriate for information-sharing for frsl can be discovered by examining the more encompassing information-seeking and information-using requirement for changing toward lrsp—namely, the pervasive solicitation and application of feedback from the present and future environment.

However, before turning to this broader subject in the next chapter, I must acknowledge an aspect of information-sharing that is already so much a part of the dialogue that I shall not expand on it here: the problem of individual privacy and freedom and the extent to which it is threatened or protected by the preemption or sharing of information, on the one hand, and by the organizations who do the preempting or sharing on the other. The issue is complex and holds deep dilemmas. How to live with these dilemmas or resolve them depends in part on what conjectures about future personal values and societal needs are emphasized as a basis for present actions. Much has been written on these issues.[5] They remain unsolved and the balance between the private and the public interest remains obscure and contentious. It is a central concern in the matter of information-sharing, but it is by no means congruent with that general problem, nor is it relevant in a great many areas where resistances to sharing information abound.

[5] See Harrison (1967); Michael (1964); Miller (1971); and Westin (1967).

On the Importance of Feedback
and the Resistances to It

ক্লক্লক্লক্লক্লক্লক্লক্লক্লক্লক্লক্লক্লক্লক্লক্লক্লক্ল

*I*nformation feedback is the *sine qua non* of cybernetic systems. It is through information feedback that a system evaluates where it is in terms of where it intends to go. It is the means by which error is detected and thereby it provides the basis for learning how to get from here to there through changes in performance that result in successive reductions in error. Of central importance for lrsp, feedback also provides the information needed for learning what now constitutes "here" and for deciding whether to continue to try to get "there," in the future. That is, it provides the basis for evaluating whether the appreciation of "here" and "there" needs to be revised. In the nature of the situation with which we are dealing, the very process of learning through feedback provides the means for making changes in definitions of "here" and "there," along with the means for linking them through time via programatic actions, and for evaluating those actions (Bauer, 1967, and Webber, 1965).

What Characterizes Feedback Appropriate for Lrsp?

Ideally, the feedback process consists of:

1. Putting into the environment "output" signals, that is, symbols, or materials, or events (which are combinations of symbols and materials) intended to produce specific results.

2. Detecting in that environment signals, presumably related to the results, that can be used to assess the effectiveness of the output signals introduced into the environment for the purpose of producing the intended results.[1]

3. Detecting other signals that can provide a context for analyzing the meaning of the gap between intended and actual results.

4. Detecting other signals that can provide a context for revising goals and objectives and hence for revising programs intended to produce specific results.

5. Gathering those signals in forms that can be interpreted.

6. Bringing them into the initiating organization (or other organizations assigned the task of feedback analysis).

7. Evaluating the meaning of the feedback in the light of extant objectives and goals and of the programs intended to meet them.

8. Disseminating that evaluation in such ways that it is *in fact acted on* by the organization so as to change or otherwise influence the output signals intended to produce specific results in the environment.

In spite of the centrality of feedback for system adaptation, most human organizations generally use a very low order of feedback under most conditions—indeed, it is often so poor or misleading as to be worse than no feedback at all. There are many reasons why this is so in organizations that are responsible to complex environments. There are deep technological and conceptual inadequacies in existing schemes for evaluating organizational impact on the environment, as was discussed in Chapter Two. There is always the question of whether turbulence, in Emery and Trist's sense, is so great as to block out evidences of relationship between organization output and environmental impact. There are ambiguities in goals and objectives that make it difficult if not impossible to specify what feedback to get. There are also contradictions and ambiguities inherent in the statutes and other directives that determine the mandate of government programs. (This situation is beginning to change, however, with the growing understanding that society is a system, not a collection of recipients for categorically funded programs.) There are time constraints and money limitations and all those other characteristics of the

---

[1] There is a generally unremarked-on subtlety in the feedback process that becomes critical in the societal situation because the matching process is so poor: "the output message must be in such a form that when it acts on the [environment] the [environment] will be able to generate a message which is usable by the feedback system for controlling the output source. [Components of systems] exist as systems because they can generate signals to which they can respond; when they cannot do this they cease to be [parts of] systems" (Michael, 1954, p. 4).

organization's operating context that permit no more than "bounded rationality," in Herbert Simon's phrase.

How the Characteristics of Feedback Information Interact with Organizational Structures for Information Processing

But other factors weave through and exacerbate these circumstances by sustaining the personal, interpersonal, and structural arrangements that make such familiar constraints more persistent and obstructive than they need to be. These are social psychological factors that revolve around the needs of the organization's members to be protected from turbulence, uncertainty, error, and sentient group instability. Doing what would need to be done to get and use better feedback for the purposes of moving toward lrsp will be resisted to the degree that it removes the social psychological advantages that organizations provide by avoiding feedback.

Even if the social psychological sources of resistance to much better feedback were removed, other sources of feedback enfeeblement would still be there and would still need to be overcome as well. However, the latter sources in some degree operate as they do because the social psychological rewards—or as H. David puts it, the benefits of calculated ignorance—discourage overcoming them. Doubtless the comforts of not knowing, because the feedback is either absent or unrevealing, have contributed to disinclinations to work hard at evaluation technology and to risk trying it in the real world. Similarly, the comforts of ignorance have made it easier to live with the disadvantages of gratuitous sub-unit autonomy and competition. So too with disinclinations to expose internal conflicts, either to resolve them or to make them work more effectively for overall organizational accomplishment vis-à-vis the environment. If attempts are made to change feedback processes in ways appropriate for lrsp, they will not succeed if the benefits of calculated ignorance as sources of resistance to change are not attended to at least as carefully as the other factors presently obstructing effective feedback.

The structural arrangements that exist between the organization and its environment, and the structural arrangements within the organization for dealing with feedback (when it does get through the organization's boundaries), contribute to the resistances to the use of feedback. "An organization is a system of structured relations. But an organization also acts, and such actions imply intellectual, rational, decision-making processes. Both organization structure and the nature of the intellectual phase of organizational life (decision making) limit the modern organization's ability to absorb feedback information, especially data regarding second-order social consequences. Learning how to perceive or detect these consequences is difficult; it is even more difficult to make these perceptions effective within the organization" (Rosenthal and Weiss, 1966, pp. 316–317).

As is true in all these matters, the interdependence of persons and structures makes precise distinctions misleading and awkward. Here the interactional amorphousness is especially pronounced in the interplay between two factors: (1) organizational doctrine and mission definition, which are, so to speak, held in the minds of men and which thereby determine what aspects of the environment men will pay attention to; and (2) the articulation of the organizational structure ("specialization, authority relations, and communication patterns"), which determines how those doctrines and definitions will be processed in transactions with the environment. Doctrine and mission tell the members what to pay attention to, but the organizational structure of expertise, of boundary-spanning, of other environmental scanners, of "receiving terminals" that seek and feed in information from the environment, all determine what in fact will be collected and introduced into the organization. The persons a bureaucrat on the interface between organization and environment chooses to listen to will depend on his definition of mission and his definition of what he can do with what he reads or hears. What he feels he can do is partially determined by how he perceives the way in which the authority system in his organization deals with information from his level and location, and by how he deals with it in view of his perceptions. I need not belabor this fairly obvious generalization.[2] But it will be useful presently to typify several important arrangements that organizations use to avoid feedback from the environment; this will help us appreciate the formidable task of dealing with resistance to feedback and hence with resistance to attempts to introduce feedback-dependent aspects of lrsp.

Within the organization, structural factors, interacting with personal and interpersonal factors, will significantly affect whether or not feedback information once obtained will be shared or encapsulated. Other factors, such as the structure of sub-unit differentiation and integration, will contribute to the capacity or incapacity, the willingness or reluctance, of members to process and distribute information so that it is useful within the time constraints that may ultimately determine its utility. I will not attempt here to show how various internal arrangements and responsibilities might affect the processing of feedback. Research on this would be important for a full understanding of the overall task involved in implementing efforts to change toward lrsp. Here I will conjecture about how organizational structures facilitate resistances to dealing with

[2] Downs (1966) delineates many interrelationships of this kind.

feedback—how they help people resist using the information itself and resist changing to structures that might facilitate that use.[3]

Ideally, feedback should help reduce uncertainty by clarifying the extent to which an intended result is presently on track and the ways in which it is not; and by clarifying and discriminating between options by feeding back into the present, so to speak, carefully worked out conjectures about the future. Sometimes this does happen, and when it does those espousing a planning perspective will gain support. But far more often feedback about the present and the future will produce irritation, exhaustion, and anxiety because it will increase uncertainty or render worthless that which was held to be certain. On the one hand, if feedback is richly reflective of the environment it will impose more information on users than they can manage, information rich in cognitive, valuative, and emotional content. If users wish to reject some of it as "irrelevant," "awkward," or "outside their responsibility," then means for sorting it out will have to be invented, and this will call for new screening procedures and new arrangements of subgroups in the organization—and the creation and implementation of these will carry heavy opportunity costs in already overburdened organizations.[4]

In this regard, it seems to me that we will face a growing problem of distinguishing signals from noise. It is generally recommended that more groups in the environment feed back more information to organizations, both as means for informing and influencing organizations and for stimulating members of the environment to participate in planning.

The law of requisite variety suggests that a system of strategic control will only succeed to the extent to which it can develop a similar level of complexity to the system it sets out to influence; it can never, however, be expected to achieve this if it is forced to rely entirely on the scanning abilities of one individual or even a single small group of individuals who occupy a central position in relation to the agencies concerned. It is here, if anywhere, that potential may exist for drawing on the diversity of perspectives which may be provided by a larger body of representatives, particularly where these are directly elected on a ward or constituency basis, and therefore have a direct motivation to keep in touch with events and

---

[3] Wilensky (1967) and Webb (1969) offer a number of suggestions about what to do structurally to reduce avoidance or distortion of feedback, as noted in Chapter Fifteen. But the problem of making the transition to those structures has not been dealt with in social psychological terms, nor is there an adequate empirical base of comparative studies demonstrating what works better than what, and why.

[4] For examples of how these overload burdens are dealt with, see Meier (1963). Also Downs (1966, Chapter 15) and Miller (1960).

pressures within defined sectors of the total community system. If the strategic control group can find effective ways of drawing on the existing scanning functions of all elected representatives, it may thereby considerably enhance its own internal capacity to identify areas of relevant connection between agencies [Friend and Jessop, 1969, p. 132].

But as the number of advocates increases and more authorities and experts take more sides, and as we see increases in the amount and variety of feedback that is asserted to be relevant for decision-making, policy formulation, evaluation, and the rest, it will become increasingly difficult to know what to pay attention to. What might be interpreted as signals, if there were enough resources to sort and compare them and enough time to do it, will instead become mere noise. The overwhelming tendency, when faced with such overloads, is to withdraw (as a person or as an organization) into familiar perspectives and styles of performing. In that case, we would be pretty much where we are now, with selected feedback used to reinforce positions rather than to facilitate societal learning. In the second place, the information will seldom be definitive, and this grossly complicates the question of what to do with it and who is responsible for the doing. For a long time to come, such information will for the most part demonstrate to the professionals involved in lrsp— and, if they are open about it, to their organizational and inter-organizational constituencies—how limited is our understanding of what is going on "out there" and how small is our ability to do anything effective about it.

How to live constructively with noisy "non-definitive" information is one of the things to be learned through lrsp efforts. A major task will involve learning what constitutes a signal that can be meaningfully transmitted into the environment; that is, what constitutes a signal that the environment will be able to recode as a function of its responses to that signal, and then transmit across environment-organization boundaries in forms that allow the organization to evaluate its activities. Many signals into the environment will turn out not to recode in these ways. Only as a result of the development of powerful theory that relates specific kinds of social change to the properties of signals will improvements in signal generation and evaluation occur; and theory development will depend on successive analyses and alterations in what at any time is hopefully referred to as "social indicator" data.

Social indicator designers are not only the ones faced with problems. Adjustments in signals into the environment and in the selection and processing of signals from the environment mean that the programs that produce these signals, and the structured relationships in the organization among programs and the functions that facilitate them, will be subject to change too. This means that personal, intellectual, and emotional commitment to a program may have to be altered or scrapped. So too, with the sentient-group supports that invariably are created by and among people associated with a given program. It means that feedback will expose the failures as well as the successes of programs and projects. This, in turn, confronts program proponents with the task of acknowledging error—indeed, of seeking it out, of embracing it—in the interests of learning how to create better programs. Feedback can raise questions about the sufficiency of original goal choices and planning for action regarding them. This will raise the harrowing question of who is accountable for information about the errors, and who can be trusted with such information. And it raises the difficult task of dealing with interpersonal and intrapersonal conflicts over goals, values, and feelings with regard to their choice and priority. In short, feedback will present all recipients with the likelihood of frequent and deep intellectual and emotional discomfort from information overload—provided they expose themselves to the feedback at all.

The personal and interpersonal burdens of adjusting preconceptions to more information, and the strains of coping with uncertainty and its repercussions in the organization, have been explored in earlier chapters; our concern here is with possible structural consequences. For example, those responsible for initiating administrative-managerial responses to the feedback face the task of reorganizing program activities in response to the feedback implications. This requires dealing with other's errors as well as one's own, with shifting mandates, status, and roles, and with removing people from programs to which they are committed and with which they have an intimate self-identification. The readjustments and rethinking will place heavy social psychological burdens on initiators and receivers. *Typical* bureaucracies are chronically and pervasively overloaded from their struggles with competing and conflicting internal empires and external demands. The idea of having to adjudicate between these *and* additional lrsp-oriented feedback, resulting from the multiple impacts of organizational output, will be too much for most people most of the time; they will tend to respond with avoidance behaviors, unless the circumstances force or reward them to do otherwise.

Structural Means Used to Avoid Feedback

It should be no surprise, then, that people have structured organizations (and organizations have structured people) to avoid unfamiliar feedback. It is worth listing these avoidance processes, because their removal will be resisted and these resistances will interfere with changing toward lrsp. Roughly put, organizations arrange to receive a minimum of turbulence-generating feedback, and to use as little as possible of that to generate further turbulence.

In the first category are such devices as structuring the organization so that sub-units are rewarded for using indicators of organizational *input* to the environment as if they represented what was going on in the environment in response to them. Use of this device has been endemic among organizations that do not use profit and related measures as their feedback signal of environmental response. Historically, this approach reflected widespread naïveté about the relationship between "input" and "output" in cybernetic systems. It also reflected the absence of the technology needed for data processing and analysis. But naïveté was sustained by a reluctance to face the consequences of abandoning it. However, this means of avoiding feedback is beginning to be undermined by growing recognition of the need for cost-benefit type analyses as a basis for public welfare program selection. Cost-benefit studies set the stage for defining the feedback needed to check the anticipated relationship between the symbols, materials, or events put into the social system and the results produced by them. Once this stage is set, expectancies and demands grow to get that feedback. But so far very little feedback has been produced because of the technical weaknesses and organizational resistances to effective utilization of PPBS and related techniques described in Chapter Two.

Meantime, the perennial argument continues to be made that *some* measure is better than no measure, and that input indicators are the best that can be done in the absence of validated theory that relates input to output. "No measure" has the virtue of signifying ignorance and therefore the need to invent and seek valid feedback. Thus recognition of ignorance is precisely what is avoided if "some" measure has become a reinforcer for the extant organizational structure and its concomitant rewards for its members. What is more, recent environment-initiated feedback in the forms of consumerism, muckraking, and protest, as well as the long-standing awareness of the potential utility of the Swedish invention of the ombudsman, demonstrate that the use of input rather than impact is a rationalization hiding the basic need to minimize personal and organizational turbulence that would be produced by impact-indicating feedback.[5]

Feedback which is disrupting because it is unfamiliar is also avoided by structuring the feedback retrieval process so that it selects from the environment only those signals that are compatible with the

[5] See Anderson (1968).

structure and norms of the organization. " 'The tendency of bureaucratic language to create in private the same images presented to the public never should be underrated.' In domestic policy surely such bogies as 'the balanced budget' have worked similar mischief. Doctrines of economic individualism, activated by phrase-making, help explain why America, unique among the rich countries, tolerated an unemployment rate of 4 per cent or more from 1954 until 1966 and has moved so reluctantly toward a humane welfare state. Francis Bacon's warning that man converts his words into idols that darken his understanding is as pertinent today as it was three centuries ago" (Wilensky, 1967, p. 22).

In the past, the environment has been placid enough, or could be treated as placid enough, that learning about highly complex and changing social issues could be minimal or at least slow.[6] Survival of the organization was dependent upon comparatively predictable intra-organizational and inter-organizational bargaining relationships between fund sources, stable constituencies, and formal internal structures—in contrast to the presently changing environment. Hence structures and norms were designed to be responsive to anticipated congressional feedback (or feedback from whatever sources the organization depended on) rather than to new environmental feedback.[7] In corporations, the familiar signals to which they are structured to respond usually have to do with profit or other profit-relevant measures such as corporate growth, market share, or public image, and the signals are sought by sub-units specializing in these preoccupations. As discussed in Chapter Four, corporations typically have not sought feedback on the extra-market consequences of the production, distribution, or consumption of their products, most notably the external costs to both non-consumers and consumers. As a result, the new consumerism and concern for the natural environment have created new sources of feedback that have been disrupting to corporations and for the most part resisted, advertising to the contrary notwithstanding. Corporate organizational structures have rewarded inattention to these matters, and therefore they are mostly populated by persons who see themselves as competent in part because they successfully fill roles that reward such inattention. Governmental agencies and governmental personnel have similarly restricted their feedback to that which is comfortable because it

[6] Schick (1969) gives a most illuminating insight into the historical circumstances of a tranquil domestic environment that encouraged the promulgation of what he calls "process politics," otherwise recognizable as "disjointed incrementalism."

[7] The classic delineation of organizational structures and norms for getting and using feedback useful to the federal budgetary process is Wildavsky (1964). Also see Seidman (1970).

is compatible with "recognizing" special constituencies and with specifying the conditions for communicating with the organizations through specific organizational sub-units or boundary spanners.[8]

An organizational need was not met by operating officials unless it or the fact that their tasks had become routine disturbed them sufficiently to interest them in making the required innovation. By the same token, external dysfunctions cannot be expected to disappear unless they are transformed into organizational needs, which means that their occurrence is so deleterious for administrators or for all officials that they are compelled to make adjustments. This raises the problem of developing democratic techniques that enable the public or its representatives to hold officials specifically accountable for the various consequences of bureaucratic operations, thus converting external dysfunctions into internal needs of the organization that disturb its personnel. The difficulty of finding solutions to this problem is matched only by the urgency of doing so [Blau, 1963, pp. 263–264].[9]

Put in another relevant perspective, only some environmental sources of support or criticism are deemed legitimate. And "legitimate" generally means those values, behaviors, and environmental auspices that are compatible with the program and information-processing structure, and are thus understandable and approved by the servicing agency. Usually, therefore, much of what an agency ought to be receiving as feedback, if it is to adapt to meet environmental needs, is screened out as unreliable, misguided, irrelevant, not within the agency's mandate, or politically infeasible.[10] At the same time, some feedback is overly responded to because it fits personal and organizational biases.

[8] "When a business or a government agency is under the administration of scientific management, its clients may feel that they are not getting the service they are entitled to. But service to the client—at least as the client perceives it—is not what keeps scientific management in business. Under modern Taylorism, management's performance is judged not by the clients' perceived welfare, but by their *demonstrable* welfare. And since the managers themselves design the criteria that demonstrate welfare, demonstrable welfare can be counted on to increase" (Thompson, 1968, p. 54).

[9] For related behavior by congressmen, see Bauer, Pool, and Dexter (1963). Also Downs (1966) is illuminating on this.

[10] "One way organizations adapt to the unreliability of information is by devising procedures for making decisions that can ignore possibly relevant information: they develop "special coding categories" (Cyert and March, 1963, p. 110). Related observations, though not interpreted in terms of legitimacy, are made under the rubric "coding scheme barrier" to communication in Frohman and Havelock (1971, Chapter 6, p. 7). They also cite several studies demonstrating this phenomenon.

This is not to say that symbols in support of established policy and comfortable prejudice inevitably serve as a substitute for policy deliberations. It is to say that facts, arguments, and propaganda directed at friends and enemies alike, in and out of an organization, can be self-convincing. Executives and politicians often become persuaded that the world of crisis journalism they create and respond to is the real world; many a decision-maker is in this way diverted from things which really happen or which are not happening but should be. Many a leader becomes captive of the rhetoric he customarily presents or of the media image he projects. Students of modern society have given too little attention to this reverse action of propaganda—the effect on the people who themselves make the news. If supplying the symbols that guide executive action is "window dressing," it is the kind of display that tells what is in the store [Wilensky, 1967, pp. 23–24].[11]

Since legitimacy criteria also function to structure and to justify the structure of organizational activities, they are a powerful means for reducing uncertainty, in Friend and Jessop's terms (see Chapter Four), about what knowledge will be needed for decision-making (UE), the anticipated state of inter-organizational relations (UR), and about the appropriate values from which to choose actions (UV). This lowered uncertainty encourages a routine perspective which in turn can be transformed into structural arrangements that reinforce the prevailing definitions and screen feedback so as to leave these definitions as little disturbed as possible. But resistances to feedback utilization, rationalized in terms of exclusive obligations to legitimate clientele, will be increasingly vulnerable as uncertainty about organizational legitimacy increases among members of the organization and as parts of the environment continue to challenge organizational legitimacy. Whether this vulnerability can be used to facilitate changing toward lrsp by intruding more effective feedback will depend on the simultaneous availability of other circumstances to be discussed in the next chapter.

Another way a prevailing definition of legitimacy is used as a feedback-reducing device is to structure the organization so that it only attends to feedback from those parts of the environment that do produce feedback compatible with the organization's output signals of symbols, things, and events. Those in the environment that do not respond to these signals do not increase organizational turbulence. By the criteria of legitimacy subscribed to, they have excluded themselves from organizational responsibility by not responding to the signals offered to them. In this situation

<hr>

[11] The most illuminating and devastating analysis and description of this situation is found in Boorstin (1964). Also see Downs (1966).

the members of the organization convince themselves and others that "they've tried" but that the environment is indifferent, or antagonistic, or unappreciative of their efforts. The fault, then, is in the environment, not in the organization's input to that environment. The fact that the environment doesn't make a corresponding "effort" to respond removes further obligations toward it on the organization's part. Such an approach permits legitimacy distinctions between the "worthy" and the "unworthy" poor, between "self-helping" and "lazy" ethnics, and between "appreciative" and "unappreciative" recipients, and it results in the familiar process of "creaming off" the environment.[12] More generally, it allows the organization to ignore or be ignorant of feedback it ought to be using as inputs to its conjectures about the future, which in turn should be affecting its goal and program choices.

In the extreme, organizations try to avoid undesired feedback by threatening to deny services or by taking punitive action. Examples of such actions are midnight check-ups by social welfare agencies; General Motors' effort to "get something on Ralph Nader"; firing an internal source of threatening feedback, be he a corporate engineer, a Defense Department critic, or a Food and Drug Administration biochemist; cutting off resources, such as funds or legitimating auspices, supplied by research-supporting agencies; or retracting a tax-free status, as the Internal Revenue Service did to the Sierra Club; or sweeping up antiwar protesters without recourse to due process.

Serious and systematic attention to feedback from the future, via future studies, is avoided by using these same devices. Future studies can be written off as illegitimate because they do not meet conventional standards of verifiability (though often they are overly legitimized by their champions, simply because they do meet other conventional professional standards of "in" jargon and logical operationalism). They remain unnoticed or unused because the organization is not structured to take in feedback from this quarter: there is no place established for it. They are ignored because organizational structure rewards management and personnel for the production of inputs that respond to existing opportunities. These, it is presumed, will take care of the future. This presumption often expresses the same kind of avoidance behavior as that which did not look closely at the assumptions that accepted other input measures as if they would correctly project impact in the environment.

Yet vicarious exposure to the future is a necessary part of the organization's feedback if it is to try to change toward lrsp. Otherwise there

[12] See Caplan and Nelson (1973). For an incisive summary of the history of American social-work attitudes toward the poor, concerning what it is "proper" to do to improve the lot of the "worthy," see Lubove (1966).

is no way to evaluate the feedback from the present in terms of anticipated impacts. Two devices serve to resist appropriate future-oriented feedback with its freight of uncertainty and problems. One means is to attend only to future-oriented feedback that is compatible with present activities and expectations. The other is to avoid gathering from the extant environment information that presages future developments which would be upsetting for the organization; that is, to avoid carrying out steps three and four in the feedback sequence (described at the beginning of this chapter). By concentrating on what is expected and familiar, the organization can overlook precursor signals that might indicate discomforting or even irresponsible incompatabilities between present actions and future outcomes. Also avoided in this way is the requirement to seek and to use continuously other more contextual conjectures about the future, which, if combined with precursor information from the present environment, probably would be even more upsetting. If we think of future studies as a form of feedback that is resisted as such, it is easier to understand why such studies are frequently commissioned but seldom used if they are incompatible with present operations and perspectives.

Sometimes feedback that has the potential for increasing uncertainty does get into an organization. Usually it is forced on it from outside or is introduced by its own boundary spanners or boundary spanners to it (such as consultants). Occasionally it is inadvertently produced, as when new senior personnel bring in a different appreciation of environmental reality. Sometimes it is produced by deliberate efforts undertaken within the organization, such as internally generated program-evaluation studies, or a decision to invite the environment to become part of the organization (for example, adding members of the environment to the organization's advisory boards). Commissioned studies of the future are one kind of effort that may be undertaken deliberately to shake up the organization, or that may inadvertently do so.

Whatever the means by which the turbulence-generating feedback is produced and however it gets into the organization, organizations are structured to attenuate, diffuse, obscure, and otherwise reduce the impact of the feedback, usually to the point of impotence. "The structure of interpersonal relationships that permits the organization to coordinate the actions of its members often blocks, or at least severely limits, communication of information between the feedback system and the rest of the organization" (Rosenthal and Weiss, 1966, p. 317). The means for doing so have been well described and documented.[13] Essentially they consist of three processes:

[13] See Wildavsky, Wilensky, Webb, Downs, and Rosenthal and Weiss, as cited in the References.

1. Progressively screening out turbulence-generating information feedback as it moves up through the system (the comments in Chapter Fifteen especially apply here).

2. Distributing the task of discovering and coping with the implications of the feedback between contending and competing subgroups who lack intention, mandate, substantive skills, or interpersonal skills to cope with the threats to values, goals, and images of competence, or to cope with the requirements for error acknowledgment and creative reprogramming and restructuring.

3. Transforming the feedback into concepts and categories that allow the decision-maker to treat it as if it were familiar and called only for application of familiar approaches and commitments. This reduces anxiety about self-competence and that of others. It also reduces anxiety about purpose. In all, information overload demands are thereby kept from becoming intolerable.

Over time an organization fabricates an idealized self-image, which becomes a sort of mythological basis for the organizational ideology that explains "what the hell we are doing." The elements of fantasy in the view of the organization involve, usually, some distortion of reality and, therefore, prejudice the evaluation of incoming information. For example, an organization easily develops the fantasy element of essential rectitude, which then leads its members to discount any information that would suggest otherwise. In some degree organizational myths are essential for continuity of purpose. If the myth of 'what the hell we are doing' is overly responsive to signals from the environment, it cannot serve as an organizational balance wheel. Yet at some point there is an optimum balance between the benefits of continuity of purpose and the costs of biased information.

. . . It seems probable that no organization actively seeks feedback information that contradicts such necessary organizational beliefs unless, of course, it is provoked to do so by some kind of crisis" [Rosenthal and Weiss, 1966, pp. 321–322].

Possible Ways of Reducing Resistance to Feedback

There are, then, many rewards deriving from the structural arrangements that protect the organization's members from the disruption encouraged by feedback, with its concomitant threats of overwhelming uncertainty, exposure of error, questions of legitimacy and purpose, and so on. Two change-over questions are posed by this situation: How can the organization overcome the resistances that protect it and its membership; and how can this be done so that the organization doesn't overrespond or underrespond to feedback from the present and the future? Indeed, this second question contains another: What would characterize an effective balance in a changing and problematic world between, overresponse and underresponse to feedback?

Whatever else is involved in dealing with these questions, certainly two capabilities are critical. First is the capability of the organization to reduce fears and anxieties about competence, purpose, status, and so on, that are elicited by the threat that if there is more feedback there will be more information available to more people about the environmental consequences of one's activities. Reducing such fears would depend on discovering how to replace the present structure and norms with ones that would sustain and reward a learning context. Then the very information that is feared, for what it might reveal about organizational and individual incompetence, would be actively sought out for the opportunity it would provide to improve. Such a shift might reduce the tendency of organizations to overrespond or underrespond to unexpected feedback. Certainly some portion of either response is simply an effort to "cover up," sometimes expressed as panic, other times as withdrawal. This shift to a learning norm of course leaves unresolved other knotty issues about allocations of effort and resources for decision-making. Hopefully, once the social psychological rewards of resisting extensive use of feedback were lowered, restraints on imaginative approaches to weakening other constraints would be reduced as well.

The second needed capability has to do with the capacity of the environment to force greater openness and responsiveness to feedback. (In what follows I am referring to the non-governmental, non-corporation components of the environment, that is, voluntary organizations and ad hoc groups.) Everything we have examined makes it clear that a very large part of the incentives to change, the counterforce to the internal resistances, will have to come from the environment and from those organizational members who, in role identification or function, link themselves to that environment. To be such a counterforce, members of the environment will have to learn what feedback it is useful to supply. This will not always be the same as what they want to supply. That is, members of the environment, organized into information-generating entities, will have to become sophisticated about what constitutes useful and valid information about their conditions and their needs and wants for change, and about how to obtain and provide such information in forms that organizations can effectively recode.[14] And they will have to become so-

---

[14] Organizations seeking useful feedback would find it in the interest of

phisticated about the structure and processes of the organizations into which they force-feed information. Elsewhere (Michael, 1971) I have described the role of voluntary organizations as "reality redefiners" and as resources for generating future-responsive policy and program-influencing information to be used as forced feedback for changing those corporate and government organizations whose actions affect various aspects of the general welfare.[15] But in order to meet the requirements for doing so, voluntary organizations will have to overcome the same internal resistances to becoming lrsp organizations as will the government agencies on which we have been focusing.

If voluntary organizations can make such changes, and a few of them are working very hard to try to do so (at least in their national offices), then they may be able to force enough newly salient information into old structures to give leverage to those proponents of lrsp within government organizations who will also be trying to make them more feedback-responsive. There are universities and even high schools that have learned, in the last few years, to respond to a larger range of feedback than they used to. In some situations they are even learning a little about how to learn to continue to respond to changes in feedback—though it has taken traumatizing crises to move them that far (Chesler and Guskin, 1970). These schools are not doing lrsp—though a few universities are beginning to begin to try to—which emphasizes that, like the other requirements for lrsp, feedback responsiveness is a necessary but not a sufficient condition. But when its ramifications are recognized, it seems to be nearer than any other requirement to being a sufficient condition as well.

---

frsl to help the environment develop its sophistication and skills regarding these requirements. Before Congress and city political establishments emasculated them, OEO's programs, which funded neighborhood development activities, were in part intended to help poor people develop such skills.

[15] The Center for a Voluntary Society in Washington, D.C., exists to facilitate these developments. Common Cause can be seen as another experiment in this spirit.

~~~~~~~ Epilogue ~~~~~~~

Outlook for Changing:
Potentials and Threats

~~~~~~~~~~~~~~~~~~~~~~~~~~~~~~~~~~~~~~

*A*s preparation for trying to respond to the many purposes for this Epilogue, it will be useful to summarize the path this book has followed. I begin then by repeating some words that were used in Chapter One to indicate where we would be going.

A Brief Review

Changing toward long range social planning would require that people working in organizations, and in the social and natural environments linked to them, find it rewarding to learn how to do these things:

1. Live with and acknowledge great uncertainty.

2. Embrace error.

3. Seek and accept the ethical responsibility and the conflict-laden interpersonal circumstances that attend goal-setting.

4. Evaluate the present in the light of anticipated futures, and commit themselves to actions in the present intended to meet such long-range anticipations.

5. Live with role stress and forego the satisfactions of stable, on-the-job, social group relationships.

6. Be open to changes in commitments and direction, as suggested

281

by changes in the conjectured pictures of the future and evaluations of ongoing activities.

To be able to learn these things will require basic changes in the ways people view themselves and others, and basic changes in the norms and structures of organizations that facilitate and reward some behaviors and punish others. To be able to learn them will also require changes in the way members of the environment view themselves and the organizations that serve them.

I have argued that changing people, organizations, and environments to meet these requirements can succeed only if long-range social planning (lrsp) is accepted as a learning process rather than as social engineering technology. I have further argued that the social psychological context for trying to change toward lrsp will be fundamentally influenced by the requirement that lrsp be treated as a future-responsive societal learning (frsl) procedure. Several reasons for this bear emphasizing by way of introducing the question of feasibility.

First, the social technologies for facilitating this learning process are underdeveloped because social science theories and the data needed to refine and test them are inadequate for understanding and delineating complex, changing social systems. Indeed it is not clear how much systematic and useful information about societal dynamics can be developed. We face, then, a long period of learning, of research and development, in order to create theory and technology applicable to lrsp.

Second, we will have to learn how to introduce the requirements for lrsp into organizations in ways that will not result in their rejection or distort them into ritual or rigid, dehumanizing, social-engineering exercises. We will have to learn *how* to change toward lrsp. We will need to learn what organizations and their members need to do to function effectively as part of a frsl arrangement, and we will need to learn how organizations and their members can change over to functioning in those ways. Our theory and methods for organizational development, for felicitously relating the needs of humans to the techniques and structures of an organization, need much research and development. The development of individuals must be articulated with the development of organizational structures that are able to redesign themselves continuously. And both individuals and organizational structures must be able to incorporate the evolving technologies of lrsp. Therefore a long period of learning what organizational development techniques to apply in order to introduce lrsp into organizations, and how to apply them, also lies ahead.

Third, a particularly difficult research and development activity will have to do with learning how to incorporate members of the environment into the lrsp process. Two reasons make incorporation mandatory. First, members of the environment share norms and expectancies that reinforce the norms, structures, and personal self-images that will produce resistance to the introduction of lrsp. Shifting the norms and expectations of the environment so that they permit or encourage organizations to experiment with learning how to meet the requirements for lrsp will itself require the environment to participate in the learning. That in turn requires the environment to be part of the learning system. Second, at all stages of lrsp there will be a need for ideas, arguments, perceptions, and information from those in the environment who presumably will gain and lose from the unfolding of particular activities guided by lrsp. But we do not know how to incorporate "inputs" from the environment in the lrsp process. What constitutes competence, relevance, and effective procedure have yet to be discovered, especially as we move into a time of partisans and confrontation politics. For more than one hundred years we have been learning how to conduct an industrial democracy. We shall have to extend the societal learning process to learn *as a society* how to learn in the situation that makes lrsp necessary. But, much more so than in the past, we shall have to be self-consciously committed to the learning process and to the learning experience as such.

Finally, we shall have to learn what things in a turbulent world can be guided and regulated, and which of them it is necessary or desirable to regulate. For none of the major societal tasks are there ready-made, tested "solutions," or even adequate coping procedures. Even when a wide-ranging "solution" can be proposed, candid examination reveals that there are no available political, fiscal, and organizational means for implementing the proposal. These need to be invented, developed through the processes of frsl. We shall have to learn what it is that we can try to manage through lrsp, as well as how to manage what we can through lrsp.

I have tried to show that the resistances to changing toward lrsp reflect images of human nature, their expressions, and the organizational means for accomplishing them, that are incompatible with the requirements for lrsp. Historically, these images of human nature have brought us to where we are. They have resulted in ways of expressing and organizing human behavior that are characterized by hierarchical organizational structures; by public organizations that try to avoid or at least minimize open contact with their relevant environments if that threatens them, and by a host of negotiating procedures that reward secretiveness; and by resource preemption, power preemption, ambiguity, disjointed incrementalism, deceit, error-denying, distrust, interpersonal distance, pseudo-interpersonal collaboration, and pseudo-emotional support. The result has been to set organizational and sub-organizational survival above anticipatory responses to the future that are appropriate for environmental development; to seek to attain and maintain power through aggressive and possessive actions; to encourage at least "petit Eichmanism," or a narrow

view of our responsibilities; to avoid feedback from the environment; and
to sidestep serious future-responsive goal-setting. In other words, we reward forms of organizational life that at best discourage effective societal
learning and at worst make it impossible. Instead, people are rewarded
for behaving in the ways that are producing an ungovernable and unsatisfying society, which is made the more unsatisfying because efforts to
counteract this situation move in the very directions that exacerbate the
situation: more novelty, distraction, image-making, security-seeking, more
"nowness," more separatist "individuality" and splintering autonomy.

How I Define Feasible

In this light, it would seem that innovators who would even attempt to move organizations toward lrsp would have to be naïve—or rec-
onciled, through deep conviction, to a struggle with long odds against
success. I intend this study to thin the ranks of the naïve. As for "technological fixes," after-the-fact laws, "marketing" of public goods and services, consumer advocates, and other such means, they seem inadequate
in themselves for meeting the larger requirement that society learn how
to self-consciously guide itself into chosen futures.[1] But they can help by
slowing down the flow of consequences from incompetent and inadequate
guidance systems, thus allowing much needed time for learning how to
institute frsl. And they can help generate an awareness of the need to
move in more deliberate, more comprehensive, and more future-responsive directions. I suspect that they are doing these things. These comments, then, are preface to what I mean when I propose that, in spite of
counterforces, moving toward frsl may just be feasible.

By "feasible" what I mean is this: there seem to be developing
circumstances that could help establish enough of a learning-by-planning
mood to moderate the growth and adverse consequences of societal en-
tropy long enough and in enough places so that we might have time to
learn to be some other kind of society, one that lives by the requirements
of frsl in order to develop humanely. What such a society might be like

---

[1] For an incisive critique of the inherent limits on marketing public
goods, see Schick (1969). See also Rivlin (1971, Chapter 6). For a critique of
the law as protection against technological impact, see Baram (1971). On the
possibilities and limits of law, see Tribe (1971 and 1971a). What comes clear
from these articles is that the proposed changes in and applications of law
would require, for their effective realization, the kind of learning through
planning activity proposed herein. Also see Dror (1970). On the limits and
usefulness of "technological fixes," see Etzioni (1968a). On the problems and
possibilities of social control of technology through greater popular participation
in decision-making, see Carroll (1971).

would depend on the kind of learning experiences undergone in getting "there."[2] As with any other learning experience there will be emergent, hence unpredictable consequences, made all the more unpredictable by the ubiquitous interjection of social events that lie outside systematic incorporation in theory.

Feasibility means to me that enough experiments could be undertaken, enough stages in the lrsp process tried out, here and there, to demonstrate enough possibilities and utilities to generate a momentum that would encourage others to try changing toward lrsp and to become environments that would support these experiments. We have begun to be more self-conscious about the need for social experiment. Feasibility would mean that some organizations and their environments were willing and able to experiment with a different image of man, and different organizational norms and structures to support that different image, for the purposes of trying to learn how to learn about changing toward lrsp. Feasibility, then, would depend on a willingness to entertain an appropriate alternate image of man, his purposes, and the means for accomplishing them; and upon the availability of circumstances that provided the occasions to try out and learn from that different way of being and doing. In what follows, I shall try to show that there *may* be the makings of an appropriate alternate image within ideas and experiences now beginning to receive serious attention. Whether this alternate "definition" of human nature would in fact be compatible with the requirements for frsl remains to be seen. Certainly it would be altered by the very effort to act in terms

---

[2] As E. Dunn argues, mankind has always evolved by building on, and learning from, an accumulating social reality. A relevant example here, because it was a self-conscious attempt to establish a societal regulator which was not complete or embedded in the society at its initiation, is the U.S. Constitution. About its genesis, R. Tugwell (1970) observes: "We tend to think today that the agreement in 1787 about the Constitution was much more unanimous than it actually was. The 1787 convention was a tumultuous one. The framers, in the interest of compromise, actually left a great many things undone; a lot of things were left to future development simply because they could not agree" (p. 53). A. Westin comments further (in personal correspondence): "The nature of 18th-century constitution-making (an exercise in the rationalism and higher law concepts of the Enlightenment of that time) was indeed to be admirably brief. The idea of framing a highly detailed, semi-statutory charter was alien to the Framers and their time. They did deliberately write in majestically vague concepts, and they did fully expect the various agencies of the Republic they were creating to give definition and meaning to the grants and denials of power they had labored over. And, they certainly did leave unspecified or only partially developed these points of basic constitutional power on which sectionalism, economic interests, and other divisions did not allow a cohesive majority to be gathered." See Westin (1962).

of it. Then I shall try to show that we can expect occasions and developments in society which, aided and abetted by this alternate image, might provide opportunities to learn about how to change toward frsl.

The Human Potential Image of Human Nature

The image of human nature I shall consider is surrounded by a penumbra of sycophants, proselytes, wishful thinkers, and millenarianists, from whom I disassociate myself. The new image is unclear at this time, partaking of a variety of sources and promulgated with sometimes contradictory and diverging emphases. It is still aborning in this changing world: the fine points and specifics and the arguments about them are unimportant for our purposes. If, in the long view of history, this image turns out to be viable, what is being thought about it now will probably appear, to future generations, as murky and fragmented as ideas about human nature that emerged between the late Middle Ages and the Age of Enlightenment now look to us.[3]

The sources of what I shall call the human potential image and philosophy derive from religious, philosophical, aesthetic, and psychological viewpoints that have persisted for so many centuries throughout the world that A. Huxley (1944) labeled it the Perennial Philosophy. Much of what appears to characterize the human potential image of human nature will seem perfectly "natural" to Americans because much of the philosophical underpinning that influenced the founders of the American revolution derived from variants of the Perennial Philosophy. "The Perennial Philosophy is not new to Western culture. It is present in the Rosicrucian and Freemasonry traditions. Its symbolism in the Great Seal of the United States, on the back of the one-dollar bill, is testimony to the role it played in the formation of this country. It also appears in the Transcendentalism of Emerson, the Creative Evolution of Bergson, and the extensive writings of William James" (Harmon, 1970).

In recent years new contributions to its formulation have come from humanistic psychology, especially from E. Fromm, C. Jung, J. Laing, A. Maslow, R. May, G. Murphy, and C. Rogers; from the theological-political-philosophical writings of such as M. Buber, H. Cox, T. de Chardin, H. Marcuse, and A. Watts; from some of the theoretical writings of behavioral scientists studying group processes and organizational development, such as C. Argyris, W. Bennis, and D. McGregor; from recent

---

[3] While the phrase "human potential image of human nature" sounds like it carries a specific definition, it does not. The "image" is a collectivity of partly congruent and generally convergent "images" at this time and should be understood as no more than that. For a survey of this situation, see "Is There a New Man?" (1971).

work with biofeedback systems that have demonstrated that humans have the ability to intervene in their "autonomic processes," thereby helping to legitimize Eastern psychology and philosophy; and from the use of chemical agents to "expand consciousness."[4] And what is very important, many executives, administrators, and professionals have discovered, when exposed to learning occasions based on these theories and perspectives, that there is much more to themselves and to others than they had realized. While some—by no means the majority of—young people have been most vocal in espousing and expressing facets of the image, the hard research and thoughts has come mostly from older members of society.[5] And while young people often find it satisfying and necessary to express themselves publicly on these matters, my experience (and that of other observers) suggests that there is a scattered but growing commitment to the tenets of the human potential philosophy among professionals, and among high-level corporate and government administrators.

These few people, as champions and as boundary spanners, may be in positions to encourage the organizational development—the improvement of interpersonal and intrapersonal skills—needed to meet the social psychological requirements for lrsp change-over efforts and the restructuring of organizations to reward those improved skills. Of course, there are far more persons in power or seeking it that do not share this emerging perspective. But with the influx of younger professionals and administrators, already exposed to these ideas in business schools and schools of planning, in departments of psychology, encounter groups, meditation sessions, and the like, their numbers will increase in the next few years. Add to this the fact that more young people are moving more rapidly into administrative roles. What is more, the image has appeal elsewhere, too: indeed, many ideas and experiments come from outside the United States (Needleman, 1972). (However, we have no idea, really, of how many people, of what kind, and where placed, it takes to "make a difference" when it comes to shifting societal perspectives.)

For the purposes of this chapter the human potential philosophy could be put roughly as follows. Human beings are part of nature, not separate from it.[6] Persons are linked to persons and to the rest of nature in ways that transcend the conscious, rational mind. Thereby humans have access to a far wider range of being and becoming than the every-

[4] See Kantor and Brown (1970); Tart (1969).

[5] For example, Buhler (1971); Drews (1970); Lasswell (1967); Graves (1970); Maslow (1968).

[6] A lucid and enlightening clarification of the difference between the conventional Western relationship of man to nature and the Zen Buddhist understanding of that relationship, one in keeping with the position being developed here, is found in Suzuki (1956, pp. 229–236).

day definitions of man and the structures of our society acknowledge or reward. These linkages and resources, if acknowledged and cultivated, encourage a drive toward compassionate and loving self-actualization, even toward transcendence, and away from exploitation of self and others; away from compulsive needs to control and manipulate; away from the canons of logic and science as the only expressions of reason; away from valuing scientific rationality over feelings and intuition; away from excessive need for possession of material things; and away from preoccupations with greater material growth and comparative social status.[7] For individuals and organizations the direction points toward openness, a much wider range of cognitive and affective experience and intercourse, and the shared development by responsible social evolution.

Some believe that the weaknesses in the conventional view of humans, as demonstrated by the declining state of the society, and the attractiveness of the human potential view of human nature, as a myth around which to reconstruct social reality, together provide the thrust for a "paradigm shift," in T. Kuhn's phrase.[8] There are indeed fascinating analogies between the conditions that lead to a fundamental change in the scientific definition of physical reality and the conditions in society today that appear to be encouraging a redefinition of social reality. But to my mind, the preconditions for the equivalent of a scientific paradigm shift do not really exist in the changing and ambiguous world of everyday society. For one thing, scientific paradigms are far more definitive than social paradigms. This makes the demonstrations of anomolies much more impressive and the need to deal with them more compelling.

"'Without the special apparatus that is constructed mainly for anticipated functions, the results that lead ultimately to novelty could not occur. And even when the apparatus exists, novelty ordinarily emerges only for the man who, knowing *with precision* what he should expect, is able to recognize that something has gone wrong. Anomaly appears only

---

[7] See Drews and Lipson (1971); Graves (1966); Gross (1971, especially pp. 287–295); Maslow (1968). (Ferkiss, 1969, pp. 205–211) outlines "a new philosophy of human existence" in terms resonant with the ideas developed herein. For a recent and detailed study of values held by one segment of the younger generation, see Morris and Small (1971). A revealing survey of attitudes held by a more heterogeneous sample of youths one year out of high school is summarized in Bachman and van Duinen (1971). For an excellent, more generalized summary of what seem to be the shifts in American values, from the perspective of the need hierarchy elaborated by Maslow, see Mitchel and Baird (1969). Periodicals exploring these ideas include *The Journal of Transpersonal Psychology,* and *The Journal of Humanistic Psychology.*

[8] For well-developed arguments favoring the "paradigm shift" hypothesis, see Kantor (1971); Persico and McEackron (1971); and Harman (1970).

against the background provided by the paradigm. The more precise and far-reaching that paradigm is, the more sensitive an indicator it provides of anomaly and hence of an occasion for paradigm change" (Kuhn, 1970, p. 65). What is valuable in the paradigm shift metaphor is the strong suggestion that a major shift in the dominant mode of appreciation (to use Vicker's term, which I prefer) may be underway, and that this will produce new questions about what humans can be and new answers to them. As a result, what are now political, economic, and social "impossibilities" might become feasible.

As I understand the contemporary version of the human potential philosophy as it is developing, it is in many ways compatible with, and indeed supportive of, the social psychological requirements for moving toward lrsp.[9] For example, being interdependent and part of nature suggests a communality, a symbiosis, that could make it less necessary to fear some loss of personal control, if others were to share a supportive sense of mutual responsibility and mutual implication. Being in nature emphasizes that each of us is unavoidably linked to and dependent on nature (including other people) and that the rest of nature is dependent on each of us. Given this mutual dependence, humans must be as responsible as they can be about their part in creating futures. But since humans are only a part of nature, what happens in the future is only partially a result of present actions. On the one hand, humans cannot expect the future to go as they would wish unless they try to guide it. On the other hand, they cannot expect the future to go the way they wish just because they try to guide it. Hence it is our responsibility to try to create a responsive future, but we cannot expect to succeed as we could if we really were in control—that is, if we were outside nature. This appreciation could make change and instability seem a more "natural" human condition because humans would not see themselves as insulated from nature, as we do when we act as if we were outside of nature—that is, conquering, or overcoming, or breaking through it. Then error-denying could seem foolish and unworthy. Embracing error could be a natural mode of adjustment, of learning, rather than a threat symbolizing loss of control, hence punishable. The anxiety attached to uncertainty could decrease if there were a sure feeling of being imbedded in the universe. This could reduce the stress caused by role ambiguities and conflicts; or stress could

---

[9] There is in some versions of the human potential image, however, a position that, of itself, is antagonistic to the requirements for frsl: the do-your-own-thing mystique, bound to the moment, insular in perspective, and at the group level committed to unconstrained group autonomy. This is not to say that there is no historical justification for demanding local autonomy and action now. But acting out that historical justification in these ways is nevertheless incompatible with the requirements for moving toward frsl.

remain high but without the anxiety now associated with losing control or being caught in error. The reduction in defensiveness evidenced by acknowledging uncertainty and embracing error could result in more mutual openness, understanding, and supportiveness. This could encourage seeking rather than avoiding feedback. A more relaxed tentativeness could replace hard-driving, compulsive forwardness.

Humans, as part of nature, would emphasize the systemic, the ecologic, the emergent, condition of man. At the same time, with emphasis on the naturalness of compassionate and loving self-actualization, one's sense of self and relatedness would be so strengthened that either excessive dependence on others or excessive preoccupation with independence from others would be unnecessary. Both of these are typical responses today; they are evidences of one's sense of being an incomplete or empty self.[10] This could lead to less emphasis on autonomy per se, more emphasis on collaboration, and thereby more boundary-spanning. Hence there could be less fear of loss of a particular sentient relationship, and more willingness to try new organizational structures.

Emphasis on the complementary utility of emotions and logic for validating experience and evaluating alternatives could encourage less defensiveness and more experiment with approaches that appealed simultaneously to both aspects of human creativeness and commitment. This could also make the arguments more open for one or another scheme for goal setting, program choice, and evaluation; and it could stimulate more occasions for trusting, and in that mood, for more social experimenting. Organizational behavior that was not directed by careful attention to alternative futures could be seen as irresponsible; it would be defined as incompatible with being part of nature, which necessarily includes in its present forms the seeds of the future. And so on.

My point is hardly to prove that such changes would in fact occur, but rather to suggest that if social reality were constructed out of this definition of the nature of man, then on the face of it there could be ample justification for and legitimation of an frsl style of being and doing as the "natural" way for humans and their institutions to perform. Nor, as I emphasized earlier, am I proposing that such a changed image would result in the removal of conflict or the elimination of power in human affairs, certainly not over the years ahead when this new image would be contending with the prevailing image of the nature of humans, and at best only occasionally substituted for it. Occasions for conflict and for the use of power would change, and the ways in which conflict and power were expressed would change too. My mood regarding the influence of

[10] For disquisitions on this, see Horney (1937); Jung (1956); Riesman and others (1955); Slater (1970); and Wheelis (1958).

the new image on conflict and power is well expressed in a statement pertaining to research on role stress written before the human potential image had attained the attention it claims today. Clearly, though, as part of the psychology of organizational behavior and change, role stress research has contributed to the present status of the new image.

"The issue, then, is not the elimination of conflict and ambiguity from organizational life; it is the containment of these conditions at levels and in forms which are at least humane, tolerable, and low in cost, and which at best might be positive in contribution to individual and organization. The present research implies four ways in which this goal might be approached: by introducing direct structural changes into organizations, by introducing new criteria of selection and placement, by increasing the tolerance and coping abilities of individuals, and by strengthening the interpersonal bonds among organizational members" (Kahn and others, 1964, p. 387).

Certain examples of approval of the human potential image of human nature deserve our attention because they come from unexpected sources where, if approval were to spread, the feasibility of trying to change toward lrsp could be substantially enhanced. Of course, public expressions of interest are not evidence of active engagement, any more than the public imagery about lrsp corresponds to what is actually happening. However, just as that imagery is influencing people to see planning in a positive light, making it an idea in good currency with increased possibilities for invention and innovation, so too with attention to the new image of man. Moreover, it is my strong impression that, inspired by the image, individuals in the most unlikely places are in fact exploring unfamiliar ways to satisfy desires that P. Slater (1970) argues are deeply and uniquely frustrated in American middle class culture:

1. The desire for community—*the wish to live in trust and fraternal cooperation with one's fellows in a total and visible collective entity.*

2. The desire for engagement—*the wish to come directly to grips with social and interpersonal problems and to confront on equal terms an environment which is not composed of ego-extensions.*

3. The desire for dependence—*the wish to share responsibility for the control of one's impulses and the direction of one's life [p. 5].*

Consider, for example, the characteristics that top executives of two major American corporations expect future managers to display—characteristics which, they emphasize, will require changes in corporate structure and norms in order to attract them.[11] One executive puts it this

[11] I am indebted to R. Raymond for this information, which was given to him by the executives referred to.

way: "High level of education; minimum loyalty to company; concern with maximum authority as individuals; desire for social concern by businesses; rejection of authoritarianism; interest in the whole environment; decreasing sense of tradition; individualistic dress and grooming; open, direct communication; acceptance of 'feelings' as essential data." An executive vice-president in one of America's largest firms sympathetically describes these characteristics as: "Openness; non-materialism; identity related to age category: I-Thou; trust; love; use of small groups; identity with alienated groups; personalization (anti-technology); moralistic concern with humanism and self-knowledge."

George C. Lodge (1972), Professor of Business Administration at Harvard Business School, has this to say:

> *The new ideas are all around us: harmony between man and nature, individual fulfillment as part of an organic social process, a right to survival and income, a sharp distinction between consumer desires and community needs, the role of the state as vision-setter and planner.*
>
> *. . . The old idea of individualism is largely a useless antique. For the majority of Americans a sense of fulfillment and happiness will derive from their place and participation in a purposeful, organic, social process; their talents and capabilities should be used to the fullest, and they should have maximum involvement in the decisions by which the process is conducted and directed.*
>
> *. . . The costs of neglect are real. It is all too likely that worker malaise and discontent will bring increased pressure for wage increases which companies may well grant, hoping that money will buy satisfaction, and thus productivity, when in fact it won't.*
>
> *. . . Paternalism won't work because there is no father and there are no children. There is only a collection of human beings with different capabilities who are needed to perform different functions. And how they are organized is something upon which they must generally agree. Perhaps the workers should select the manager, in some cases.*
>
> *. . . Whatever the techniques, this transition will place a serious burden on existing management. In many instances, managers may in fact be deciding whether or not to relinquish their own jobs and authority in the name of a more efficient and useful collective [p. 4].*

It is reasonable to assume that the *Wall Street Journal* chooses its non-financial news articles to appeal especially to its readers. Consider then that the *Journal* featured a completely serious page-one article that ran for two full columns describing research that can be interpreted as indicating that plants can sense human feelings toward them as well as the biological state of other animals (Martin, 1972).

In the last few years *Science* magazine has begun to publish articles concerned with states of being and images of reality that simply would have been out of bounds a few years earlier. Consider such titles as "A Cartography of the Ecstatic and Meditative States" (Fischer, 1971), by an experimental psychiatrist and pharmacologist; or "Sensuous-Intellectual Complementarity in Science," (Blackburn, 1971), by a chemist; or "States of Consciousness and State Specific Sciences," by an experimental psychologist (Tart, 1972). Whether the editors and referees share the views of the authors, what is significant is that they now believe the views are proper subject matter for *Science,* and that enough readers will find them interesting and appropriate to merit space that is heavily competed for. Whether or not positive views about the human potential image are widely held, it appears that those who see themselves as idea disseminators and opinion influencers believe that they are widely held. And, very likely, that is one means by which prophecies can become self-fulfilling.

Other more familiar topics are fully compatible with the perspectives emphasized in the human potential image, and these would depend on frsl for their resolution. These include concerns about the natural environment and an "ecological ethic" (in L. Caldwell's term) ; commitments to radical change in the status of the dispossessed, the marginal, and minorities; strong control of technology for social welfare; and the reassessment of science as the crowning expression of man's competences and of the ethical consequences of it. Much of what is discussed, proposed, and implemented with regard to these issues tacitly accepts the prevailing definition of human beings, though quite a few critics either subscribe to versions of the human potential image or deplore the prevailing one. At any rate, whatever the assumptions about man's being, preoccupation with these powerful social issues certainly will not discourage perceiving new and additional human potentials and other social realities that might engender much less resistance to attempts to change toward lrsp.

The human potential image seems to be a fact and its spread seems likely. "The recognition of the divine in man is widely diffused through the literature of religion and of mysticism. What is not so generally visible, is that an identical recognition is now spreading through the journals of psychology. In fact, there is a convergence of religion, psychology, and education. They share a growing unity of concern beyond the proper forming of a social self in each human. Their concern now is with the cultivation of the subjective self that also lives in every man"

(Kantor, 1970, p. 28). The extent to which this image could facilitate efforts to change toward frsl is speculation, but on the face of it, it also seems likely. The next question is: are there societal circumstances that are likely to expand the plausibility of the human potential image and provide occasions for the credibility of the philosophy to be demonstrated?

Before discussing specific situations that may enhance feasibility, let us acknowledge the ubiquitous role of inadvertence—the occasional influence in the direction of lrsp that might be exerted by persons, technologies, or roles introduced into organizations for different purposes altogether, or at most for lrsp ritual or imagery.[12] Persons may at any time find themselves involved in lrsp-tending efforts as a result of the circumstances we shall look at now.

Organizational Development as Facilitating Frsl

I have referred throughout to growing recognition of this approach in corporations, third-sector organizations, and in principle, if not nearly as much in practice, in government. Among the elites of established organizations there is growing appreciation of the utility and the validity of the findings of behavioral science to the effect that fulfillment of higher human needs and aspirations is increasingly necessary for effective organizational performance. More and more executives are aware of the arguments, and sometimes the evidence, that openness, trust, and all the rest "pay off." Bennis (1966) sees those espousing organizational development as reflecting the following philosophy: "(1) A new concept of *man*, based on increased knowledge of his complex and shifting needs, which replaces the oversimplified, innocent push-button or inert idea of man.

(2) A new concept of *power*, based on collaboration and reason, which replaces a model of power based on coercion and fear.

(3) A new concept of *organizational values*, based on an humanistic existential orientation, which replaces the depersonalized, mechanistic value system." He adds immediately (and I second him), "I do not mean that these transformations of man, power, organizational values are fully accepted, or even understood to say nothing of implemented in day-to-day organizational affairs. These changes may be light-years away from actual adoption. I do mean that they have gained wide *intellectual* acceptance in enlightened management quarters, that they have caused a terrific amount of rethinking and search behavior on the part of many organizational planners, and that they have been used as a basis for policy formulation by certain large organizations, mainly industrial leviathans, but also by many other non-industrial institutions" (pp. 188–189).

[12] For some relevant examples of inadvertent change, see Costello (1971).

There is no reason to believe the direction of this trend will reverse; when practiced it usually proves rewarding and it recruits executives, managers, and professionals who are searching for a more rewarding human condition.[13] Since it seems to improve performance, it also appeals to the conventional view of humans and the conventional goals of organizations, particularly corporations.[14] But as more business school graduates who have been exposed to the processes and philosophy, and who themselves are products of the middle-class search for meaning, move into positions of authority and influence, emphasis on compatibility with the human potential image should increase. Increased use in other sectors should help legitimize its application in government, especially when younger generations of bureaucrats, political appointees, professionals, and consultants move into authority and influence and as legislators partake of similar experiences and ideas before assuming their elected positions.

There is another favorable consequence of the growing emphasis on organizational development that merits our recognition. It must be evident that the social psychological requirements for changing toward lrsp would also be functional for organizations or their components that will be uninvolved in activities needing long-range social planning; examples might be some distribution and service-dispensing components of large organizations. Such organizations are increasingly investing in organizational development. The greater the number of people and organizations that find it rewarding to behave in some of the ways needed to move toward lrsp, the more likely, it would seem, that there will evolve networks of organizations and people sympathetic to lrsp and willing to risk collaboration in ways that would at least be less resistant to lrsp efforts. The more that organizations find they can work together, the less the uncertainty they must bear about what other organizations are going to do, about sabotage and double-dealing. Under such circumstances, the atmosphere surrounding tactics and strategy for preserving and extending orga-

---

[13] There may be another felicitous process at work here, though I know of no research concerning it. As organizational development becomes more a part of the ideas in good currency that both junior and senior executives are exposed to and educated in (as is happening through increasing numbers of civil service seminars, business school courses, and management training conferences), it should be easier for these executives and administrators to acknowledge the social psychological sources of resistance to changes in the direction of lrsp. Being less "uptight" about them, that is, seeing them as natural properties of conventional norms and structures, they may feel freer to initiate and support efforts to overcome them. Ideas in good currency gain acceptance because it becomes increasingly legitimate and desirable to see oneself and be seen as sharing them. Thus the willingness to innovate may grow.

[14] As an example, in addition to those found in Likert, Bennis, and Argyris, see Marrow, Bowers, and Seashore (1967).

nizational autonomy is likely to change. Non-government organizations have often found that more can be accomplished with less effort by enlarging participation in management and policy decisions—if organizational development has preceded such enlargements. So, too, organizations may find more satisfactions, including a kind of exhilarating autonomy of competence and direction, through collaboration based on the sort of behavior and structures argued for here than they now find in the typical defensive, closed, and narrowly protective organizational behavior. Some sources of turbulence might be reduced, as a result, and the satisfactions this provides could encourage more movement toward behavior and structures sympathetic to trying to change toward lrsp or to trying to help other organizations do so.

Social Crises and Disasters as Facilitators of Frsl

One consequence of our inability to regulate our society, at least as it is presently operated, will be frequent crises and disasters. Some will be sudden, like an urban insurrection or a lethal inversion layer. Others will be cumulative like Vietnam, mercury poisoning, or power shortages. Such crises and disasters could have important potentials for encouraging moves toward lrsp.

First, crises and disasters will demonstrate that leaders and administrators are unable to carry out successfully the solutions to social problems they claim to have. It will be clearer to more people, as disasters and crises accumulate, that those who run the government really don't understand the problems: that they are unable to operate their own organizations productively and creatively, and that they are unable to guide coherently and felicitously the natural and social environments for which they accept or claim responsibility. In spite of all the technological and managerial resources they have or claim to have, it will be evident that they are unable to make things work the way they promise they can and then claim they have. It will become unavoidably evident that in an increasingly complex world, conventionally behaving leaders and executives are simply incompetent or inadequate.

Second, some seeking to lead may try to do so by acknowledging to their environments that they are uncertain about what to do because they are uncertain about what is happening in the present, to say nothing of the future, hoping thereby to exhibit honesty, courage, wisdom, and humility.[15] They may also choose to embrace error rather than deny it,

---

[15] Of course, those who are seeking to lead may themselves subscribe to the new image of man. As the conventional paths to political offices, and the qualifications for them, widen, under the impact of the legitimacy-dissolving

pointing out that *all* leaders are in fact inadequate on the basis of their records but haven't the courage or honesty to admit it. Having embraced error and acknowledged uncertainty, they may invite their followers to share in *learning* a way through.[16] This approach would terrify and revolt people who, in their uncertainty and fear of error, need the kind of leader who believes he knows and acts as if he knows. "Anxieties are provoked when one hears about the danger of external attack, or the imminent collapse of the economic system, or the disintegration of his sound, virtuous country. These factors mobilize a sense of anxiety and a sense of the need for action. They also make one perceive his own limitations. Now suppose this anxiety-ridden, helpless citizen can attach himself to an effective leader, can identify with him. He lessens his own anxiety and no longer feels so helpless" (Hall, 1968, p. 61).

But among those subscribing to or susceptible to the human potential image there is, along with a respect for candor, an appreciation that complex situations can be experienced in many ways, leading to quite different versions of "telling it like it is." Some loss of control doesn't upset them. They accept error more easily as part of the human condition, as something to be learned from. And they believe that control, such as it is, is best exercised through participative processes that share power and purpose. While many in this group have never tested their beliefs against the need to get large things done with finite resources and time, it increasingly includes senior people who have had responsibility in the midst of complexity in all kinds of organizations. Such people could encourage those leaders who want to move toward lrsp and they could help sustain the efforts made to do so.

Third, it is during the aftermath of disasters that organizations are most subject to drastic restructuring and redirecting.[17] The environment that sustained their norms and operating style is changed: either it does not provide the expected feedback or it provides unexpected feedback. Indeed, a disaster can be thought of as the withdrawal of sustaining feedback. Lacking these regulating, constraining, inputs the organization is vulnerable to metamorphoses. Usually an organization "reorganizes"

---

forces and the changing experiences of members of the environment, those who never before had access to political offices will fill them. Radical young people on city councils and black mayors are only the beginning.

[16] The typical spokesman argues for a program as if he *knows* what the problem is and knows how to solve it. Our spokesman would have to argue for a program on the grounds that we really don't know what will work, but that on the basis of this particular analysis (including a certain conjectured future), this activity seems worth trying for the purpose of finding out more about what we are involved in and what might be done.

[17] An excellent review of all aspects of disaster behavior is Barton and Merton (1963).

itself into essentially what it was, and so does its environment. But things need not work that way. The disaster of the Great Depression resulted in a permanent shift in the norms and structure of the federal government in the direction of developing and supplying public welfare services. The disaster of World War II for Europe contributed to the creation of the European Trade Community. The disasters of the urban uprisings intensified attention to racist norms and structures. The disasters of student uprisings have led in some places to changes in the structure and norms of university governance.[18]

However, recovery into a transformed structure and norm system that could encourage the social psychological processes able to meet the requirements for changing toward lrsp is almost certain to fail unless much preplanning is done. Among many other things, this preplanning would have to include training for interpersonal competence. Without such skills, trying to use the disaster as a lever to move toward lrsp would be virtually impossible. Many people, pushed by their experience with the disaster or the crisis, will feel an intensified need to keep things under control. At the same time, the fluid post-disaster context will seem both an opportunity in which to capture control and a threat that control is slipping away. Both perceptions will intensify pre-disaster behavior patterns acting in the service of pre-disaster norms. However, organizations that believe themselves right and healthy are unlikely to do such preplanning, or provide funds for it, because that would imply an inability to avoid disaster. Acknowledging such impotence is more than most leaders can manage, either publicly or privately. Therefore, in the event of a disaster we will have to depend on the skills available in organizations that had undertaken organizational development previously, for reasons other than disaster planning. However, it might also be that if they possessed these skills—including, crucially, self-understanding—leaders could face acknowledging the likelihood of impotence to avert disaster. (I know some who acknowledge this today.) With that strength they might be able to initiate some contingency planning that would facilitate moves toward lrsp when disasters occur.

Another characteristic of the social psychology of crises and disaster must be acknowledged. In the crisis stage preceding disaster, members of organizations tend to retreat into forms of behavior that have been well learned because they were successful in the past—unless they have been trained to avoid doing so. They are very likely to cut themselves off from information they should have to cope with the reality of the looming disaster. Instead, they will selectively attend to information that is com-

[18] On exploiting crises for facilitating change, see Gross (1967); and Lawrence (1969).

patible with their previously learned successful behavior, including hierarchical command procedures. These procedures are followed because they have a history of success that leads back to childhood.[19] Such behavior increases distrust in the environment and heightens a sense of beleagueredness. It would make post-disaster experiments with frsl highly unlikely.

Social Indicators, Social Experiments, and Distributive Equity as Facilitators of Frsl

Those seeking more efficient government, more agency productivity and accountability, more "bang for the buck" in social investments, and those seeking more humane and rewarding government in the public interest share a growing appreciation of the potential utility of data collected to evaluate the social state of the nation. To this we may add the thrust of consumerism, volunteerism, concern with the natural environment, and the pressures for decentralization of such social services as public health, education, and welfare for the poor into quasi-autonomous neighborhood and lay-organized activities. These circumstances, which are facilitated by the human potential image and encourage its growth, would seem to hold opportunities for frsl.

These differing interests and groupings will disagree strongly and often about whether the right data are being collected to estimate particular social conditions, and they will disagree strongly about whether the correct interpretations are being made from a given set of data. Intense arguments will be inevitable, at least as long as models of what constitute social processes and their causal interrelations are underdeveloped and unevaluated.[20] In the absence of error-embracing and acknowledgment of uncertainty, and in the absence of guiding future perspectives, these arguments will most likely bog down in familiar disarray, and decisions will probably be made in familiar but increasingly unacceptable ways. Instead of this outcome, these differences could be used as the basis for

[19] There are exceptions to this inclination, as there are to all forms of human conduct. Allison (1971) points out that President Kennedy's personal approach to the Cuban missile crisis was to be more, rather than less, exploratory, and apparently his information enlarged rather than narrowed his perspective. Even then there were strong tendencies, in some of his immediate advisors, to narrow the information inputs and options rather than to enlarge them. Allison's book is also a most stimulating study of the limits and assets of three alternative theoretical perspectives for illuminating the relationship between bureaucracy, policy, and decision-making under stress. It complements the position argued here. Also see Hermann (1963).

[20] See Henriot (1971); Chapman (1968); Gamson (1968); Heilbroner (1971); and Michael (1968).

competing and collaborative societal experiments at the very local level as well as on a regional and national scale. To go beyond ad hoc experiments would require moving toward meeting the requirements for frsl. If this were seen as the desirable direction in which to go, the human potential image, as a model of appropriate norms and behavior, would make it easier to work with the uncertainties and conflicts inherent in changing toward frsl.

At the same time, as argued earlier, social indicator data will force more organizations, especially government, to face up to questions of distributive equity more directly and comprehensively than ever before. Government agencies and many private organizations face futures in which increasing data and advocate skills will force them to make preoccupation with the public interest unavoidably paramount. Inevitably, then, they will have to try to anticipate the costs and benefits to the social and natural environment of conditions that could increase or reduce equity for one or another group, and they will have to seek or at least cope with feedback relevant for their actions. In other words, they will have to move toward long-range social planning. A willingness by management to indulge if not to support the new image of humankind—especially if it becomes an idea of some currency—would make it easier to survive the crunch of environmental pressures on one side and internal resistances to lrsp on the other. Those inside and out who do subscribe to the new image would be strengthened in their efforts to undertake actions aimed at facilitating moves toward lrsp. If these efforts began to be rewarding, indulgence could change to commitment.

Planning as a Facilitator of Frsl

It is hard to imagine the idea of lrsp weakening if society holds together enough to be outraged and terrified by its disarray. Measured by the number of publications, popular concern with the future would seem apparent.[21] More academics and more students are taking an interest in policy research and future studies. Organizations in and out of government are making new efforts to set goals and are thinking about reexamining organizational structures and evaluating activities.[22] Advocate plan-

---

[21] However, without research we do not know how much is serious interest, how much simply Sunday supplement curiosity, how much various attempts to relieve generalized anxiety or rationalize it, and how much is simply promotion.

[22] A recent and sophisticated analysis and critique of the present status of future research and its overlap with policy studies, and related topics, as well as a description of what types of studies are being done by whom, is found in McHale and Cordell (1971). Three examples of organizational efforts to look

ning and counter-planning are almost institutionalized. Consulting service firms are increasing in all these areas. More people are being caught up in the idea, in and out of government, that there is a need for lrsp and that we should try to do it. And positions of authority and responsibility will be filled by increasing numbers of younger persons who, by virtue of their advanced stage of personal development will believe in these changes and will intend to act to facilitate them.[23] It seems to me, then, that an elaborated idea in good currency about planning may develop: that if we are to plan, we must change ourselves in the direction of believing in and acting out the human potential image of social reality.

B. Gross (1971) having reviewed the evolution of planning and having conjectured about societal trends, concludes with a statement that well expresses what I expect to be one appealing idea in good currency regarding long-range social planning: "Genuine human rationality is essentially a process of learning and . . . any learning process involves not only the acquisition of knowledge and skills but also the development of new values and interests. In this sense, if we are to escape the icy grip of technocratic planning, we must develop a humanist style of *learning through planning* and a theory of planning as widespread *social learning*. This is what we must learn if we are to escape the new superhighways to post-industrial serfdom and begin to release the vast potentials for humanist reconstruction" (p. 294).[24]

Feasible But How Hopeful?

Even taken together, these potentially supportive circumstances are pathetically thin reeds to lean on, or to weave into a hope that lrsp as a means of societal learning could become pervasive in, say, the next two decades. As of now, the human potential view of man is attractive primarily to the intellectually or economically affluent. Most people apparently "don't know what they're missing" from the perspective of their conventional viewpoint. For most people, survival, security, belonging, and esteem are much more attractive goals than self-actualization. P. and B. Berger (1971) have argued that if those espousing variants of the new

---

afresh at where they might go are: The Detroit Edison Company, Wayne State University, and Doxiadis Associates, (*The Urban Detroit Area Effort,* 1969); Hahn (1968); and *Diplomacy for the 70's* (1970).

[23] With regard to the relationship of social psychological characteristics to need patterns, as a function of one's location and experience in social or class groups in this society, see the theories of A. Maslow, C. Graves, and R. Kantor as elucidated and extended in Kantor (1969, especially pp. 59–66).

[24] Another eloquent and pertinent argument along related lines is in Morris (1948, pp. 151–154).

image cannot find congenial circumstances within conventional norms and structures, they will be quite adequately replaced, according to the familiar process of circulation of the elites, by people who have no doubts about the sufficiency of the conventional norms for being and doing. "There is no reason to think that 'the system' will be unable to make the necessary accommodations. Should Yale become hopelessly 'greened,' Wall Street will get used to recruits from Fordham or Wichita State. Italians or Southern Baptists will have no trouble running the Rand Corporation" (p. 23).

This suggests that for many years it will probably be much easier for the many in power who hold to the traditional definitions of the nature of humans, to ignore the requirements for frsl, and to try to plan where they can in the spirit of social engineering—what Gross calls "technocratic planning." Social engineering may well be attempted where coercion, manipulation, and control seem right and reasonable to those holding to the traditional image of human beings, where it could seem feasible and correct to social-engineer, for example, the control of delinquency, crime, drug abuse, or job training for the undertrained.[25] One can hope that out of the inevitable failures that would result, failures due as much to their inhumanity as to the inadequacy of a social engineering approach, would come appreciation of the need to move away from the conventional image of the nature of humans and the norms of organizational and interpersonal behavior that reflect it. But the denoument might more likely lead to the rejection of any kind of planning in favor of authoritarian leadership.

Bennis, who was among the most optimistic about the impact of organizational development, as caused by and causing a shift in values that would encourage self-actualization, has described in a most instructive and error-embracing article some fundamental organizational dilemmas he now sees us faced with: "the threat to legitimacy of authority, the tensions between populist and elitist functions and interdependence and complicity in the environment, the need for fresh metaphors, the discontinuities between microsystems and macrosystems, and the baffling competition between forces that support and those that suppress the adoption of democratic ideology" (Bennis, 1970, p. 604). Some of these dilemmas

---

[25] A social engineering approach could be undertaken within conventional organization structures and norms, avoiding contact with the environment, substituting technological ritual and pseudo data for acknowledging uncertainty or embracing error, and so on. Organizational resistances would be minimal because planning these activities would be treated as if no changes in men or organizations were required to do it—just more exotic engineering techniques applied to planning for, rather than with, the environment.

are deepened by the progress of the new image of man, making its way amidst the expressions of the older one. And we can each add our visions of countertrends and conditions in the society that would be almost certain to overwhelm the circumstances I have suggested as supportive for changes toward lrsp. To my mind, the most threatening is the likelihood that social crises and disasters will be dealt with in ways that will destroy the opportunities, the new definition of social reality, and the proponents needed to create the conditions for future-responsive societal learning. The authors of a highly authoritative study on attitudes toward violence indicate one such potential source of destruction. "The fact that almost 50 percent of American men felt that shooting was a good way of handling campus disturbances 'almost always' or at least 'sometimes' is particularly disturbing. . . . That 20 percent of American men considered it appropriate for the police to kill in these circumstances indicates the ease with which many people will accept violence to maintain order even when force so used is entirely out of proportion to the precipitating incidents. The data imply that willingness to reach for a gun is easily evoked" (Blumenthal and others, 1972, p. 243).

But the fact is that we really don't understand the processes of change in this society, which is so complex that it has no historical precedent: that is why we must turn to frsl. We don't know what it takes to make a difference, to produce a change, in the definition of social reality that is akin to T. Kuhn's paradigm shift. We don't know how to measure or perceive clearly the dialectics of trend and counter-trend, value and counter-value, image and counter-image.

For example, it is easy to assert that although the Perennial Philosophy is perennial, it has never been realized except by a few, and that what is really going on is a perennial welling-up of that part of human nature that finds comfort in fantasies of being more than we can be. It is easy to demonstrate that in large groups at least, humans have never behaved according to the human potential image, no matter how much they might have aspired to. It is easy to conclude that they won't and can't this time around either. Indeed, the bulk of this book would support that position.

But it is also arguable that there never has been a convergence of circumstances like those we now face, where more and more people of all ages know how enormous are our powers, how rudimentary our abilities to control them, and how precarious and finite the natural and social environments in which we must act out this struggle with ourselves. It can be argued that by knowing these things, and by recognizing the existential circumstances which reveal them, we are creating a social setting different from any that existed in the past. Moreover, growing numbers of people know that they know, and know that growing numbers of other people *also* know, that our societal condition is historically unique. This may provide for the first time a real potential for beginning to redefine our natures and for beginning to create social arrangements that validate and sustain that definition. It took the circumstance of agriculture to make civilization possible, with its concomitant changes in the definition of man. It took the circumstances of technology to produce the density and complexity of interactions that characterize our society—including our increasingly shared dissatisfactions with the more prevalent definitions of human nature and our increasing shared aspirations for something akin to the Perennial Philosophy.

As a basis for learning to become a future-responsive learning society, by learning how to do long-range social planning, this is not much to go on. But if the thesis of this book seems reasonable, we had better make the most of it.

List of Respondents

(Affiliations as of the time of the interview. Some respondents chose to remain anonymous.)

Joseph F. Abely, Jr.
Controller
General Foods Corp.
White Plains, N.Y.

David Ackerman
Senior Behavioral Scientist
Stanford Research Institute
Menlo Park, California

Marvin Adelson
Professor, School of Architecture &
    Urban Planning
University of California
    at Los Angeles

Chris Argyris
Professor
Department of Administrative
    Sciences
Yale University

Herbert Auerbach
Vice President
Descon-Concordia Ltd.
Montreal, Canada

Paul Baran
Vice President
Institute for the Future
Palo Alto, California

Arthur Barber
President
Institute of Politics and Planning
Arlington, Virginia

Richard Barber
Director
Transportation Planning Study
National Academy of Sciences

Russell Bartels
Office of the Mayor
Bureau of the Budget
New York City

Raymond Bauer
Professor
Graduate School of Business
    Administration
Harvard University

305

Warren G. Bennis
Vice President for
  Academic Development
State University of New York
  at Buffalo

Robert Biller
Professor
Graduate School of Public Policy
University of California at Berkeley

Gordon Binder
Graduate Student (and ex-Staff
  Intern Environmental
  Protection Agency)
University of Michigan

John Brandel
Deputy Assistant Secretary for
  Program Evaluation
U.S. Department of Health,
  Education, and Welfare

William C. Bryant
Associate Executive Editor
U.S. News and World Report
Washington, D.C.

Robert Burco
Public Policy Analyst
Berkeley, California

David S. Bushnell
Research Director
Project Focus
Washington, D.C.

William Byron
Associate Commissioner
Administration and Fiscal
  Management
N.Y. State Department of
  Mental Hygiene

John Caffrey
Director
Commission on Administrative Affairs
American Council on Education

Lynton Caldwell
Professor
Department of Political Science
University of Indiana

Donald Campbell
Professor
Department of Psychology
Northwestern University

Nathan Caplan
CRUSK, Institute for Social
  Research
University of Michigan

Bayard Catron
Graduate Student
University of California at Berkeley

Bernard Cazes
Commissariat General du Plan
  d'Equipement et de La
  Productivité
Paris, France

C. West Churchman
Research Philosopher and
  Professor of Business
  Administration
University of California at Berkeley

Matthew Coffee
Special Assistant to the
  Director
Corporation for Public
  Broadcasting
Washington, D.C.

Timothy Costello
Deputy Mayor
New York City

Douglas Costle
Woodrow Wilson Fellow
Smithsonian Institution

Arch D. Crouch
Principal City Planner
Los Angeles, California

James Crowfoot
Consultant
Organizational Development Group
Lutheran Synod of Illinois

Michel Crozier
Director
Centre de Sociologie des Organisations
Paris, France

James Dator
Professor
Department of Political Science
University of Hawaii

Henry David
Executive Secretary
Division of Behavioral Sciences
National Academy of Sciences

Paul Davidoff
Director
Suburban Action Institute
White Plains, N.Y.

John Dixon
Director
Center for a Voluntary Society
Washington, D.C.

Gilbert Donahue
Labor Management Services
    Administration
U.S. Department of Labor

Charles Dresher
Manager
Information Systems
Los Angeles Technical Services Corp.

Yehezkel Dror
Rand Corporation
Santa Monica, California

Leonard Duhl
Associate Director
Program on Social Policy
College of Environmental Design
University of California at Berkeley

Richard Duke
Director
Environmental Simulation Laboratory
University of Michigan

Matthew Dumont
Director
Center for Studies of
    Metropolitan Problems
National Institute of Mental Health

Robert Ehler
Professor
Urban and Policy Sciences Program
College of Engineering
State University of New York
    at Stony Brook

Duane Elgin
Commission on Population Growth
    and the American Future
Washington, D.C.

Edward H. Erath
President
Los Angeles Technical
    Services Corporation

Martin Ernst
Vice President
Management Science Division
A. D. Little, Inc.

Carl Eugster
Head
Corporate Development
CIBA-GEIGY AO
Basel, Switzerland

Keith Evans
Budget Systems Coordinator
Office of Vice President
    for Academic Affairs
University of Michigan

Lansing Fair
Director
Developing Great Lakes
    Megalopolis Research Project

William Finley
Vice President
Community Planning & Research
The Rouse Company
Columbia, Md.

Jack Fisher
Associate Director
Center for Urban Studies
Wayne State University

John Ford
President's Commission on
  Management Improvement

John Forester
Graduate Student
University of California at Berkeley

Harley Frankel
Executive Assistant to
  the Commissioner of
  Education, HEW

Winston Franklin
Vice President, Planning
Charles F. Kettering Foundation

Louis Friedland
Associate Dean
School of Liberal Arts
Wayne State University

John Friedmann
Chairman
Urban Planning Program
University of California
  at Los Angeles

Dennis Gabor
Professor
Applied Electron Physics
Imperial College of Science and
  Technology
London, England

Sheldon Gans
Vice President
Marshall Kaplan, Gans, and Kahn
San Francisco, California

Jack Gibbons
Director
ORNL-NSF
Environmental Program
Oakridge National Laboratory

Gideonse Hendrik
Staff Member
Senate Subcommittee on Executive
  Reorganization and Government
  Research
Washington, D.C.

Clifford Glover
Directorate for Scientific Affairs
OECD
Paris, France

Robert Goe
Special Assistant to the Mayor
Los Angeles, California

Theodore Gordon
President
The Futures Group
Glastenbury, Conn.

Andre Grandsard
Directeur D'Etudes
Compagnie D'Etudes Industrielles
  et D'Amenagment du Territoire
Paris, France

Bertram Gross
Professor
Department of Urban Affairs
Hunter College
New York City

Robert Grosse
Director
Health Planning Program
University of Michigan

Walter Hahn
Special Assistant for Planning
  to the Secretary of Commerce
Washington, D.C.

Calvin Hamilton
Chief of City Planning
Los Angeles, California

Wallace Hamilton
Institutional Development
The Rouse Company
Columbia, Md.

James Hardy
Associate Executive Director
YMCA, National Headquarters
New York City

Willis Harman
Educational Policy Research Center
Stanford Research Institute
Menlo Park, California

Robert Heilbroner
New School for Social Research
New York City

Kurt Hellfach
General Electric Company
New York City

Dee Henderson
Associate Head
Special Programs Department
Graduate School
U.S. Department of Agriculture

David Hertz
McKinsey & Company, Inc.
New York City

Towsend Hoopes
Cresap, McCormick, and Paget
Washington, D.C.

Ida Hoose
Space Sciences Laboratory
University of California at Berkeley

Morton Hoppenfeld
Vice President
American City Corporation
Columbia, Md.

Alan Jacobs
Director of Planning
San Francisco, California

Erich Jantsch
College of Environmental Design
University of California at Berkeley

Robert Jungk
Technische Universitat
West Berlin, Germany

Alfred Kahn
Professor
Columbia University School
 of Social Work
New York City

Robert Kahn
Director
Survey Research Center
Institute for Social Research
University of Michigan

Marvin Kelkstein
Director
Technical Assistance Office
State University of New York
 at Stony Brook

Robert Kantor
Educational Policy Research Center
Stanford Research Institute

Marshall Kaplan
President
Marshall Kaplan, Gans, and Kahn
San Francisco, California

Stephen Kaplan
Professor
Department of Psychology
University of Michigan

George Kozmetsky
Dean
College of Business Administration
University of Texas
Austin, Texas

Jody Ladio
Senior
Residential College
University of Michigan

Todd La Porte
Professor
Department of Political Science
University of California at Berkeley

Kai Lee
Postdoctoral Fellow
Institute of Governmental Studies
University of California at Berkeley

Robert Levine
Assistant Director
Research Plans, Programs, and
    Evaluation
U.S. Office of Economic Opportunity

Ronald Lippitt
Program Director
CRUSK, Institute for Social Research
University of Michigan

Ralph Littlestone
Chief
Planning Branch
National Institute of Mental Health

John Maddux
Special Assistant to the President
International Bank for
    Reconstruction & Development

Floyd Mann
Director
Center for Research on Utilization
    of Scientific Knowledge, ISR
University of Michigan

Robert Marans
Past Supervisor of Environmental
    Design Studies (Transportation
    and Land Use Study)
Detroit Regional Planning Commission

O. W. Markley
Educational Policy Research Center
Stanford Research Institute

Joseph Margolin
Director
Educational Policy Group
Program of Policy Studies in
    Science and Technology
George Washington University

M. Benjamin Matalon
Charge de Recherches
C.E.R.A.U.
Puteaux, France

John McHale
Director
Center for Integrative Studies
State University of New York
    at Binghamton

William Medina
Director
Executive-Development Program
U.S. Civil Service Commission

Dennis Medows
Research Program on Technology
    and Public Policy
Dartmouth College

Richard L. Meier
Professor
College of Environmental Design
University of California at Berkeley

Daniel Metlay
Graduate Student
University of California at Berkeley

Michael Michaelis
Director
A. D. Little, Inc.
Washington, D.C.

Alan Miller
Commissioner
New York State Department of
    Mental Hygiene

Arnold Mitchell
Assistant Director
Educational Policy Research Center
Stanford Research Center

Lawrence Mohr
Professor
Institute for Public Policy Studies
University of Michigan

Charles Morris
Professor
Department of Philosophy
University of Florida
Gainesville, Fla.

Claire Nader
Associate Director
ORNL-NSF
Environmental Program
Oakridge National Laboratory

Charlotte Neagle
Intern
Detroit City Planning Commission

Robert Newman
Corporate Headquarters
General Electric Company
New York City

Mancur Olsen
Deputy Assistant Secretary
Department of Health, Education,
    and Welfare

Robert Patton
Associate Commissioner
Office of Program Planning
    and Coordination
N.Y. State Department of
    Mental Hygiene

Harvey Perloff
Dean
School of Architecture and
    Urban Planning
University of California at Los Angeles

Jeffrey Pressman
Department of Political Science
University of California at Berkeley

Daniel Rader
Chief, Planning Section
State Department of Mental Health
Raleigh, N.C.

Philburn Ratoosh
Professor Department of Psychology
California State University,
    San Francisco

Paul Ray
Lecturer
Urban Planning
University of Michigan

Richard Raymond
President
Portola Institute
Menlo Park, California

A. Kenneth Rice
Center for Applied Social Research
Tavistock Institute of Human
    Relations
London, England

Arliss Roaden
Vice Provost and Dean, Graduate
    School
Ohio State University

Andrew Rouse
Director
Resources Planning Staff
Executive Office of the President
U.S. Bureau of the Budget

William Royce
Senior Behavioral Scientist
Stanford Research Institute

Irving Rubin
Director
Transportation and Land Use Study
Detroit Regional Planning Commission

Rudy Ruggles
Office of Exploratory Planning
International Business Machines
    Corporation

Bryce Russell
Corporate Planning Staff
Ford Motor Company

Donald Schon
President
Organization for Social and
    Technological Innovation
Cambridge, Mass.

Herbert Shepherd
Consultant on Group Processes
Stamford, Conn.

W. W. Simmons
Director
Exploratory Planning
International Business Machines
  Corporation

Robert Solo
Professor
Department of Economics
Michigan State University

Jay Starling
Graduate Student
University of California at Berkeley

Herbert Striner
Dean
College of Continuing Education
American University

James Sundberg
Graduate Student
Institute of Urban and
  Regional Planning
University of California at Berkeley

Michael Tate
Assistant Director
PPBS Training
Financial Management and
PPBS Training Center
U.S. Civil Service Commission

Michael Timpane
Program Analyst
Office of Program Evaluation
U.S. Department of Health,
  Education, and Welfare

Jeffrey Tirengel
Graduate Student (and ex-Staff
  Intern NIMH)
University of Michigan

Wilber Thompson
Professor
Department of Economics
Wayne State University

Geoffrey Vickers
Goering-on-Thames, England

Dwight Waldo
Professor
Department of Political Science
Syracuse University

Richard Walton
Professor
Graduate School of Business
  Administration
Harvard University

Graham Watt
City Manager
Dayton, Ohio

Melvin Webber
Director
Center for Planning and
  Development Research
University of California at Berkeley

Alan Westin
Director
Center for Research and Education
  in American Liberties
Columbia University and
  Teachers College

Charles Williams
Staff Director
National Goals Research Staff

Ian Wilson
Consultant
Business Environment Studies
General Electric Company
New York City

Langdon Winner
Graduate Student
University of California at Berkeley

Paul Ylvisaker
Director
New Jersey Department of
  Community Affairs

References

ABELSON, P. "The National Goals Research Staff Report." *Science,* 1970, *169.*

ACKOFF, R. *The Concept of Corporate Planning.* New York: Wiley-Interscience, 1970.

ALLISON, G. *Essence of Decision.* Boston: Little, Brown, 1971.

ANDERSON, S. (Ed.) *Ombudsmen for American Government?* Englewood Cliffs, N.J.: Prentice-Hall, 1968.

Annual Report. New York: Social Science Research Council, 1968–1969.

ARONSON, E. "The Theory of Cognitive Dissonance: a Current Perspective." In L. Berkowitz (Ed.), *Advances in Experimental Social Psychology.* New York: Academic Press, 1969, Vol. IV.

ARCHIBALD, K. "Three Views of the Expert's Role in Policymaking: Systems Analysis, Incrementalism, and the Clinical Approach." *Policy Sciences,* 1970, *1.*

ARENDT, H. *The Human Condition.* Chicago: University of Chicago Press, 1958.

ARENDT, H. *Eichmann in Jerusalem: A Report on the Banality of Evil.* New York: Viking, 1963.

ARGYRIS, C. *Interpersonal Competence and Organizational Effectiveness.* Homewood, Ill.: Dorsey Press, 1962.

ARGYRIS, C. "The Incompleteness of Social-Psychological Theory: Examples from Small Group, Cognitive Consistency, and Attribution Research." *American Psychologist,* 1969, *24*(10).

ARGYRIS, C. "Resistance to Rational Management Systems." *Innovation,* 1970 (10). (In 1972 *Innovation* merged with *Business and Society Review.*)

ARGYRIS, C. *Applicability of Organizational Sociology.* New York: Cambridge University Press, 1972.

ARNSTEIN, S. "A Ladder of Citizen Participation." *Journal of the American Institute of Planners,* July 1969, *35.*

ARNSTEIN, S. "Maximum Feasible Manipulation." Third Conference on Crises, Conflict, and Creativity, National Academy of Public Administration, July 1970.

313

ASHBY, W. R. *An Introduction to Cybernetics*. London: Chapman and Hall, 1956.

BACHMAN, J., AND VAN DUINEN, E. *Youth Look at National Problems*. Ann Arbor: Institute for Social Research, 1971.

BALDRIDGE, J. "Images of the Future and Organizational Change: The Case of New York University." In W. Bell and J. Mau, *The Sociology of the Future*. New York: Russell Sage Foundation, 1971.

BANFIELD, E. "Ends and Means in Planning." In S. Mallick and E. VanNess (Eds.), *Concepts and Issues in Administrative Behavior*. Englewood Cliffs, N.J.: Prentice-Hall, 1962.

BARAM, M. "Social Control of Science and Technology." *Science*, 1971, *172*.

BARNARD, C. *The Functions of the Executive*. Cambridge: Harvard University Press, 1938.

BARRETT, J. "Power Influence and Control in Organizations." In S. E. Seashore and R. J. McNeill, *Management of Urban Crises*. New York: The Free Press, 1971.

BART, P. "The Myth of a Value-Free Psychiatry." In W. Bell and J. Mau (Eds.), *The Sociology of the Future*. New York: Russell Sage Foundation, 1971.

BARTON, A., AND MERTON, R. *Social Organization Under Stress: A Sociological Review of Disaster Studies*. Washington, D.C.: National Academy of Sciences, National Research Council, 1963.

BAUER, R. (Ed.) *Social Indicators*. Cambridge: M.I.T. Press, 1966.

BAUER, R. "Societal Feedback." *The Annals of the American Academy of Political and Social Science*, September 1967, *373*.

BAURER, R., POOL, I. DE SOLA, AND DEXTER, L. *American Business and Public Policy*. New York: Atherton, 1963.

BAUER, R., WITH ROSENBLOOM, R., AND SHARP, L., and the assistance of others. *Second Order Consequences: A Methodological Essay on the Impact of Technology*. Cambridge: M.I.T. Press, 1969.

BAUMAN, Z. "The Limitations of 'Perfect Planning'." In B. Gross (Ed.), *Action Under Planning*. New York: McGraw-Hill, 1967.

BAZELON, D. "Psychology's Roles and Contributions in Problems of Crime, Delinquency, and Corrections." Address to the American Association of Correctional Psychologists' Conference. Washington, D.C.: Mimeographed, January 1972.

BEARD, C. *The Supreme Court and the Constitution*. Englewood Cliffs, N.J.: Prentice-Hall, 1962.

BECKHARD, R. *Organization Development: Strategies and Models*. Reading, Mass.: Addison-Wesley, 1969.

BELL, D. "Twelve Modes of Prediction—A Preliminary Sorting of Approaches in the Social Sciences." *Daedalus*, 1964, *93*,(3).

BELL, D. "The Cultural Contradictions of Capitalism." *The Public Interest*, Fall 1970, (21).

BELL, W., AND MAU, J. "Images of the Future: Theory and Research Strategies." In W. Bell and J. Mau, *The Sociology of the Future*. New York: Russell Sage Foundation, 1971.

BELL, W., AND MAU, J. *The Sociology of the Future.* New York: Russell Sage Foundation, 1971.

BENNIS, W. *Changing Organizations.* New York: McGraw-Hill, 1966.

BENNIS, W. *Organization Development: Its Nature, Origins, and Prospects.* Reading, Mass.: Addison-Wesley, 1969.

BENNIS, W. "A Funny Thing Happened on the Way to the Future." *American Psychologist,* 1970, *25*(7).

BENNIS, W., BENNE, K., AND CHIN, R. *The Planning of Change.* New York: Holt, Rinehart and Winston, 1962 and 1969 (revised).

BENNIS, W., AND SLATER, P. *The Temporary Society.* New York: Harper and Row, 1968.

BERGER, P., AND BERGER, B. "The Eve of the Bluing of America." *The New York Times.* February 15, 1971.

BERGER, P., AND LUCKMANN, T. *The Social Construction of Reality.* Garden City, N.Y.: Anchor Books, 1966.

BERLIN, I. *The Hedgehog and the Fox.* New York: New American Library, 1957.

BERLYNE, D. *Conflict, Arousal, and Curiosity.* New York: McGraw-Hill, 1960.

BERNSTEIN, M. *The Job of the Federal Executive.* Washington, D.C.: Brookings Institution, 1958.

BILLER, R. "Converting Knowledge Into Action: The Dilemma and Opportunity of the Post Industrial Society." In J. Jun and W. Storm (Eds.), *Tomorrow's Organizations: Challenges and Strategies.* Glenview, Ill.: Scott, Foresman, in press 1973.

BION, W. *Experiences in Groups.* New York: Basic Books, 1959.

BIRCH, D. "The Model-Building Process and Its Interaction with Organizations: Two Exploratory Field Studies Involving Mathematical Decision Models." Thesis. Graduate School of Business Administration, Harvard University, Jan. 1966.

BLACKBURN, T. "Sensuous-Intellectual Complementarity in Science." *Science,* 1971, *172.*

BLAKE, R., AND MOUTON, J. "Grid Organizational Development." *Personnel Administration,* Jan.-Feb. 1967.

BLAKE, R., AND MOUTON, J. *Corporate Excellence Through Grid Organizational Development.* Houston, Tex.: Gulf, 1968.

BLAU, P. *The Dynamics of Bureaucracy: A Study of Interpersonal Relations in Two Government Agencies.* Chicago: University of Chicago Press, 1963.

BLUMENTHAL, M., KAHN, R., ANDREWS, F., AND HEAD, K. *Justifying Violence: Attitudes of American Men.* Ann Arbor: Institute for Social Research, University of Michigan, 1972.

BLUMER, H. "Social Problems as Collective Behavior." *Social Problems,* 1971, *18.*

BOETTINGER, H. "Big Gap in Economic Theory." *Harvard Business Review,* 1967, *45*(4).

BOORSTIN, D. *The Image: A Guide to Pseudo-Events in America.* New York: Harper and Row, 1964.

BORGATTA, E. "Research Problems in Evaluation of Health Service Demonstrations." *Milbank Memorial Fund Quarterly,* Oct. 1966, *44,* Part II.

BOULDING, K. *The Image.* Ann Arbor: The University of Michigan Press, 1956.

BOULDING, K. "Ethics of Rational Decision." *Management Science,* 1966, *12*(6).

BOWER, J. *Managing the Resource Allocation Process: A Study in Corporate Planning and Investment.* Boston: Harvard Business School, 1970.

BOWERS, D. "Perspectives in Organizational Development." CRUSK-ISR Working Paper. Ann Arbor: Center for Research on Utilization of Scientific Knowledge, Institute for Social Research, University of Michigan, 1971.

BRINTON, C. *Shaping of the Modern Mind.* New York: Mentor Books, 1953.

BROOKS, H. "Science and the Allocation of Resources." *American Psychologist,* March 1967, *22.*

BRZEZINSKI, Z. *Between Two Ages: America's Role in the Technetronic Era.* New York: The Viking Press, 1970.

BUCKLEY, W. (Ed.) *Sociology and Modern Systems Theory.* Englewood Cliffs, N.J.: Prentice-Hall, 1967.

BUCKLEY, W. (Ed.) *Modern Systems Research for the Behavioral Scientist.* Chicago: Aldine, 1968.

BUHLER, C. "Basic Theoretical Concepts of Humanistic Psychology." *American Psychologist,* 1971, *26*(4).

BURCO, R. "The Assessment of Technology as a Problem in the Distribution of Technical Expertise." Private paper, December 1971.

BURNS, T., AND STALKER, G. *The Management of Innovation.* London: Tavistock, 1961.

BUTKIS, A. "The New Youth Movement." *Dunn's,* 1971 *98*(2).

CAHN, E., AND CAHN, J. "Citizen Participation." In H. Spiegel (Ed.), *Citizen Participation in Urban Development.* Washington, D.C.: NTL Institute for Applied Behavioral Science, 1968.

CALDWELL, L. *Environment: A Challenge for Modern Society.* Garden City, N.Y.: The Natural History Press, 1970.

CALDWELL, L. *In Defense of Earth: International Protection of the Biosphere.* Bloomington, Ind.: Indiana University Press, 1972.

CAMPBELL, D. "Methods for the Experimenting Society." Paper delivered to the American Psychological Association meetings, Washington, D.C., September 1971. To appear in the *American Psychologist.*

CAMPBELL, J. *The Hero with a Thousand Faces.* Princeton, N.J.: Bollingen Series No. 17, 1968.

CAMPBELL, J. *The Flight of the Wild Gander: Explorations in the Mythological Dimension.* New York: Viking, 1969.

CAPLAN, N. "The Impact of Social Research on Policy Decisions." Invited address to the American Society for Public Opinion Research, May 19, 1971, Pasadena, California. Ann Arbor: Center for Research on Utilization of Scientific Knowledge, Institute for Social Research, University of Michigan.

CAPLAN, N., AND NELSON, S. "On Being Useful: The Nature and Uses of Psychological Research on Social Problems." *American Psychologist,* 1973, *28*(3).

CARROLL, J. "Participatory Technology." *Science,* 1971, *171.*

CAZES, B. "The Promise and Limits of Social Indicators." *European Business,* Summer 1972, (34).

"Change in the Corporations." By the Editors. *Harvard Today,* March 1972, p. 4.

CHAPMAN, J. "Voluntary Association and the Political Theory of Pluralism." In J. Pennock and J. Chapman (Eds.), *Voluntary Associations: Nomos XI.* New York: Atherton, 1968.

CHARLESWORTH, J. (Ed.) "Ethics in America: Norms and Deviations." *The Annals of the American Academy,* 1966, *31*(3).

CHESLER, M., AND GUSKIN, A. "Intervention in High School Crises: Consultant Roles." Ann Arbor: Educational Change Team, School of Education, University of Michigan, 1970.

CHURCHMAN, C. W. *Challenge to Reason.* New York: McGraw-Hill, 1967.

CHURCHMAN, C. W. *The Systems Approach.* New York: Dell, 1968.

CHURCHMAN, C. W. "Operations Research as a Profession." *Management Science,* 1970, *17*(2).

CHURCHMAN, C. W., AND EMERY, F. "On Various Approaches to the Study of Organizations." In J. Lawrence (Ed.), *Operational Research and the Social Sciences.* London: Tavistock, 1966.

CLAIBORNE, R. Review of R. Titmuss, *The Gift Relationship.* In "Book World," *Washington Post,* May 9, 1971, p. 4.

CLARK, K. "Problems of Power and Social Change: Toward a Relevant Social Pathology." *Journal of Social Issues,* 1965, *21*(3).

CLARK, T. "The Concept of Power: Some Overemphasized and Underrecognized Dimensions—An Examination with Special Reference to the Social Community." *Social Science Quarterly,* December 1967.

CLEVELAND, H. *The Future Executive: A Guide for Tomorrow's Managers.* New York: Harper and Row, 1972.

COHEN, A., STOTLAND, E., AND WOLFE, D. "An Experimental Investigation of Need for Cognition." *Journal of Abnormal and Social Psychology,* 1959 (51).

COLM, G., AND GULICK, L. *Program Planning for National Goals.* Washington, D.C.: National Planning Association, 1968.

Concepts for Los Angeles. Los Angeles: City Planning Department, 1967.

COSER, L. *Functions of Social Conflict.* Glencoe: The Free Press, 1956.

COSER, L. *Continuities in the Study of Social Conflict.* New York: The Free Press, 1967.

COSTELLO, T. "Change in Municipal Government: A View from the Inside." *Journal of Applied Behavioral Science,* 1971, *7*(2).

COTTLE, T. "Temporal Correlates of the Achievement Value and Manifest Anxiety." *Journal of Consulting and Clinical Psychology,* 1969, *33*(5).

COTTRELL, L., AND SHELDON, E. "Problems of Collaboration Between Social Scientists and the Practicing Professions." *The Annals of the American Academy of Political and Social Science,* March 1963, *346.*

CRECINE, J. *Defense Budgeting: Organizational Adaptation to External Constraints.* Prepared for the United States Air Force Project Rand. Santa Monica, Calif.: The Rand Corporation, March 1970.

CROWE, B. "The Tragedy of the Commons Revisited." *Science,* 1969, *166.*

CROWFOOT, J. "Planning and Social Systems Organizations as a Special Case." Working paper, Center for Research on Utilization of Scientific Knowledge. Ann Arbor: Institute for Social Research, 1972.

CROZIER, M. *The Bureaucratic Phenomenon.* Chicago: University of Chicago Press, 1964.

CYERT, R., AND MARCH, J. *A Behavioral Theory of the Firm.* Englewood Cliffs, N.J.: Prentice-Hall, 1963.

DAHL, R. "The Concept of Power." *Behavioral Science,* 1957, (2).

DALE, E. "The 'Unfavorables'." *New York Sunday Times,* Financial Section, November 7, 1971.

DAVID, H. "Assumptions About Man and Society and Historical Constructs in Futures Research." *Futures,* 1970, *2*(3).

DEARDEN, J. "Myth of Real-Time Management Information." *Harvard Business Review,* 1966, *44*(3).

DE HOGHTON, C., PAGE, W., AND STREATFEILD, G. . . . *And Now the Future: A PEP Survey of Futures Studies.* London: PEP, 1971.

DE JOUVENEL, B. *The Art of Conjecture.* New York: Basic Books, 1967.

DEL GUIDICE, D. *The Potential for Developing a Local Goals-Setting Model and NGRS [National Goals Research Staff] Involvement Therein.* National Academy of Public Administration, 1970.

DEUTSCH, K. *The Nerves of Government.* New York: The Free Press, 1966.

DEUTSCH, M. "An Experimental Study of the Effects of Cooperation and Competition Upon Group Processes." *Human Relations,* 1949, 2.

DEUTSCH, M. "The Effect of Motivational Orientation Upon Trust and Suspicion." *Human Relations,* 1960, *13.*

DIAL, O. *Urban Information Systems: A Bibliographic Essay.* Urban Systems Laboratory, M.I.T. Cambridge, Mass.: 1968.

DI BONA, C. "Where Is Systems Analysis?" CNA 451–67, Revised. Washington, D.C.: Center for Naval Analysis, 1967.

Diplomacy for the 70's: A Program of Management Reform for the Department of State. Department of State. Washington, D.C.: U.S. Government Printing Office, 1970.

Discussion Paper: Planning Goals for the Los Angeles Metropolis. Los Angeles: City Planning Department, 1967.

DOWNS, A. *Inside Bureaucracy.* Boston: Little, Brown, 1966.

DOWNS, A. "A Realistic Look at the Final Payoffs From Urban Data Systems." *Public Administration Review,* 1967 27(3).

DREWS, E. *Policy Implications of a Hierarchy of Values.* Menlo Park, Calif.: Educational Policy Research Center, Stanford Research Institute, 1970.

DREWS, E., AND LIPSON, L. *Values and Humanity.* New York: St. Martin's Press, 1971.

DRIVER, M., AND STREUFERT, S. The General Incongruity Adaptation Level (GIAL) Hypothesis–II. Incongruity Motivation to Affect, Cognition, and Activation-Arousal Theory. Paper No. 148. Lafayette, Ind.: Institute for Research in the Behavioral, Economic, and Management Sciences, Purdue University, 1966.

DROR, Y. "Muddling Through—'Science' or Inertia?" *Public Administration Review*, 1964, *24*(3).

DROR, Y. *Public Policymaking Reexamined.* San Francisco: Chandler, 1968.

DROR, Y. "Law as a Tool of Directed Social Change." *American Behavioral Scientist*, 1970, *13*(4).

DRUCKER, P. *The Practice of Management.* New York: Harper and Row, 1954.

DUHL, L. "Creation of Forecasting and Planning Mechanisms." American Academy of Arts and Sciences, Commission on the Year 2000. Unpublished paper.

DUMONT, M. *The Absurd Healer: Perspectives of a Community Psychiatrist.* New York: Science House, 1968.

DUNCAN, O. "Social Forecasting: The State of the Art." *The Public Interest,* Fall 1968 (17).

DUNN, E. *Economic and Social Development: A Process of Social Learning.* Baltimore: Johns Hopkins, 1971.

EDELMAN, M. *The Symbolic Uses of Politics.* Chicago: University of Illinois Press, 1964.

EDELSTON, H., AND KOLODNER, F. "Are the Poor Capable of Planning for Themselves?" In H. Spiegel (Ed.), *Citizen Participation in Urban Development.* Washington, D.C.: NTL Institute for Applied Behavioral Science, 1968.

EMERY, F. "The Next Thirty Years: Concepts, Methods, and Anticipations." *Human Relations,* 1967, *20*.

EMERY, F., AND TRIST, E. "The Causal Texture of Organizational Environments." *Human Relations,* 1965, *18*.

ERBER, E. (Ed.) *Urban Planning in Transition.* New York: Grossman, 1970.

"To Establish a Select Senate Committee on Technology and the Human Environment." Hearings before the Subcommittee on Intergovernmental Relations. Washington, D.C.: U.S. Government Printing Office, March 1967.

ETZIONI, A. " 'Shortcuts' to Social Change?" *The Public Interest,* Summer 1968a (12).

ETZIONI, A. *The Active Society.* New York: The Free Press, 1968.

ETZIONI, A., AND LEHMAN, E. "Some Dangers in 'Valid' Social Measurement." *The Annals of the American Academy,* September 1967, *373*.

EVAN, W. "The Organization-Set: Toward a Theory of Interorganizational Relations." In J. Thompson (Ed.), *Approaches to Organizational Design.* Pittsburgh: University of Pittsburgh Press, 1966.

EWING, D. *The Human Side of Planning: Tool or Tyrant?* New York: Macmillan, 1969.

Experimental Symposia on Cultural Futurology, American Anthropological Association, Office of Applied Social Science and the Future, University of Minnesota, 1970, 1971.

FERKISS, V. *Technological Man.* New York: Braziller, 1969.

FISCHER, R. "A Cartography of the Ecstatic and Meditative States." *Science,* 1971, *174*.

FLACKS, R. "Protest or Conform: Some Social Psychological Perspectives on Legitimacy." *Journal of Applied Behavioral Science,* 1969, *5*(2).

FRAISSE, P. *The Psychology of Time.* New York: Harper and Row, 1963.

FRENCH, J., AND CAPLAN, R. "Psychosocial Factors in Coronary Heart Disease." *Industrial Medicine,* 1970, *39*(9).

FRENCH, J., AND RAVEN, B.. "The Basis of Social Power." In Cartwright, D. (Ed.) *Studies in Social Power.* New York: Harper and Row, 1968.

FRIEDLANDER, F. "The Primacy of Trust as a Facilitator of Further Group Accomplishment." *Journal of Applied Behavioral Science,* 1970, *6*(4).

FRIEDMANN, J. "The Future of Comprehensive Urban Planning: A Critique." *Public Administration Review,* 1971, *31*(3).

FRIEDMANN, J. *Retracking America: A Theory of Transactive Planning.* Garden City, N.Y.: Anchor Press–Doubleday, 1973.

FRIEND, J., AND JESSOP, W. *Local Government and Strategic Choice.* London: Tavistock Publications; Sage Publications, 1969.

FROHMAN, M., AND HAVELOCK, R. "The Organizational Context of Dissemination and Utilization." In R. Havelock and others, *Planning for Innovation.* Ann Arbor: Institute for Social Research, Center on Utilization of Scientific Knowledge, 1971.

FROMM, E. *Escape from Freedom.* New York: Holt, Rinehart and Winston, 1941.

Full Opportunity and Social Accounting Act. Hearings before the Subcommittee on Government Research of the Committee on Government Operations. Washington, D.C.: U.S. Government Printing Office, 1967.

GABOR, D. *Inventing the Future.* New York: Knopf, 1964.

GAMSON, W. *Power and Discontent.* Homewood, Ill.: Dorsey Press, 1968.

GANS, H. "The Need for Planners Trained in Policy Formation." In E. Erber (Ed.), *Urban Planning in Transition.* New York: Grossman, 1970.

GARDNER, J. "America in the Twenty-Third Century. *New York Times,* Editorial Page, July 27, 1968.

GEORGE, A. "Power as a Compensatory Value for Political Leaders." *Journal of Social Issues,* 1968, *24.*

GEORGOPOULOS, B. "An Open-System Theory Model for Organizational Research." In A. Negandhi and J. Schwitter (Eds.), *Organizational Behavior Models.* Kent, Ohio: Kent State University, 1970.

GLATT, E. AND SHELLEY, M. *The Research Society,* New York: Gordon and Breach, 1969.

GOODING, J. "It Pays to Wake Up the Blue-Collar Worker." *Fortune,* September 1970.

GORDON, W. *Synectics.* New York: Harper and Row, 1961.

GORE, W. *Administrative Decision-Making: A Heuristic Model.* New York: Wiley, 1966.

GRAVES, C. "Deterioration of Work Standards." *Harvard Business Review,* 1966, *44*(5).

GRAVES, C. "Levels of Existence: An Open System Theory of Values." *Journal of Humanistic Psychology,* 1970, *10*(2).

GRINSPOON, L. "Interpersonal Constraints and the Decision Maker." In R. Fisher (Ed.), *International Conflict and Behavioral Science*. New York: Basic Books, 1964.

GROSS, B. *The Managing of Organizations*. New York: The Free Press, 1964.

GROSS, B. "Activating National Plans." In B. Gross (Ed.), *Action Under Planning*. New York: McGraw-Hill, 1967.

GROSS, B. "Friendly Fascism: A Model for America." *Social Policy*, November–December 1970, *1*.

GROSS, B. *Management Strategy for Economic and Social Development*. Working Paper prepared for the United Nations Interregional Seminar on the Use of Modern Management Techniques in the Public Administration of Developing Countries, Washington, D.C. ESA/PA/MMTS/27. New York: United Nations, 1970.

GROSS, B. "Planning in an Era of Social Revolution." *Public Administration Review*, 1971, *31*(3).

GROSS, B., AND SPAINGER, M. (Eds.) *Social Intelligence for America's Future: Explorations in Societal Problems*. Boston: Allyn and Bacon, 1969.

GUSKIN, A., MICHAEL, D., AND CROWFOOT, J. "The Implications for the Change-Over to Long-Range Planning of the Rise of the Advocate Planner." Working Paper 2. Center for Research on Utilization of Scientific Knowledge, Institute for Social Research, University of Michigan, 1970.

GUTTENTAG, M. "Models and Methods in Evaluation Research." *Journal of Theory of Social Behavior*, 1972, *1*(1).

HABERSTROH, C. "Control as an Organizational Process." In W. Buckley (Ed.), *Modern Systems Research for the Behavioral Scientist*. Chicago: Aldine, 1968.

HAGE, J., AND AIKEN, M. *Social Change in Complex Organizations*. New York: Random House, 1970.

HAHN, W. *The Department of Commerce: Its Past Present and Future*. A Task Force Report. Washington, D.C.: The Department of Commerce, December 1968.

HALL, M. "A Conversation with Harold Dwight Lasswell: The Psychology of Politics." *Psychology Today*, 1968, *2*(5).

HALL, W. "Strategic Planning Models . . . Are Top Managers Really Finding Them Useful?" Graduate School of Business Administration, University of Michigan, 1972. (Limited circulation.)

HALPERIN, M. "Why Bureaucrats Play Games." Washington, D.C.: The Brookings Institution Reprint, 1971.

HANS, H. "The Need for Planners Trained in Policy Formation." In E. Erber (Ed.), *Urban Planning in Transition*. New York: Grossman, 1970.

HARDIN, G. "The Tragedy of the Commons." *Science*, 1968, *162*.

HARMAN, W. "Nature of Our Changing Society: Implications for Schools." In P. Piele and T. Eidell (Eds.), *Social and Technological Change: Implications for Education*. Eugene, Ore.: Center for the Advanced Study of Educational Administration, University of Oregon, 1970.

HARRISON, A. *The Problem of Privacy in the Computer Age: An Annotated*

Bibliography. Memorandum RM-5495-PR/RC. Santa Monica: The Rand Corporation, 1967.

HAVELOCK, R. "Specialized Knowledge Linking Models." In R. Havelock and others, *Planning for Innovation.* Ann Arbor: Institute for Social Research, Center for Research on Utilization of Scientific Knowledge, 1971.

HAVELOCK, R., with the collaboration of A. Guskin, M. Frohman, M. Havelock, M. Hill, and J. Huber. *Planning for Innovation.* Ann Arbor: Institute for Social Research, Center for Research on Utilization of Scientific Knowledge, 1971.

HEILBRONER, R. *The Future as History.* New York: Grove Press, 1959.

HEILBRONER, R. *The Making of Economic Society.* Englewood Cliffs, N.J.: Prentice-Hall, 1962.

HEILBRONER, R. "On the Limited 'Relevance' of Economics." *The Public Interest,* Fall 1970, (21).

HEILBRONER, R. "Phase II of the Capitalist System." *The New York Times Magazine,* November 28, 1971.

HENRIOT, P. "Political Implications of Social Indicators." Paper presented at the Annual Meeting of the American Political Science Association. Chicago, September 1971. Seattle: Seattle University, 1971.

HERMANN, C. "Some Consequences of Crises Which Limit the Viability of Organizations." *Administrative Science Quarterly,* 1963, *8*(1).

HERTZ, D. "Has Management Science Reached a Dead End?" *Innovation* (now *Business Society Review*), 1971 (25).

HEYDEBRAND, W. "Administration of Social Change." *Public Administration Review,* 1964, *24*(3).

HIRSCHMAN, A. *Exit, Voice, and Loyalty: Responses to Decline in Firms, Organizations, and States.* Cambridge: Harvard University Press, 1970.

HIRSCHMAN, A., AND LINDBLOM, C. "Economic Development, Research and Development, Policy Making: Some Converging Views." *Behavioral Science,* 1962, *7*(2).

HOFFER, E. *The Ordeal of Change.* New York: Harper and Row, 1963.

HOLT, J. *The Underachieving School.* New York: Dell, 1970.

HOOK, S. *The Hero in History.* Boston: Beacon Press, 1943.

HOOPES, T. *The Limits of Intervention: An Inside Account of How the Johnson Policy of Escalation in Vietnam was Reversed.* New York: David McKay, 1969.

HOOS, I. *A Critical Review of Systems Analysis: The California Experience.* NASA Report CR-61350. Berkeley: University of California, 1968.

HOOS, I. "A Realistic Look at the Systems Approach to Social Problems." *Datamation,* 1969, *15*(2). In the journal section, "The Forum."

HORNEY, K. *The Neurotic Personality of Our Time.* New York: Norton, 1937.

HUBER, B. "Studies of the Future: A Selected and Annotated Bibliography." In W. Bell and J. Mau (Eds.), *The Sociology of the Future.* New York: Russell Sage Foundation, 1971.

HUNT, R. "Technology and Organization." *Academy of Management Journal,* September 1970.

HUNT, R. "Role and Role Conflict." In Hollander, E., and Hunt R. (Eds.)

Current Perspectives in Social Psychology. New York: Oxford University Press, 1971.

HUXLEY, A. *The Perennial Philosophy.* New York: Harper and Row, 1944.

HYMAN, H. "Reference Groups." In *International Encyclopedia of the Social Sciences.* Vol. XIII. New York: Crowell Collier and Macmillan, 1968.

Information Technology: Some Critical Implications for Decision Makers. New York: The Conference Board, Inc., 1972.

"Is There a New Man?" *The Center Magazine,* 1971, *4*(6).

JANIS, I. "Groupthink Among Policy Makers." In N. Sanford and C. Comstock (Eds.), *Sanctions for Evil.* San Francisco: Jossey-Bass, 1971a.

JANIS, I. "Groupthink." *Psychology Today,* November, 1971.

JANTSCH, E. "From Forecasting and Planning to Policy Sciences." Paper for presentation at the AAAS Annual Meeting, Boston, December 26–31, 1969.

JANTSCH, E. (Ed.) *Perspectives of Planning.* Paris: Organization for Economic Co-operation and Development, 1969a.

JANTSCH, E. *Technological Planning and Social Futures.* London: Associated Business Programs Limited, 1972.

JONES, E. *Systems Approaches to Multi-Variable Socioeconomic Problems: An Appraisal.* Staff Discussion Paper 103, Program of Policy Studies in Science and Technology. Washington, D.C.: The George Washington University, 1968.

JONES, R. "The Model as a Decision Maker's Dilemma." *Public Administration Review,* 1964, *24*(3).

JUNG, C. *Two Essays on Analytical Psychology.* Cleveland: World Publishing Co., 1956.

KAHN, A. *Theory and Practice of Social Planning.* New York: Russell Sage Foundation, 1969.

KAHN, R. "The Justification of Violence: Social Problems and Social Solutions." *Journal of the Society for the Psychological Study of Social Issues,* 1972, *28.*

KAHN, R., AND BOULDING, E. (Eds.) *Power and Conflict in Organizations.* New York: Basic Books, 1964.

KAHN, R., WOLFE, D., QUINN, R., SNOEK, J. AND ROSENTHAL, R. *Organizational Stress: Studies in Role Conflict and Ambiguity.* New York: Wiley, 1964.

KANTOR, R. *Psychological Theories and Social Groupings.* Research Memorandum EPRC-6747-5. Menlo Park, Calif.: Stanford Research Institute, 1969.

KANTOR, R. "The Affective Domain and Beyond." *Journal for the Study of Consciousness,* 1970, *3*(1).

KANTOR, R. *Implications of a Moral Science.* Memorandum Report EPRC 6747-14. Menlo Park, Calif.: Educational Policy Research Center, Stanford Research Institute, 1971.

KANTOR, R. "Moral Science." Menlo Park, Calif.: Stanford Research Institute, 1971.

KAPLAN, M. "The Role of the Planner in Urban Areas: Modest, Intuitive Claims for Advocacy." San Francisco: Address to the National Conference on Social Welfare, 1968.

KAPLAN, S. *Cognitive Maps in Perception and Thought.* Ann Arbor: University of Michigan, 1970.

KATZ, D., AND GEORGOPOULOS, B. "Organizations in a Changing World." *Journal of Applied Behavioral Science,* 1971, 7(3).

KATZ, D., AND KAHN, R. *The Social Psychology of Organizations.* New York: John Wiley, 1966.

KAYSEN, C. "Model-Makers and Decision-Makers: Economists and the Policy Process." *The Public Interest,* Summer 1968 (12).

KIEFER, D. "Industry Maps Tomorrow's Technology." *Chemical and Engineering News,* 1972, 50(9).

KLUCKHOHN, C., AND KELLY, W. "The Concept of Culture." In R. Linton (Ed.), *The Science of Man in the World Crisis.* New York: Columbia University Press, 1945.

KNIGHT, F. *Risk Uncertainty and Profit.* Chicago: University of Chicago Press, 1921.

KOHN, M. "Bureaucratic Man." *New Society,* October 28, 1971.

KUHN, T. *The Structure of Scientific Revolution.* Chicago: University of Chicago Press, 1970. Second Edition.

LA PORTE, T. *Organizational Response to Complexity: Research and Development as Organized Inquiry and Action—Part I.* Working Paper No. 141. Berkeley: Center for Planning and Development Research, Institute of Urban and Regional Development, University of California, 1971.

LASSWELL, H. *Power and Personality.* New York: W. W. Norton, 1948.

LASSWELL, H. "The Changing Image of Human Nature." *The American Journal of Psychoanalysis,* 1967, 26(2).

LASSWELL, H. "A Note on 'Types' of Political Personality: Nuclear, Co-Relational, Developmental." *Journal of Social Issues,* 1968, 24(3).

LASSWELL, H., AND CLEVELAND, H. *The Ethic of Power.* New York: Harper and Row, 1962.

LASSWELL, H., AND KAPLAN, A. *Power and Society.* New Haven: Yale University Press, 1950.

LAWRENCE, J. (Ed.) *Operational Research and the Social Sciences.* London: Tavistock, 1966.

LAWRENCE, P. "The Uses of Crises: Dynamics of Ghetto Organization Development." In R. Rosenbloom and R. Marris (Eds.), *Social Innovation in the City.* Cambridge: Harvard University Press, 1969.

LAWRENCE, P., AND LORSCH, J. *Organization and Environment: Managing Differentiation and Integration.* Cambridge: Harvard University Press, 1967.

LEAVITT, H. "Applied Organizational Change in Industry: Structural Technological, and Humanistic Approaches." In March, J. (Ed.) *Handbook of Organizations,* Chicago: Rand McNally, 1965.

LEE, I. *The Language of Wisdom and Folly.* New York: Harper and Bros., 1949.

LEVINE, S., AND WHITE, P. "Exchange as a Conceptual Framework for the Study of Interorganizational Relationships." *Administrative Science Quarterly,* 1961, 5(4).

LEVINE, S., WHITE, P., AND PAUL, B. "Community Interorganizational Problems in Providing Medical Care and Social Services." *American Journal of Public Health,* 1963, *53*(8).

LEWIN, K. "Feedback Problems of Social Diagnosis and Action." In W. Buckley (Ed.), *Modern Systems Research for the Behavioral Scientist.* Chicago: Aldine, 1968.

LICHTMAN, C., AND HUNT, R. "Personality and Organization Theory: A Review of Some Conceptual Literature." *Psychological Bulletin,* 1971, *76.*

LIKERT, R. *New Patterns of Management.* New York: McGraw-Hill, 1961.

LINDBLOM, C. "Contexts for Change and Strategy: A Reply." *Public Administration Review,* 1964, *24*(3).

LINDBLOM, C. *The Intelligence of Democracy: Decision Making Through Mutual Adjustment.* New York: The Free Press, 1965.

LINDBLOM, C. "The Science of 'Muddling Through'." In E. Schneier (Ed.), *Policy Making in American Government.* New York: Basic Books, 1969.

LITWAK, E., AND HYLTON, L. "Interorganizational Analysis: A Hypothesis on Coordinating Agencies." *Administrative Science Quarterly,* 1962, *6*(4).

LONG, N. "The Local Community as an Ecology of Games." *American Journal of Sociology,* 1958, *64*(3).

LONG, N. "The Administrative Organization as a Political System." In S. Mallick and E. Van Ness (Eds.), *Concepts and Issues in Administrative Behavior.* Englewood Cliffs, N.J.: Prentice-Hall, 1962.

LOWI, T. *The End of Liberalism.* New York: W. W. Norton, 1969.

LOWI, T. "Government and Politics: Blurring of Sector Lines." In *Information Technology.* New York: The Conference Board, 1972.

LUBOVE, R. "Social Work and the Life of the Poor." *The Nation.* May 1966, *202.*

MAIMON, Z. "Second-Order Consequences—A Presentation of a Concept." Discussion Paper. Detroit: Center for Urban Studies, Wayne State University, May 1971.

MAIMON, Z. "Some Aspects of the Treatment of Costs and Benefits in Social Psychology." Discussion Paper. Detroit: Center for Urban Studies, Wayne State University, May 1971.

MANSFIELD, H. "Federal Executive Reorganization: Thirty Years of Experience." *Public Administration Review,* 1969, *29*(4).

MARINI, F. (Ed.) *Toward a New Public Administration.* Scranton, Pa.: Chandler, 1971.

MARKLEY, O. W., CURRY, D., AND RINK, D. "Contemporary Societal Problems." Research Report EPRC 6747-2. Educational Policy Research Center, 1971.

MARRIS, P., AND REIN, M. *Dilemmas of Social Reform.* New York: Atherton, 1967.

MARROW, A., BOWERS, D., AND SEASHORE, S. *Management by Participation.* New York: Harper and Row, 1967.

MARTIN, R. "Be Kind to Your Plants or You Could Cause a Violet to Shrink." *Wall Street Journal,* February 2, 1972.

MARTINO, J. "Forecasting the Survival of the Forecaster." *The Futurist,* 1971.

MARX, F. *The Administrative State.* Chicago: University of Chicago Press, 1957.

MASLOW, A. *Toward a Psychology of Being.* Princeton: Van Nostrand, 1968.

MAY, R. *Man's Search for Himself.* New York: Norton, 1953.

MAY, R. (Ed.) *Symbolism in Religion and Literature.* New York: Braziller, 1959.

MAY, R. "Reality Beyond Rationalism." In Smith, G. Kerry (Ed.), *Agony and Promise: Current Issues in Higher Education 1969.* San Francisco: Jossey-Bass, 1969.

MAYO, E. *The Human Problems of an Industrial Civilization.* New York: Macmillan, 1933.

MC CLEERY, M. "On Remarks Taken Out of Context." *Public Administration Review,* 1964, *24*(3).

MC CLUSKY, H. "The Adult as Learner." In S. Seashore and R. McNeill (Eds.), *The Management of Urban Crisis.* New York: The Free Press, 1971.

MC HALE, J., AND CORDELL, M. *Typological Survey of Futures Research in the U.S.* Binghamton, N.Y.: Center for Integrative Studies, State University of New York, 1971.

MC KEAN, R., AND ANSHEN, M. "Problems, Limitations, and Risks." In D. Novick (Ed.), *Program Budgeting: Program Analysis and the Federal Budget.* Santa Monica, Calif.: The Rand Corporation, 1965.

MC NAMARA, R. *Address to the Board of Governors.* Washington, D.C.: International Bank for Reconstruction and Development, 1970a.

MC NAMARA, R. *Address to the Columbia University Conference on International Economic Development.* Washington, D.C.: International Bank for Reconstruction and Development, 1970.

MC QUADE, W. "What Stress Can Do to You." *Fortune,* 1972, *85*(1).

MC WHINNEY, W. "Organizational Form, Decision Modalities, and the Environment." *Human Relations,* 1968, *21*(3).

MEAD, G. *Mind, Self, and Society.* Chicago: University of Chicago Press, 1934.

MEAD, M., AND BYERS, P. *The Small Conference.* The Hague, The Netherlands: Mouton, 1968.

MEADOWS, D., MEADOWS, D., RANDERS, J., AND BEHRENS, W. *The Limits of Growth.* New York: Universe Books, 1972.

MEIER, R. "Information Input Overload." *Libri,* 1963, *13*.

MERTENS, H., AND GROSS, B. (Eds.) "Symposium on Changing Styles of Planning in Post-Industrial America." *Public Administration Review,* May-June 1971, *31*(3).

MEYER, M. "Two Authority Structures of Bureaucratic Organization." *Administrative Science Quarterly,* 1968, *13*(2).

MICHAEL, D. "Civilian Behavior Under Atomic Bombardment." *Bulletin of the Atomic Scientists,* May 1955, *11*.

MICHAEL, D. "Cybernetics and Human Behavior." Bethesda, Md.: Army Medical Service Graduate School, Walter Reed Army Medical Center, 1954.

MICHAEL, D. "Psychopathology of Nuclear War." *Bulletin by the Atomic Scientists,* May 1962, *18*.

MICHAEL, D. "Speculations on the Relation of the Computer to Individual Freedom and the Right to Privacy." *The George Washington Law Review,* 1964, *33*(1).

MICHAEL, D. "On Coping with Complexity: Planning and Politics." *Daedalus,* 1968, *97*(4).

MICHAEL, D. *The Unprepared Society: Planning for a Precarious Future.* New York: Basic Books, 1968.

MICHAEL, D. "Influencing Public Policy: The Changing Roles of Voluntary Associations." *Journal of Current Social Issues,* 1971, *9*(6).

MICHAEL, D. "The Individual: Enriched or Impoverished, Master or Servant?" *Information Technology: Some Critical Implications for Decision Makers.* New York: The Conference Board, Inc., 1972.

MILLER, A. "Business Morality: Some Unanswered (and Perhaps Unanswerable) Questions." *The Annals of the American Academy,* 1966, *363.*

MILLER, A. *The Dossier Society.* Ann Arbor: University of Michigan Press, 1971.

MILLER, E., AND RICE, A. K. *Systems of Organization.* London: Tavistock, 1967.

MILLER, J. "Information Input, Overload, and Psychopathology." *American Journal of Psychiatry,* 1960, *116.*

MILLWARD, R. "PPBS: Problems of Implementation." *Journal of the American Institute of Planners,* 1968, *34*(2).

MILSUM, J. "The Technosphere, The Biosphere, The Sociosphere." *IEEE Spectrum,* 1968, *5*(6).

MITCHELL, A., AND BAIRD, M. *American Values.* Long Range Planning Service, Report 378. Menlo Park, Calif.: Stanford Research Institute, 1969.

MOCKLER, R. "Theory and Practice of Planning." *Harvard Business Review,* 1970, *48*(2).

MOHR, L. "Determinants of Innovation in Organizations." *The American Political Science Review,* 1969, *62*(1).

MORRIS, C. *The Open Self.* New York: Prentice-Hall, 1948.

MORRIS, C., AND SMALL, L. "Changes in Conceptions of the Good Life by American College Students from 1950 to 1970." *Journal of Personality and Social Psychology,* 1971, *20*(2).

MOSHER, F. "The Public Service in the Temporary Society." *Public Administration Review,* 1971, *31*(1).

MOYNIHAN, D. *Maximum Feasible Misunderstanding.* New York: The Free Press, 1969.

MOYNIHAN, D. "Counselor's Statement." *Toward Balanced Growth: Quantity with Quality.* Report of the National Goals Research Staff. Washington, D.C.: U.S. Government Printing Office, 1970.

MOYNIHAN, D. "Eliteland." *Psychology Today,* 1970, *4*(4).

MUMFORD, L. *The Transformations of Man.* New York: Harper Bros., 1956.

MUNSINGER, H., AND KESSEN, W. "Uncertainty, Structure, and Preference." *Psychological Monographs: General and Applied,* 1964, *78.*

MYRDAL, G. "The World Poverty Problem." *Encyclopedia Britannica Annual World Book,* 1972.

NEEDLEMAN, J. *The New Religions.* New York: Simon and Schuster Pocket Books, 1972.

NELSON, R., PECK, M., AND KALACHEK, E. *Technology, Economic Growth, and Public Policy.* Washington, D.C.: The Brookings Institution, 1967.

The New York City Rand Institute: A Review, January 1968–June 1970. New York: New York City Rand Institute, 1970.

NOVAK, M. *The Experience of Nothingness.* New York: Harper and Row, 1970.

Our Future Business Environment: Developing Trends and Changing Institutions.
ERM-85A. General Electric Company, 1968.

OZBEKHAN, H. "Toward a General Theory of Planning." In E. Jantsch (Ed.),
Perspectives of Planning. Paris: Organization for Economic Co-operation
and Development, 1969.

PARSONS, T. *Structure and Process in Modern Societies.* New York: The Free
Press, 1960.

PEABODY, R., AND ROURKE, F. "Public Bureaucracies." In J. March (Ed.), *Handbook of Organizations.* Chicago: Rand McNally,1965.

PECCEI, A. "How to Survive on the Planet Earth." *Successo* (International Edition). Milan, 1971, 2.

PERSICO, C., AND MC EACKRON, N. *Forces for Societal Transformation in the
United States, 1950–2000.* SRI Project 6747, Vol. 1. Menlo Park, Calif.:
Stanford Research Institute, 1971.

PICKERING, G. *Voluntarism and the American Way.* Occasional Paper 7. Washington, D.C.: Center for a Voluntary Society, 1970.

The Planning-Programming-Budgeting System: Progress and Potentials. Hearings
before the Subcommittee on Economy in Government of the Joint Economic Committee. Washington, D.C.: U.S. Government Printing Office,
1967.

PLATT, J. "Lock-ins and Multiple Lock-ins in Collective Behavior." *American
Scientist,* 1969, *57*(2).

PLATT, J. "What We Must Do." *Science,* 1969, *149.*

PLATT, J. *Hierarchical Restructuring.* Ann Arbor: University of Michigan,
Mental Health Research Institute Communication 269, 1970.

POLAK, F. *The Image of the Future,* Vol. II. Translated by E. Boulding. The
Netherlands: A. W. Sijhoff, 1961.

POLANYI, M. *The Tacit Dimension.* New York: Doubleday, 1966.

POUNDS, W. *The Process of Problem Finding.* Cambridge: Massachusetts Institute of Technology, 1965. Unpublished manuscript.

RATOOSH, P. "Experimental Studies of Implementation." In J. Lawrence (Ed.),
Operational Research and the Social Sciences. London: Tavistock, 1966.

READ, W. *Factors Affecting Upward Communication at Middle Management
Levels in Industrial Organizations.* University of Michigan, 1959. Unpublished dissertation.

READ, W. "Upward Communication in Industrial Hierarchies." *Human Relations,*
1962, *15.*

REIN, M. "Social Planning: The Search for Legitimacy." *Journal of the American Institute of Planners,* 1969, *35.*

REIN, M. "Social Policy Analysis as the Interpretation of Beliefs." *Journal of the
American Institute of Planners.* September 1971, *37.*

RICE, A. K. *Learning for Leadership.* London: Tavistock, 1965.

RIESMAN, D., GLAZER, N., AND DENNEY, R. *The Lonely Crowd.* New York:
Doubleday Anchor Books, 1955.

RITTEL, H., AND WEBBER, M. *Dilemmas in a General Theory of Planning.* Working Paper N. 194, Institute of Urban and Regional Development, University of California, Berkeley, 1972.

RIVLIN, A. *The Planning, Programing, and Budgeting System in the Department of Health, Education, and Welfare: Some Lessons from Experience.* Washington, D.C.: The Brookings Institution, 1969.

RIVLIN, A. *Systematic Thinking for Social Action.* Washington, D.C.: The Brookings Institution, 1971.

ROKEACH, M. *Beliefs, Attitudes, and Values.* San Francisco: Jossey-Bass, 1968.

ROETHLISBERGER, F. *Management and Morale.* Cambridge: Harvard University Press, 1941.

ROETHLISBERGER, F., AND DICKSON, W., with the assistance of Wright, H. *Management and the Worker.* Cambridge: Harvard University Press, 1946.

ROGERS, E., WITH SHOEMAKER, F. *Diffusion of Innovations.* New York: The Free Press, 1971.

ROSENTHAL, R. *Experimenter Effects in Behavioral Research.* New York: Appleton Century Crofts, 1966.

ROSENTHAL, R., AND WEISS, R. "Problems of Organizational Feedback Processes." In R. Bauer (Ed.), *Social Indicators.* Cambridge: M.I.T. Press, 1966.

ROSS, R., AND GUSKIN, A. "Advocacy and Democracy: Towards a Research Program." Working paper, Center for Research on Utilization of Scientific Knowledge. Ann Arbor: Institute for Social Research, 1972.

ROTTER, J. "Generalized Expectancies for Interpersonal Trust." *American Psychologist,* 1971, *26*(5).

SALOMEN, J. "Science Policy and Its Myths." *Futures,* 1971, *3*(1).

SCHEIN, E. *Process Consultation: Its Role in Organization Development.* Reading, Mass.: Addison-Wesley, 1969.

SCHICK, A. "Systems Politics and Systems Budgeting." *Public Administration Review,* 1969, *24*(1).

SCHICK, A. "Can the States Improve Their Budgeting?" Brookings Research Report 120. Washington, D.C.: The Brookings Institution, 1971.

SCHON, D. *Technology and Change: The Impact of Invention and Innovation on American Social and Economic Development.* New York: Dell, 1967.

SCHON, D. *Beyond the Stable State.* New York: Random House, 1971.

SCHRODER, H., DRIVER, M., AND STIEUFERT, S. *Human Information Processing.* New York: Holt, Rinehart and Winston, 1967.

SCHULTZE, C. *The Politics and Economics of Public Spending.* Washington, D.C.: The Brookings Institution, 1968.

SCODEL, A., RATOOSH, P., AND MINAS, J. *Some Personality Correlates of Decision Making Under Conditions of Risk.* Reprint 1. Berkeley: Institute of Industrial Relations, University of California, 1960.

SEASHORE, S., AND MC NEILL, R. (Eds.) *The Management of Urban Crisis.* New York: The Free Press, 1971.

SEIDMAN, H. *Politics, Position, and Power: The Dynamics of Federal Organization.* New York: Oxford University Press, 1970.

SHAPLEY, D. "Professional Societies: Identity Crisis Threatens on Bread and Butter Issues." *Science,* May 19, 1972, *176.*

SHELDON, E., AND FREEMAN, H. "Notes on Social Indicators: Promises and Potential." *Policy Sciences,* 1970, *1*(1).

SHONFIELD, A. *Modern Capitalism: The Changing Balance of Public and Private Power.* New York: Oxford University Press, 1965.

SIMON, H. "On the Concept of Organizational Goal." *Administrative Science Quarterly,* 1964, *9*(1).

SIMON, H. "Administrative Behavior." *International Encyclopedia of the Social Sciences,* Vol. I. New York: Crowell Collier and Macmillan, 1968.

SLATER, P. *The Pursuit of Loneliness.* Boston: Beacon Press, 1970.

SMELSER, N. *Theory of Collective Behavior.* New York: The Free Press, 1972.

SOFER, C. *The Organization From Within.* Chicago: Quadrangle Books, 1962.

SOLO, R. *Economic Organizations and Social Systems.* New York: Bobbs-Merrill, 1967.

SOLO, R. "New Maths and Old Stabilities." *Saturday Review,* January 22, 1972.

SPERLICH, P. *Conflict and Harmony in Human Affairs: Cross-Pressures and Political Behavior.* Chicago: Rand McNally, 1971.

SPILHAUS, A. "Ecolibrium." *Science,* February 18, 1972, *175.*

STABLER, C. "Changing Times: For Many Corporations, Social Responsibility Is Now a Major Concern." *Wall Street Journal,* October 29, 1971.

STAGNER, R. "Decision-Making and Conflict Resolution." In S. Seashore and R. McNeill, *The Management of Urban Crisis.* New York: The Free Press, 1971.

STEINER, G. *Top Management Planning.* Toronto: Collier-Macmillan, 1969.

STRASSMANN, P. "Managing the Evolution to Advanced Information Systems." Presented at the Tenth American Meeting of the Institute of Management Sciences, Atlanta, Georgia. Stamford, Conn.: Xerox Corporation, 1969.

SUCHMAN, E. *Evaluative Research: Principles and Practice in Public Service and Social Action Programs.* New York: Russell Sage Foundation, 1967.

SUZUKI, D. *Zen Buddhism.* W. Barrett, Ed. Garden City, N.Y.: Doubleday and Co., 1956.

TANNENBAUM, A. *Control in Organizations.* New York: McGraw-Hill, 1968.

TART, C. *Altered States of Consciousness.* New York: Wiley, 1969.

TART, C. "States of Consciousness and State-Specific Sciences." *Science,* 1972, *176.*

TEAD, O. "The Ethical Challenge of Modern Administration." In H. Cleveland and H. Laswell (Eds.), *Ethics and Bigness.* New York: Harper and Row, 1962.

TERKEL, S. "Servants of the State." *Harper's Magazine,* 1972, *244.*

TERREBERRY, S. "The Evolution of Organizational Environments." *Administrative Science Quarterly,* 1968, *12*(4).

THANT, U. "At the United Nations." *The American Way,* 1970, *3.*

THOMAS, T., AND MC KINNEY, D. *Accountability in Education.* Research Memorandum, EPRC-6747-15. Menlo Park, Calif.: Stanford Research Institute, 1972.

THOMPSON, J. "Decision-Making, the Firm, and the Market." In W. Cooper, H. Leavitt, and M. Shelly (Eds.), *New Perspectives in Organizational Research.* New York: Wiley, 1964.

THOMPSON, J. *Organizations in Action: Social Science Bases of Administrative Theory.* New York: McGraw-Hill, 1967.

THOMPSON, J., AND TUDEN, A. "Strategies, Structures, and Processes of Organizational Decision." In J. Thompson and others (Eds.), *Comparative Studies in Administration.* Pittsburgh: University of Pittsburgh Press, 1959.

THOMPSON, V. "How Scientific Management Thwarts Innovation." *Trans-action,* 1968, *5*(7).

THOMPSON, W. *A Preface to Urban Economics.* Baltimore: Johns Hopkins Paperbacks, 1965.

TRIBE, L. "Towards a New Technological Ethic: The Role of Legal Liability." *Impact of Science on Society,* 1971a, *21*(3).

TRIBE, L. "Legal Frameworks for the Assessment and Control of Technology." *Minerva,* 1961, *9*(2).

TRIPATHI, R. *A Review of Conceptualizations of Organizational Environment and Studies of Environment-Organization Relationships.* Manuscript prepared for the University of Michigan's Organizational Psychology Program, December 1971.

TUGWELL, R. "Drafting a Model Constitution." *The Center Magazine,* 1970, *3*(5).

Urban and Regional Information Systems: Support for Planning in Metropolitan Areas, M/MP-71, U.S. Department of Housing and Urban Development. Washington, D.C.: U.S. Government Printing Office, 1968.

The Urban Detroit Area Effort: The Substance of Findings of the UDA Research Project. Athens, Greece: Doxiadis Associates, 1969.

VANDIVIER, K. "The Aircraft Brake Scandal." *Harpers Magazine,* 1972, *244.*

VICKERS, G. *The Art of Judgment.* New York: Basic Books, 1965.

VICKERS, G. "The Multi-Valued Choice." In L. Thayer (Ed.), *Communication Concepts and Perspectives.* New York: Spartan Books, 1967.

VICKERS, G. *Freedom in a Rocking Boat.* Middlesex, England: Penguin Books, 1970.

VICKERS, G. "The Management of Conflict." *Futures,* 1972, *4*(2).

WADE, N. "Freedom of Information: Officials Thwart Public Right to Know." *Science,* Feb. 4, 1972, *175.*

WALTON, R. "Theory of Conflict in Lateral Organizational Relationships." In J. Lawrence (Ed.), *Operational Research and the Social Sciences.* London: Tavistock, 1966.

WALTON, R. *Interpersonal Peacemaking: Confrontations and Third-Party Consultation.* Reading, Mass.: Addison-Wesley, 1969.

WARREN, R. "Interorganizational Field as a Focus of Investigation." Waltham, Mass.: Brandeis University, 1968.

WARWICK, D. "Socialization and Personality." In S. Seashore and R. McNeill (Eds.), *The Management of Urban Crisis.* New York: The Free Press, 1971.

WEBB, E. *Individual and Organizational Forces Influencing the Interpretation of Indicators.* Research Paper P-488. Arlington, Va.: Institute for Defense Analyses, Science and Technology Division, 1969.

WEBBER, M. "The Roles of Intelligence Systems in Urban-Systems Planning." *Journal of the American Institute of Planners*, 1965, *31*(4).

WEBBER, M. "Planning in an Environment of Change." *The Town Planning Review*, 1968, *39*(3).

WESTIN, A. (Ed.) *Information Technology in a Democracy.* Cambridge: Harvard University Press, 1971.

WESTIN, A. "Introduction." In C. Beard, *The Supreme Court and the Constitution.* Englewood Cliffs, N.J.: Prentice-Hall, 1962.

WESTIN, A. *Privacy and Freedom.* New York: Atheneum, 1967.

WESTIN, A. "Information Technology and Public Decision-Making." In *Harvard University Program on Technology and Society, 1964–1972, A Final Review.* Cambridge: Harvard University Press, 1972.

"What Goals?" New York Times, July 21, 1970, p. 34.

WHEELIS, A. *Quest for Identity.* New York: Norton, 1958.

WIELAND, G. "The Determinants of Clarity in Organization Goals." *Human Relations,* 1969, *22*(2).

WILDAVSKY, A. *The Politics of the Budgetary Process.* Boston: Little, Brown, 1964.

WILENSKY, H. *Organizational Intelligence: Knowledge and Policy in Government and Industry.* New York: Basic Books, 1967.

WILKINS, L., AND GITCHOFF, T. "Trends and Projections in Social Control Systems." *The Annals of the American Academy of Political and Social Science,* 1969, *381.*

WILSON, D., AND WILSON, A. *Toward the Institutionalization of Change.* Working Paper 11. Middletown, Conn.: Institute for the Future, 1970.

WOHLSTETTER, R. *Pearl Harbor: Warning and Decision.* Stanford: Stanford University Press, 1962.

ZIMBARDO, P., AND EABESEN, E. *Influencing Attitudes and Changing Behavior, A Basic Introduction to Relevant Methodology, Theory and Applications.* Reading, Mass.: Addison-Wesley, 1969.

Index

A

Abortion, legalization of, 140, 177

Accountability: and error, 139–141; and feedback, 271; and organization restructuring, 200

Advocate planners: as boundary spanners, 239, 242; professionals assuming roles as, 204–205; and uncertainty, 130; as voluntary organizations, 34

Alaskan pipeline, 46

American Motors Corporation: and synthetic competition procedures, 209n

"Antagonistic cooperation," and interpersonal incompetence, 183

Anxiety. *See* Social Psychology, changing to lrsp; Management; Uncertainty, anxiety produced by

"Appreciation," and changeover to lrsp, 67–68

ARGYRIS, C., 24, 184–188, 195, 258–259, 261

"Authority innovation-decisions," 73

Autism, 112, 112n

B

BACON, FRANCIS, 162, 275

"Bargain decision process," in interpersonal relations, 197

Behavior; Argyris on interpersonal, 24; organizational, 8n

BENNIS, W., 183–184, 188, 191, 195–196, 294, 302

Bicentennial Commission, 147n.4

Black militancy, 25

"Bounded rationality," in feedback, 267

Boundary spanning, 237–254; ambivalence toward, 248, 249–250, 254; burdens of, 250–254; defection in, 246–247; and environmental feedback, 239–240, 244, 248; and interpersonal relations, 230, 251n, 252; as generator of organizational turbulence, 238, 240, 245, 247–248, 253n.12; in government, 239n.2, 248, 248n; incentives of, 250–254; and data increase, 239–240; "knowledge-linking roles" in, 242–243; management anxiety over, 247–248, 249; Miller and Rice on, 250; need for, in organizational restructuring, 200, 207, 209, 233, 237, 239–240, 252; "omniscience" in, 252–253; and Presidential Commissions, 245; resistance to, 237–238, 240–241, 242, 244–250; role stress in, 246, 246n.5, 250; in turbulent environments, 244; and uncertainty, 240; Wilensky on, 241–243; and work overload, 251